These letters, written almost fifty years ago by a young man to his wife, speak to us with quite startling and extraordinary relevance today. He gave his life in trying to defeat Hitler by giving Germany a second Reformation—not of the soul this time, but of the fundamental spirit of democracy. Now, in the summer of 1990, all the great questions he raised are finally being confronted as the two halves of his country face their common future at last.

Count Helmuth James von Moltke was an authentic German hero. Descended on his father's side from the ancient Prussian nobility (his father's great-uncle was Bismarck's legendary Field Marshal) and on his mother's side from vigorously liberal South African stock, he grew up in a family noted for its probity and progressive views. Trained in Berlin and at London's Inner Temple, Moltke became a brilliant lawyer, and was already much involved in helping Jews and other refugees to escape from Germany when war broke out. He then joined the Abwehr (the German intelligence service) at the age of thirty-two as legal adviser to the High Command of the Armed Services. The Abwehr, under its chief, Admiral Wilhelm Canaris, was the focal point of resistance to Hitler in the very heart of Berlin. Passionately opposed to Nazism, but unable, by both his deep Christian faith and his political foresight, to condone the use of violence in the struggle against the regime, Moltke turned his formidable talents and training loose in two great campaigns. By wielding his legal expertise like a bureaucratic monkey wrench to counter the deportation and murder of Jews and the execution of captured soldiers, he saved untold lives. And as the war dragged on, he brought together in secret at his country estate, Kreisau, the best possible minds among fellow resisters to plan the building of a new Germany—with a totally new democratic tradition—that would have to be ready to take responsibility for itself when chaos and defeat overtook Hitler.

(continued on back flap)

KNOPF
75
YEARS·OF·PUBLISHING

Letters to Freya

Helmuth James von Moltke

Letters to Freya

1939–1945

Edited and Translated from the German

by Beate Ruhm von Oppen

ALFRED A. KNOPF   NEW YORK   1990

Library of Congress Cataloging-in-Publication Data
Moltke, Helmuth James, Graf von, 1907–1945.
[Briefe an Freya. English]
Letters to Freya : 1939–1945 / Helmuth James von Moltke ; edited and translated
from the German by Beate Ruhm von Oppen.—1st American ed.
p.   cm.
Translation of: Briefe an Freya.
Includes bibliographical references.
ISBN 0-394-57923-2
1. Moltke, Helmuth James, Graf von, 1907–1945—Correspondence.
2. Moltke, Freya von—Correspondence.
3. Nationalists—Germany—Correspondence. 4. Anti-Nazi movement—Germany.
5. World War, 1939–1945—Personal narratives, German.
I. Ruhm von Oppen, Beate.   II. Title.
DD247.M6A4   1990
943.086'092—dc20   89-45268   CIP

Manufactured in the United States of America
Published June 22, 1990
Second Printing, October 1990

Grateful acknowledgment is made to Julian Frisby
for his translation of the commentaries by Freya von Moltke that appear
on pages 385–386 and 396–397.

FRONTISPIECE: Helmuth James von Moltke.
Drawing by M. Schneefuss, 1930.

Letters to Freya

Introduction

When, on 11 October 1944, after nearly nine months in jail, Helmuth James von Moltke was served with his arrest warrant, which accused him of treason, he expected to live only a few more days, though in fact his trial did not take place until three months later. He wrote a farewell letter to his two boys (one aged three, the other not quite six) in which he told them the cause of his condemnation. ". . . Throughout an entire life, even at school, I have fought against a spirit of narrowness and unfreedom, of arrogance and lack of respect for others, of intolerance and the absolute, the merciless consistency among the Germans, which found its expression in the National Socialist state. I exerted myself to help to overcome this spirit with its evil consequences, such as excessive nationalism, racial persecution, lack of faith, and materialism." He continued that from their point of view the Nazis were therefore right in killing him. But they were wrong to kill him inasmuch as he had always opposed acts of violence, like the attempted coup of 20 July 1944, for a number of reasons, but chiefly because it would not change the mentality behind the Third Reich.

Eight days later, he wrote another letter to his boys, to add something that only he could tell them about their mother. ". . . Ever since National Socialism came to power, I have done my best to mitigate the consequences for its victims and to prepare for a change. I was driven to it by my conscience, and, after all, it is a task for a man. From 1933 on, I have therefore had to make material sacrifices and to run personal risks. In all these years Freya, who was the one who suffered most from these sacrifices and who always had to be concerned that I would be arrested, imprisoned, or killed, never hindered me in what I considered necessary, or made it harder in any way. She was always ready to accept everything; she was always ready to make sacrifices if it was necessary. And I tell you: that is much more than I did. For running risks oneself, which one knows, is nothing compared with the readiness to let the person with whom one's life is joined run risks one cannot gauge. And it is much more, too, than the wife of a warrior accepts, for she has no choice; one word from Freya might have held me back from many an undertaking."

A year later, when Freya von Moltke left Kreisau in Silesia—now Krzyzowa, and Polish—in the autumn of 1945 with her two little boys, she was not able to take much with her, but took what she later called her "greatest treasure," her husband's letters. He had been sentenced to death and executed in January. There were about sixteen hundred letters, covering the years 1929–45. They were a surprisingly manageable package. The handwriting of this very tall man was tiny. She had kept them hidden in her beehives in case the house was searched.

George Kennan has called Moltke "the greatest person, morally, and the largest and most enlightened in his concepts that [he] met on either side of the battle-lines in the Second World War." He concluded his vivid account of him and of their dealings with these words: "I record all this because the image of this lonely, struggling man, one of the few genuine Protestant-Christian martyrs of our time, had remained for me over the intervening years a pillar of moral conscience and an unfailing source of political and intellectual inspiration." [1]

Biography[2]

Helmuth James von Moltke was born on 11 March 1907, the first child of Count Helmuth von Moltke (1876–1939), who was a great-nephew of the "great" Moltke of Bismarck's wars, and Dorothy, née Rose Innes (1885–1935), the only child of Sir James Rose Innes (1855–1942) and his wife, Jessie, née Pringle. Sir James, the revered grandfather—always referred to as "Daddy"—had been Attorney General under Cecil Rhodes and finally retired as Chief Justice of South Africa. He was a man of great probity and progressive views. His wife and eighteen-year-old daughter

1. George F. Kennan, *Memoirs 1925–1950* (Boston, 1967), pp. 121–22.
2. For a fuller account see Michael Balfour and Julian Frisby, *Helmuth von Moltke: A Leader Against Hitler* (London, 1972; New York, 1973).

had visited Europe in 1904 and come to Creisau (as it was spelled until 1928) as paying guests. It was a considerable hardship for her parents that their only child then decided to stay and marry the twenty-nine-year-old new owner of the estate, who proposed to her when, in 1905, his father died.

Dorothy was an affectionate daughter and a faithful correspondent. Her regular letters about her life with the "Young Teuton" and the five children that were born at two-year intervals are most lively and informative and by no means confined to children, farm, and husband, but full of observations on the political and economic developments in Germany. Her views were, like those of her parents, liberal.

Kreisau, together with the neighbouring estates Nieder-Grädtz and Wierischau, comprised about a thousand acres. Field Marshal Moltke, the "great" Moltke, had acquired them with money granted him by his grateful King after the Prussian war against Austria in 1866. By East Elbian standards it was a modest estate. The Field Marshal was widowed in 1868. There were no children. On his death, in 1891, the entailed estate went to his nephew, Wilhelm, and when *he* died, in 1905, to his eldest son, Helmuth. An estate that had been added was leased to a younger brother, a bachelor, and on his death to *his* nephew Hans Adolf von Moltke, who bought it in 1942.

The nearest town was Schweidnitz. Breslau (now Wrocław) was about thirty miles away. The village had four hundred souls, a school, and a Catholic church; the Protestant church was in Grädtz.

The family lived in the Schloss until 1928, when, for reasons of economy, they moved to the Berghaus, a smaller house on a rise a little distance away.

Conditions at Kreisau were comfortable before the First World War, less so during it, and almost penurious after it. But that never interfered with the richness of life or the hospitality of the family. The house welcomed not only all members of the Moltke clan, but many interesting guests, who contributed at least as much to the education of the children as their schools. Plays were staged (with young Helmuth keener on directing than acting), literature was read aloud; the father sang Schubert, Brahms, and Strauss. Until the coming of the Republic he had a seat in the Herrenhaus, the upper chamber of Parliament in Berlin.

Both parents were Christian Scientists and the translators of Mary Baker Eddy's *Science and Health* into German; the father even became a healer and teacher in the sect. The children, however, grew up as Lutherans; after Helmuth there was Joachim Wolfgang ("Jowo," born 1909), then Wilhelm Viggo ("Willo," 1911–87), Carl Bernd ("C.B.," 1913–41), and Asta Maria (born 1915).

Helmuth went to school in Schweidnitz, then to a boarding school, which he hated because of its collective spirit, and finally, living with relatives, to a school in Potsdam. It left him free to spend time in Berlin, act as interpreter to some American journalists, and enjoy the cultural life there.

He then embarked on studies in law, politics, social history, the history of socialism, and a little journalism. He studied at Breslau, Berlin, and Vienna and had in mind a career in politics—at the age of twenty he applied to the League of Nations—or the law, probably as a judge, to emulate his admired grandfather.

His concern for social conditions was intense. He did vacation work under the administrator Karl Ohle, a Social Democrat, in Waldenburg, a hard-stricken district in Silesia. In 1928 he joined with his cousin Carl Dietrich von Trotha and Horst von Einsiedel, a friend of "C.D.," to discuss ways of helping to alleviate the misery in the area. They found allies in their professors Eugen Rosenstock (-Huessy), who was also a fiery social reformer and promoter of adult education; Schulze-Gaevernitz; and Hans Peters. The voluntary work camp for young farmers, workers and students, which the twenty-one-year-old Moltke helped to prepare and organize at Löwenberg in March 1928, was one of several. He did not take part in any of the later ones but kept in touch with some of the people he had met in that context, who included the Member of Parliament for Waldenburg, the later Reich Chancellor Heinrich Brüning (to whom the young Moltke had gone for funds for the work camp), and several of the members of the anti-Nazi group of post-war planners he started in 1940.

While studying in Berlin he would eat at a canteen initiated by Dr. Eugenie Schwarzwald, a woman of immense energy and resourcefulness in helping others, who became best known for her schools in Vienna. Having taken her degree in Zurich, she was appalled at the exclusion of women from higher education in Austria and founded a school where girls, too, could prepare for university entrance. It was a wonderful place, where Kokoschka taught art and Egon Wellesz music.

Her husband, Dr. Hermann Schwarzwald, served in prominent positions in the Austrian administration and as head of the Anglo-American Bank. Their house was a meeting place for artists, scholars, and writers, such as Arnold Schönberg, Adolf Loos, Bertolt Brecht and his wife, Helene Weigel, Carl Zuckmayer and Alice Herdan, Karl Kraus, Karin Michaelis, and the very young Rudolf Serkin. (A decade later, after the Anschluss, Moltke helped the Schwarzwalds, who were Jewish, to get out of Austria, as he helped many others who were persecuted on "racial" or political grounds.)

It was in the soup kitchen in the former imperial palace in Berlin that the young Helmuth von Moltke had been introduced to "Frau Doktor" Schwarzwald by the brother of a former schoolmate, Hans Deichmann. She invited him to come to Vienna and to her summer house at the old Hotel Seeblick in Grundlsee in Styria, where the Schwarzwalds' many friends, among them many young people, spent happy and affordable holidays. It was here that Helmuth met Freya Deichmann in the summer of 1929, when she was eighteen—and chaperoned by her mother—and he twenty-two.

The meeting with Freya, daughter of the Cologne banker Carl Theodor Deichmann, initiated the correspondence which he was to cherish throughout his life. In his first letter, of 1 September 1929, he wrote that he had never so looked forward to writing a letter in his life. He instantly realized how they complemented each other, eagerly awaited and treasured her letters, and once described them as dewdrops on a parched plant.

He had considered becoming the assistant of his friend Edgar Mowrer, then Berlin correspondent of the Chicago *Daily News,* or else going to New York to work at the New York *Evening Post.* Instead he decided to start work in the statistical department of the *Berliner Handelsgesellschaft.* In his free time he enjoyed discussions with his friends and the lively cultural scene of Berlin.

There was an abrupt end to this pleasant beginning. In October 1929 the manager of Kreisau died, and the estate was discovered to be in total disorder and deep debt. Helmuth's father called on his eldest son to put it in order. The ensuing months were extremely strenuous. He became his father's plenipotentiary, analyzed the complex and menacing situation, and persuaded the creditors to give him a year in which to prove that they stood to benefit from his management. His legal training was, of course, invaluable; his clear mind, strict self-discipline, and prodigious capacity for work no less.

Among his chief worries were the dependent small farmers and the need to reduce the work force and the wages of the workers who remained. He hated being "the executor of the capitalist system." But he never lost his nerve and found "immense satisfaction in being able to create something out of chaos."

There soon was an additional task. He started the practical phase of his law studies as Referendar. He managed to squeeze the work of eighteen or nineteen hours into fourteen hours per day. This iron discipline enabled him later, when he studied English law in London, to compress a two-year curriculum into six weeks. By October 1930 the worst was over, and he enjoyed the new work of reconstruction, rationalization, financing, and economic management at Kreisau.

Helmuth and Freya had met again at Grundlsee in August. In the spring of 1930, Freya had visited him at Kreisau with her brother Hans; in June 1931, Helmuth visited her in the Rhineland. He did not want to marry or to be responsible for bringing children into the world. Freya, who was only twenty, was in no hurry either.

But they did marry on 18 October 1931, quietly and in the company of only a few family members. Only Helmuth's parents and his brother Willo could afford to come to the Rhineland. The Deichmann Bank was on the point of liquidation and Freya's father was dying.

Practical reasons seem to have prompted the decision to marry at that moment: Helmuth's mother wanted to visit her parents for six months, and Freya was able to take over the household at Kreisau. As late as 17 June Helmuth had found wedlock "too big a word" and asked her: "Will you be content with the fact that we are just two students who prefer living together to living alone?"

In October 1932 the two students moved into a tiny flat in the Bendlerstrasse in Berlin. Freya continued the law studies she had begun in Cologne and got her doctorate in 1935. She never practised law.

The crisis at Kreisau had coincided with the world economic crisis signalled by the Wall Street crash; and now came the lethal crisis of the Weimar Republic.

Helmuth had been aware of the potential for catastrophe. The trade unionist Franz Josef Furtwängler, who met him during this time, described him thus: "No politician saw as clearly as this young legal genius how the millions of unemployed were ushering in an era of revolution and the horrors of war. In the millions of idle workers, the unemployed young academics, the dispossessed farmers, and bankrupt businessmen he saw even then the end of the social order as it had evolved, with all the revolutionary consequences that were bound to follow 'one way or another.' "[1]

Until Hitler's advent to power in 1933, Moltke worked as Referendar in the law office of Erich Koch-Weser (of the Democratic Party) and Alfred Carlebach. He then joined with Karl von Lewinski in an office specializing in international private law; in July 1938 he and Lewinski parted and he joined another international lawyer, Paul Leverkühn. He had no desire to become a judge under the Nazis. Furtwängler described the change: "When I later emigrated to Hungary, he occasionally smuggled reports on the situation out to me, in which he described the shrivelling up of human values as the worst consequence of the totalitarian regime. The young man who had enjoyed life had become a serious man.

1. Franz Josef Furtwängler, *Männer, die ich sah und kannte* (Hamburg, 1951), p. 127.

The driving force in his character was a deeply religious feeling for his fellow men. And yet he was the sharpest legal intellect I had ever encountered."[1]

Only people who did not know him very well, but whom he liked, could see him as one who enjoyed life. He was, as he wrote at the end of his life, a complicated man, but one who did not permit himself to succumb to his periodic doubts about the meaning of life. His tremendous energy might mislead one on that point.

After 1933 there were the added political complications, the question not only whether there was any point in staying in Germany, but increasingly whether remaining there—while keeping his distance from the Nazi regime—did not involve him in culpability, because it helped to maintain a façade behind which the most horrendous things were happening. On the other hand, he was able to help the persecuted and did what he could. Above all he was attached to Kreisau, which, despite the burden of debt and the hostility of the Nazi farmers' organization, not only was an economic base that kept him relatively independent, but became more and more of an oasis.

The beginning of the Third Reich came while he was still a Referendar and in the winter of 1933–34 he had to spend some weeks in a camp devoted to the ideological indoctrination and pre-military training of young lawyers. In the midst of it he stayed aloof and found sympathizers who helped to embarrass the appointed indoctrinator, especially in the "racial" interpretation of history, and to substitute periods of listening to records of classical music for the prescribed reading of Nazi literature. Being the tallest, he had to intone the marching songs, and wrote to Freya that Heine would have turned in his grave.

What made the camp at Jüterbog bearable was the prospect of a long trip to South Africa with Freya. They relished the comparative freedom, seeing his grandparents, meeting their friends. Even on the ship on the outward voyage, he used the freedom from censorship to write three long letters about conditions in Germany to friends in Scandinavia. They were women he had met in the Schwarzwald circle. The letter to Helene Weigel was the wittiest and gave an almost Brechtian description of his life in the camp. One to Maria Lazar is politically the most interesting. In it he deals with those "who are not persecuted in Germany" and "whom the Party still has to woo." According to him, "this privileged caste" consisted of "the high Catholic clergy and the lower Catholic clergy in South and West Germany, the Protestant clergymen of the Pastors' Emergency

1. Ibid., pp. 127–28.

League,[1] the big landowners; some Catholic professors of every faculty; some private bankers and big industrialists, though the latter only in very small numbers; and finally some independent people with an inherited or acquired name." Clearly he was speaking here not of a growth potential for the Party, but of opposition and actual or potential resistance. He did not mention the military.

The return in the autumn was overshadowed by the developments of the summer. During the week-end of 30 June there had been the bloody purge that eliminated Ernst Röhm and other stormtrooper (SA) leaders as well as other political "undesirables," such as the former Reich Chancellor General von Schleicher and his wife, two close collaborators of the Vice Chancellor Franz von Papen, and the Catholic Action leader Erich Klausener. By the time Moltke returned, the much more dangerous rival of the SA, Himmler's SS, had begun its ascendancy, which brought the gradual change from authoritarian *Gleichschaltung* ("coordination") to totalitarian rule. In early August the ancient President von Hindenburg had died and Hitler had assumed his office and merged it with the chancellorship, while keeping the leadership of the Party. The armed forces had to take an oath swearing personal allegiance to Hitler, not to the defence of the constitution.

The question of what to do now had become more serious, the answer more difficult. Moltke went out on reconnaissance to see what the chances of international work were for him in Europe. He visited the League of Nations, but found it disappointing. All the people there saw themselves as representatives of their countries and not as officials of the League, and worked to further their careers accordingly. The only true internationalists were "those Germans, Russians, and Italians who are not Nazis, Bolshies, or Fascists and have broken off relations with their countries without leaving the Secretariat"—but their freedom of movement was limited because their passports were not being renewed.

His visit to the International Court at The Hague was more promising. He had a good talk with the Secretary of the Court, the Swede Åke Hammarskjöld,[2] who instantly grasped Moltke's situation, which resembled that of his former colleague Berthold von Stauffenberg, who had had to relinquish his post under German pressure. During his subsequent visit to England Moltke realized that the study of British law, with the aim of being called to the British bar, was the most promising prospect.

1. The group founded by Martin Niemöller in the autumn of 1933 to combat Nazification of the Protestant church and the application of "racial" criteria among its ministers; in 1934 it became the Confessing Church.
2. Brother of Dag Hammarskjöld, the later Secretary General of the United Nations.

He applied for admission to the Inner Temple and during the next few years not only read for the bar, but paid fairly frequent visits to England to eat the required dinners. His first visit to England had been in 1934, on the way back from South Africa. He had met Lionel Curtis, a friend of the Rose Innes family, co-founder of the (Royal) Institute of International Affairs at Chatham House and Fellow of All Souls College in Oxford. Moltke had told Curtis about the work camps and Curtis had told him something about the time he spent as a young man with Lord Milner in South Africa and about his later experiences at the armistice and peace negotiations in 1918–19. Curtis introduced him to many interesting and prominent people. Moltke used the opportunities thus offered to inform himself and to enlighten the "Appeasers" he met at All Souls about the true character and aims of the Third Reich. One brief meeting with Lord Lothian, a friend and collaborator of Lionel Curtis, led to a long letter to Curtis on 12 July 1935, in which he marshalled the arguments against Lothian's view that it was British and French mistakes after the war, especially the Treaty of Versailles and the French occupation of the Ruhr in 1923, that were responsible for the growth of the Nazi movement; Moltke did not believe that the Nazis would gradually turn into a respectable government or that a policy of concessions could promote this end. He was convinced that Lothian had fallen victim to German propaganda. He was afraid that the policy of appeasement would gain popularity in England and lead the German government to believe that Britain would remain neutral in case of war.

Lothian took a long time to see that appeasement only emboldened the Nazis. There were indeed many who shared his view. They included Lady Astor, the American-born Member of Parliament, whose country house gave its name to the "Cliveden Set," the "Germanophiles" she gathered around her. The budding young German diplomat Adam von Trott zu Solz, a Rhodes Scholar, whom Moltke had met in England, went there as late as June 1939 and wrote a long report intended to stop Hitler from going to war.[1]

Appeasement was not confined to politicians. Arthur Headlam, the Anglican Bishop of Gloucester and Chairman of the Church of England Council on Foreign Relations, whom Moltke met at All Souls, was convinced that this young German was determined to keep up the church struggle in Germany only because he thought it would injure National Socialism. The Bishop was therefore sceptical of his warnings about an exacerbation of Nazi persecution of the Protestant churches, which

---

1. Text in *Documents on German Foreign Policy* (hereafter *DGFP*), series D, vol. VI, no. 497. For Trott see n. 5 to letter of 19 September 1939.

Moltke correctly foresaw in November 1935 as likely to occur after the Berlin Olympic Games of 1936.

Fortunately there were other Anglican clerics, notably George Bell, the Bishop of Chichester, who maintained close contact with Dietrich Bonhoeffer and with the provisional World Council of Churches in Geneva and who sent his Dean to Germany to observe the trial of Martin Niemöller in 1937.

Moltke was appalled by the popular and international success of the Olympic Games and horrified at the heedlessness of the masses who attended them and who rejoiced in the phoney internationalism the Nazis put on for the occasion. It was this willing self-surrender that frightened him. What he minded most was that many people of whom he thought well joined in and did not see how disgusting, degrading, and dangerous it all was. His only consolation was the prospect of another trip to South Africa.

But new difficulties awaited him after his return. His deeply loved mother had died in June 1935. She left behind a lonely widower, who decided to marry one of his Christian Science pupils in December 1937. It was not only the memory of his mother that caused her eldest son to be aghast at this development, but the practical, including financial, consequences. Kreisau was still in debt. He fought hard to keep the new Countess Moltke out of Kreisau and to preserve the peace of the Berghaus. His father died in March 1939; the widow survived the war.

As Moltke had foreseen, the policy of appeasement did indeed lead to further German threats. Austria was annexed in March 1938 and became part of Greater Germany. In September Czechoslovakia was dismembered. The Munich agreement gave the strategically important Sudeten area, which was inhabited by ethnic Germans, to Germany. Hitler said he had no further territorial claims, but marched into Prague in March 1939. This was the turning point. Great Britain and France concluded a treaty of mutual assistance with Poland, the obvious next victim, and declared war on Germany on 3 September, after the Germans had marched into Poland.

Moltke had also foreseen the radicalization of Nazi domestic policy. The flood of refugees from the German orbit increased, especially after the coordinated, nation-wide anti-Jewish excesses of November 1938. He was extremely busy helping people to get out.

By the time the war came, he had passed his English bar exams and found an office in London. He now made the best of his experience of international and especially British law, and joined the Foreign Division of the Abwehr, the German intelligence service, as legal adviser to the High Command of the Armed Services (Oberkommando der Wehrmacht: OKW).

The Abwehr, under its chief, Admiral Wilhelm Canaris, was the focal point of much opposition to the regime. Both Canaris himself and his right-hand man, Colonel (later Major General) Hans Oster, as well as other wartime members of the Abwehr, were executed before the end of the war. There was increasing rivalry between the Abwehr and the intelligence branch of the SS, the SD (Sicherheitsdienst: Security Service).

In the early phase of the war, Moltke concentrated on the prevention of breaches of international law and the protection of neutrals. It was very hard, almost impossible, to affect strategic planning. But he was clearly involved in the efforts to get Hitler to cancel or at least postpone plans for a campaign in the West after the defeat and partition of Poland. There was little that could be done by the Wehrmacht to stop the atrocities committed by the SS against the Polish leadership, clergy, and Jews. He did, however, fight for the recognition of Polish prisoners of war as such and of the Poles who fought on with the French and British after escaping abroad, as combatants. Throughout, Moltke's endeavour was to extend the protection of the Wehrmacht to people who would otherwise fall prey to the SS.

He knew about and was to some extent involved in the efforts of opponents of the regime inside and outside the Abwehr to put out feelers in Britain for a negotiated peace after the hoped-for elimination of Hitler. The emissary was yet another member of the Abwehr, the Munich lawyer Josef Müller, who went to Rome, where the Pope, Pius XII, was willing to vouch for the *bona fides* of the group and act as intermediary to the British Ambassador at the Holy See.

But nothing could stop Hitler's course of aggression. Germany occupied Denmark and Norway in April 1940 and attacked Holland, Belgium, Luxembourg, and France in May. The rapid defeat of the French disarmed and disoriented the domestic opposition in Germany. Hitler stood at the zenith of his popularity and power.

It was in part to overcome his own depression and that of other opponents of the regime at this moment of what he called "the triumph of evil" that Moltke began, in the summer of 1940, the systematic collection of like-minded men to discuss the principles on which Germany should be rebuilt after Hitler, in a liberated Europe. (It was the Gestapo which, much later, called the group "Kreisau Circle," when interrogators found out about it in the investigations after the failed plot of 20 July 1944.) With some of these men he had had discussions months and years before. More than half of them he knew from the time of the work camps. They came from very diverse backgrounds.

Moltke took particular care to include socialists and representatives of the churches, two groups he saw as fundamental to the rebuilding of a better Germany. Likewise, he was concerned to bring representatives of the (majority) Protestant and (minority) Catholic churches together. Undoubtedly it was his realization of the political harm done by the religious schism in Germany, and its exploitation by the Nazis, that prompted these efforts. It was typical that this Protestant son of Christian Scientists read papal encyclicals on the Sunday war was declared. Hitler's electoral base had been predominantly Protestant, the Protestant churches were stridently nationalistic, and the so-called "German Christians" had shown how German Protestantism could shade into racism and neo-paganism.

In addition to his official job in the Abwehr and the increasing activity in connection with these "Kreisau" discussions and plans, he still had his private law practice, with an indispensable secretary, Katharina Breslauer, who could deal with his more confidential appointments too, and he kept a watchful though distant eye on the farming operations at Kreisau, always longing to be there, rarely able to go for a week-end or a working vacation.

His rank in the Abwehr corresponded roughly to that of a major. He was a Kriegsverwaltungsrat (an administrative rank) and did not have to wear uniform and never did, though repeatedly urged to do so. His name no doubt helped, both in his work and in preserving his freedom—until his arrest in January 1944. The name of Bismarck's general still had an aura in the Third Reich.

Before the war Moltke had written articles for the periodical of the Kaiser Wilhelm Institute for Public and International Law. The deputy director of the Institute, Ernst Martin Schmitz, became his colleague in the Abwehr. The chief of the Foreign Division there was a politically nondescript naval captain, Leopold Bürkner. The International Law Group could only give advice, not directives or orders. Yet it managed to make its voice heard and occasionally listened to. Moltke's letter of 18 November 1939 shows an early measure of success, but also the intense and discreet struggle that had to be kept up. In March 1940 there was a "big row" with his bosses—in which, however, he prevailed.

After the fall of France he had to work hard to maintain his own morale and confidence in British victory. He embarked on a reading programme: Spinoza, Voltaire, Kant. The Bible now meant more to him than it used to and struck him as very topical.

He continued to work on Alexander Kirk, the American Chargé d'Affaires in Berlin, to counteract the American tendencies to isolationism, which were being fostered assiduously by the American Ambassador in London, Joseph Kennedy. When Kirk left Berlin in October 1940, he handed over this "most delicate and valuable of his clandestine 'contacts' among the German oppositionists" to George Kennan, who later wrote that "it was, in fact, largely from Moltke that [Kirk] had derived his conviction that the war, all early German triumphs notwithstanding, would end badly for Germany. . . . Even at that time—in 1940 and 1941—he had looked beyond the whole sordid arrogance and the apparent triumphs of the Hitler regime; he had seen through to the ultimate catastrophe and had put himself to the anguish of accepting it and accommodating himself to it inwardly, preparing himself—as he would eventually have liked to prepare his people—for the necessity of starting all over again, albeit in defeat and humiliation, to erect a new national edifice on a new and better moral foundation."[1] He read the *Federalist Papers* and envisaged a federal structure for Germany and Europe. Kennan was particularly impressed by the way Moltke had risen above the pettiness and primitivism of latter-day nationalism.[2]

The German attack on the Soviet Union in June 1941 ended the year in which Britain and the Commonwealth stood alone against Hitler's Europe. The attack began the ideological and total war. As long as the Hitler-Stalin Pact of August 1939 was in force, National Socialist Germany had fought the Western "plutocracies." Now came the struggle against "Jewish Bolshevism." It was a fight not only for *Lebensraum*, the land and the natural and human resources of the Soviet Union, but for the destruction of communism and those who were taken or alleged to embody it, not only partisans and obstructive civilians, but Jews, all Jews. These were left to the Einsatzgruppen or task forces of the Security Police and SD to deal with. Soon it was not only Jews in the Soviet Union, but Jews from Germany and countries occupied or allied with Germany. Deportations from Berlin began in October 1941. In January 1942 the "final solution of the Jewish question" was initiated for the whole of Europe. By then Moltke had heard of SS men with nervous breakdowns. In October 1942 he heard the first reliable report about an extermination camp, one of the places that worked with poison gas. In May 1943 he saw the cloud of smoke above the Warsaw ghetto on his only trip to occupied Poland.

The "evacuation" and "resettlement" of Jews was carried out by the police and SS and did not fall in the competence of the Abwehr and its International Law Group. But there was one occasion when Moltke was asked to attend a meeting at the Ministry of Foreign Affairs on this matter, of bureaucrats representing several ministries. He seized the opportunity to exert all his strength and powers of persuasion to halt the machinery of spoliation and deportation, or at least to prevent its legalization. He succeeded for a few days. The sequence of letters from the 8th to the 14th of November 1941 shows the strain. The Abwehr was not represented at the Wannsee Conference in January 1942.

1. Kennan, *Memoirs*, p. 119.
2. Ibid., p. 121.

At the same time Moltke fought for the lives of Soviet prisoners of war, who were also dying in large numbers and who *were* the concern of the armed forces. Here, too, he mentioned the fact that the Foreign Division of the Abwehr had not been consulted about the orders. Though he pleaded for respect for international law and humanity, he knew that arguments for expedience and reciprocity were more effective. The earlier German practices were not modified until it could be proved that there were German prisoners in Russian hands. They needed the help of the International Red Cross, which therefore had to be given access to Soviet prisoners in German camps. Another factor that made for change in the German methods was the manpower shortage. Prisoners were needed for work and could therefore not be left to starve. Yet millions of them died.

Elsewhere in occupied Europe, too, all resistance was now treated as "communist insurrection." Moltke's efforts turned increasingly to preventing the killing of hostages. He negotiated not only with generals of the Wehrmacht, but also with those of the SS, like Wilhelm Harster in Holland and Werner Best in Denmark. His visit to Best, the Reich Plenipotentiary in Denmark, coincided with the largely abortive round-up of Danish Jews. Moltke was able to contribute something to the rescue of most of them, though less than the local German shipping attaché, Georg Ferdinand Duckwitz.

Trips to occupied or neutral countries always served more than one purpose. Everywhere he looked for allies, people who were willing to work against the escalation of the war and of German atrocities and oppression. He also found, especially in Holland and Scandinavia, sympathy for the endeavours of the "Kreisauers" and their post-war plans.

This secret working group had grown considerably since the summer of 1940. The summer of 1941 saw the beginning of Moltke's regular exchanges of news and views with Konrad von Preysing, the Catholic Bishop of Berlin, who was also kept informed about the deliberations of the Kreisauers and contributed comments.

The first members of the group—Yorck, Einsiedel, Peters, Gablentz, Trott—were joined by the socialists Adolf Reichwein, Carlo Mierendorff, and Theodor Haubach. Hans Bernd von Haeften, a member of the Foreign Service and a committed Protestant, joined in 1941, as did the somewhat older Theodor Steltzer, another lively Protestant, who was stationed in Norway, and the Protestant prison chaplain Harald Poelchau. Karl Ludwig Guttenberg established the connection with the Munich Jesuits, their Provincial, Augustin Rösch, and Fathers Alfred Delp and Lothar König. The last two joined in 1942, as did Eugen Gerstenmaier, Konsistorialrat in the Protestant church, the "man in Berlin" of the Protestant Bishop of Württemberg, Theophil Wurm, who since the summer of 1941 had become the acknowledged, though unofficial, head of the Confessing and "Intact" Church. The Catholic Paulus van Husen, another later addition, took a leading part in drafting the plans for punishing Nazi criminals.

The Kreisauers mostly met in Berlin, in small groups—of often only two or three—in the centrally located small apartment above a garage at Derfflingerstrasse 10, which Moltke shared with his (usually absent) brother-in-law, Carl Deichmann. But meetings were also held, especially when more people were involved, at the house of the Yorcks in Hortensienstrasse, Berlin Lichterfelde-West. This was the venue of the meeting with the group around Carl Goerdeler in January 1943, whose plans Moltke rejected as too backward-looking and half-hearted. He referred to that group as "Their Excellencies."

The first of the three big meetings at Kreisau took place in May 1942 and dealt with questions of political structure, education, university reform, and the relations of church and state.

The second Kreisau meeting, in October 1942, was preceded by intensive preliminary talks, especially between the socialist Mierendorff and the trade unionists Leuschner and Maass on the one hand and the Jesuits Rösch, Delp, and König on the other, in order to achieve a consensus between Social Democrat and Christian trade unionists and churchmen. Wilhelm Leuschner and Hermann Maass, who deputized for him at the Kreisau meeting, favoured one big, united trade union, whereas the Kreisauers preferred works unions, to activate local initiative and avoid the centralization that the federalist constitution plans were intended to counteract on the political plane. "Small communities" were to restore to the individual a sense of having some say and responsibility.

Preparatory talks for the third and last Kreisau meeting, in June 1943, overlapped with continuing discussions of the results of the second meeting. There were deliberations and documents on the punishment of Nazi criminals[1] and on the "translation to the European plane" of the federal plans drawn up for Germany. In April 1941 Moltke had written a document on the shape of a peace settlement after a German defeat. At that time he postulated "a unitary European sovereignty from Portugal to a point as far east as possible, with a division of the entire continent into smaller, non-sovereign political units."[2] At that time he also foresaw an Anglo-Saxon Union.

---

1. Ger van Roon, *Neuordnung im Widerstand: Der Kreisauer Kreis innerhalb der deutschen Widerstandsbewegung* (Munich, 1967); abridged English ed., trans. Peter Ludlow, *German Resistance under Hitler: Count von Moltke and the Kreisau Circle* (London, New York, 1971), 343–47.
2. See van Roon, pp. 317–28, especially p. 322.

By June 1943 the political landscape had changed considerably. The German defeats at Stalingrad and in Tunisia, the demand for an unconditional surrender proclaimed by Roosevelt and Churchill at their Casablanca Conference in January 1943, the conflict between the Soviet Union and the "London" Poles, the tensions between Russia and the Western Allies, and Russian attempts to woo the Germans were some of the factors that now had to be taken into account. In addition German policies in occupied Europe had made any German initiatives in planning for a united Europe after the war more difficult. But it turned out that some European resistance groups also saw a need for German participation in a freely united Europe.

Little of this was made explicit in the agreed Kreisau documents; much of it is reflected in the letters.

Dietrich Bonhoeffer, in his essay reviewing the first ten years of Nazi rule, which he wrote at Christmas 1942, a few months before his arrest, thought the cure of stupidity—or, rather, the conversion of those whom the overwhelming impression of power had stupefied—impossible unless preceded by an act of liberation, that is, by a coup d'état;[1] Moltke saw in a coup the danger of a new legend of stab-in-the-back, like the one that had done so much political harm in Germany after 1918. That is why he held a clear military defeat to be necessary. It was to prepare for this eventuality, above all, that the Kreisauers continued in the summer of 1943 to work for a new Germany in a new Europe and looked for suitable men, "regional commissioners" who could accept responsibility once the moment had arrived, in the time of transition.

All these plans and personnel questions meant travels, which, as before, were mostly connected with official missions or camouflaged as such, as were two trips to Turkey in July and December 1943, when he tried in vain to bring about a meeting with Alexander Kirk.

Earlier attempts to persuade the British to station a trustworthy intermediary—perhaps Moltke's friend Michael Balfour—in Stockholm, for liaison with the German opposition, had proved equally fruitless. A long letter Moltke wrote to Lionel Curtis in March 1943 never reached him. The Swede to whom it was entrusted for forwarding thought it too risky. It rested in a Swedish archive until it was published in 1970.[2]

But it gives, even now, a vivid and detailed picture of what the internal

---

1. See Eberhard Bethge, ed., *Dietrich Bonhoeffer: Letters and Papers from Prison* (enlarged ed., New York, 1972), pp. 8–9.
2. Henrik Lindgren, "Adam von Trotts Reisen nach Schweden 1942–1944: Ein Beitrag zur Frage der Auslandsverbindungen des deutschen Widerstandes," in *Vierteljahrshefte für Zeitgeschichte*, 18 (1970), 274—91. See n. 1 (p. 279) to letter of 18 March 1943. For the full text, see pp. 281—90.

opponents of the Third Reich were up against. Among the handicaps Moltke listed three that distinguished them from the resistance in countries occupied by Germany: lack of unity, lack of men, and lack of communications. In the occupied countries—except, perhaps, in France—most people were united against the occupiers. In Germany there were many who had profited from the Third Reich and many who had supported the Nazis at first and now saw no way out. Even more could not bear the thought of a German defeat and the dire consequences painted for them by German and British propaganda. There were hardly any younger men left in the country to spearhead a revolution: only millions of foreign workers and the men of the Gestapo and SS. The women were overworked and preoccupied with the difficulties of wartime life. Lack of communication was the worst: it was not safe to use the phone or the postal service; messengers, even if available, could be intercepted; and it was risky to speak freely even with people one trusted, because of the Gestapo's methods of surveillance and interrogation. British broadcasts were being listened to (despite the penalties if one was caught), but their propaganda was sometimes inept. The regime, the letter continued, was successful in keeping the army largely ignorant of what went on in Germany. The population was kept ignorant of such things as the killing of the Jews and thought they were just being segregated and sent east. People would not believe the truth if it were told and would take it for enemy propaganda.—Nineteen guillotines were at work inside Germany and no one knew the numbers of executions or deaths in concentration camps. The opposition kept losing men, and these deaths were hushed up by their families. Even the martyr was classed as a common criminal. But there was sabotage, especially in the bureaucracy, and the lives of victims were being saved.—It was a mistake to have placed any hope in the generals. "The main sociological reason," the letter said, "is that we need a revolution, not a coup d'état, and no revolution of the kind we need will give generals the same scope and position as the Nazis have given them and give them today."—But the opposition had done two things that would count in the long run: it mobilized the churches and cleared the road for a decentralized Germany. The protests of bishops had become known abroad; what mattered more, however, was the steady work of the clergy in maintaining principles in the face of all the propaganda and other pressures exerted against them. The notion of decentralizing Germany, which had seemed utopian only a couple of years before, had become a commonplace.—The punishment of political criminals would be popular in view of the large number of their German victims. Their punishment should be left to Germans, lest they be turned into national heroes.—The danger of communism was real. Intellectuals were more prone to it than workers. The workers who might go commu-

nist were Nazis now and might simply switch to communism. Older and
skilled workers were fed up with all kinds of totalitarianism. The middle
class were most affected by the lure of one kind of totalitarianism or another, the Prussian landed gentry least. The higher nobility in South and
West Germany were prone to the disease; the urbanized nobility were
part of the middle class—which tended, if anti-Nazi, to be pro-Bolshevist
or pro-Russian.

There then followed the plea "for a stable connection between the German opposition and Great Britain," one *not* based on secret-service relations for the extraction of information, not for the discussion of peace
terms, but one that could be helpful in the internal war against Hitler
inside Germany.

Nothing came of this appeal. The "memorized" version that reached
London in the summer was feeble and faulty and even the original would
not, in all likelihood, have led to a modification of Churchill's directive to
ignore all German approaches. The Foreign Office records show that
these were assumed to be aimed at splitting the Allies or arguing for a
soft peace.

The increasingly crowded and difficult last months before Moltke's arrest were also made more strenuous by the escalation of Allied air raids.
The central offices of the Abwehr moved to the new OKW headquarters
at Zossen, outside Berlin. Moltke continued to work in Berlin with a
small group. When the apartment at Derfflingerstrasse was bombed, he
was staying with the Yorcks.

The immediate cause, or occasion, of his arrest on 19 January 1944
was the arrest of his colleague Otto Kiep, whom he had warned that he
was under surveillance. The Gestapo learned of the warning, and that
was reason enough to arrest the warner. The real reason lay deeper: in
the fight of the SD against Canaris and the Abwehr. It was, despite all
caution and circumspection, in any case unlikely that Moltke would be
allowed to carry on his opposition against the principles and practices of
the Third Reich indefinitely, despite the protection of his illustrious
name.

No charges were preferred at first, and the confinement was called
"protective custody." After a few days of interrogation at Gestapo headquarters in Prinz-Albrecht-Strasse in Berlin, he was sent to a prison on
the outskirts of the women's concentration camp at Ravensbrück. His letters from there had to pass the censor. They describe a fairly comfortable
captivity—except, of course, for the proximity of the camp. Life was relatively companionable. He and Marie-Louise (Puppi) Sarre and his
brother Willo's friend, Isa Vermehren, cheered each other up and sang
and whistled a rich repertoire of songs, hymns, and French chansons. (Isa

Vermehren had been a cabaret singer and later became a nun and a teacher.) He not only was subject to prison discipline, but kept up his own programme of readings and physical exercise, so as to keep fit in body and soul. His readings extended from horticulture and the letters of Field Marshal von Moltke to the Bible and Hymnal.

Freya was allowed to visit him a few times and they were able not only to discuss family and farm affairs, but also, more discreetly, his present situation. His Abwehr office was still allowed to give him some papers to work on and by the summer it looked as if he might be released.

But the failed plot of 20 July changed all that. Yorck and other Kreisauers had joined the group of plotters preparing a coup d'état under the leadership of Colonel Claus Schenk Graf von Stauffenberg. Yorck was in the first group of defendants before the People's Court and was hanged on 8 August. In the course of widespread and intensive interrogations of people connected, or assumed to be connected, with the plot, the Gestapo learnt more and more names—sometimes as a result of torture—of men who had worked against the regime with Moltke, who himself was never subjected to such "special methods of interrogation," unless one includes deprivation of sleep among them. Although he had been under arrest for six months before the attempt, although his critical attitude towards Goerdeler and his group of plotters was known, Moltke was seen more and more as leader and driving force.

As these suspicions mounted, Moltke was brought back to Berlin in September, and now to Tegel prison, where once more he found many— all too many—friends, but where he was shackled and hardly able to communicate with the others. Yet the resourceful and intrepid Harald Poelchau was able, as prison chaplain—whose connection with the Kreisauers was never discovered—to visit them all and to help the harmonization of their statements and lines of defence. He also conveyed letters between Helmuth and Freya, who was allowed to visit her husband a few more times. She spent the last few weeks in Berlin, to be close at hand and to see what could still be done. She called on the Gestapo chief, Heinrich Müller, who told her that the Third Reich would not make the mistake that was made in 1918, of letting the internal enemies live. Moltke had to die, but the family would not be touched. (Families of the plotters were imprisoned wholesale and children taken from their mothers, to be sent to the interior under false names. There had even been threats of collective extermination by such leading Nazis as Himmler and Ley, who called for the extirpation of the "blue-blooded swine.") Moltke's trial took place from 9 to 11 January, the execution on 23 January 1945.

The letters describing the trial are the only ones that were intended not only for Freya but also for other contemporaries and for posterity. The earlier prison letters are too private for publication. They add little of political or historical, though a good deal of human, interest.

He had prepared himself for his trial legally and psychologically. The arrest warrant (for a man already in jail) came in October. It accused him of having tried, together with others, to change the constitution of the Reich by violence and thereby aiding and abetting foreign powers in wartime. This meant high treason and the death penalty. Paragraphs 80, 81, 91b, 73, and 47 of the penal code were adduced as applicable. These paragraphs do not appear in the judgment but instead, clearly as a result of his astute defence, paragraphs 83 and 139 (failing to report treasonous activities) and paragraph 5 (defeatism) of the Special Penal Ordinance for War are cited.

Moltke's letters about his trial show relief, gratitude, and elation. He found himself standing before his judge "not as a Protestant, not as a big landowner, not as a nobleman, not as a Prussian, not as a German . . . but as a Christian and nothing else." In this—secret—trial the judge had admitted the incompatibility of Christianity and National Socialism. It was an incompatibility the regime had always been at pains to conceal or deny, however much its actions bespoke its hostility.

He never obtruded his faith on others—not even on his own children, whom, in his farewell letter, he asked only to respect faith where they found it. Having, during the cataclysmic autumn of 1941, suggested introducing grace before meals, he did not insist when Freya did not agree.

It was during that same autumn that he realized his own better understanding of "Christian principles." And when he had a chance to write to his English friend Lionel Curtis the following spring, he mentioned the fact that he now saw the necessity of faith, as he did not before the war. "Today I know that I was wrong, completely wrong. You know that I have fought the Nazis from the first day, but the amount of risk and readiness for sacrifice which is asked from us now, and that which may be asked from us tomorrow, require more than right ethical principles, especially as we know that the success of our fight will probably mean a total collapse as a national unit. But we are ready to face this."

But what, he asked, was to come after this reign of terror and horror? People would need a picture beyond the terrifying and hopeless immediate future, one they could strive and work for. "For us," he wrote, "Europe after the war is less a problem of frontiers and soldiers, of top-heavy organisations or grand plans, but Europe after the war is a question of how the picture of man can be re-established in the breasts of our fellow-citizens."[1]

---

1. Balfour and Frisby, *Moltke*, p. 158. English in the original letter.

That was what the Kreisauers worked on, to restore the sense of humanity to people who had experienced its destruction; in practice this also meant discussions of a possible polity that would help to undo that destruction.

The German experience had brought even socialists to an appreciation of the positive role of religion in politics. Whatever the shortcomings of the churches in the face of rampant nationalism, whatever their failures when racism turned murderous, more people now saw in Christianity a sheet-anchor of ethics in the political storm.

The presiding judge of the People's Court, Roland Freisler, was wrong when he berated Moltke in court for taking his orders "from the guardians of the Beyond" and thus from the enemy. It was Moltke who sought out the Catholic Bishop of Berlin, and Moltke who in 1943 wrote to Curtis that the anti-Nazi opposition had "mobilised the churches," which, whatever some of their public pronouncements—and some of their more courageous ones had actually been noted abroad—worked quietly and steadily to uphold the principles of humanity.

His own concern to alleviate present sufferings is a persistent strain in the letters. There were limits to what he could do. And just as, before the war, he had voiced misgivings about staying in Germany and helping to maintain a façade behind which horrors were enacted, he sometimes hoped, during the war, that he would be thrown out of his job for his opposition. Yet it was clear that he could do more where he was.

It is this complex predicament the letters illuminate. They show what those desperate times demanded and how one "whole man," a man of integrity, responded. They also show his gratitude for the good companions he found in the struggle. He saw that it was usually he who had to go ahead and set an example in his official activities; and in the work of the Kreisau Circle he planned, coordinated, allocated tasks, prodded where necessary, and maintained direction and momentum. But with these friends the mode was a pooling of experience and discussion to arrive at agreed positions and plans.

The letters show how he grew with the challenges. There is, despite the complexity of his many undertakings, a continuity of intent, to mitigate the horrors by all the means in his power and to prepare for a better future.

They show how he lived and what he thought. They show how he needed Freya and the daily exchange with her. What we have here is not a diary with an interlocutor, but one side of a dialogue.

The life he sums up so movingly in his last letter is here laid open. However all-engulfing Hitler's twelve-year millennium may have seemed while it raged, here is the voice of conscience from inside.

Editorial Note

The letters Moltke wrote during and after his trial were published—with some omissions—in English in the quarterly *The Round Table* in June 1946, and soon afterward the Oxford University Press published the English and the German text as a little book.[1] Material from other letters was used in Ger van Roon's basic work on Moltke and his circle, as well as in the biography by two English friends of Moltke's, Michael Balfour and Julian Frisby. It was after the publication of that book that the need for an independent publication of the letters became clear.

When I prepared the German edition of the letters it was obvious that the wartime letters were the most important, though the earlier letters, too, had a great deal of human and historical interest. Although the German edition runs to over six hundred pages, it had to be selective even for the war years, when Helmuth and Freya exchanged letters almost daily. But in order to make available one of the richest and most significant sources on Hitler's rule and what it took to oppose it inside Germany, the German edition retained, for instance, every mention of Moltke's circle of opponents of the regime.

The American edition is shorter than the German and does not stick to the rule of preserving every mention of a "Kreisauer." It also omits almost all references to German sources, which those wishing to consult them can find in the German edition. I hope I have kept enough of family, farming, and financial matters, enough of his frequent mentions of food (he was a competent, though frugal, cook), health, the weather (mostly in connection with agriculture or the air war), even some of his references to Freya's bees, which he once described as his "favourite object of meditation," to show how he lived, thought, and felt, not only what he did.

One remark about the style of the translation: when no mid-Atlantic compromise was possible and I had to choose between British and American English, I chose the former. Moltke's own English—which was good, though not flawless[2]—was that of his South African mother. It would have been wrong to make him sound American.

I must thank the National Endowment for the Humanities and the Harris and Eliza Kempner Foundation for supporting my work on this

---

1. *A German of the Resistance: The Last Letters of Count Helmuth James von Moltke* (London, 2nd ed., 1948).
2. The letter written in English to Lionel Curtis reproduced on pages 281–290 is a good example.

edition. Among those to whom I owe thanks for readings and comments I should like to mention Claire Nix and Eva Brann. My chief thanks are due to Freya von Moltke: for her trust, for her great hospitality during the time of transcription and translation, for her help in comparing transcripts and originals and both with the translation, and above all for her friendship.

Annapolis, Maryland

3 June 1989

"Vienna, 1928, I suppose—more or less. Taken in the house of
Dr. Hermann and Dr. Eugenie Schwarzwald. Before I knew him.
We met first in 1929."—F.M.

Freya, "South Africa, 1934,
on a visit to the grandparents.
Taken by friends there.
Not much more to say.
Obviously I was happy."—F.M.

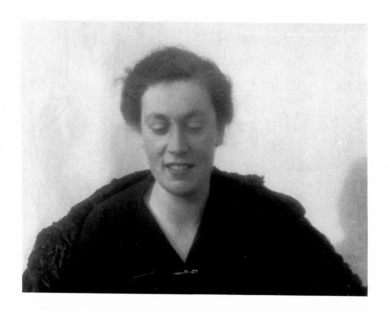

"We [Caspar, Konrad, and Freya] got out of Silesia and into Berlin
with the help of the British. We got out of Berlin (to Frankfurt) with
the help of the Americans. At Christmas 1945 we were in Switzerland. At this stage the photo must have been taken."—F.M.

South Africa, 1934. "Helmuth James trying to explain to some nice but naïve white Afrikaans farmers 'up-country' what National Socialism really meant. (I shall never forget it!)"—F.M.

South Africa, 1934. "There you now see the whole story. From left to right: the two 'Boers'; Dr. Jean von der Poel, professor of history at Capetown University, and Dr. Petronella van Heerden, a gynecologist and farmer herself—the friends with whom we travelled."—F.M.

Schloß Moltke - Kreisau, Kreis Schweidnitz

Kreisau, now called Krzyzowa. "A postcard to be bought in stores—in a small general store at Kreisau, but surely also in our next town, Schweidnitz, now Svidnica. Kreisau, because of the Field Marshal Helmuth von Moltke, was always a sightseeing goal for Germans generally."—F.M.

Kreisau. "Veranda of the Berghaus, i.e., house on the hill. The family lived there from 1928 onwards—not in the Schloss anymore (too expensive to heat; the family had some very hard years). This small house was much beloved. It had big, generous rooms downstairs and many small bedrooms upstairs. It is here that the three meetings took place that gave the resistance group its name."—F.M.

Helmuth James with Caspar
(born in November 1937), Kreisau,
Christmas 1938.

Freya with Caspar on the
veranda of the Berghaus
at Kreisau, 1938.

"1942, I would say. The veranda
of the Berghaus, Kreisau, from
the other side. In summertime,
as you well see, we lived out
there. From left to right:
a young cousin of Freya's,
visiting; Katharina Breslauer,
Helmuth James's secretary
in Berlin, also visiting; Caspar;
Konrad, in a pen; and Freya."
—F.M.

Freya with Konrad
(born in September 1941)
on the veranda of the
Berghaus at Kreisau, 1942.

Helmuth James with Konrad at
the dinner table at Kreisau, 1942.

"Helmuth James and Freya walking
on the estate (an endless pleasure!),
here passing a meadow full of
Kreisau cows, 1942."—F.M.

Freya with Konrad on the veranda
of the Berghaus at Kreisau,
shelling peas, 1943–44.

"Konrad (left) and Caspar.
Their father had this photo with
him in prison at Ravensbrück.
1943–44."—F.M.

"1942? Helmuth James working
in his beloved garden around
the Berghaus at Kreisau;
Freya's feet."—F.M.

10 January 1945: the trial.

Letters

1939

My love, last night I was with Kirk,[1] and while I was still there the telephone rang with the news of the German-Russian pact.[2] In the pessimistic atmosphere of this city every novelty of this kind comes as a relief. The feeling is: Thank God that at least something is happening. I've not heard anything about the pact and in any case am very sceptical. I incline to the view that it is a *coup de théâtre* that doesn't change much. But some here go as far as saying that a real partition of Poland was

1. Alexander Comstock Kirk, American chargé d'affaires. M. had first met him at his friend Wallace Deuel's, who was the Berlin correspondent of the Chicago *Daily News*. The meeting led to a frequent exchange of views. This is how M. described the scene in a letter of 26 July 1939: "Yesterday it was very nice with Kirk. He has rented Frau von Pannwitz's house: one vast hall after another, and he quite alone in the midst of it all. Very funny; a little like the theatre. In one of the large halls with a conservatory behind French windows and a view of the park beyond, there was a table in the centre, lit with candles; and we sat there, and three servants waited on us, who spoke nothing but Italian. Just like a film. But he is a nice man."
2. The agreement by the German and Soviet governments to conclude a Non-Aggression Pact was announced by the German News Agency late at night on 21 August. Ribbentrop and Molotov signed it in Moscow on 23 August (Text in *DGFP*, D, VII, no. 228). The secret protocol on spheres of interest and the "case of a territorial-political transformation of Poland" only became known later (Text in *DGFP*, D, VII, no. 229).

agreed.—Otherwise the mood here is such that everybody expects war to break out in a few days, surely before the end of this week. I am not prepared to believe that and feel comfortable in my disbelief.

Yesterday I felt wretched the whole afternoon. Heaven knows why. I think I'll go to Suchantke.[1]—The affair for which I had to leave on Sunday turned out to be far from ripe, and I wasn't able to do anything. That was very annoying.—Today I'm having lunch with the Hülsens,[2] and Einsiedel[3] will visit me in the evening. Tomorrow I hope to get hold of Hans Adolf[4] so as to bring my information up to date, and on Thursday I'm eating with Kirk again. That is very useful for me at the moment.

For the time being I have no plans either for Switzerland or for London. I'll talk with Einsiedel tonight and take counsel; he was planning to come to Kreisau on Sunday.—Farewell, my love, be well and continue your affection for your husband, Jäm.[5]

Three hours later: I'm working through a pile of papers A.M.[6] sent me, concerning [Powell?]. Look what I found. I think Uncle Helmuth[7] made that speech.

Berlin, 23 August 1939

. . . The general situation is far from clear. I still think that nothing has changed, unless a partition of Poland has been agreed upon with the Russians. That is quite possible, and I've heard it maintained by a good source. But it strikes me as so obviously idiotic from the Russian point of view that I can't imagine it to be true.

Domestically the consequences of the new course are incalculable and most disagreeable for us. The economic situation will hardly be improved by having a few million Poles for breakfast, digestive trouble will increase,

1. His doctor.

2. Leonore von Hülsen (1875–1961), sister of M.'s father, and her son, Hans Carl.

3. Horst von Einsiedel (1905–48?), old friend from student and voluntary-work-camp days; economist in the Chemical Industries Administration; took part in the second and third meetings at Kreisau; escaped arrest after 20 July 1944; arrested by Soviet authorities shortly after taking on the Industrial Planning Division in the Central Administration of the Soviet Zone of Occupation; died in captivity.

4. Hans Adolf von Moltke (1884–1943), cousin of M.'s father; German Ambassador in Warsaw until the outbreak of war, in Madrid 1943—see letter of 12 January 1943.

5. For "James," the name he had from the loved and revered father of his mother.

6. Anne-Marie (Elisabeth) Gräfin Moltke, since twenty months earlier the second wife, since March 1939 the widow of his father, also referred to as "Pension Annie."

7. Helmuth von Moltke (1848–1916), uncle of M.'s father; colonel general and chief of German General Staff at the beginning of the First World War; nephew of the "great" Moltke.

and things will gradually become more and more uncomfortable. It may mean that in effect the Rhine becomes the frontier of Europe.—But I don't yet see all that either, because I don't think the Poles will lay down their arms without a fight, unless the Russians conclude a regular offensive alliance with us. Neither do I believe that the British and French will stay out. But we shall see.

Berlin, 24 August 1939

. . . The city is full of rumours. The latest view is that things will start tonight and that we have agreed with the Russians to restore the pre-war frontiers. Your husband seems to be the only person in Berlin who thinks that, apart from the general nervousness, there is no reason to abandon the earlier assessment of the situation. The AA[1] in particular seems to have succumbed to a mass psychosis that war is coming, must come, and at once or almost at once. All this strikes me as nonsense.

I got on quite nicely with my work during the day; in particular I had a serious conversation with Prof. Schmitz,[2] Bruns's[3] deputy, on questions of British law; I found it very interesting. Apart from that I had a meeting and did some clearing up.

Berlin, 2 September 1939

. . . I haven't heard much so far. Developments must have been completely crazy, and we seem to have lost our nerve at the last moment. Moreover I have the impression that no one can imagine what a big European war will be like. Lack of imagination and lack of knowledge seem to go hand in hand. . . .

As for further developments, these are the conjectures here: the British and French will start shooting tomorrow; there is a hope that Italy will stay neutral and not go over to the French; but that possibility seems by no means excluded.—The week's delay is explained by the fact that last Friday, the 25th, the Italians suddenly declared they didn't want to join in. Ciano[4] is said to have made himself unavailable by telephone and to have kept issuing statements that he could not be reached, and he did not receive the German Ambassador either.

1. Auswärtiges Amt: Ministry of Foreign Affairs.
2. Dr. Ernst Martin Schmitz, deputy director of the Kaiser Wilhelm Institute for Public and International Law; during the war, member of the International Law Group of the Abwehr.
3. Dr. Viktor Bruns, director of the Kaiser Wilhelm Institute for Public and International Law.
4. Count Galeazzo Ciano (1903–44), Italian Foreign Minister, Mussolini's son-in-law.

Berlin, 3 September 1939

So today is Sunday. So far one's mood isn't warlike; it is just a feeling of misery. I went to bed early last night, read a few *Times*es and then a little in the encyclicals of Leo XIII and Pius XI,[1] and then slept moderately well. Einsiedel came this morning. Visibly depressed. Then I saw Hans Adolf and talked with him about possible employment for me. But he was rather negative. Still, I'm to make a note for him on what I am especially good at and he'll have a look round at the AA. His opinion seems to be that anti-aircraft gunnery is the right activity for me.—People here actually seem to believe that they can conduct a war with an administrative machine that's already creaking.

Please tell Zeumer[2] the following: we must expect production of artificial fertilizers to be cut down and that of nitrogen to stop, because the coal to generate the electricity required won't be available any more. He should therefore buy not only feedstuff but fertilizers too. We'll manage to finance that somehow.

The atmosphere here is terrible. A mixture of resignation and mourning. There is nothing at all positive in it.—By the way, I've meanwhile ascertained beyond a doubt that we wanted to march early on Saturday the 26th. The orders had been given and were only revoked Friday evening. I don't know whether it is true that it was because Musso[lini] refused to go along. But I know the other date as surely as one can know anything. . . .

Berlin, 4 September 1939

. . . The mood here amounts, at times, to physical sickness. It could not be worse. I think I am now sure of this much: The plans for deployment and everything else rested on two assurances given by the AA to the army and the Führer: (a) that the British and French would not fight, (b) that the Italians would fight on our side. It was on these assumptions that the attack was planned for early on Saturday 26 August. Only in the course of the 25th did the AA conclude that presupposition (a) was wrong, and only in the afternoon of the 25th that presupposition (b) was wrong too. Whereupon the army declared that the attack would now have to be postponed, because deployment plans would have to be changed. So every-

1. Almost certainly the encyclicals "*Rerum Novarum*" (1891) and "*Quadragesimo Anno*" (1931), which dealt with social and economic policy; perhaps also the encyclical against National Socialism and the Third Reich, "*Mit brennender Sorge*" (1937).
2. Adolf Zeumer, the *Inspektor* (manager) at Kreisau, an early admirer of the Nazis, but loyal to the Moltkes.

thing was postponed for nearly a week. The army, however, was certain that time was now working for the others, that England was planning to strangle us and that it would therefore be wrong to postpone these measures for months. So the army contented itself with those few days. To put it plainly: we've simply stumbled into this war.

Yesterday I had lunch by myself at the Adlon, because I wanted to soothe myself with good food. A few tables away from me were Henderson,[1] Coulondre,[2] Kirk, at another table Miss Webb[3] with two secretaries of the Embassy. But I kept myself out of sight. A curious feeling. This morning as I arrived at my office the French were just departing. . . .

I have the impression that nobody has any notion of how this war is to be conducted. They seem to be waiting to see what form the British and French attacks take; whether there is a big air war in the West, or what else.—But nobody takes a rosy view of the situation.

Berlin NW 7, Pariser Platz 7[4]   *5 September 1939*

Your two letters of the 3rd and 4th arrived simultaneously today. So I'm spoilt today.—This war has a ghostly unreality. The people don't support it. I happened to pass when Henderson left the Wilhelmstrasse yesterday. There were about 300 to 400 people, but no sound of disapproval, no whistling, not a word to be heard; you felt that they might applaud any moment. Quite incomprehensible. People are apathetic. It's like a *danse macabre* performed on the stage by persons unknown; nobody seems to feel that he'll be the next one crushed by the machine. It is the machine-like quality, the human disengagement, that takes the drive out of this war. It is bound to take the enthusiasm out of victory, perhaps the sting out of defeat too. What a war that starts with threats against those who are to sacrifice their belongings, their lives, their friends, husbands, wives, sons, and daughters.

And the top that is to run this gigantic enterprise is deficient in everything. Did you notice that in the last German Note to the British Government Palestine is called a protectorate?[5] Who writes such notes? How can a man at such a desk not know that Palestine is a mandate, a mistake that Frl. Breslauer[6] wouldn't let pass if I made it while dictating?—Noth-

1. Sir Nevile Henderson, British Ambassador.
2. Robert Coulondre, French Ambassador.
3. British acquaintance.
4. Law-office stationery.
5. See *DGFP*, D, VIII, no. 561.
6. His secretary, Katharina Breslauer.

ing is prepared, nothing has been considered but the military machine. But soldiers can never win this war; they can lose it; only civilians can win it.—Nobody seems to have thought about getting raw materials from overseas, about protecting German property in neutral countries from enemy seizure.—This is what happened yesterday: the British news agencies reported that we sank a steamship in the Hebrides[1] without rescuing the passengers, that is, violated the convention on submarine warfare. We denied it. But how: five different government offices gave five American journalists five different versions, containing things that (a) contradicted each other and (b) could not be known to the office issuing the report. Moreover we have also cut off telephone and telegraph facilities for foreign journalists, so that none of these versions could reach the U.S.A. in less than 48 hours, that is, after the British version had dominated the press for two days. Result: all America believes in another Lusitania case.[2] Ah yes, I forgot to say that the ship was British, but the passengers were Americans returning to the U.S.A. . . .

Berlin, 6 September 1939

. . . At the moment I am haunted as by a phantom by a plan to coordinate, under Bruns, legal consultation on international law for army, navy, Ministry of Economics, and Foreign Ministry and to get assigned Prizes and the British section. I hope it isn't a mirage. Since yesterday afternoon I've been unable to think of anything else, because I sense a great, interesting, and salutary task there. Forgive your husband for his one-track mind and continue your affection for him. . . .

Berlin, 7 September 1939

There's been no letter from you yesterday or today. What's the meaning? Is there no more postal service from Silesia—it's hardly possible.

Since yesterday an infectious optimism has spread in the well-known way of mass psychology; the optimistic assumption is that the people of France won't fight; it is claimed that French soldiers put big placards on their bunkers, in German: "If you don't shoot, we won't start." The story seems too fantastic. Still, it is true that nearly a week after the outbreak of the war the French and British have not yet done anything to come to

1. The British steamer *Athenia* had been sunk by German U-boats two hundred miles north-west of Ireland. Twenty-eight of the 112 passengers killed were Americans.
2. The American ship *Lusitania* was sunk by German U-boats in 1914; in that case, too, German propaganda blamed Churchill, in 1914 as in 1939 First Lord of the Admiralty.

the aid of their ally. I still explain it to myself by preparations for deployment and similar considerations. But these explanations won't hold water
much longer, and then it will simply be an unimaginably bad policy on
the part of the other side to allow the enemy to finish off each adversary
one at a time. But we shall see.

I think I've promoted my plans as far as it's possible for me. Bruns and
Schmitz are now negotiating with various offices of the Wehrmacht to get
the whole Institute put under Wehrmacht auspices. As soon as that has
been achieved, and I think it will be, Bruns will ask for me as assistant—
or, rather, the army has already been asked—and then I'll be working
under the auspices of the Institute, that is, in an innocuous place. . . .

Berlin, 14 September 1939

This was a nice day, with interesting work. Very depressing; but the
encouraging thing is that Sch[mitz] and I drill away until the sorry facts
are laid open. We'd written a beautiful draft for a publication, and it was
eliminated in the usual way and something impossible substituted. That
happened two days ago and all foreign papers have carried this published
statement and it was their best propaganda; we hoped people might have
learnt something from this. Far from it! The newly formed Sea War Committee met in the afternoon. It wasn't as good as I'd hoped, but quite
encouraging. Now I'm spending the evening on economic warfare. . . .

DER REICHSKRIEGSMINISTER UND
OBERBEFEHLSHABER DER WEHRMACHT[1]

Berlin W 35, Tirpitzufer 72–76   *15 September 1939*

You see who is writing to you. Today I was suddenly told that I am on
night duty, so that I can't go to my office to write to you. . . .

A regulation that came today says that wartime officials don't have to
wear uniform. A blessing!—I'm quite absorbed by my work at the moment, because it is so important to organize it correctly. Here the work is
increasing. They're getting used to consulting us and then throwing our
advice to the winds.

Now, my love, I must quickly get back to work. . . .

1. Stationery of the defunct War Ministry.

Berlin, 16 September 1939

The night was peaceful. But the papers that came in the morning showed that all our repeated advice had been thrown to the winds in the answer to Chamberlain.[1] Well, we've got used to that.—I went home at about 10 and, after some telephoning, breakfast, and bath, I slept very well until 1. Schmitz and Stauffenberg[2] came at 1.30. I hope to be able to use Derfflingerstrasse 10 to maintain, improve, and strengthen the connections of the international lawyers with one another. . . .

Berlin, 19 September 1939

There was only one event during my night watch, and it involved the departure of German officers for Moscow.[3] That was highly dramatic and I am very curious to see how the affair ends. I feel a bit like Hannibal *ante portas* and very much wonder if our compatriots will share that feeling when they learn the facts.[4] . . .

Trott[5] and Bielenberg[6] came to lunch at 1. . . .

Berlin, 21 September 1939

. . . Events continue to be dramatic. It seems to me that the great event of this year will not be the absorption of Bohemia or the dismemberment of Poland but the fact that Russia will lay hands on the Baltic States and the Balkans to prevent our expanding, economically as well, to the north-east and south-east. That, at least, is how it looks, and it seems to me that we have made possible an encirclement that was previously impossible because of Russia's remoteness. . . .

1. Sir Neville Chamberlain (1869–1940), British Prime Minister 1937–40.
2. Berthold Schenk Graf von Stauffenberg (1905–44), Marineoberrichter (naval judge), member of the Kaiser Wilhelm Institute and co-editor of its periodical; during the war in the international-law section of the Seekriegsleitung (navy). Brother and confidant of Claus Schenk Graf von Stauffenberg (q.v.); executed in August 1944.
3. See *DGFP*, D, VIII, no. 70.
4. The partition of Poland.
5. Adam von Trott zu Solz (1909–44), known from pre-war encounters in England, where Trott was a Rhodes Scholar; during the war he served in the Information Division of the Foreign Ministry and was head of its special section on India (cf. n. 2 [p. 149] to letter of 12 July 1941); used the foreign travel made possible by his position to work for the Kreisau Circle and the German opposition in general. Executed in August 1944. See Christopher Sykes, *Troubled Loyalty: A Biography of Adam von Trott zu Solz* (London, 1968).
6. Peter Bielenberg, friend of Trott's, lawyer, then in the Ministry of Economic Affairs. See Christabel Bielenberg, *The Past Is Myself* (London, 1968); republished as *Christabel* by Penguin Books, 1988.

DER REICHSKRIEGSMINISTER . . .

Berlin, 23 September 1939

Yesterday I got my pay as major.[1] I get 4.80 per day. That's what you call a princely salary; it is based on the assumption that one still has some other salary in addition. But no matter. Meanwhile the oath has also been administered to me.

. . . Fritsch has been killed in action.[2] I don't know if we'll be told. Since he wasn't employed, he marched off with the regiment bestowed on him, in which, however, he had no position of command, and put himself at the head of an infantry assault column near Warsaw; that's where he was killed. They had to use a company to recover the body.—In the end result it is a triumph for the epigones.[3] . . .

DER REICHSKRIEGSMINISTER . . .

Berlin, 26 September 1939

. . . All is quiet again for once. I'm plodding through the *Trading with the Enemy Act*[4] at the Institute and hope to have more or less finished it by the middle of the week.—Here at the OKW there is little work. There isn't much initiative and if the people at the top show no interest in questions of international law, everything here is dormant. But the machine is being run in and people are getting used to consulting us in current transactions, though as a rule too late.

Berlin, 28 September 1939

. . . Hans Adolf visited me at the OKW the other day and was obviously impressed by the martial style. I was much amused. In any case he said we should have a meal together, and he'll come to Derfflingerstrasse tomorrow or the day after. Frl. Saager[5] has already chilled a chicken. The recent faint shadow has thus been erased by the colonels, admirals, army

1. He remained a Kriegverwaltungsrat to the end, did not have to wear uniform, and never did, though repeatedly urged to do so. Cf. letter of 18 October 1939.
2. Colonel General Werner Freiherr von Fritsch, until 4 February 1938 commander-in-chief of the army; his removal, on a trumped-up charge of homosexuality, had been a significant step in the consolidation of Hitler's power.
3. In German: *Epigonen*, a term sometimes used for Party generals.
4. The basic British law on economic warfare.
5. The housekeeper at Derfflingerstrasse.

captains, navy captains—all with red stripes[1]—who drifted through the room when H.A. was there.

My work is still far from satisfactory, and the main task is still for Schmitz and me to gain elbow-room in order to be able really to achieve anything. It will take a long time yet, because nobody can see clearly in the general muddle. . . .

Berlin, 29 September 1939

. . . H.A. came to lunch at Derfflingerstrasse. I think he found the food satisfactory: there was a delicious chicken Frl. Saager had captured somewhere; he was more talkative than usual, especially on the settlement in the East.[2] He said he'd phone again next week. As far as I'm concerned, I'd quite like to have some regular contact. One reason for his greater talkativeness now, of course, is the fact that I too am now sworn to secrecy and that he wants to learn about the military side from me. I wonder how that will develop. . . .

Today I've been three weeks with the OKW. To me it seems like a year, and everybody I ask feels as if we'd been at war for an eternity. When one considers that it hasn't really started yet, that it probably won't start in earnest for six months, one could feel sick. It is too horrible to realize. It can only be fought off by not thinking about it.

Berlin, 30 September 1939

. . . This has been a terribly strenuous day. In the early morning there was a big case in naval law[3] that really infuriated me. A first-rate piece of stupidity. I was defeated in open battle but we, especially I, did what could be done. You'll see it in the papers, starting tomorrow. Hardly was that over when we got a question on air law, then one on economic warfare, and finally one relating to land warfare. Switching from one to the other is incredibly strenuous. . . .

I've been at my office for an hour and a half now and am going to the Institute later. I always like that best. I spend a peaceful 4, 5 hours there with no telephone nearby and nobody who can want anything from me

1. General Staff officers had red stripes on their trousers.
2. For Hans Adolf von Moltke's official view on it see *DGFP*, D, VIII, no. 137; for the German-Soviet Boundary and Friendship Treaty of 28 September 1939, with its confidential and secret protocols, see ibid., nos. 157–60; for Hitler's Directive of 30 September 1939, ibid., no. 170.
3. It probably concerned the lifting of restrictions on the U-boat war against enemy merchant vessels in British waters.

directly. That is very agreeable and somewhat restores the disturbed peace.—Talking of peace: I'm afraid that the war will start within a month.[1] I still can't imagine it. A good thing that Silesia is where it is.

Berlin, 10 October 1939

. . . Nothing much has happened since you left. Last night I worked at the Institute till 10 and then read a little after supper at home. It was 11.30 when I went to sleep. Late, don't you think?—Since yesterday there's been a suggestion in the news that the war may come to an end after all. That would be welcome relief, even if it were only a short peace. For this one month has been quite enough. But I don't know if there's anything in it. The British government seems to argue that even if they win the war Bolshevism in some form would come to the Rhine or even cross it. This would be intolerable, and even a defeat in war would be preferable.—Perhaps this means that we'll now oppose Russian presumptions a little more energetically. . . .

Berlin, 13 October 1939

The catastrophe is rushing towards us. I've reached the point where I can no longer see anything standing between us and this catastrophe. Only a miracle can give us a brief respite, a postponement of a few months. Does a man like Zeumer see now what has happened, or does he still not see it? I must confess that I did not imagine the scale of what's ahead. Stay with the work at Kreisau and look the other way—it's the best thing one can do. . . .

Berlin, 14 October 1939

. . . The last 24 hours were interesting in that I had two sharp altercations in the department, one on questions of warfare at sea, the other on the duty to report unfavourable developments, too, to superiors and especially to the top echelons of the services. In the first discussion the navy people[2] were incredibly stubborn and dense. The second one was sensational: I was told that it is our duty to avoid a crisis of nerves, that there-

1. On 27 September Hitler had told the commanders of three armed services that he intended to attack in the West.
2. On 10 October Admiral Raeder, the commander-in-chief of the navy, had proposed the occupation of Norway and urged an intensification of the war at sea, in disregard of existing international law and of the rights of neutrals.

fore we must be selective in what we pass on to those above us. Lovely, don't you agree? I count myself lucky that in all my own, purely technical work I have no responsibility of that kind. . . .

Berlin, 18 October 1939

. . . Yes, my love, it is a sad jubilee,[1] because the chance of keeping our own fate out of the general catastrophe will be rather small in the future. Still, it remains a jubilee, which has only gained by association with the grandparents and Mami.

. . . Today I was handed my certificate of appointment as Kriegsverwaltungsrat amid malicious remarks by Schmitz and Tafel.[2] Otherwise nothing happened at the Office. There's lots of bad news, but we'll have to get used to that. I'm to give a talk on the seizure of enemy property to people in the various ministries concerned. But it will probably be a week from now. That basically pleases me; it gives me a chance to prevent some nonsense. Otherwise not much has happened in that area. . . .

Berlin, 20 October 1939

. . . It was 1.45 before I returned from that meeting and Einsiedel, C.D.,[3] and Gauger[4] were already waiting. We had an agreeable meal together and talked about the prospects of the Christian world. C.D. looked unwell. . . .

There's nothing pleasant to report. Things are beginning to develop in the South that were already under way or concluded in the North-East.[5] Perhaps they're directed rather against Russia and result from the pressure of the Russian threat; but against us, too, because the little ones down there have seen that we sacrificed other little ones to our friends. But things won't go so quickly there.

1. The 18th of October was their eighth wedding anniversary and also the anniversary of the wedding of his mother and of her parents.
2. Major Wilhelm Tafel, head of the International Law Group, opponent of the regime, related to the Bonhoeffers.
3. Carl Dietrich von Trotha (1907–52), M.'s cousin who had taken part in the organization of the voluntary work camps and who later participated in the work of the Kreisau Circle, mostly in conjunction with his friend Horst von Einsiedel; economist in the Ministry of Economic Affairs.
4. Martin Gauger (1905–41), legal adviser of the Confessing Church—cf. letter of 1 June 1940.
5. The Soviet Union had concluded agreements of mutual assistance with the Baltic States and occupied bases there. It now began to exert pressure on the Balkan States.

Berlin, 22 October 1939

. . . The dread of coming events weighs on everybody; some are depressed, others feel a need to be merry and for as much food and drink as possible. Business seems to be flourishing for the ladies on Kurfürstendamm, too. When I went to meet the Jowos[1] last Sunday, I got red flashlight signals every other step. . . .

Berlin, 25 October 1939

. . . I had to dispose of a few enquiries at the Institute, and then I worked without interruption on the *Trading with the Enemy Act*. It's a very interesting subject, because it is so closely interwoven with questions of strategy and of general law.
. . . Everything continues as before. More and more people recognize the calamity that's rolling towards us and as morale in general worsens my own spirits rise.—Incidentally, next time you come bring the gas mask with you. Let Schwester[2] give it to you without anybody hearing about it. I don't think it out of the question that things may start by then, and Kreisau really doesn't need it. . . .

Berlin, 29 October 1939

. . . The gas mask you're to bring for yourself. I have my own from the OKW. At the moment, incidentally, it looks as if another little postponement has been achieved. If only it were until spring, at least. Everything is easier to take in the summer than in winter.
Yesterday at the Kieps'[3] there was a real tea party. Not at all the thing for me. K. had told me that his people, i.e., the people from his department, would be there. And so they were. But there was also a crowd of other people who didn't interest me at all. Still, I made the acquaintance of Warlimont.[4] He's the chief of the Operational Section of the OKW, on

1. His brother Joachim Wolfgang (born 1909), an art historian and a gallery curator in peacetime, an army officer in the war, and his wife, Inge, née von Dippe.
2. Ida Hübner, *Diakonisse*, the Lutheran parish nurse who had done social work at Kreisau since 1907, especially with children.
3. Otto Kiep (1886–1944), diplomat; 1931–34 Consul General in New York, 1936–38 German member of the Non-Intervention Committee for the Spanish Civil War, 1939–44 liaison officer between AA and OKW. His arrest on 16 January 1944 led to M.'s arrest three days later. Executed 26 August 1944.
4. Colonel, later General Walter Warlimont, deputy chief of the Operations Branch of the OKW and chief of the National Defence Section. See Walter Warlimont, *Inside Hitler's Headquarters 1939–45*, trans. R. H. Barry (New York–Washington, 1964).

a level with Canaris.[1] It turned out that he came to Kreisau from Wei-gelsdorf in '26. And Elka[2] was a relief. She didn't seem charmed by the proceedings either. We ate together at the Taverne afterwards.

Today I'm on Sunday duty, that means staying at home at Derfflinger-strasse. Wehl[3] and Leverkühn[4] are coming later, to talk about the future of the office. As soon as they've gone I'll start working on my report, so that I get the structure done today.—So far no date has been set for it. It's not to be presented to the Reich Ministry of Economics but to a com-mittee on the law of war and economic war.[5]

Incidentally, I've heard meanwhile that there are no objections to my having leave from 22 December to 4 January. Of course the final decision can't be made until we know the situation in December. But it's worth a lot that the mere thought wasn't indignantly rejected.

My love, I'll talk to you on the phone again tonight and you'll be here in a few days. My love, we have to get through these years of sadness now, it can't be helped, and then the worst is still to come. Whether there will be anything left then, heaven only knows.

Berlin, 30 October 1939

The calm day I expected became a stormy one. At 10 in the morning the draft of a new law landed on my desk and had to be dealt with today: I found myself in total disagreement. I had to obstruct it massively, and the result so far is a meeting tomorrow of all the ministries concerned, at which your husband must play the leading role. I wonder how it will end. . . .

Berlin, 31 October 1939

. . . I spent the major part of the morning doing battle in various min-istries. I was horrified by the irresponsibility and sloppiness with which laws are being made these days. It is really shattering. It doesn't matter much, because nobody ever calls an official to account. . . .

1. Admiral Wilhelm Canaris (1887–1945), chief of the Abwehr since 1935; opponent of the regime; removed from office February 1944, hanged at Flossenbürg 9 April 1945.
2. Elka von Wedel, relative of F.M.'s.
3. Berlin lawyer who shared an office with M. and Leverkühn.
4. Paul Leverkühn, lawyer with whom M. shared the office at Pariser Platz 7; served with the Abwehr during the war.
5. The Special Committee for Economic Warfare—Sonderstab für Handelskrieg und wirt-schaftliche Kampfmassnahmen (HWK)—had been set up in the OKW on 23 October 1939.

Berlin, 10 November 1939

Another very long day, and it is far from over. My new assignment in fact brings me to grips with one of the biggest questions of general policy and I may be in a position to prevent harm, at least in matters of detail. Because of the scale of the question even details have a range I would never have thought possible, affecting thousands and tens of thousands of people. I got the job this morning and have been at it since; it is now 7. Now I must work on the final composition, and most of the night will be over before that is finished. Then I'll have to fight for the acceptance of my opinion in all the offices, and I see no prospect of being through with that before the middle of next week.

Fortunately my report is finished; today I corrected the last pages and copies are being made of the beginning today. I'll probably present it at the end of next week. I wonder how it will go.—But when I think of the peaceful days that ended only two days ago,[1] they seem to me already very far away, for suddenly everything bears in on me at once.—But those days were lovely, and without them the time now would be an unrelieved burden. . . .

Berlin, 11 November 1939

. . . Lately, that is since Wednesday, I've slept badly, because I've been too worked up about my jobs. Fighting for human lives[2] is gratifying, but also terribly agitating. Tomorrow I look like spending practically the whole day speaking to the chiefs and with that begins the big battle it-self. . . .

Berlin, 12 November 1939

This morning I went to the OKW at 9; now it is 5 and I have just got away; but as far as it's possible today, I have achieved a success. I expect every day this week will be the same. I opened the meeting with a presentation that took nearly 2 hours, much of it dealing with questions of strategy, a field in which I don't feel exactly at home. But it went well and

1. Freya had visited him in Berlin.
2. Apart from the conduct of the war at sea, there was now the question of Polish soldiers interned in neutral countries, and that of exit from the part of Poland that had become the German-occupied Government General, set up on 7 October. The German "cleansing operations" there meant that the chance to leave was a matter of survival for the Polish leadership, for aristocrats, priests, academics, and Jews, who were being massacred system-atically by the SS.

I convinced the people in my division who matter most in the first instance. This is an important step, for from now on I represent not just my own position but that of my division. The next step is to convince the two other divisions of the OKW,[1] and then my position will at last be the position of the OKW. It will take the whole week. But I have prepared the thing so well that I should succeed.

I keep getting bad news now in the area of greatest concern to me.[2] Very bad news . . .

I'm beginning to be tired. I think I must still get used to the new responsibility. I hope to learn how to bear it better than I'm doing now. At the moment it excites me too much; I couldn't stand that in the long run. It is a blessing that I have Schmitz beside me. He is someone with whom I can always discuss things. . . .

Berlin, 13 November 1939

. . . This morning I gave yet another report on this subject; it is 12 now, and there will be a little midday break. The battle resumes at 3. I very much wonder what I'll achieve. The worst disaster that was imminent seems to have been called off.[3] But that still seems like a miracle, and one hardly dares believe it. Yet it seems to be so. If so, we have at least gained a little time and can hope to escape the worst in that respect. . . .

Berlin, 16 November 1939

. . . We made a 3-hour presentation. Your husband was really exhausted, but he seems to have carried his point. Slowly I'm beginning to see how I can at least torpedo one of these mad measures. But it will take more work. . . .

. . . My love, I must go. This strikes me as a miserable letter, but at the moment my head is so full of possibilities of preventing the worst, at least in limited areas, that I can hardly think of anything else.

1. Probably the legal division (Wehrmacht-Rechtsabteilung) and the Economics and Armaments Office (Wehrwirtschafts- und Rüstungsamt).
2. The planned Western offensive; on 7 November it had been fixed for the 15th; on the 9th it had been postponed. But there was cause for concern, since Hitler had, on 5 November, turned very sharply on Brauchitsch, the commander-in-chief of the army, who tried to argue against the offensive.
3. Another postponement of the Western offensive, which also became less likely now because of unfavourable weather.

Berlin, 17 November 1939

I slept wretchedly because I'm too excited about a possibility of averting the catastrophe that seems imminent.—A slight possibility has appeared in the last few days, and perhaps it can be developed.[1] This has
blotted out all my other thoughts. The day is nearly over; it is 6 in the
evening; I got several steps closer to my goal today. However, since I can't
act on my own and must confine myself to supplying others with arguments driving them to action, every step takes unspeakable effort.—Now
I've finished here. I'll go to the Institute, where I'll try to concentrate on
a few reports I have to deal with there.

This morning I put up the picture postcards you gave me opposite my
desk here. I'd had them up at my own office. So this room has gained
greatly. Altogether Schmitz and I are very slowly making it look lived-in.
Meanwhile I've even got used to his clouds of smoke. But he's very unhappy because he's so depressed. Fundamentally I have already stopped
being depressed and am trying to learn from this disaster and save what
can be saved. But it gets him down badly. . . .

Berlin, 18 November 1939

The most exciting week of my life so far is over. And the disaster has
been postponed.[2] I don't know what it means, I don't know how much I
contributed, but the result is there. It feels like a real Saturday afternoon.
Tomorrow I'll have to clear up what had to be neglected during the week.
Of course I'm still at the short end of the lever, a mere stump of the short
end, and when I want to move the lever, the long end, it costs quite dis-
proportionate exertions; what's more, the long arm must not be allowed
to notice it.—Despite this limitation my chance of averting some things

1. This may be a reference to the first favourable results of the mission of Josef Müller, a
Bavarian lawyer and, during the war, member of the Abwehr, to the Vatican. The conspiracy
against Hitler had revived, notably as a result of the German atrocities in Poland and Hitler's
threat of a Western offensive. Müller was sent to Rome to try to establish there a connection
with the Western Allies and to seek assurances that they would not exploit unrest in Germany for military operations or the imposition of another unacceptable peace like the Treaty
of Versailles. Pope Pius XII, who had served as nuncio in Germany for many years, liked
the Germans and disliked the Nazis; he decided to depart from his official neutrality and,
in accordance with the request of the German conspirators, to be a guarantor of their good
faith vis-à-vis the British government. See Owen Chadwick, *Britain and the Vatican During
the Second World War* (Cambridge, 1986), pp. 86–100, and Peter Hoffmann, *The History of
the German Resistance*, trans. Richard Barry (Cambridge, Mass., 1977), pp. 158–64.
2. A (new) postponement of either the Western offensive or of the intensification of the war
against merchant vessels—see Memorandum by Ambassador Ritter of 17 November 1939
in *DGFP*, D, VIII, no. 367.

is greater than ever before. This week I've really talked only to Schmitz. Last night, after what I wanted had happened, I gave the file containing the written record of my efforts in notes, memoranda, and letters to the senior member of our group, Col. Fonck,[1] who'd so far had no inkling of my activity. Ten minutes later—he could only have glanced at the contents superficially—he came in and said quite excitedly: Look here, it seems to me that the centre of gravity in the direction of the war has shifted to the International Law Group. However exaggerated and downright idiotic the sentence was, it still brought home to me the change in my position in a week and a half.—But today I'll go to bed early and sleep with a Phanodorm.

As far as my personal welfare is concerned, I look after it, want for nothing, eat amply and well, and do no more than is absolutely necessary. But as long as I feel that by taking pains and by using all my strength I can prevent or delay disaster threatening tens of thousands, maybe hundreds of thousands, that effort takes precedence. That can't be helped. . . .

Berlin, 20 November 1939

. . . There's less work today. In general I want to take it easy this week in order to be fresh for my report on Thursday. The audience will consist mainly of senior officials of the ministries, some admirals and ambassadors. A very exalted gathering. It will be very funny. . . .

Berlin, 25 November 1939

Yesterday I didn't write. From early in the day till late at night I fought a war measure in a minority of 1:25. It was a brutal strain, particularly since the others continually used against me a Führer Order, which is already out.[2] So the decision yesterday went against me. This morning I took the matter to my chief[3] and got his complete backing; with this backing I resumed the fight this morning, and towards 2 o'clock I reached the point where the representatives of some sections began to waver and wanted to discuss the matter with their ministers once more. As soon as that has been done there's to be another meeting, that is either tonight or tomorrow morning.—Meanwhile I've mobilized the lawyers from the

1. Colonel Fonck had been in charge of the section on international law in the War Ministry some years before the war.
2. See Hitler's Directives No. 7 of 18 October 1939 (*DGFP*, D, VIII, no. 276), No. 8 of 20 November 1939 (ibid., no. 377), No. 9 of 29 November 1939 (ibid., no. 399).
3. Captain, later Rear Admiral Leopold Bürkner, chief of the Abteilung Ausland (Foreign Division) in the Abwehr.

other sections. They would never have found the courage to rebel by themselves, but the fact that a senior military officer was backing us gave them the necessary courage. As the matter now stands I've succeeded in weakening their stand, and so I hope I may yet prevail against the twenty-five-fold odds. I can hardly believe that I managed to get this far; but now that this hardest part of the road is behind me, I have hope. But I feel terribly exhausted.

Otherwise I have nothing to tell you. I wondered whether I should ask you to bundle up the Baron[1] and come here, because a new crisis is looming, and I don't know how everything will look in two weeks' time. But I decided against it. By the way, you must give as reason for any change in your plans the fact that I had an exceptional amount of work at the time originally intended.

After some snow in the night it's warmer here today. I can't judge if the weather will permit work in the fields; but it should be possible, and I hope the sugar beet can still be got in.

Farewell, my love, your husband is drained, but he hopes to recover quickly and he's pleased at the success so far.

Berlin, 27 November 1939

Today I won my case. But it was like winning a victory over a hydra. I chopped off one of the monster's heads, and 10 new ones have grown in its place. In any case I felt so wretched after this victory that I went home and had tea. Here I sit writing on my knees and waiting for Frl. Breslauer, who is coming here to work. I simply feel weak.—I'll go to bed soon and shall take a Phanodorm.

It's pouring here. Yesterday and the day before were the same. In the morning and evening there is some slush, rain during the day. The weather is some comfort, but whether it will help I don't know. It seems to me that only miracles can help us now. . . .

Berlin, 28 November 1939

After the hectic events of the last few days preceding the final decision today—the discussion with the Führer begins in an hour[2]—it strikes me as an anticlimax to be dealing again with normal everyday things.

1. Nickname for (Helmuth) Caspar (born 1937).
2. Cf. n. 2 (p. 46) to letter of 25 November. Hitler's directive of 29 November on economic warfare against Britain was much milder than Raeder's proposals and the directives of 18 October and 20 November.

Yesterday in particular I felt that I didn't have the necessary resilience. But today I got used to it again, and it may well be that tomorrow nothing remains but even greater care than before in guarding my key to the safe. . . .

Berlin, 9 December 1939

Yesterday evening I won a victory over Ritter[1] without doing much; he had to beat a retreat on quite an important question in the face of a concentric attack by all present. He'd simply overplayed his hand. How much this means for the future is not yet clear.

Monday will see another Major Engagement. I therefore made careful preparations today for the Monday battle and shall go to the chief tomorrow, Sunday, morning. On the whole the chances look better to me than before. In any case the past week has brought round some who were not on my side originally. . . . [2]

Berlin, 10 December 1939

Yesterday afternoon Schuster[3] sent one of his people to inform me that he has come round to my view of the question on which I put up such a hard fight; since that was a new factor, he wanted to put the question on the agenda for Monday, when other questions have to be discussed; I am therefore to state my case once more.—Now I am curious how it will go on. This move shifts the main burden of the struggle from me to the admiral, who carries more weight but is also more vulnerable, because he has something to lose. . . .

Berlin, 11 December 1939

. . . Today from 12.30 till 3.30 we had a meeting from which I emerged with a satisfactory victory. Ritter retired with the comment that the art of war required flexibility and so did the art of economic warfare. I hope this chapter is now closed.—At the same time we opened a new chapter, in

1. Dr. Karl Ritter, Ambassador specializing in economic questions, represented the AA in the Special Committee for Economic Warfare (HWK)—cf. n. 5 to letter of 29 October—and advocated the circumvention of international law; in 1949 sentenced to four years' imprisonment in the Wilhelmstrasse (Ministries) Trial at Nuremberg.
2. See letter of 11 December.
3. Admiral Karlgeorg Schuster, head of the Sonderstab HWK—cf. n. 5 to letter of 29 October—until May 1940, then Admiral South-East, later commander-in-chief of Marineobergruppenkommando South.

which I was able to operate more successfully. The matter is being reviewed and I confidently hope it will go better. Now that I have prevailed in the first dramatic clash, what follows should be easier. It seems so and Ritter was already much more tame. . . .[1]

Berlin, 13 December 1939

Look, my love, what lovely letters arrived today. They had come to Carl,[2] who sent them from Cologne. I find the two last words in Daddy's[3] letter the most moving.—That was my chief joy this morning. But I had an altogether pleasant day, since my hope for a quicker end to this war has had good nourishment.[4] I'm ready to bet now that we'll celebrate the next Christmas in the messy aftermath of war. . . .

Berlin, 17 December 1939

. . . Last night[5] was very nice, as always. I'm already harvesting the first fruits of what I sowed in September and October.[6] Altogether, when I survey these 4 months, I find that I've never before prevented so much evil and achieved so much good. It astounds me. And the agreeable part of it is that nobody will ever find out about it or take note of it, so that nobody will see ways to oppose it. My holiday mood persists. It's very bad of me, but after the exertions of the last months, and especially the last few weeks, I must let myself go a bit if I'm not to get completely overwrought.—I'm still debating with myself whether I should start something at the Institute next week or not.

Today will be very quiet. I'll work here at my office till lunchtime, perhaps till 2 or 3. Then I'll go home to eat, continue to read and work at home, have tea, telephone with Pim, have supper, and go to sleep. The only human voice I'll hear all day will be the voice of my Pim on the telephone. Those are the days I treasure. For 36 hours one is left com-

1. Next day he reported, "Ritter's second project has blown up."
2. Carl Deichmann, his brother-in-law, who travelled abroad on business.
3. His maternal grandfather, Sir James Rose Innes (1855–1942); 1890–93 Attorney General of the Cape, 1902–10 Chief Justice of the Transvaal, 1914–27 Chief Justice of the Supreme Court of South Africa.
4. Cf. letter of 17 November.
5. A visit to Kirk.
6. According to George Kennan, "It was largely from Moltke that [Kirk] had derived his conviction that the war, all German triumphs notwithstanding, would end badly for Germany" (*Memoirs 1925–1950* [Boston, 1967], pp. 119–20). This was to become an even greater feat after the fall of France, and all the more necessary as the American Ambassador in London, Joseph Kennedy, advocated the opposite view.

pletely in peace and can't be distracted. Oddly enough I enjoy such days only in fine weather. When it rains, they irritate me.

I've just received the protocols of the conference at Sydney in 1938,[1] which was attended by Curtis,[2] Lothian,[3] and others. I want to study them over Christmas.—But I do hope we have fine weather at Christmas, because I'd like to be out as much as possible—I do nothing but sit indoors now.

Yes, my love, I'm very anxious to see how everything looks. I am full of joyful anticipation. . . .

Berlin, 19 December 1939

. . . Tonight I plan to tackle a longer job on the subject of territorial waters, and home is better for that than the Institute, where somebody always asks me this or that. I'm being made something of an information office on every conceivable aspect of British law. . . .

Berlin, 20 December 1939

. . . Yesterday I was suddenly seized by fear that a certain action I'd managed to block—not in open battle but by my mere presence—would be taken while I was away. I thought I'd seen signs that deliberate advantage would be taken of my absence. So I sat down and quickly wrote a memo[4] on it, to commit at least my own department to my point of view. . . .

1. The Commonwealth Conference in Sydney in early September 1938.
2. See n. 5 to letter of 18 April 1940.
3. Philip Henry Kerr (1882–1940), since 1930 Marquess of Lothian; worked in South Africa as a young man (member of "Milner's Kindergarten"); 1910–16 editor of *The Round Table*; 1916–21 worked under Lloyd George; since 1925 Secretary of the Rhodes Trust; 1939–40 British Ambassador in Washington. Cf. Introduction, p. 11.
4. Presumably it concerned Poles—both civilians and soldiers—interned in neutral countries, who were threatened with transfer to Germany as prisoners of war or, if not recognized as such, as political prisoners subject to internment in German concentration camps.

1940

. . . The atmosphere here is bad as always. In a week we're certain to
be in one of the crises that keep coming, and one never knows how things
will look afterwards. I'm appalled by the early signs of a lack of discipline.
In the second-class waiting room Inge[2] and I were sitting at a table near
the door with a major. 200 soldiers, who were sitting in the waiting room,
must have passed us, and about 10 of them saluted. The rest looked at
the major with curiosity and passed without saluting. Yesterday at 7
I went to Herr Becker to have my hair cut. He did it himself, because
almost all his people have been called up. Suddenly his assistant came
up to the table beside me and shaved himself. Herr Becker said nothing. After having done his hair and brushed himself the young man left,
and Herr B. apologized to me with a very red face. He couldn't say anything, he said, for if he did they'd run to the Labour Front.[3]

1. Erroneously dated 6.1.39.
2. His sister-in-law, the wife of his brother Joachim Wolfgang (Jowo).
3. The Deutsche Arbeitsfront (DAF) was the monolithic union established after the elimination of trade unions in 1933.

Berlin, 15 January 1940[1]

The miracle that saved us[2] has amazing, even catastrophic dimensions. It is not yet possible to assess what the consequences will be. . . .

Berlin, 16 January 1940[3]

It was announced this morning that it will get cold again, and it is already icy. Unfortunately this has made the other projects a matter of acute concern, and we'll have to live in a state of uncertainty until Sunday.—I spent the morning at the OKW. I had lunch with Peter Yorck,[4] Davy's[5] brother, at his place. He lives near the botanical gardens, in a tiny house[6] which is furnished very nicely. I think we found ourselves very much in agreement and I'll be seeing more of him. . . .

Berlin, 17 January 1940[7]

. . . I'm to write another 2 articles for the journal, one on the *Trading with the Enemy Act* and one on the Order-in-Council directed against German exports. In addition I submitted a big programme for economic warfare. So I'm doing quite a bit that I enjoy, which in the given circumstances is useful too.

During the last few days I have been appalled to see how a tendency to

1. Erroneously dated 15.1.39.
2. After an emergency landing by two Luftwaffe majors, documents on the Western offensive—fixed for 17 January—had fallen into Belgian hands. They caused Belgium and Holland to put their forces on alert. Hitler ordered the cessation of the preparatory deployment, and on 16 January postponed the attack in the West to the spring.
3. Erroneously dated 16.1.39.
4. Peter Graf Yorck von Wartenburg (1904–44), descendant of General Yorck, who in 1812 brought Prussia to the side of Russia against Napoleon in the Convention of Tauroggen. After taking a law degree, Peter Yorck became a civil servant from 1935 on at the Oberpräsidium Breslau, then in the Reich Price Commissariat in Berlin. After the removal of his chief, Josef Wagner, from office in November 1941, Yorck, who had taken part in the Polish campaign as a reserve lieutenant, worked in the armaments administration. His aversion to the National Socialist regime had led to conspiratorial activities since the late thirties. From the summer of 1940 on, Moltke and Yorck began the systematic gathering of the circle of anti-Nazis later known as the Kreisau Circle. Yorck continued its work after M.'s arrest in January 1944, bringing it into closer connection with his kinsman Claus Stauffenberg's plans for a coup d'état. He was sentenced to death and executed on 8 August 1944.
5. Davida von Moltke, née von Yorck, was the wife of Hans Adolf von Moltke.
6. The house at Hortensienstrasse 50 became the venue of many discussions of the "Kreisauers." When the heavy bombing of Berlin began in 1943, M. lived there. It was his official address when he was arrested.
7. Erroneously dated 17.1.39.

underrate the British has spread. Since I think that this underestimation is apt to impair the chances of peace I want to counter it, especially since I caused this attitude by pointing out some British articles describing their difficulties and giving some extracts from them. I concluded from them that with their usual matter-of-factness the British had recognized dangers inherent in the present economic tendency and that mistakes were to be corrected soon. The others considered these articles symptoms of weakness, on the grounds that the British would never admit to a weakness unless it was very serious. These people are stricken by blindness. The most fantastic part is that the naval operations staff, who have not had any successes for some time now, seriously held in their own conference that this weakness was due to their performance. That is a very dangerous illusion. . . .

Berlin, 19 January 1940

Today I got a lot of things going at the OKW which I wanted to get going. Everything went smoothly for once. At the same time Schmitz was able to put in a good word in a rather important place for the preservation of Belgian and Dutch neutrality.[1] Preventive action on this point is always to the good. So we are both quite pleased with our day. . . .

Berlin, 23 January 1940

. . . The disaster has now been finally called off. Finally means for quite a while, probably months. I have a tremendous feeling of relief. Furthermore, to accustom us to constant change from quite low to quite high and vice versa, a tiny bit of silver lining[2] has appeared in the last three days. It is very small, but the first of its kind since the 1st of September. Your husband does not dare to hope, but is in the fortunate position of being able to help a tiny little bit to extend the silver lining. . . .

1. It had been known since 13 January at the latest—see letter of 15 January—that the Belgians and the Dutch knew of the German intention to violate their neutrality. But Colonel Hans Oster of the Central Division of the Abwehr—see letter of 15 October 1941— had even before that date regularly informed the Dutch military attaché in Berlin of German invasion plans and continued to do so.
2. Probably a reference to efforts of the opponents of the regime to use the mediation of the Pope to put out peace feelers to England—see n. 1 to letter of 17 November 1939—and Peter Hoffmann, *The History of the German Resistance*, trans. Richard Barry (Cambridge, Mass., 1977), pp. 159ff. Trott was active in America along similar lines—see Christopher Sykes, *Troubled Loyalties: A Biography of Adam von Trott zu Solz* (London, 1968), pp. 287–331. M. at that stage seems still to have hoped that the generals would resist a German Western offensive.

Berlin, 25 January 1940

. . . Yesterday I spent the whole day at the OKW working on one thing. I always like that best. I got them to look up the precedents from the last war and did one of these things really thoroughly. At 5 I took it to the chief, expecting him to peruse and sign it quickly. To be on the safe side, I said he should phone the head of naval operations to make sure that no hash was made of the matter before we could do anything. And lo and behold, we just managed to catch on to it. It was about to be badly bungled. So we lost no time and managed to apply a brake. That is always gratifying. . . .

Berlin, 27 January 1940

. . . Schmitz was alone at the OKW today and seems to have had considerable fights. He came to the Institute, where I was working, about 1, and was still quite worked up. I have acquired so much routine by now that I take it all more calmly than he. . . .

Berlin, 28 January 1940

. . . Your husband is full of hopes. We undoubtedly have a madly strenuous half year ahead. But the prospects of a favourable outcome are better today than at any time since 1 September 1939. It seems that the days you were here last[1] were a turning point, because of the events I reported. There is still no reason to do more than hope. But at least we can now hope.

Yesterday at Kiep's I had a long talk with Schuster. He was very nice to me. I gave him a piece of advice. I'd long intended to, but was a bit worried about it. It was advice on how to do his work. But he was obviously pleased by it, which makes me think that I must have confirmed thoughts of his own. He told me I must always make such suggestions and always come to see him when I had anything of the sort. That is very friendly, don't you think?

Berlin, 29 January 1940

There were three letters from you today, including yesterday's. Only the one of the 26th is missing now. Today was rushed, with lots of work. But

1. F.M. had been in Berlin 11–14 January.

on the whole quite satisfactory. I had lunch with Yorck at Derfflingerstrasse again. Now it is 7.10, and Waetjen[1] and Einsiedel are coming to
supper with me at 7.30. I have quickly booked a call to you and then want
to leave.—Schuster asked me today if I want to join him. I wonder if
anything will come of it. A lot will depend on a meeting tomorrow where
an operational plan of your husband's will be discussed. If they decide to
study it seriously I'll probably change over, and Schmitz will get my
work. . . .

Berlin, 9 February 1940

This will only be a very short line. I had expected a quiet day; instead
it became very stormy. At 11 I had to go to a meeting with Schuster at
which some very important questions were discussed, and at 2.30 there
was already another meeting, "in the most restricted military circle,"
where I was the only participant below the rank of general. So it was
pretty funny. Afterwards I had to brief Bürkner and before I knew it it
was 5. I decided to go home and have some tea. I've just done that—
unfortunately without you. . . .

Berlin, 10 February 1940

. . . It's a really beautiful winter day: cold and sunny. I had my breakfast
by daylight for the first time. This progress pleases me.—I couldn't eat
with Peters[2] yesterday because I was involved in those meetings. So I'll
eat with him in town today instead. I am not yet at the Institute, because
we are to have another address by Canaris. . . .

1. Eduard Waetjen, who had an American mother, was a Berlin lawyer with whom M. now
shared the law office at Viktoriastrasse; he worked for the Abwehr during the war, mostly in
Switzerland, where he had dealings with the OSS. Cf. Walter Laqueur and Richard Breit-
man, *Breaking the Silence* (New York, 1986), pp. 177, 180, 192, 197, 201, 212–14, 259.
2. Hans Peters (1896–1966), civil servant and university teacher, known to M. since his
student and work-camp days. Decorated in the First World War, captain, later major in the
Air Command, finally relegated to anti-aircraft defence because of political unreliability.
Active Catholic layman, helped to establish connection with Bishop Preysing (q.v.), participant in two meetings at Kreisau. In 1945 co-founder of the Christian Democratic Union
(CDU) in Hamburg; 1946–48 member of Berlin City Parliament and professor at Berlin
University and Polytechnic; 1949–66 professor at the University of Cologne, some of the
time as Dean and Rector.

Berlin, 12 February 1940

. . . So half of me was ceded to Schuster today. I wonder what will come of it. In any case it is a step in the right direction, I think. . . .

[Berlin], 13 February 1940[1]

Today I started work with Schuster and now spend half a day here and half a day with Schmitz. The new work opens up considerable possibilities, I think. I very much wonder how it will develop. In any case it is much more likely than hitherto that I get at all the decisive things. For here we are a staff of only 5 people[2] in addition to Schuster, which will produce much closer collaboration than in the big Abteilung Ausland. . . .

This evening I'm going to the Yorcks'. Mütterchen[3] is coming tomorrow night. I happen to have a lot of work now. But I'm glad, because the prospects of doing something useful are better now than they have been for a long time.

Berlin, 14 February 1940

. . . Then I hurried to my new Office, where I worked till 10.30. I have a nice room there, facing Bendlerstrasse. It is an old house with a big hall and marble staircase. Then I hurried to my old place at the Tirpitzufer,[4] where I had things to do till 12. Finally I was back at Bendlerstrasse from 12 till 1.15. So now I have 4 offices and 4 secretaries. . . .

It was a crazy day. But slowly everything will fall into place and it will become less strenuous. Now I want to be there if Schuster needs me. After a month or two I'll know the rhythm of work there, and they'll know my methods, and then my constant presence won't matter so much.

Ah yes: it is likely that the German people will be called upon to make a birthday present to the Führer[5] of all objects made of non-ferrous metals, i.e., copper, bronze, nickel, tin, zinc, etc. Please think ahead what we want to give, what replacements you may need, what it would be better not to give. Anything belonging to the last category would surely be very useful in the archive[6]. . . .

1. Erroneously dated 14.2.40.
2. Captain (Navy) Weichold was chief of staff until summer 1940, Major Kayser for the army until about 1942, Colonel Veltgens for the Luftwaffe, Captain Vesper for the navy.
3. His mother-in-law, Ada Deichmann, née von Schnitzler.
4. The OKW building, which was also the seat of the Abwehr, was at the corner of Tirpitzufer and Bendlerstrasse, now Reichpietschufer and Stauffenbergstrasse.
5. Hitler's fifty-first birthday was on 20 April 1940.
6. The Moltke Archive, which contained relics of the Field Marshal, in a room of the Schloss at Kreisau.

Berlin, 15 February 1940

... There was a lot of work today, and yet it was quiet. I spent the day partly at Schmitz's, partly here at Schuster's. It is quite remarkable to be suddenly in a place where one gets operational plans automatically, as a matter of course, when previously one only saw them in bits and pieces after making an effort.[1] Today in a report I cited an operational proposal made earlier which I'd always known. I was told, coolly, that this was simply improper, and that I was permitted to cite only the operational order. That's something not even Canaris got regularly in my former office. ...

Berlin, 18 February 1940

... I am still very worried. Last month's hopes have vanished, and instead a large number of unfortunate facts have come together. At the same time the stupidity in some high military quarters is so blatant that it is unbelievable. Against these sad spectacles in the public sector the fact that I am now in a somewhat more useful position is only of minor importance.

Berlin, 20 February 1940

... This has been a full day, and it is far from finished. The *Altmark*[2] occupied us intensely, but all the questions of naval warfare in the spring and early summer cause a lot of work. So your husband really has to work hard at the moment. Schmitz too, by the way. Today I had lunch at the mess, and it was disgusting. I had only some soup, because I felt that, for the time being, the rest was still beneath my dignity. In the afternoon we had a meeting, and when that was over, shortly after 6, I felt famished and had some tea, which I am still sipping. Einsiedel is coming a little later and will have supper with me. For tomorrow I have a fantastic programme: firstly preparations for a big meeting on Thursday afternoon,

1. This was especially important since Hitler had on 11 January issued a very restrictive order on security.
2. On 16 February the British destroyer *Cossack* had attacked the German supply ship *Altmark* in Norwegian territorial waters and rescued about three hundred British seamen. The Norwegian government protested against this violation of neutrality. The British seamen had been captured from ships sunk by the pocket battleship *Graf Spee*, which had been badly damaged in an engagement in the River Plate estuary on 13 December 1939 and, after first taking refuge in Montevideo, had scuttled itself on 17 December.

i.e., drawing up the agenda, drafting Schuster's speech, and discussing both *opera* with Weichold and Schuster; secondly a report for the foreign and economic groups of my department on the present state of economic warfare and on operational objectives in that war; thirdly a talk to Schuster's staff on the *Altmark* case and its implications in international law. Each of these assignments would fill a day, and the devil only knows how I can squeeze them into one day, together with current business. . . .

Berlin, 21 February 1940

The day has passed astonishingly mercifully. It is now 5.30 and I'm already sitting at home and have had my tea. I do, however, have to get down to my property declaration and similar things, or I would not have come home this early. Deuel is coming about 8. Yes, my preparatory work for tomorrow's meeting was accepted in essentials, so that there was no need for revision; and my talk on the state of the economic war won't be until 2 p.m. tomorrow; and the talk on the *Altmark* was bad, as could be expected. So I managed to get through the day.

This morning the telephone rang. I thought: Aha, my Pim, and promptly said 210276. But lo and behold, it was Inge, quite shaken, telling me that Jowo is being sent to the Russian border and would not be able to telephone from there. I tried to console her by saying that it meant he probably wouldn't be sent to the Western Front for quite a while, but she refused to be comforted. . . .

Berlin, 22 February 1940

. . . I have really nothing to tell you. Really nothing is happening. One waits for spring and the disaster spring will bring. The chances of avoiding it are constantly decreasing and becoming less likely. I have got to the point where I can hardly think of anything else. It isn't at all pleasant. . . .

Berlin, 2 March 1940

You only left this morning and when I go home now, there will be no Pimmes. That is sad. But it was so lovely with you here and you're returning soon, my love. . . .

Berlin, 4 March 1940[1]

. . . The Welles[2] conversations don't seem to have produced much. Yesterday afternoon he talked with Schacht.[3] It's a devilish jam. But I believe less than ever in an attack in the West. Yet how is this paralysis to be overcome? . . .

Berlin, 5 March 1940

. . . Today I had lunch with Kiep and a few gentlemen from our department. It was nice and unexciting. I have arranged that Kiep and I are to brief Admiral Schuster jointly on foreign affairs, and so I now have an official link with Kiep as well.

Here everything looks all grey again. The prospects for a change of direction which seemed open at the beginning of the year have vanished again. It is strange that even I am still convinced, contrary to all the facts, that this won't go on for long. If I ask myself honestly why, I can't give an answer, and yet I feel that it is more than a hope.

Here is a letter from Julian.[4] As usual, though less informative. Carl cut out a bit saying that his position is difficult, for on the one hand he is convinced that *these Germans simply must be kicked in the pants*, on the other hand, *"you know, that it is not in my nature to kick anybody in his pants."*[5] Find out Julian's birthday from Asta.[6] Perhaps we can send him a birthday parcel.

Berlin, 6 March 1940

. . . The meeting yesterday went splendidly and like clockwork; though everyone expected it to last from two to two and a half hours, we finished

1. Erroneously dated 5.3.40.
2. President Roosevelt had sent Sumner Welles, Under-Secretary at the State Department, to Europe on a peace mission. See George Kennan, *Memoirs 1925–1950* (Boston, 1967), pp. 115f; David Dilkes, ed., *The Diaries of Sir Alexander Cadogan, O.M., 1938–1945* (New York, 1972), pp. 250, 252ff., 260; *The Von Hassell Diaries 1938–1944: The Story of the Forces Against Hitler Inside Germany, as Recorded by Ambassador Ulrich von Hassell, a Leader of the Movement*, intro. Allen Welsh Dulles (Garden City, N.Y., 1947), pp. 112ff., 117, 120–23, 125.
3. Hjalmar (Horace Greeley) Schacht (1877–1970), President of the Reichsbank 1924–30 and 1933–39, Minister of Economics 1934–37, Minister Without Portfolio 1937–43; acquitted at Nuremberg.
4. Julian Frisby, old friend of the Moltke family, co-author with Michael Balfour of the biography *Helmuth von Moltke: A Leader Against Hitler* (London, 1972).
5. The italicized phrases are in English in the original.
6. M.'s sister, Asta Maria.

in an hour and ten minutes. I'm very pleased that this first job of mine went off so obviously well, especially since the subject was a terrible apple of discord until quite recently. . . .

Berlin, 7 March 1940

. . . Tell me, did Asta tell Zeumer that she's going away? She must please do it, because he'll have to train someone to replace her. I assume that lots of people will be called up soon and then he's alone with Asta. The idyll of having Asta as a substitute for Luchter[1] can't last for

Here I was interrupted and now it is evening. There was a big row and I wonder whether they'll decide to throw me out at last. Once more I was defeated in the large group, deserted by Bürkner this time, on a question which in my view will have quite a decisive influence on the German position in the post-war world. As important as the Polish question,[2] in a different field.[3] When the meeting was over I went to Weichold and said I had been left in a minority of one against x. But I remained unconvinced and asked permission to exercise the right of every official to have his dissenting opinion put on record. Big row: I was an officer and had no such right but simply the duty to obey. I said I was sorry, but this was a question of responsibility before history, which to me had priority over the duty to obey. The matter came before the admiral,[4] and after 5 minutes he endorsed my opinion. He obviously had shared it all along, at any rate had wavered, and my resistance had strengthened his courage. He naturally hadn't been able to say anything, having to register and harmonize the opinions of the others without stating a standpoint of his own.

Result: the admiral will represent the opinion of the sections officially but will have his personal dissent recorded in the minutes and will also speak to these minutes before the Führer. This naturally left no reason for putting forward my own dissenting opinion and removed me from the firing line. But whether the admiral will survive it, figuratively speaking, I don't know.

Well, my love, the above is only for you. Now I must work, and fast, for this fight has cost me a lot of time.

[P.S.] Brandenburg No. 5 in D major.

1. An employee at Kreisau.
2. Possibly the question of recognizing as belligerents Poles who had joined Polish forces abroad; or the depredations of the SS in Poland.
3. Either the forthcoming German invasion of Denmark and Norway or German reprisals against British efforts to impede German exports—see *DGFP*, D, VIII, no. 662.
4. Schuster.

Berlin, 8 March 1940

Today I celebrated a great triumph. Yesterday's battle continued today, and all the military stars were mobilized. Schuster succeeded finally in getting Keitel[1] onto my line, and Keitel succeeded in getting the Führer onto my line, and at 6.30 came a Führer Order[2] with my conclusion and with my arguments. It is a scandal that such a thing can happen without the whole government falling apart, for it really isn't feasible to have one minister sabotage the collective decision of all the other ministers. But a great disaster has been averted, and despite everything it gives me great satisfaction to think that many non-German women have your husband to thank for the continued existence of theirs. For at bottom this decision is entirely and solely your husband's against all the other ministries, and against my own superiors. Isn't that gratifying?—Incidentally, only 5 people know about it: Schuster, Weichold, Bürkner, Tafel, Schmitz. So keep it to yourself. . . .

Berlin, 10 March 1940

Yesterday again my head was like a perpetuum mobile. I would not drop the things which are its main official concern. The struggle to prevent needless destruction absorbs me so completely that sometimes I can't think of anything else. All last week stood under two slogans I had coined, which had both hit home. One is: Destruction that wins the war is warfare; destruction that doesn't open a prospect of winning the war is barbarism. And the other is this: I want to win the war, you want successes to report; the two are incompatible.—It is a remarkable discovery that even in warfare only ethical principles have any prospect of proving right. Whoever thinks otherwise has simply not thought it through.

At bottom my attitude to this war is that of an executor who is horrified to see heirs fighting over an inheritance that grows less and less because of the dispute. He sees the heirs putting all their energy into this quarrel, and forgetting how to work usefully, and finally not only squandering their inheritance in the litigation but also wasting their own abilities in the battle. One sees all this and is obliged to try every way that may lead out of the quarrel. Every time one hopes there may be some way or other, it turns out not to be a way. And when one has once more seen that it isn't a way, one thinks perhaps one didn't try everything, didn't search and consider and investigate carefully enough.

1. General, later Field Marshal, Wilhelm Keitel (1882–1946), chief of the OKW. Sentenced to death at Nuremberg.
2. See *DGFP*, D, VIII, no. 662.

Once again I found myself in this vicious circle and I wasn't even able to listen properly to the *Eroica*, which I put on yesterday. . . .

Berlin, 12 March 1940

. . . Since Saturday I have been once more involved in a big fight against a certain strategic plan.[1] I really made a terrific effort, but, alas, without any success. Tomorrow I want to take a break, because I simply can't go on any more. I'm so tired that I have a headache, and there's no point in that.—Today I have thought out a new tactic to get the project taken up again. For that I must first get certain people, among them Bürkner, Schuster, and Weichold, to read an old article by Schmitz. That will give me some breathing space and nothing will happen until next week. . . .

Berlin, 13 March 1940

. . . I gave myself a lazy day today. I did work hard in the morning, but lunched here with Eddy[2] and Nostitz,[3] very well, incidentally, because Frl. Saager, to outdo Pim, had baked another cake. It was very funny. Then I went to Amelang to enquire about Aesop's Fables. They didn't have them. Instead I found 4 volumes of the little red leather Temple edition of Shakespeare, of which we have some, too: Pericles, Lucrece, Henry IV, parts I and II. Please have a look to see whether we have these 4 volumes. If not, I'll buy them. They are in excellent condition. Then I strolled along Tauentzienstrasse to look for your purse.[4] But there was nothing worth considering. One more hideous than the other. Then I went home and worked till 7; now I'm writing to you, and then Deuel is coming. There you have the whole day.

There is really nothing to tell you. It is raining and not at all nice outside. I talked at length to the admiral today on international law and strategy. He always listens in a very friendly way, though I can't help calling some military measures mistakes.

Now I'll listen to some of my new records.[5] My head is tired with writing and reading.

1. Perhaps the invasion of Denmark and Norway, for which Hitler had issued a directive on 1 March; it emphasized the need for secrecy and surprise.
2. Eduard Waetjen.
3. Legation Counsellor Gottfried von Nostitz of the Ministry of Foreign Affairs, from 1941 Consul in Geneva. Active in work against the regime, especially in connection with peace feelers via the Vatican—see *Hassell Diaries*, 19 March 1940.
4. Probably for F.M.'s birthday on 29 March.
5. F.M. had given him records for his birthday on 11 March.

Berlin, 17 March 1940

Today is a long and quiet day; or so at least I hope, for it is still morning. Your husband got up slowly, washed a little, had a delicious breakfast, and then listened to the Suite in B minor. I've already got very fond of it. Then I read the Bible a little more, an activity I pursue with more enjoyment now than ever before. It used to be all stories to me, at least the Old Testament, but now it is all contemporary to me. I find it much more gripping than ever before. I used to be annoyed by the long-drawn-out inessentials and the brevity of the essentials, but now I have learnt that what matters can be expressed in one sentence or not at all. Therefore, when anyone tries to stretch out something essential, it's a sure sign that he can't say it at all.

I want to stay at home all day today. I feel the need to see no one for a change, not even in the street. First I want to write letters. I have a lot to write. It is likely to take till after lunch. Then I must read a little essay on the Paris Conference of 1856,[1] then I want to listen to some music, and finally I must finish a little article of mine. So the day will be over before I know it. . . .

Berlin W 35, Viktoriastrasse 33[2]   *11 April 1940*

. . . It was lovely to have you here. But the times just aren't nice now. No one can claim that.—But don't take it to heart, my love.

I am tired, but that is agreeable. It diminishes the ability to react to all the unpleasantness.—Tonight is very critical, and starting at noon tomorrow we should be able to see a bit more clearly.[3]

Berlin W 35, Viktoriastrasse 33   *12 April 1940*

. . . The general situation is still unclear, though on the whole better than it was, militarily. By dint of much brooding I have found a possible solution to the riddle of the strategic purpose of this operation. Even if it is only possible to occupy Southern Norway it may perhaps tie down considerable enemy naval forces in the North Sea and in the North Atlantic. These naval forces can only be taken from the Mediterranean. That in-

1. At the end of the Crimean War there had been an attempt at a new regulation of the war at sea, especially regarding the definition of blockade and the protection of neutral commerce.
2. Stationery of his law office.
3. Despite the German-Danish Non-Aggression Pact of 31 May 1939, the German occupation of Denmark and Norway had begun on 9 April. The Norwegians resisted.

creases Italy's prospects of standing up to the Allies. It isn't enough to enable the Italians to take an active part,[1] but it is enough to prevent an Allied enterprise, even from the Eastern Mediterranean.

It strikes me as far-fetched, but it would at least be a tolerable explanation for an operation which otherwise is hard to understand. . . .

Berlin, 13 April 1940

Your letter of the day before yesterday, with all the news, is here. It doesn't sound as bad as we'd expected. But please insist on the pigs being weighed.—About the tractor, I told you everything on the phone. The matter is very urgent.

Hans Adolf has just left now, at 4.30. From that you see that we had a nice conversation. Our views seem to be getting closer to each other. Here is another letter from Granny. I now take it that Willo[2] has arrived in the U.S.A. He has been sent there for construction by his firm. Then there is a letter about the wreath from the Kaiser.[3] Please do what's needed and send the letter back to me so that I can thank them.

. . . The process by which Denmark is gradually to be made like Poland begins today.[4] I did what I could to prevent it; but when I first heard about it the people who should have done something had already given their consent. Otherwise the situation is unchanged. . . .

Berlin, 14 April 1940

. . . I'd intended to go to the Institute today. But I'll stay here. First I went to the Office in the morning to find out how things were going. I got into conversation with Bürkner on the strategic aspects of this present operation. It took an hour; unfortunately it was more use to him than to me. I started by complaining that we are continually being informed only of the How of operations, while the really interesting Why is withheld from us, so that we are reduced to guess work. I found this to be so time and again. It seems to be a trait of the German character to evade the Whether in important matters and to push the How into the foreground and to rejoice in doing that so well and never to ask whether it should be

1. At a meeting on 18 March Hitler had divulged to Mussolini his plans for the Western offensive. Mussolini told him that Italy was prepared to enter the war. This did not happen, however, until 10 June.
2. See n. 2 (p. 67) to letter of 18 April.
3. A wreath dedicated by the Kaiser from his Dutch exile to the memory of Field Marshal Moltke.
4. Denmark was now to get a reliable Nazi as Reich Plenipotentiary and an equally dependable military commander.

done at all. The Germans seem to have a pronounced gift for tactics, and seem to be hopeless at strategy.

Translated into military terms this flaw means that these men, rejoicing in operations and victories, quite lose sight of the goal of winning the war. Instead of pondering whether a solution will bring the winning of the war nearer, they think only of the best solution for each question. I've seen someone start as from a dream when I asked naïvely whether he thought his suggestion was calculated to promote the winning of the war. It's really only Schuster and Weichold I haven't found making this mistake.

It's the same with this operation in the North. I've already asked quite a number of people why we occupied Norway. Not one has been able to give a satisfactory answer. But not only did the answer leave me unsatisfied, no, I noticed every time at the end of the conversation that my interlocutor wasn't satisfied by the answer either, or, rather, was no longer satisfied. For the time being I actually have a better solution than the others; only this possible solution doesn't seem to have dawned on anyone; it would demand certain preparations which have not been made.

So on this question I lingered in conversation with Bürkner. Then Canaris joined us and we started all over again. But C. really is very primitive in military matters. . . .

Berlin, 15 April 1940[1]

. . . I haven't read any newspapers for days. Today I was talking to a man whose judgment I respect but who has to rely on the press for his information. His perspective on events differed from mine by 180°, and his comments embarrassed me greatly. It was downright funny. I wonder what the papers are saying.

I am filled to the brim with present and especially with the expectation of coming events.[2] It seems to me that everything is going much faster than I ever imagined, and a process that would normally take years or decades will be compressed into the next six months. I cannot shake off the notion that I must think and plan constantly so as to keep a step ahead of events. I hope the beginning of May isn't too late for my two weeks; they are likely to be my last leave for quite some time. . . .

Berlin, 16 April 1940

. . . I have a frantic amount to do, and very much more to come. There are suddenly things which I can't refuse to be done at my own office, too,

1. Erroneously dated 16.4.40.
2. British troops landed in Norway on 14 April and on the Faroe Islands on 16 April; but the Western offensive was drawing closer too.

and here at the Office an enormous job is looming up. The saying "*Si vis bellum para pacem*" has suddenly found a hearing in the highest quarters, and since we, that is I, invented it, we are now to implement it. But that means overlooking (a) that the saying no longer applies to the present stage of the war and (b) that economic action is called for, not long-term planning. The latter we could have done rather well; for the former we are quite unsuited. I don't yet know how to put this task in the right hands.

⟋. . . I had lunch with Kiep, who is gradually getting more and more depressed. Tonight Yorck is coming to Derfflingerstrasse. . . .

Berlin, 18 April 1940

. . . Last night I had an exciting dream. I was sent to Holland on duty and had a week-end there. So I decided to go to London with an American passport, the passport of a friend who did not appear in the dream. I arrived in London Saturday morning and went from Liverpool Street[1] to 5 [Duke of] York Street,[2] where I surprised Michael[3] at his morning toilet. He had to go to his office, and I went to the Temple and sat down in John Foster's[4] room, where I did some telephoning and was visited by various friends and acquaintances. L.C.,[5] unfortunately, was not in London. For some military reason or other I was not to go to Oxford, and he said he'd come up. On Sunday we walked through London, through the parks, which were already very springlike. C. had become a bit fatter but was well and chipper.—For some inexplicable reason I missed the night train, which was to have brought me back to my work at The Hague on

1. During his English law studies before the war M. used to arrive there after crossing the Channel from Hook of Holland to Harwich.

2. 5 Duke of York Street was round the corner from Chatham House (10 St. James's Square). Lionel Curtis had his London pied-à-terre there and had lent it to M. before the war, especially during his intensive preparations for his bar exams in the summer of 1938.

3. Michael Balfour, English friend of M.'s, co-author with Julian Frisby of the biography *Helmuth von Moltke*. During the war he worked in the Political Warfare Executive, later became professor of history at the University of East Anglia.

4. British barrister in whose rooms in the Inner Temple M. had been planning to set up his London practice.

5. Lionel Curtis (1872–1955), Fellow of All Souls College, co-founder of the quarterly *The Round Table* and the influential group of the same name which was dedicated to the cause of the British Empire and Commonwealth; co-founder of the (Royal) Institute of International Affairs (Chatham House). He had worked in Africa under the Governor General Lord Milner after the Boer War, as did Philip Kerr, the later Lord Lothian (q.v.). Curtis's interests developed from the creation of the South African Union to the federation of the British Dominions to a world federation (see letter of 7 September 1941). His weightiest publication was a history of the world entitled *Civitas Dei* (London, 1934–37). See also Introduction, p. 11.

Monday morning. This was the disagreeable end of an otherwise very nice dream: I felt compelled to choose between two alternatives: being shot as a spy in England or as a traitor in Germany. And so I woke up.

The enclosed letter from Michael is especially nice, and Daddy's[1] letter is touching too.—Willo:[2] it can't be kept a secret; his firm sent him to America to carry out construction he's working on. Whether he'll then go to Mexico we can leave open for the time being. Annoying that Herr Deichmann let it become known. . . .

Today is warm and clear here. Still only 8° in the morning, but welcome progress all the same. The occasion for my wanting to have you out of Berlin before Friday has been postponed a second time. For how long?

Berlin, 22 April 1940

. . . Today was ghastly again because we are now beginning to behave in Norway as in Poland. It is ghastly. The SS have been sent in and you'll soon see the organizational changes in the papers.[3] And the military go along. I am terribly depressed.

The spring warmth is wonderful. One day more beautiful than another. There are lots of birds, and the leaves are already opening. I'm fed up with being always shut up in this city; it is almost a feeling of claustro-phobia, that I'll never get out again. . . .

Hamburg, 25 April 1940

. . . I really shouldn't leave, for there is a lot to do; but since everything concerning the North is so badly awry that my doing this or that better would make no difference, I don't give a damn. And in the sphere acces-sible to me at the moment there are, in the North, no more human lives at stake.

But above all, my love, I look forward to coming home at last.

Hamburg, 26 April 1940

We are just leaving Hamburg. In two minutes we leave the hotel. That's nice. The meeting lasted from 10 till 3 without interruption because one

1. His grandfather in South Africa.
2. M.'s brother Wilhelm Viggo (1911–87) had emigrated for political reasons and worked in Sweden as an architect; he went on to America, where he settled and became a town planner and professor of architecture at Harvard. He was of military age and beyond the reach of the German authorities.
3. On 24 April Gauleiter Josef Terboven (1898–1945) became Reich Commissar for Norway. A Norwegian government in exile was formed in London on 5 May.

case was settled out of court; we'd expected that it would take from 10 to 1 and from 3 to 5 or 6. So we can return, quite unexpectedly, today. Since I need every minute in Berlin, I am pleased.

The session was none too edifying. The chairman made an inquisitorial impression, not like a judge, and the judgments were without exception badly argued. One judgment is undoubtedly quite wrong. One could see that the lawyers felt they were confronting invincible prejudice. One of the speeches was good, by an old lawyer who pleaded like an old-fashioned liberal [name illegible].

Incidentally, this is the land of milk and honey, compared with Berlin. In the restaurants they don't take bread coupons and fat coupons; sugar is kept in big pots. Meanwhile, I'm sitting with Stauffenberg in the train at Altona. We came out here because we didn't have a reserved compartment for this train.

Berlin, 29 April 1940

I didn't write yesterday because at 6 o'clock I discovered a mistake in a memorandum that was to give the reasons for a decision that had already been formulated as an order, and it undermined the whole thing. I then sat over it till 12. Today all hell has broken loose. I must finish this memorandum before I leave, and the order is already wrong.

But I have declared I'll go even if the world collapses.

Breslau, 19 May 1940

. . . My love, it was so lovely with you and I felt so agreeably sheltered.

Now a terrible time is coming, and heaven only knows how things will look when I come back. There will be difficulties at Kreisau, but from my point of view they look rather like a pleasant distraction.

Heaven knows what I am in Berlin for. The main purpose of my work is gone.[1] Well, I must wait and see. But you are my love and that at least is a firm point.

I hope that the question of workers can be settled so that the awful pressure is relieved.

---

1. On 10 May the German Western offensive had begun, which violated the neutrality of Holland, Belgium, and Luxembourg. The Dutch armed forces capitulated on the 15th; Queen Wilhelmina and her ministers formed a government in exile in London. On 18 May Artur Seyss-Inquart became Reich Commissar for the Netherlands. Chamberlain had resigned on the first day of the offensive. Churchill succeeded him as Prime Minister and formed a coalition Cabinet.

Berlin, 20 May 1940

The first day away from home is nearly over. It is 7 o'clock, and I'm sitting at Viktoriastrasse[1] after spending the whole day gathering information on the general picture. The picture tonight is of a complete collapse of the French front in the North-West resulting from an outright military failure of the French, especially of their leadership. Gamelin[2] has failed his exam. The superiority of the Luftwaffe admittedly played a big part, but a big real mistake was made. Incomprehensible! And it will have enormous consequences. But we still have to wait a few days.

Berlin, 21 May 1940

. . . You ask how I am. What do you expect? I am threshing empty straw on a side track, for everything I might have been able to do has been overtaken by events. That is, naturally, unpleasant. But what am I to do? I am in the machine now and must wait to see how I get out again. Moreover I would have liked so very much to stay at Kreisau. I don't think there was ever a time when I was so reluctant to leave, because I cannot imagine at all how things will look when I come back. I'd much prefer to do nothing at all at the moment, because I can see nothing I can usefully do. Everything is in flux, and in a few days, weeks, months, all presuppositions will have been turned upside down.

And yet I have heaps of work. That's the annoying thing. I have a very hard week ahead of me and late evenings will be the rule. When all that is taken into account, I am really quite well. Your husband is well and dissatisfied, nailed to the spot and in need of departure for Kreisau. This is a time that has to be endured. . . .

Berlin, 24 May 1940

I am feeling more sick every day. I only begin to recover after leaving the Office. I'll return to my old habit of working at the Institute twice a week. That at least is peaceful. Well, after this not very cheerful beginning I must go to a meeting. 100,000 Dutchmen are said to have been killed in action, there is no railway running in Holland.

The meeting which started at 5 was over at 7.30. Schuster, who was there, drove me home. It was a topic I'd once set in motion, on 10 Janu-

---

1. Since the beginning of the year his law office had been at Viktoriastrasse 33, Berlin W35.
2. On 19 May General Gamelin was succeeded by General Weygand as commander-in-chief. In June Weygand was appointed Minister of National Defence in Marshal Pétain's government.

ary,[1] under the motto *"si vis bellum para pacem,"* which I'd promoted
against stiff resistance, and which, now that it has lost its real meaning,
suddenly interests everybody, because now we can dictate, where I
wanted to plan. I didn't say a word, but it was very painful for me to see
my argument for post-war cooperation now being misused to suck the
conquered dry. My arguments of 4 months ago, which nobody really
wanted to hear then, were now being echoed from all sides as the ultimate wisdom; even in the Führer's letter to the King of Sweden[2] there is
a whole paragraph dealing with this question, and a sentence taken from
a memorandum of your husband's. So this project is wholly corrupted by
the power which now supports it. After the war it will be useless, because
it has been compromised. It is as though one designed a house for a lot
of guests and collected the building materials, but at the moment the
guests came to inspect the building the workmen took the materials and
threw them at their heads. It is an awful pity. . . .

Berlin, 25 May 1940

Today once more I did almost no work. I expect I'll gradually pull myself together again. In the afternoon I want to go to the Institute, and
perhaps I'll feel better there. It's never happened to me before that an
external situation I had to face made me physically sick. It is very odd.
Sometimes I can't eat, sometimes I feel like throwing up, and sometimes
it's diarrhoea. I consider these phenomena with interest and detachment
and only relate them as curiosities.

This is another fine day. Warm and clear. This morning there were the
first raids on land targets in Southern England. Carl got his visa for
Switzerland today and intends to leave next week. I am actually glad of
that, for though we get on very well together, I now want a week alone
without seeing anybody in order to master my own weakness. All the
people I see I use as distractions and thus never get on with it. All of
Kreisau, too, was not only lovely and lovable, but also a distraction, and I
must now get the better of this thing.

Berlin, 26 May 1940

. . . Last night I met A.C.K.[3] He asked how you were and sends his best
regards. He said: *"Do you want to know my solution? It is a flood without*

1. Probably his suggestion to promote intra-European trade.
2. On 24 April Hitler had assured King Gustav V that he would respect the neutrality of
Sweden and stressed the importance of a new economic policy in the Baltic. See *DGFP,*
D, X, no. 161.
3. Kirk.

an ark."[1] No, I don't want to float here, in Berlin; for that I find the other people too disgusting.—I don't know yet what to do with the time gained. I thought I might learn Spanish. But I'd prefer to work at something that required more concentration. The trouble is, however, that everything one does, even if it's historical or philosophical, whether it is Tolstoy or the Bible, seems so uncannily topical.

I have a very great worry: that this war will expand unimaginably. That the U.S.A. will be drawn in, either by helping the Allies or because the British want to conduct the war from Canada, whereupon the U.S.A. simply has to go along. If that happens, and if Europe, partly willingly, partly unwillingly, comes under our rule, the war will be transformed into a struggle between the Western Hemisphere and Europe, a war which can last 100 years and need not end, and which will only reduce the existence of us all. Then we are prisoners of Europe who cannot let themselves be seen anywhere else. Carl and I today examined the question where in the world we can still show ourselves without being imprisoned or kept out. Except for Italy we were unable to discover a single country.

Many thanks, my love, for the report on flowers and shrubs. I hope everything succeeds. I had the impression that the new lilac would do nicely at the very back of our plantation. The one that always comes a bit later. Cut the bushes back a bit. I didn't cut much last year, and they are apt to become long and straggly and not to form enough flowers. The same goes for the little flowering *prunus;* I left the two long shoots because I was afraid it would otherwise not get enough light between the lilac and jasmine. Please also see to it that the little lilac bush in front, the one with the delicate branches, gets enough air, and cut the old lilac on its south side and the robust little bush which covers its northern side back enough to allow the little one to develop. If and when the little one grows well, I'd go as far as taking away the whole big branch of the old one.

My love, I'll stop. It is so nice to talk with you.

Berlin, 27 May 1940

. . . So Schuster left for good today; he's been designated Admiral Commanding in Holland, Belgium, and Northern France. Weichold succeeds him as chief. Today Carl and I had lunch with Trott[2] and Peters at Derfflingerstrasse. Peters was filled with innocence, as always; he wishes to be remembered to you.

1. English in the original.
2. Trott had returned from his American trip—cf. n. 2 to letter of 23 January—and had then been ill.

I've started reading Voltaire's *Charles XII.* I'll do lots of reading of that kind now and do it everywhere, in the office too and at the Institute. In both places I can concentrate better than at Derfflingerstrasse.

Berlin, 28 May 1940

I've retired again to the Institute, where I'm reading a few things in peace. It is pleasantly quiet and secluded here, and I consider this afternoon a success. This morning I was at the Office without doing anything of note; I had lunch with Üx.[1]

Üx told me something I had only a vague notion of, that Hans Adolf has been put to work on the papers found in Belgium and Holland. So he's doing intelligence again. I find that simply ghastly and I can't understand why he lends himself to such work.

It's another warm and sunny day. A glorious day. I hope that it is the same at Kreisau, and I hope that the Poles have come at last. Several times a day I see the Berghaus in the sun with the flowering lilac. It just appears. That's never happened to me before, and can probably be explained only by the fact that nothing really interests me.

There is nothing to tell you. Schmitz is likely to return in the next few days and I'm already much looking forward to having him sitting opposite me. During the quiet time for which I'm hoping now, I'll actually benefit more from his presence than before. . . .

Berlin, 29 May 1940

. . . We are suffering a great misfortune: Wagner[2] has definitely been deposed and Schulenburg[3] with him. Bracht[4] has been appointed in his place and said in his speech on assuming office: "The period of objective decisions is over; now there will be National Socialist government." The fall of Wagner is a great and grievous loss for Silesia.

1. Edgar Freiherr von Uexküll, a wartime member of the Abwehr.
2. Josef Wagner (1899–1945) was a moderate National Socialist; Oberpräsident and Gauleiter of Silesia; he remained Reich Commissar for Price Policy until 1941. See n. 4 to letter of 16 January.
3. Fritz-Dietlof Graf von der Schulenburg (1902–44). Joined the NSDAP in 1932, but later opposed it; 1937–39 Vice President of Berlin Police; 1939–40 Vice President in Breslau; then lieutenant in the Wehrmacht, released for administrative tasks 1942–43. He was a member of Yorck's circle of friends and planners and acted as a liaison with the Goerdeler and military groups of plotters. He also took a lively part in the deliberations of the Kreisau Circle. Executed 10 August 1944.
4. Fritz Bracht, Gauleiter of Silesia, old Nazi and high officer in the SA and SS.

Otherwise there is really nothing to report. Your husband is doing reasonably well. I keep thinking that all of you at Kreisau will probably be quite well off for a while still. I imagine it like a harbour; I hope it remains one. . . .

Berlin, 1 June 1940

Yesterday I wasn't able to write to you properly that I'd waited in vain for Gauger Thursday night. He had committed suicide. It was quite a while ago; and my request to come in the evening had never reached him, but I hadn't been notified either. I'll tell you the reasons when you come. You can imagine that I was badly affected by this news.[1]

Today I saw Suchantke again, and he gave me some injection. He does have the air of a miracle doctor. But I have the kind of confidence in him which is half the cure. Altogether I'm looking after my health now. On Monday I'm seeing the eye doctor. Tuesday Schramm. I hope that when you arrive you'll find a normal husband again.

It's lunchtime now. I'm expecting Friede and Jaenicke[2] from the Institute, to discuss the question of the Belgian capitulation with them. They'll eat here, then we'll discuss, and then I'll retire for Saturday/Sunday, remove the telephone, and do nothing but lie back, read, and play the gramophone. I hope I'll be better by Monday.

As for the question of our allegedly putting our heads in the sand at Kreisau, I have this to say: It is our duty to recognize what is obnoxious, to analyze it, and to rise above it in a synthesis which enables us to make use of it. Whoever looks the other way for lack of the ability to recognize it or of the strength to surmount what he has recognized, is indeed putting his head in the sand. Whether one registers details and discusses them, whether one hears them on Thursday or on Friday, doesn't matter at all. On the contrary, the rage for detailed information leads to attaching excessive importance to detail and neglecting the equally important task of sublimating the facts and bringing them into proper perspective. If one chases after details, one won't have the strength to prevail over them. It is certain that this strength is greater in a calm atmosphere than in a hectic one, and anyone able to spread this atmosphere of peace around himself is a live support and driving force in the right direction. Peace is not *complacency*.[3] Whoever lets black be white and evil good for

1. Gauger had fled to Holland, having faked evidence of suicide; his persecutors caught up with him, and he died in German captivity. Cf. letter of 20 October 1939.
2. Günther Jaenicke, member of the Kaiser Wilhelm Institute and reserve lieutenant.
3. English in the original.

the sake of outward calm does not deserve peace and is putting his head in the sand. But whoever knows at all times the difference between good and evil and does not doubt it, however great the triumph of evil[1] seems to be, has laid the first stone for the overcoming of evil. That is why a peaceful atmosphere is of enormous importance and must not be endangered.

My love, it is funny that I of all people should write that to you just now, when I can't quite get to grips with anything myself. But perhaps that is why I know it so well. I hope I shall have regained the necessary confidence by the 8th. But you must defend the methods that have kept the Berghaus so peaceful and not make any compromise in this respect.

I'm just beginning to read a book on the history of philosophy,[2] which contains the following dedication:

TO MY WIFE

Grow strong, my comrade . . . that you may stand
Unshaken when I fall; that I may know
The shattered fragments of my song will come
At last to finer melody in you;
That I may tell my heart that you begin
Where, passing, I leave off, and fathom more.

Berlin, 2 June 1940

. . . I am glad I went to Suchantke. Even if the drops and injections are nothing but humbug, the very fact that what plagued me was treated simply as an illness brought improvement.

The Times of 21 May reports a case in which Viktor Wolff appeared. So he is at home, at any rate.[3] Otherwise there's nothing of family interest, so to speak, that I can discover.

1. The expression recurred in a letter to Yorck of 17 June, which initiated the work of the Kreisau Circle. In his reply of 7 July Yorck took exception to M.'s description of the German victory as "the triumph of evil"—see Ger van Roon, *German Resistance to Hitler: Count von Moltke and the Kreisau Circle*, trans. Peter Ludlow (London, 1971), pp. 291–95.
2. Will Durant, *The Story of Philosophy: The Lives and Opinions of the Greater Philosophers* (New York, 1924).
3. Son of Martin Wolff, F.M.'s law professor. The family had emigrated to England. Fear of a German invasion led to the internment and, for many, the deportation overseas of German nationals, although most of these "enemy aliens" were refugees from Germany. Many of them later served in the British armed forces.

Berlin, 3 June 1940

. . . This morning I saw Müller-Stüber. Result: the eyes are excellent
and the vision sharp, a little farsighted, so that, as he said, I'll need reading glasses in 10 years. I'm not to protect them from the sun so much and
should wear less strongly tinted sun-glasses. Otherwise he said that he'd
conclude from the state of my eyes that my general condition was out of
balance. When I agreed, he said the eyes would lose their tiredness as
soon as my general condition improves.

. . . At the Office I do hardly anything any more. I read the information
and *The Times*. Schmitz returns tomorrow, and I'll chat with him.—
I don't think I have anything else to report.

Berlin, 4 June 1940

. . . Yesterday Einsiedel and I went to Furtwängler's.[1] I had promised it
long ago and it was as refreshing as always. Today I am going to the
Yorcks'. Üx has invited you and me alone to supper on Monday and I have
accepted. The Kieps want us to come out Sunday afternoon. I left it
open. . . .

Berlin, 5 June 1940

Last night I was at the Yorcks' with Schulenburg, until 12. It was nice
and interesting, only a little long. So I am a little tired today. But it makes
no difference. . . .

Berlin, 15 June 1940

Your letter of yesterday had already come before I left. That was very
nice, for it made me feel quite *au courant*. I can't understand M.D.[2] as
regards Paris.[3] Her views are not only not shared by our people, including
most of the officers I meet here, but also not shared by the public one
meets here. Fantastic, terrific—and that exhausts the subject. In the war
of '14/'18 a fraction of this success would have touched off many times
this enthusiasm. Clearly M.D. and Grandmother Schnitzler,[4] too, still
react in terms of the last war.

Einsiedel came last night and we talked until about 10. Then I went to

1. See n. 1 to letter of 10 September.
2. Abbreviation of "Mütterchen Deichmann"—i.e., his mother-in-law.
3. Paris had been taken without a fight on 14 June.
4. F.M.'s maternal grandmother, Fany (Stephanie) von Schnitzler.

bed and slept deliciously. For the first time in a long while high-quality sleep. So today looks much pleasanter than yesterday. . . .

I don't think I have anything else to report. The days pass and I wait. I do know exactly what I consider right and good, but I'm waiting to see if any starting point can be found for action in accordance with this knowledge.

Berlin, 16 June 1940

. . . I spent the whole morning reading. So these are peaceful days. I've recovered my peace now and read with satisfaction and concentration. What happens outside hardly touches me any more, it suddenly falls into place, doesn't get me worked up any more, but is simply a phenomenon like any other. I wonder if this state can be maintained. Surely it will depend on physical and accidental factors, but I am optimistic. In two or three weeks' time I hope to fill my days normally again, and that it was ever different will seem to me a confused dream.

I've suddenly plunged into Spinoza[1] and I read him at the Institute. I owe much of my improvement to him. I must ask Edith[2] if she can get me an edition.

Berlin, 17 June 1940

. . . I talked to Bürkner today, and I can stay away Friday and Saturday. On Monday I must be here. I'll write you exactly when I'm coming.— Weichold is being sent to Rome. That's sad for me. Admiral Groos[3] is coming in his place. He is an educated and intelligent man, but without much military standing. That is a pity.

Events are happening thick and fast. The Russian entry into Lithuania will probably be followed by parallel actions in Estonia and Latvia.[4] That can't be helpful for us.—H.A. is now the Führer's closest foreign-policy adviser. He is at Führer Headquarters, not at Ribbentrop's[5] HQ. He is likely to emerge from this war as Staatssekretär in the AA.[6]

1. Baruch/Benedict Spinoza was, of course, detested in the Third Reich.
2. Edith Henssel, friend of the family and a book dealer.
3. Admiral Otto Groos became head of the Sonderstab HWK.
4. On 14 June Lithuania accepted a Russian ultimatum; Russia occupied Kaunas and Vilna and on 15 June the Lithuanian state ceased to exist. On 16 June there were Russian ultimata to Estonia and Latvia; on 17 June both countries were occupied by Soviet troops.
5. Joachim von Ribbentrop (1893–1946), Minister of Foreign Affairs since 1938. Sentenced to death at Nuremberg.
6. He died as German Ambassador in Madrid—see letter of 12 January 1943 and n. 5 to letter of 5 April 1943.

The peace plans[1] sound terrible. There can only be one comment on all one hears: *it could not have been worse.*[2]

Nothing else to report, I think. Just imagine, I crowed too soon. I slept badly again and am furious. But I suppose it will get better.

Berlin, 18 June 1940

I am very rushed, with masses of work suddenly pouring in on me now that I want to go home the day after tomorrow. I don't yet know how I am to get through. Moreover, before I leave, I am to address 2 admirals,[3] each one separately, on the prospects for development of international law in relation to economic warfare. . . .

Berlin, 25 June 1940

. . . Schmitz is in good spirits. He seems to do a lot of rowing and altogether to take everything lightly. I saw Kiep briefly today. He is resigned, like everybody else. I have the impression that we are rushing for a common currency for the whole of Europe. That would be progress, of course, and, one would hope, of lasting significance. The Russian danger[4] looks less menacing than last week.

My new chief, Admiral Groos, makes his entrance at Bendlerstrasse today. He will take charge at 3 p.m. I think he is a very nice and educated man, a historian in the first place. . . .

Berlin, 27 June 1940

. . . This morning Schmitz and I fought hard in the Academy for German Law for the rights and status of the Poles in the area we occupy. Some really incredible theses were put forward, and Schmitz and I took turns responding. It was simply shocking. It's no use, unfortunately, but at least our honour was saved. . . .

1. Hitler and Mussolini discussed conditions for the armistice with France, which was concluded on 22 June.
2. English in the original.
3. One of them may have been Admiral Gladisch, who was to become chairman of a committee for the development of the law of war—a committee suggested by Schmitz and M. on 20 June, and accepted by Keitel. Cf. letter of 22 July.
4. On 26 June the Soviet Union demanded the cession of Bessarabia and northern Bukovina from Roumania. The ultimatum was accepted on 27 June, whereupon the Red Army occupied these territories.

Berlin, 28 June 1940

... I'm reading chiefly Spinoza now.—Today we had our first staff meeting with Admiral Groos. I really liked him. Matter-of-fact, educated, yet with a little more backbone than Schuster.—There is talk now of my going to Wiesbaden for the armistice negotiations and the preparation of the peace negotiations. I've made the condition that I must appear there as the only lawyer for the Wehrmacht and leave the moment another is consulted. Should that be accepted, I still wouldn't want to go, but would leave the position thus secured to Schmitz. First he is the better man, and second I have set myself so many little tasks here that I'd rather not leave Berlin and the libraries. And at Wiesbaden I'd be even farther away from Kreisau.

Your husband is decidedly well. He reads easily again and feels healthy and all he does goes quite smoothly. I hope this means that the May crisis has been finally overcome.

Otherwise I have nothing to report.

Berlin, 30 June 1940

... When I was leaving home I decided to look in at the Office and talk with the chief and intrigue a bit against Wiesbaden.[1] Besides, I wanted to promote Schmitz's and my separate plans a little. And that's what I did, and I'm now writing at the Office so that the letter can go at a reasonable time today.

It's glorious summer weather here. Admittedly a bit close, but satisfyingly warm. I'd like to be with you. But a peaceful day at the Institute is the nicest thing I can have here. I'm simply devouring the Spinoza. It is so very well written. As for the political theory, it's a mixture of perennial wisdom, utopias, and absurdities. In the more general reflections there is more of the first, in the specific treatises more of the second. What interests me, because I never knew it, is that there is no important philosopher who advocates any constitution but an aristocratic one.

Now, my love, I must go. Your husband is well. He is actually better than before the May crisis, because he has no expectations now and therefore lives without tension, more contemplative than active.

Berlin, 1 July 1940

... Fortunately the Wiesbaden thing seems to pass me by. Kiep and I have decided instead to travel by car through France in the second half

---

1. He means the plan to send him to the armistice negotiations—cf. letter of 28 June. He did not want to leave Berlin, which was the ideal base for the intensifying work of the Kreisau Circle.

of August. I included Brussels in order to visit P.W.[1] if it hasn't been possible to move him by then. Unfortunately we can't take our dear wives with us.

Nothing else has happened really.

Berlin, 2 July 1940

... Nothing has happened here. It is marvellous to watch the squabble of the various offices over the booty in the occupied territories—i.e., mainly over organization and thus jurisdiction and thus influence; only someone as personally uninvolved in it as I can enjoy so heartily this clash of the vultures.

Wiesbaden is sure to be off, because the conditions I set can't be met. I certainly couldn't do any useful work there.—Today Schmitz and I put up a big fight against the slave trade, that is, trade in people whom we propose to hand over in exchange for similar services.

I want to go home early today and read a bit. I've just had lunch with the newly married Trott.[2] ...

Berlin, 3 July 1940

... Your husband continues to be in satisfactory shape. He is not yet quite as fit as at the beginning of the year, but his inner equilibrium is excellent, and I'm glad it's all over, especially when I see the others, like Einsiedel, Trott, Waetjen, Kessel,[3] etc., who are still downcast all the time.

Berlin, 13 July 1940

Yesterday's meeting was long and annoying. Annoying because all the civilians there acted as if the war was going to be won in 4 to 8 weeks, no further efforts were required, and paradise was round the corner. Ghastly. Therefore nothing came of it, and I wrote a note to the admiral today proposing to drop the subject[4] since the civilian officials are already drunk with victory. ...

1. Ada Deichmann's friend P. W. Müller, who lived in Belgium.
2. Adam Trott had married Clarita Tiefenbacher in early June.
3. Albrecht von Kessel, Legation Secretary, member of the diplomatic service whom M. had first met in Switzerland in 1935; friend of Yorck's.
4. F.M. had been in Berlin and knew what the subject was. It may have been the study and development of the law of war—cf. n. 3 to letter of 18 June.

Berlin, 14 July 1940

. . . I expect I'll stay here till lunch and then go to the Institute to chew a little more on Spinoza. At present I have no desire at all to see anybody but am content with the two gentlemen Spinoza and Kant. I feel I am in the very best company there.—But I'd like to be with you.

Farewell, my love, I hope you and your household are well, the people & children, the fowl, the plants, the flowers, the bees. Keep well, give my love to all, keep your head above water, don't do too much yourself, keep your patience and serenity, give my love to all.

Berlin, 15 July 1940

. . . I had a very peaceful Sunday. Herr Deichmann didn't stay to lunch, so that I was alone; then I made some coffee and went to the Institute. There I read Spinoza: after some slow chapters two enormously exciting ones which were simply magnificent. In fact they were so exciting that when I went home and to bed at 9.30 I couldn't go to sleep for a long time. The writing, too, is so outstanding. I've asked Frl. Breslauer to make a copy for you of an extract, which she's typing today. But I don't know whether the extract conveys anything when one doesn't know the full text. . . .

Berlin, 17 July 1940

. . . I have just arrived and found your letter, with a lot of interesting news.

But you write on Monday that you are tired, and yesterday you rang me up towards 11 and your voice didn't sound at all fresh and lively. You *must* go to bed early if you get up early and are active the whole day. You really must stick to that, and the others will have to accommodate themselves. Once you are tired you work less well, therefore take more time, and become more tired and discontented. It is a vicious circle which one must not enter, because it is hard to find a way out again.

I heard on the phone that today an order came from Keitel saying that in preparing for a possible peace Schmitz and I are to have a free hand on questions of the international law of war.[1] That isn't much but it is something. I hope we can turn it into a kind of special assignment that will largely free us from regular work. It could become interesting, if we were to succeed in making something more of it.

1. Cf. n. 3 to letter of 18 June, and letter of 22 July.

... The chief event ahead of us is Friday's meeting of the Reichstag and the war that will start afterwards. The most important battle will probably be over in 2 months, and then we shall be able to see what are the further prospects for the war. . . .

Berlin, 18 July 1940

... I wonder very much how the attack on England[1] will develop. Only a few days separate us from the event, I think, and once it gets started, the outcome will not long be in doubt. Every day I feel relieved that the harvest prospects are better than my previous expectations. There is no point in assuming anything until the harvest is in, but nevertheless it is more agreeable to have hopes than to have none from the outset. . . .

Berlin, 19 July 1940

... I have a meeting with v.d. Gablentz,[2] a new man, who's to replace Gauger. I already know him and wanted us to get him when the Special Committee[3] was expanding. Weichold had more or less settled it with him and told me, when our work got less and the whole thing came to nothing. . . .

Berlin, 21 July 1940

... I read the speech[4] with great interest, because everything that had been prepared was not in it. I can only understand the speech to mean that others attribute more weight to the pending negotiations than I do.— When I read about the 12 field marshals[5] I thought the effect must have

1. He may have meant the planned invasion of Britain, but he was probably referring to the air raids that were to prepare it. The Battle of Britain, which continued for weeks, was first aimed at the destruction of the RAF, then switched to raids on London and other big cities. The decisive air battle was on 15 September.
2. Otto Heinrich von der Gablentz (1898–1972), constitutional lawyer and economist, religious (or conservative) socialist, active in the ecumenical movement. After leaving the Ministry of Economics in 1934, he worked in the administration of the chemical industry. He knew a number of Kreisauers from before the war. After the war he was a professor at the University of Berlin.
3. Cf. n. 5 to letter of 29 October 1939.
4. Hitler's Reichstag speech of 19 July. English translation in Adolf Hitler, *My New Order*, ed. Raoul de Roussy de Sales (New York, 1973), pp. 809–38.
5. The high point in the Reichstag meeting was the nomination of a dozen field marshals and one Reich marshal—Göring—to mark "the most glorious victory of all time" (thus Hitler in a proclamation to the German people on 24 June).

been great hilarity. Far from it. I hear that they were received quite seriously everywhere and nobody sees anything funny in this abundance. I had expected that Brauchitsch[1] and Keitel would be considered sufficient.

Berlin, 22 July 1940

Your letter with the ear of grain arrived today. I'm not too much impressed. It had 46 grains, as compared with up to 60 in good years, and the grains themselves didn't strike me as very big. But it is hard to judge by a single ear.—So I'll arrive Friday night at 12 and leave Monday morning. Then I have another request: If possible I'd like to have a look inside the beehives. Do you have a mask I can use, or can I use Stäsche's? . . . the beehives. Do you have a mask I can use, or can I use Stäsche's? . . .

It now looks as if I'll have work very quickly, lots of it. First the proposal to reformulate the international law of war has been approved by my Field Marshal[2] and is to get going. The work will go to a commission of Schmitz, Stauffenberg, and myself, under the chairmanship of Admiral Gladisch.[3] That will be something to tackle. As if that were not enough, Schmitz and I are apparently to be assigned to another commission of all branches of the armed services for the preparation of peace negotiations. That would also be a *full time job*[4] and my present *otium cum dignitate* would then certainly be at an end.

I have a feeling that the decisive phase of the war is still nearly a month away and that this relative peace will be maintained for a month. In any case there's nothing we can do but wait. . . .

Berlin, 23 July 1940

. . . Last night I was at Kirk's for supper. It was very nice and we talked till about 11. I had a princely ride home and then I felt suddenly the urge to write something down. So I only got to bed at 12.30, but slept well and today was fresh and chipper, admittedly animated by the prospect of talking with you on the telephone in a minute.

Once more there is a lot to do; the work is just as useless, but somewhat more pleasant; at any rate it has some intellectual attraction once more.

1. Walther von Brauchitsch (1881–1948), commander-in-chief of the army from February 1938 (as successor of Fritsch) until 19 December 1941, when Hitler assumed the command himself.
2. Keitel. It was the answer to the proposal of 20 June—see n. 3 to letter of 18 June.
3. Admiral Walter Gladisch, Reich Commissar at the Oberprisenhof, the Supreme Prize Court. Cf. letter of 18 June.
4. English in the original.

Today I'm having lunch with Stauffenberg; Yorck comes tonight. Tomorrow lunch with Kessel; Deuel in the evening.

Berlin, 30 July 1940

. . . Whether and how I am to represent the Wehrmacht in the preparation for peace negotiations is still an open question. But something seems to be brewing behind my back. In any case Tafel spoke to me about it, and a letter of Canaris's, with which I had nothing whatever to do, has been indexed under the reference number of my section. All that is very funny. I remain passive and await events.

Berlin, 31 July 1940

. . . Meanwhile we have fixed our itinerary. I've asked Grandmother Schnitzler whether we can spend the first night 6/7th with her; the second night in Brussels, which we want to reach on the 7th at noon after inspecting Eben Emael.[1] At 6 a.m. on the 8th to Tourcoing, where I've told Jowo we're coming, then via Ypres, Dunkirk, Calais, Dieppe to Rouen. Early on the 9th to Paris; on the 10th to Metz via Compiègne,[2] Reims, Verdun; on the 11th to Strasbourg; and home on the 12th. I actually want to eat with Hans[3] in Frankfurt on the 12th. I'll call Pim early on the 13th. . . .

Berlin, 2 August 1940

. . . Yes, a new and important month has started. I don't believe in an attack before the second half of the month. Even so it will be bad enough. In any case, a vital part of the war will be clearly surveyable in 8 weeks, i.e., at the end of my leave in September. . . .

Last night I was at Mutzenbecher's to meet people trying to get posts as governors of our future colonies. Subject of the whole evening: the uniform of the German colonial troops. I doubled up with laughter inside, but I am now informed on all details, from the combinations to the shorts, number of nails on the shoes, colour of badges, and signs of rank,

1. A Belgian fort which had been taken at the very beginning of the Western offensive by a combination of gliders and infantry.
2. Compiègne was the locality where the Germans had capitulated in 1918 and where—in the same railway carriage—the Franco-German armistice had been concluded on 22 June 1940.
3. His brother-in-law Hans Deichmann, who worked for I. G. Farben, mostly in Italy, and later used this work for cooperation with the Italian resistance.

to details regarding the pith helmet. Yesterday these gentlemen finally inspected and decided on the uniform; it will be shown to Brauchitsch today. Uniforms for 30,000 men will be ready in 2 months. Please keep this to yourself and Asta and don't spread it. But it really is a beauty. . . .

Berlin, 3 August 1940

. . . C.B.[1] has become a corporal today. I've just telephoned with him because I wanted the addresses of the Librairie Fischbacher[2] and Ljena.[3] He didn't know the Fischbacher address. He said his addresses are in his room at Kreisau. In the bottom drawer in a yellow folder. He authorizes you to have a look there. Could you look and copy any that may interest me? I particularly want Ljena's because I could probably get all the other addresses from her. All I want is to hear how they all are. . . .

Berlin, 4 August 1940

. . . It is a glorious summer day: quiet, light cloud, warm. I wish I were at Kreisau. But I wish even more that this weather might last a week or 10 days and help the harvest. That will decide, among other things, whether the big outlay on the Stahllanz and the Bulldogg will already pay off this year. That reminds me: please find out whether there has been any progress in the matter of the workers' dwellings in Nieder-Gräditz. I'd very much like to pay something back to Comes. Then I remember something else: please tell Jowo, but alone, that I implore him to be discreet and not to say anything even indirectly—because the aunts are too dangerous, Frede-Ilse[4] too. . . .

So I'll come in the evening of the 16th. The Yorcks[5] may come, as agreed last time, and possibly Waetjen, too. In September, when I'm on leave, we'll visit the Yorcks for a week-end when he comes to Silesia.

Otherwise, I have, I think, nothing to report. Basically I am well. My nerves are less involved in what's ahead than they have been for a long time; in short, I think I excel in the role of a spectator at my own funeral. I am better in this role, it seems to me, than most of the people I see. . . .

1. His youngest brother, Carl Bernd (1913–41).
2. Parisian publisher. A son of the family had spent the summer of 1939 at Kreisau, after Carl Bernd had stayed with the Fischbachers in France.
3. Friend from the Schwarzwald circle.
4. Wife of Carl Viggo von Moltke—see n. 1 (p. 179) to letter of 8 November 1941.
5. Peter Yorck and his wife, Marion, née Winter, who became a judge in a juvenile court in Berlin after the war.

Girsberg, 7 August 1940

Carl and I had hit on the version that he was unable to get a berth to Cologne in the evening of the 6th and that we took him along as a sort of stranded traveller. He simply occupied one of the vacant seats, and it worked very well. Nobody minded. We left at 6 and picked up Kiep, whose suitcase gave us a lot of trouble because we couldn't get it into the luggage space. So the three of us were already 5 minutes late at the meeting place, where Count Schlieffen[1] in major's uniform and Woermann[2] in his diplomatic uniform walked up and down, shivering. But they bore it with dignity. Woermann's uniform corresponds to that of a general, without shoulder tabs; thus much gold, and as Kiep instantly said to him: *molto distinguido.* So we set off. First through very poor land as far as Magdeburg. There was *very* little standing in the fields. Then through the Magdeburg Börde, where a *great* deal was standing in the fields, though I saw no potatoes like ours, but incredibly good wheat and marvellous sugar beets. Then came the very nice stretch soon after Hanover, through the hilly countryside. Near Bielefeld, of all places, the distinguished gentleman felt hungry and we made a detour to Bielefeld, where we ate quite well. It was only 12. About 1 we went on. We all slept a little, and I woke up when we'd just left Hamm and were travelling "above" the Ruhr area. For the Autobahn is always a little higher and gives one a broad view over the industrial area. Near Dortmund we saw an enormous gas works standing as askew as the Tower of Pisa, it must have been hit by a bomb. At 3.15 we were in Cologne. When we'd finished our coffee in Cologne Herr Deichmann returned from his business and we all drove to the Girsberg, where we arrived at 5 and had the familiar tea. Grandmother Schnitzler was marvellous as always and in positively high spirits. We then went for a walk on paths that reminded me of you. It was very nice.

Brussels, 7 August 1940

. . . We set out at 6.30, but unfortunately in the rain. We passed a few positions of the West Wall, which it was quite interesting to see, and went through Schleiden-Losheim, Malmédy-Spa, Liège. Too bad there was fog most of the time, so that once we lost our way and saw nothing of the beauty of the region. Towards Liège the peaceful landscape looked as if it had been struck at intervals without rhyme or reason by a fist, or perhaps as if the famous seven-league boots had come down every seven

1. Probably Graf Karl Wilhelm von Schlieffen, who was killed in action in 1945.
2. Ernst Woermann, head of the Political Division of the Foreign Ministry.

miles. And in those places all is thoroughly smashed. The bridges blown up near Liège have all been repaired so that one has to look quite carefully to see that they are not the original ones. The destruction is always in localities. In some places 2 or 3 houses at the entrance, sometimes in the centre, sometimes at the exit. Sometimes single churches have been hit by one or two artillery shells in towns otherwise intact.

The region is charming and Lille[1] itself is very nicely situated. The bridges across the Ourthe are all standing, the bridges across the Meuse are all blown up, and traffic still crosses by a rather primitive wooden emergency bridge. But work is in progress on all bridges. There is much life in the streets, the shops seem already barer than in normal times, but by our standards fabulously well stocked. While waiting for permits to see the fortifications we had two fried eggs and hot coffee. Then we drove to a Fort Fleuron that held out until about 23 May. It is an old fort on the Meuse, facing Germany, intended for defence against an advance from Aachen. Inside the fort is primitive and very damp and narrow. There are ladders into the artillery turrets. The fortress had been attacked by dive-bombers and had been hit directly by 20 of the heaviest bombs. Very deep craters. None of the bombs pierced the concrete structure, but several of them had caused considerable breaches; one hit beside the command post must have lifted it up, though it was a concrete block certainly not less than 15 m by 10 m by 15 m. It was completely shattered inside. It was still possible to walk there, but the floor and walls had deep cracks and the ceiling had fallen in places. My overall impression is that the Stuka[2] attack was carefully aimed and very effective, but that the installation itself had not been properly thought through and fell short in effectiveness and defensibility.

Woermann and Schlieffen drove on to Eben Emael,[3] while Kiep and I decided to go straight on to Brussels. . . .

Le Touquet, 8 August 1940

. . . The library at Louvain [was] completely gutted, the outer walls still standing. But everywhere it was the returning refugees or prisoners who made the deepest impression. Sad, exhausted, depressed, they looked at the ruins where houses had been not long before, when they left. Nobody was meeting them, and they were obviously not eager to reach their houses or what was left of them. Totalitarian war seems to repeat the pattern of domestic policy. It leaves material values intact and destroys

1. He means Liège.
2. Stuka: *Sturzkampfflieger*, dive-bomber.
3. Cf. n. 1 to letter of 31 July.

human beings. One feels that everywhere. If it destroyed material values, the people, whose thinking is mostly limited by their perceptions, would know how and against what to defend themselves. As it is, the inner destruction has no correlative in the perceived world of things, of matter. So they fail to grasp the process and the possible means of countering it or renewing themselves.

The other thing that made the drive from Liège to Brussels so very interesting was the quality of agriculture. I have never seen such fields and do not believe there could be such fields in Germany. For such fields are possible only where agricultural labour has a high standard, and our present policies will never achieve that. . . .

Paris, 9 August 1940

The others called me away to supper. Then we sat together, walked a bit, slept, and this morning Kiep and I drove off to Paris. But I resume where I left off.

On the way from Liège to Brussels I bought some magnificent fruit, which was plentiful everywhere. A fat, friendly old woman first sold me the 2 kg of assorted plums for which I asked. Then she said, pointing to a display of magnificent blue plums: *J'ai des raisins merveilleux! Simplement merveilleux! Achetez en un! C'est une nouvelle espèce, la plus parfaite qu'on a jamais cultivé!* And then, with a cheerful laugh: *Oh, c'est le raisin Léopold, on doit en acheter un!* And I had to agree with her.

Brussels. We had princely accommodation, in the best hotel. We arrived at 3 and first of all ate lunch. The city makes a splendid impression as one passes through the gardens and parks and finally reaches the inner city. It is quite different from other big cities: however beautiful their centres, there are always slums on the perimeter. But here we entered through parks, I drove to P.W.'s through parks, and through parks we departed.

Paris, 9 August 1940 continued

The city [Brussels] is full of people, it is teeming, and it is hard to imagine that many people could be away. Of course the soldiers strengthen this impression. Admittedly one sees no "better" people in the streets. The remaining plebs are friendly, obviously interested in the soldiers, and relations between the men and the Belgian girls are in accordance with normal rules. P.W.[1] said one could no longer walk in the parks

1. See n. 1 to letter of 1 July.

in the evening because the goings-on were like the zoo: nothing is hidden, everyone witnesses everything.

To our eyes the shops seem filled to bursting with splendours. But when one looks more closely, one finds that the back shelves are quite empty and the profusion is mere appearance. It is like a hive with only a few bees: only the nearest combs are filled with honey, most are already empty. The buying up is quite shameless. All the officers and probably the men, too, buy all they can—and that in a country facing famine and scarcity of goods such as have no precedent in Western Europe. This is so striking that the following incident occurred: On the way from Brussels to Dunkirk, no, between Dunkirk and Boulogne, we could not find a restaurant and wanted to buy something to eat in a bakery. The others bought bread, and I looked for other things, like fruit. In a shop I saw half a round cheese, but only one. I thought that might be ideal to add to dry bread and was about to go in. But I was so embarrassed, because it was obviously the last cheese and the shop had otherwise been stripped, that I turned and went away. It was only when I really could not find anything but dry bread that I decided to buy a piece of the cheese.—Everything, incidentally, is sold on ration cards, also the foods that are unrationed with us. Only vegetables and fruit are unrationed. The Germans get cards for ample amounts, the Belgians are kept quite short: 250 gr. bread a week, 100 gr. butter, also less meat than we get. In addition it is a fact that for a fortnight there have been no butter rations, because there simply was none (P.W.'s information, corroborated by Falkenhausen[1]).—The buying up by Germans is said to have taken two particularly nasty forms: Strength-Through-Joy[2] trips by Rhenish housewives, no one knowing where they got their permits; and purchases by officers complete with briefcases and orderlies. That evidently caused particularly bad blood, and those two forms have ceased. But there is not much left either.

After lunch I drove out to P.W.'s and sent away the car. I had to trust to luck, for there is no telephone in the city, but it worked out well. I omit this visit because I am going to write to Mütterchen about it and shall send you a copy of that letter.

1. General Alexander Freiherr von Falkenhausen (1878–1966), highly decorated (Pour le Mérite) in the First World War; since 28 June 1940 military commander in Belgium and Northern France; 1934–39 military adviser to Chiang Kai-shek, then commanding general in Dresden. He had been in contact with opponents of the regime for some time. Dismissed shortly before 20 July 1944 and arrested soon after. Liberated by the Allies, but sentenced for war crimes (cf. letter of 21 October 1941) by a Belgian court in 1951; released before his sentence was fully served, on account of earlier imprisonment.
2. Kraft durch Freude, the recreational organization of the German Labour Front. One of its many activities was tourism for the masses.

P.W. accompanied me to my hotel, where I arrived at 7, just in time to clean up and get ready for dinner. At 7.25 we were picked up by two cars and taken first to Falkenhausen's hotel, where there were drinks in which I did not join so as not to have to go on drinking. The following were present in addition to us 4 and Falkenhausen: the chief of the Civil Administration, a man with the rank of general who was a cousin of Freya Kleist[1] and had been at her wedding in Kreisau; the chief of staff, Herr von Harbou;[2] two men from the AA; and the 4 departmental heads of the Military Administration and the military command posts. We then drove in several cars to a restaurant out in the park opposite P.W.'s house, where we had a fantastic dinner: caviar, ham in burgundy, duck, crepes. With it there were excellent things to drink: vodka, a claret Enfant Jésus, champagne, and Armagnac. I did not have any of it, but the others seemed to be in seventh heaven. Afterwards, about half past eleven, we went back to Falkenhausen's hotel, where whisky and beer were provided. Woermann was thoroughly tight and most of the others, including Kiep, were distinctly tipsy, so that Falkenhausen and I were the only ones left sober. For the two hours from 11.30 to 1.30 we talked mostly alone. I welcomed this, because at dinner I had unavoidably sat too far away from him for talk.

Paris, 10 August 1940

The dinner conversation was of middling quality. I was able to learn something about the economic situation, which, on the food sector, is very bad, but otherwise it was altogether mediocre. I was annoyed anyway by the opulent meal in a country on the verge of starvation and that naturally disturbed me, because I didn't want to be rude, but neither did I want to leave the impression that I approved of this affair. But after they apologized I got over that, and the two late hours with Falkenhausen were very nice, with the others *hors de concours* from alcohol. He is an outstanding and courageous man and we talked mostly about the economic situation of Belgium, our spoliation of the country and its economic and political consequences. Finally he told me where he sees the limits of his collaboration and the point at which he will refuse to take any further part. From a human point of view it was all very encouraging, and it was interesting, though on the whole nothing new. It was, rather, a corroboration filled with details I was in no position to know. It was nice, too, that he told me he made a tour of the fields of Belgium every week, along field roads and paths, to inform himself of the state of the crops and to

1. An acquaintance.
2. Bodo von Harbou, colonel in the General Staff.

help with the means at his disposal where work has come to a standstill. The only thing he told me that did not fit the picture was that he considers the unemployment figures low.—We talked in considerable detail about the refugee question and he said that he insisted on the return of refugees and prisoners so firmly, and to a large extent successfully, because he wanted families reunited and thus pacified, and because he thought they would stand up to unavoidable hardships better together. The man's focus is entirely on human beings, not on any *"gloire"* or *"grandeur."* He is obviously deeply concerned about our behaving again in a way that makes our position untenable. I remember one thing he said: "I always tell my colleagues passing through, 'Your task is to destroy as quickly and thoroughly as possible, and for that you get honours and decorations; my task is to repair as quickly and thoroughly as possible, but that process, in contrast to your activity, is slow and brings no public recognition.' "

Then we talked about Chiang. But I want to have breakfast now and go on writing afterwards.

Nancy, 11 August 1940

. . . Back to Falkenhausen and China. Woermann, who was sitting on my other side, prodded him. W. was quite tipsy and championed real Ribbentrop doctrines which amounted to this: *a.* We must set the Japanese against the English, for that is good policy; *b.* The Japanese presence in China does not prevent our having an economic say there; *c.* Chiang Kai-shek will be defeated shortly. Falkenhausen replied as follows: *a.* To set the Japanese upon the British is a crime against the white race, the British are the bulwark of Europe in the Far East and we must on no account defeat them so badly that they are not able to maintain their Far Eastern positions; altogether the British are the only decent race and a good deal better than we; it is a shame to set all the bad upon the good; *b.*—I must stop.

Frankfurt, 12 August 1940

I am sitting in the I. G. [Farben] administrative building in a room of Hans's[1] and in an hour we want to go to Dornholzhausen. But I want to continue with Falkenhausen.

b. To have the Japanese in China, in Hong Kong, Siam, etc., would mean that we could not even export there any more. Furthermore it

---

1. Hans Deichmann, his brother-in-law.

would mean that Europeans would have nothing more to say in the Far East and that this largest potential market in the world would be entirely closed to us; *c.* Chiang Kai-shek is well on the way to winning the war; unless we fall on his rear, cut him off from his friends, and support the Japanese. F. declared: I don't say this because Chiang is my man and I know he has no equal in China, nor do I say it because I am a friend of the Chinese: I say it because I consider any other policy detrimental for Germany. Even if I were not convinced that in Japan we are backing the wrong horse because there is no [responsible] man there, I would always advise backing China because of the dangers a Japanese victory would bring.

That was the core of the conversation. Your husband was delighted and strongly supported F. Woermann, who pleaded the Ribbentrop thesis with élan, presently had his back to the wall and was reduced to defending himself with axioms on power politics, to which F. and I merely listened with an indulgent smile. This conversation also led Herr von Harbou to sing a hymn of praise for the British, so that British ears around the world should have been ringing. In any case he stated his view that a policy that involved us in war with Britain was ipso facto criminal.

After a few hours' sleep we left Brussels at 6.30, at first in the direction of La Panne. On our way we visited the 1914/18 battlefields of Flanders and the main war cemeteries. The drive was interesting because it showed clearly the tremendous importance of the few elevations in this plain, for instance the Kemmel, which we climbed. But now signs of this year's battle were increasing. The destruction in villages and towns was somewhat more extensive, all the bridges had been blown up, so that we were always crossing emergency bridges, and beside the road overturned and burnt-out British and French vehicles were more and more frequent. Almost all the vehicles we lost had been cleared away. Only once did I see a shot-up German tank. Just before La Panne we passed the first collecting point for wrecked vehicles. There were hundreds, possibly thousands, of cars, trucks, armoured vehicles of all sizes. Almost all of them were burnt out, because the British and French had put fire to all the vehicles they had to abandon. In La Panne itself, a harbour which had served for embarkations, there was merely a vast amount of war materiel, all useless. Anti-aircraft guns, machine guns, motor bicycles, anti-tank guns, etc. From the place where we stopped on the beach we could see a sunken British warship. I took it for a destroyer, a soldier claimed it was a torpedo-boat destroyer, therefore somewhat bigger. Otherwise there were no sunken ships to be seen.

From La Panne we drove parallel to the beach not far from the shore. It was the same picture everywhere. At one place we saw a shot-down

German plane and a French one. Then we reached Dunkirk.[1] We found few houses totally destroyed, but almost all were without a roof and gutted inside. Some houses had only their outer walls standing, while everything inside had collapsed. It was a scene of hopeless desolation, more so than in the completely destroyed towns of Northern France, because a heap of rubble is less accusing than the skeleton of a house. What we saw showed clearly that Dunkirk had been destroyed mainly by artillery and not by dive-bombers. The only way I can explain it is that the British maintained air mastery over Dunkirk as long as necessary for embarkation.

The harbour of Dunkirk is the most desolate scene of destruction. The sea sluices, which the British destroyed, are still blocked by two ships that collided, all over the harbour there are destroyed, burnt-out, overturned ships, and when we were there most of the harbour was dry at low tide, which made it especially desolate. But the most remarkable observation I made was that it seems impossible to destroy quays. Bombs had made big craters in the quays, which had been partly filled in in the meantime; but the quay walls had not been affected even by near hits. This means that harbours can be destroyed only by destroying sea sluices where they are needed, destroying installations, and obstructing traffic by sinking ships in the harbour. Of these three possibilities the first and second are very difficult and the third not exactly easy either.

The population of Dunkirk evidently stayed there and made a deplorable impression: ragged, dirty, living in rooms without furniture or window panes, famished. A ghastly spectacle. I remember a woman looking out of the first floor of a house that no longer had a roof or upper floor; her flat had no windows left and was gutted inside. But she was looking out to call to her children.

Frankfurt, 12 August 1940 continued

From Dunkirk we drove along the coast to Boulogne. It was an enchanting drive. Meanwhile it was 1 or 1.30 and the sun on the landside shone on the sea. First one drives behind low dunes. But about 15–20 km beyond Calais the road rises and winds along high above the sea, cutting off spits, and every now and then descending to the sea again, in narrow curves. It is an enchanting, bare seascape. The full glare of the sun was shining down on a sea smooth as glass and quite deserted, because not even fishermen dare go out. From the heights the English coast was vis-

1. Dunkirk had been the scene of the rescue of much of the British Expeditionary Force and many Frenchmen.

ible in the haze, and I was much moved by the thought that there, within sight, are so many of our friends, and that we cannot meet.

This part of the trip was of special interest, however, for the military preparations. Fighter planes circle constantly above the entire area from Calais to Boulogne. They look for enemy planes and are responsible for keeping them out. One also passes a number of airfields. Otherwise this barren region of dunes is alive with tens of thousands of Germans who, under the general denominator of the Todt Organization[1]

Berlin, 13 August 1940

We have telephoned and I got your long letter. Of course the weather is a nuisance, but it is good that we got in the barley at least. Today it is grey and dry here. The wet weather after all has its merits for the pasture, for rape, potatoes, sugar beet. With the larger number of machines and the reduced grain area we shall probably manage somehow. Perhaps it will clear up over the week-end.—The air offensive against England began this morning. I expect it will take about two weeks before one can form a picture. I don't feel good about it. But the fact that the assault has now started points to a favourable weather estimate. But I shall make more enquiries before I come on Friday.

Pierre's death[2] affected me deeply. I did not expect it at all. In the morning of the 10th, before going to a meeting with Schuster, I passed the bookshop. It was still closed. Just before departing I went back once more and entered the small, old-fashioned, but obviously well-kept shop. A slender elderly lady came towards me and said: *Bonjour Monsieur.* I said: *Je suis venu pour chercher un ami, qui vous connaissait probablement, un Pierre Fischbacher.—Qui êtes-vous donc?* she asked me. I told her my name. Oh, she said, *je sais, il comptait vous et votre femme parmi ses amis. Eh bien, il est tombé.* I thought I had not heard right. She saw that I was moved and asked me to sit with her at the back of the shop, which I did. There she told me that he was killed near Sedan. I said, *Ah, ça veut dire avant la catastrophe, c'est enfin mieux pour lui.—Oui,* she said, *il est tombé plein d'espoir.* She also told me what details were known: his brother was in the fighting only kilometres away. The body has not been found, so that he was among the missing and there was still a shadow of hope. She clearly thought very highly of him. She said: *Voyez, c'est trop triste. Il était si brillant, si gai, il était le meilleur de toute la famille. Nous tous aurions donné notre vie pour sauver la sienne. Je dirai à ses parents*

1. The text breaks off.
2. He had mentioned the death of Pierre Fischbacher on the telephone.

que vous êtes venu et que vous aussi êtes très triste. I gave her our address and asked her to write to us if he turned up again after all. I also said that I would always be prepared to do anything for Pierre's family that might help them. There you have the whole sad story. I had nobody to whom I could tell it and so I kept it to myself, but I had to think of Pierre all day, how exactly a year ago he was picking raspberries at Kreisau, singing: "*mourir pour la patrie.*"

So now I'll continue where Hans interrupted to take me to Homburg.

Under the general classification Todt Organization all the big German construction firms are working there on gun emplacements, airfields, embarkation piers, etc. Tens of thousands of German workmen are employed in these dunes and cliffs and are making the area bristle with arms. Rails have been laid, gigantic building sites are being excavated, and everything is protected against air reconnaissance by camouflage covers. It is really impressive. Truck after truck brings up more materiel and men. And beyond it all one sees the coast of England, the goal of all these endeavours. The senselessness of this unproductive effort is especially plain there.—For the rest it seems to be a ghostly repetition of 1810, when probably a similar number of people were engaged at the same place with the same aim.

In the harbour of Boulogne there were German minesweepers and speed boats, very cleverly camouflaged. They had camouflage nets to protect them against aircraft and a curious blue-white, grey, and dark-grey paint against being seen from the water. Here we had to refuel, and since that took some time, we had some coffee. Then we drove on to Le Touquet, where we arrived at 8 and found quite decent accommodation in a small hotel. We had had only dry bread and cheese for lunch and were therefore ravenous when we finally sat down to a meal at 9. But then we were rewarded with a really good meal: cold salmon trout with mayonnaise, mutton with mint sauce, chaudeau. After a little while we went to bed. The guard on duty told us that the British had landed a few nights before and had taken the German guard with them. Le Touquet, incidentally, is a typical seaside resort, of the better kind, with a fine beach and houses that are well looked after. Behind the row of beach hotels there are relatively luxurious villas owned by summer residents.

The next morning—9 August—Kiep and I drove to Paris. At first the picture was exactly the same as on the previous days: Separate groups of houses are completely destroyed, especially at river crossings and the entrances and exits of towns, and otherwise the landscape seems almost untouched. The fields are unimaginably bad, full of weeds, a little poor grain, some areas not planted at all, root crops dirty with weeds. Sugar beet left partly thinned, the villages up to Abbeville quite empty, with only

German soldiers there. The few things growing in the fields have there-fore not been harvested. Livestock is ranging over the fields and eats what can be found. In one place I saw 20 to 30 white horses standing in about 50 acres of clover completely wild. It looked very strange. And I am sure everything that could be removed has been already. There is something ghostly about the emptiness. After Abbeville things gradually get better. The farther into the country one gets the more people have returned, and gradually the harvest there gets moving. Everywhere one sees returning refugees: people with hopeless, sad faces. They come on all kinds of ve-hicles and seem all to look alike: tired, dirty, ragged, some obviously tear-stained. Coming through a town, they look furtively at the rubble heaps, not knowing whether they will find their own houses in the same state. One sees some digging about in the rubble, and others relieved to have found their houses unharmed.—Where the refugees have returned, pro-visions are a big problem. There simply are no shops, at any rate no shops with anything in them. Wherever there is food, people stand in queues. Gas, water, electricity simply don't exist. Everything else is missing too, because the abandoned dwellings are partly gutted, partly cleared out. The refugees mostly bring bedding back with them. Beyond Beauvais there are already schools again. Children were on the way to rooms where teaching is going on. But a boy of Caspar's age running after a hoop on a sidewalk and enjoying himself, while not a house remained standing to left or right, is a pathetic spectacle. On most rubble heaps men are work-ing to clear up and to salvage what can be used.

Beauvais is the most demolished town we saw. The cathedral is stand-ing, but nothing else of the inner city. It is just heaps of brick rubble. One may suddenly see a bit of wall with a sign, "Boucherie." In the streets there were craters made by mortar shells and now filled with rubble. The town was worked over by dive-bombers and must have been hell; Amiens is said to look just the same. The rubble of destroyed houses lies all over the streets. The ways for the cars have been dug through the rubble, as we dig paths through the snow in the winter.—The population, which now has to clear away these heaps of rubble, is decidedly friendly. When one stops and wonders where to turn in the rubble, which looks the same everywhere, someone always jumps up and willingly gives information. There is no feeling of unfriendliness.

Outside the built-up areas the roads are in excellent shape, except for bridges, which were almost all blown up and have been replaced by emer-gency bridges. On the whole drive I did not see a single shell crater on the open road. That was surprising, too. The only explanation I can think of is that we attacked columns with machine guns, but not with bombs. This hypothesis was supported by a conversation I shall report later. The vehicles lying beside the roads never show hits by shells, nor do the tanks. Yet the best have long since been removed. The only possible explanation is that our activity caused very few enemy losses in vehicles and that most vehicles became unusable without it, could not be repaired, and were driven to the side and set on fire so as not to fall into our hands. Wilhelm[1] confirmed this, at least in regard to the tanks.

The whole route to Paris runs through beautiful rolling country. Nothing exciting, but charming and animated by the change between hills and dales, woods, fields, and meadows, and by diverse brooks and streams. The closer one gets to Paris the more normal conditions are. During the last hour one really sees no more signs of destruction. Everything looks quite normal. The only thing striking is the German guard posted in virtually every village. People seem to pursue their normal activities, there are no more queues in front of shops, but one meets treks of refugees. The approach to Paris is strictly controlled in order to prevent the surrounding troops from inundating the city. After getting through the many formalities we finally landed at the Ritz Hotel, where each of us had a princely room with a bath. I rang up Wilhelm, who is stationed outside at Fontainebleau, and had lunch with him and Kiep. The others came later. Before eating, I tried to see Ljena, but the building in which she lives and all the neighbouring buildings were completely shut up: all blinds down, the doors blocked and bolted, and even the concierges away. So I had to give up.

My Paris programme was very rich: On the 9th I had lunch with Wilhelm and Kiep, and afterwards W. and I walked along the Seine; a Yugoslav friend of Hans's, Sajovic, came at 5 and stayed until 7.30, at 8 we were picked up for dinner with the permanent representatives of the OKW in Paris and Embassy people at a Restaurant Le Doyen. Next morning I tried to reach Fischbacher's, at 10 I saw Schuster; immediately after, at 11, Weichold, who just happened to be there; at 11.45 I had another official talk; at 12 I was at Fischbacher's, and at 12.15 I drove to Fontainebleau. We were to have eaten with the new Ambassador, Herr Abetz,[2] but Kiep and I had had enough, left Woermann and Schlieffen in the lurch, and drove instead to Wilhelm's for lunch, which we enjoyed very much.

Before I go into detail I want to try and give my general impression, made up partly of observations and partly of reports. Control of the troops

---

1. Wilhelm von Trotha, a cousin.

2. Otto Abetz (1903–58), since the middle of June AA representative with the military commander in Paris, later Ambassador in Paris. In 1949 sentenced to twenty years' hard labour by a French court. Released 1954.

is very strict, which is a blessing. You don't see soldiers driving with girls, and the few who misbehave receive incredibly harsh punishments. A major who was drunk is said to have been sentenced by the Commandant of Paris to 60 days' arrest. German civilians and Party representatives, on the other hand, make a rather ugly impression. One sees high Party functionaries with their wives traversing the town in big cars on shopping expeditions. Yes, the subject of shopping: Wilhelm told me about a general who bought fur coats for himself and his wife; this, he said, had shaken his own, Wilhelm's, principles as well. The most disgusting are the people from Berlin and other parts of the Reich who come to Paris for a day to stock up on everything imaginable. As a German one can no longer enter a shop.

The attitude of the population towards the changing of the guard and similar spectacles is reserved, but obviously on the whole sickeningly friendly. I have not been able to observe anything of the sort myself, but everybody confirms unanimously that the women, for instance, were positively queuing up to get a German soldier into bed, evidently from a feeling that he was the stronger and that it was more fun with the stronger man. I sensed the same thing, though I observed nothing of the sort myself. The people one sees on the streets don't seem downcast. But of course one has to remember that only a small part of the upper middle class, the backbone of the nation, remains in Paris. That seems to be indicated, at least by my visit to the Avenue de Ségur; but the fact that the Fischbachers were back speaks against it, and Sajovic also claimed that all his acquaintances were back.

Berlin, 13 August 1940 continued

Be that as it may, one sees many discharged French soldiers in the streets who do not strike one as dejected, and on the whole one senses that even before the fighting began French powers of resistance were very weak.—Actually that is the most important impression I brought back, that French morale was simply non-existent. Aircraft did not take off when the Germans attacked, units deserted under the leadership of their officers, the troops in fortifications and tanks struck arms at the slightest hint of an attack. This assessment is shared by Sajovic, who went with the refugees from Paris to beyond Bordeaux, Wilhelm, our people in Paris, and a regimental staff with whom we had a meal on the 11th, who had the breaching of the Maginot Line[1] to their credit. It is the subject that

1. The system of fortifications on the French eastern border, which was to make France unassailable from the Swiss to the Belgian border and which was in large part outflanked by the German offensive.

keeps recurring. I put my question to all these people in this form: Do you agree that two-thirds of the victory can be attributed to the French lack of fighting morale? The answers were: Sajovic: No, 99%; our people: No, 100%, because in equipment they were many times superior to us, especially in anti-tank warfare; Wilhelm: The French tanks had the better armour, we had better tactics, and the French had no morale; the staff of the regiment at the Maginot Line: 50% lack of fighting morale + 30% the fact that the French evacuated the glacis of the defence works before we attacked; it is true they did so only because they knew that the morale of their troops was not up to fighting in open terrain.—And this lack of backbone, from Pétain to the last man, is evident now, too: in the fact, for instance, that Laval[1] invites Abetz to lunch, while we could not do such a thing until after the ratification of the peace treaty; and in the fact that the individual Frenchwoman tends to prefer the German billeted on her to her husband, who returns defeated. Thus it is a moral debacle, and Sajovic only said: You can't live in such a plague spot. Though I have lived here since 1920 I am going back to Yugoslavia.

Berlin, 14 August 1940

... Tomorrow Schmitz is going to Bordeaux and Brest with Jaenicke to study the records of the French prize courts. I shall then be alone, so to speak. But I told Tafel I was leaving on Friday all the same. I hope it works. Now I want to tell you about my various conversations in Paris.

First I had a very nice talk with Wilhelm. The most interesting part I've told you already, I think; that was his enthusiasm for the superiority of the German tanks. He is now setting up new tank formations and bringing the tank division up to strength again in personnel and materiel. All he told me was good, interesting, even if confined to the strictly military domain. On Saturday, the 10th of August, Kiep and I had a meal with him at Fontainebleau and there, too, everything was just right and arranged in his characteristic way. The food was good and well cooked, and we ambled about in the garden of the villa he shares with an officer, with the special mess of his staff downstairs. His quarters there are very comfortable and suitable and well furnished with everything necessary. When he heard that I was taking nothing back for you because I refused to enter shops, he entrusted to me a box of soap for you, which will reach you Friday.

1. Pierre Laval (1883–1945), French Prime Minister 1931–32 and 1935–36, Minister President under Marshal Pétain in Vichy 1940—see letter of 16 December—and again from 1942 on. Sentenced to death for treason in 1945.

My most interesting conversation was with Hans's friend Sajovic. He is a Yugoslav, was employed by the I.G. in their French firm, and looked after it during the war in France. So he was suspected of belonging to the 5th column and decided to flee south from Paris to escape the possible murder of all suspect elements. He therefore piled the papers of the I.G. into a truck, got into his car, and departed in the direction of Bordeaux. Because he made this decision very late, he was one of the last to leave Paris. He got into this trek of many hundreds of thousands, a thing unheard of in Europe, which moved south in columns of 4 cars abreast. He had food with him. Water was scarce and cost 5 francs a glass in the beginning and 15 francs in the end. The first 100 km took 20 hours.

The trek consisted of civilians and soldiers. The civilians were women, children, and older men in about equal proportions. The soldiers were simply refugees in uniform; they did not obey officers' orders, and the officers had ceased trying to give orders; all military discipline was gone. But the soldiers' behaviour was insolent. Shouting *"Nous sommes des soldats,"* they kept themselves supplied with petrol when others only got a few litres; when their vehicles became useless they managed to requisition cars and other vehicles and eject the owners. The trek was also joined, from both sides, by soldiers in still-existing formations supposed to form a holding position south of Paris. All the soldiers stood on their prerogatives, not to fight but only to flee. Usually two officers occupied a car, the one in front with a girl in his free arm, the other in the back with one in each arm. Public order had dissolved, the police had ceased to function. So the trek pushed gradually forward.

German aircraft appeared from time to time, sometimes attacking soldiers and military vehicles in the trek, sometimes bridges, buildings, and similar objectives. He saw innumerable such attacks, several not more than 50 m away from him, and he was once wounded himself. Tanks, buildings, and bridges were attacked with bombs, moving columns were attacked with machine guns. Before firing their machine guns, the aircraft had always flown over the column once, and everyone had run off the road into the fields; then machine-gun fire from the planes rendered the vehicles useless without much loss of human life. Crippled vehicles were then simply pushed over into the ditches and set on fire. He was wounded in a bombing attack. He heard the aircraft approach and hurried to the side, towards a house. The house in which he wanted to take refuge was hit immediately above him just as he was entering. The impact and dispersion of the bomb left many dead and about 25 wounded around him. He himself, standing in the dead angle of the bomb, was knocked down by the blast but only hit by a few fragments. There was a field hospital beside the house that was hit. He went to it, and others brought the dead, dying, and wounded there. But there were no doctors, only two nurse's aides who burst into hysterical screams at the sight of the wounded and dead, at which the stretcher-bearers, the wounded and dying, also began to scream. Though weakened by loss of blood, he fled from the house. Outside a man who had studied some medicine gave him an emergency dressing, which was sufficient because he only had flesh wounds. He then got into his car and drove on.—He said the behaviour of the uniformed refugees was unbelievable. When a plane was heard approaching, they jumped yelling from their vehicles, pushed aside women, children, old people, and their own girls in the stream of refugees, and took cover in the fields. The civilians were much more helpful to one another.

Shortly after he was wounded his truck had a flat tire and the repair was bound to take some time. Because he could be of no use, weakened as he now was, he had gone on and agreed with the truck driver that they would meet in front of the Mairie in Bordeaux. He learnt later that the government had taken its seat in Bordeaux, so that the administrative quarter was sure to be cordoned off, and he feared that he would never find his truck. But when he reached Bordeaux, there was such indescribable confusion and lack of any semblance of organization that he was able to stop in front of the Mairie and wait 24 hours for the other man. The two vehicles then drove on together as far as Argenton.

Since the spectacle of disorder got worse and worse and morale was in process of total dissolution, he decided to try to return to the German-occupied part of the country. He could not find a French frontline, but he was anxious about the last kilometres nearest the German line of fire. Driving along the road, however, he suddenly saw a gigantic German soldier sitting on a tree stump holding his rifle between his crossed legs, and taking no notice of him. He thereupon put his hand to his hat, and his salute was answered by a negligent gesture; thus he penetrated the German "front" and nobody bothered with him any more. He found his apartment and his office in Paris undamaged.

He summed up his overall view as follows: I'll go to Yugoslavia as soon as I get an exit permit; you can't live in a country where men have no courage and will to work and whose women are faithless. This country can only recover under a Bolshevist regime, once equality in poverty has prepared the ground.

My conversations with Germans were uninteresting, except for those, for instance, with Schuster and Weichold, concerned exclusively with military questions, especially with the present operation against England and with the preparation for war against England next spring. What is significant about these conversations is that obviously no soldier with any knowledge of the situation believes in the success of the operation now in progress, so that all reckon with a long war. But haven't the knowledge-able soldiers been wrong so far, and may there not, contrary to all assess-ments, be a moral collapse in Britain? I don't think so. Falkenhausen summed up his view as follows: "If I had not already seen several military miracles this year, I would call this operation hopeless."

That brings me to the end in Paris. Kiep and I played truant and did not go to the Embassy breakfast but drove to Fontainebleau. The town looks very nice. Of its 18,000 inhabitants 14,000 have already returned. It all looks like Potsdam with a little more money. The gardens are well tended, the houses well kept. The Palace has beautiful proportions, though I don't like a lot of the detail. Black prisoners of war are working in the gardens. It all makes a tremendously peaceful impression. The street in which Halder[1] and Brauchitsch have their seat is cordoned off, but elsewhere civilians move freely and come and go as they please. One also sees discharged French soldiers in uniform. German soldiers are hardly to be seen, because access to Fontainebleau is, even for generals, by special permit only, in order to provide the necessary quiet for the General Staff. No signs of defence such as anti-aircraft guns, fighter planes, etc., are visible. It seems that they are unnecessary, because the General Staff is scattered all over town and therefore is not a promising target for air attack. The whole thing is idyllic and one could only wish for such accommodation. Clearly the OKH[2] has an excellent quarter-master who has succeeded in settling everything most satisfactorily with the local administration and thus in securing good relations between the military and the civilian population.

Now I must stop. I shall write again tomorrow . . . and see you the day after.

Berlin, 15 August 1940

It is 9 o'clock, and the day has only just ended. It was filled with more things than the number of hours in it and I only got through it at excessive speed. Except for lunch, devoted to intensive conversation with a new man, Reichsgerichtsrat von Dohnanyi,[3] there was not a single calm mo-

1. Colonel General Franz Halder (1884–1972), chief of staff of the army 1938–42.
2. Oberkommando des Heeres: High Command of the Army.
3. Hans von Dohnanyi (1902–45), Judge Advocate in the Supreme (Reich) Court; during the war Sonderführer in the Abwehr, where he worked closely with Hans Oster (q.v.), active opponent of the regime from the beginning; brother-in-law of Klaus and Dietrich Bonhoef-fer and, like them, executed shortly before the end of the war.

ment.—I am bringing this letter with me and am writing it only in order to give you a complete account.

About Paris I have something more, which I think I forgot. It is the attitude of the population towards the government in Vichy[1] and towards us in general. Towards us it is an attitude of wait and see: if we make a successful attack on England before the autumn, the French will support us because they see no alternative. If we make an unsuccessful attack or postpone the attack, they will mostly be against us. Both these attitudes will be based less on any firm insight than on speculation like a gambler's. As for the government in Vichy: those who are fundamentally anti-German reject it as incapable of maintaining itself against Germany and undignified in its behaviour; those who would like an understanding with Germany reject it for reasons of domestic policy and say to themselves that this mixture of dotards and schemers is unlikely to achieve a real accord with Germany, being incapable of carrying out internal reconstruction.

I shall now continue from Fontainebleau. We now drove through a nice countryside, partly agricultural, partly overgrown with "Pusch," partly wooded, past Provins nearly to Montmirail. Again the fields were a dreadful sight: badly planted, but also generally badly cultivated, full of weeds, the fruit famished, straw puny, ears of grain barely visible, the harvest behindhand. The only thing I liked in the agriculture of that region was the carts used in the harvest. They were one-horse, two-wheel vehicles with rungs fore and aft, not at the sides, which makes them much easier to load. Shortly before reaching Montmirail we came to the most westerly point of the German advance of 1914. Kiep had a horse patrol in that area. One evening after dark he came from such a patrol and was asked to report to his army chief, Bülow,[2] in a barn at Vauxchamps near Montmirail, where Bülow was deliberating with Hentsch[3] about a retreat. Kiep had to report and then fell asleep. When he woke in the morning, the order to retreat had been given in that barn, the order that may have decided the last world war. We got out at Vauxchamps and inspected the barn. The farmer came and spoke to us. But he was a new owner who had taken over in 1925 and knew nothing of former days. From Vauxchamps to Verdun and on to Pont-à-Mousson, we followed the front of 1914. War graves right and left; tens of thousands here, more tens of thousands there. There are more men buried in the main cemetery at

1. Since July the seat of the French government under the aged General Pétain in the unoccupied part of France.

2. General of the Second Army in the Battle of the Marne, 1914.

3. General von Moltke, chief of the General Staff, had sent Lieutenant Colonel Hentsch to the flanking armies.

Douaumont than Germans and French together lost in the present campaign. Every war has its horrors, and in this war so far the emphasis is not on those killed in action. I got the impression that at most not more than 20 to 25,000 Frenchmen have been killed this time, few officers among them.

I don't think I mentioned Sajovic's comment that he has a staff of 80. Roughly 40 of them were at the front, 17 as officers. The husband of one of the secretaries was killed in the skirmishing in November '39, otherwise he knew of no casualties in the families of his employees, and all 40 soldiers were unharmed.

At Verdun we drove to Fort Douaumont, where Kiep had been stationed at first. About 800,000 men were killed there during the last war on both sides. A dreadful mountain and fought for quite senselessly. Incidentally, not a fort in the present meaning of the word. But from the top there is a fine view of wide, rolling landscape, wooded, criss-crossed by rivers, lightened by meadows, pastures, and fields, animated by villages and hamlets. It is a peaceful view, for there was practically no fighting here this time. The fighting consisted in blowing up bridges.

After Verdun the land begins to be a bit more thickly settled. One sees that one is approaching an industrial region and from Pont-à-Mousson onward as far as Nancy one really drives constantly past houses. It is like Langenbielau. This part of the Moselle looks like the Rhine near Basel: a broad, big, calm, flowing river. The river valley is narrow, not much broader than the valley of the Weistritz above the dam, and made even narrower where the shores are built up. From time to time the valley broadens, leaving room for wide, good meadows; there are also some vineyards, but on the whole no intensive agriculture. A region emphatically dominated by industry. At Nancy, where Kiep and I arrived alone because the others, coming directly from Paris, got there only at 11.30 at night, we were very well received by Field Marshal Witzleben.[1] The headquarters of the Army Command [AOK] are in the Grand Hotel, which lies on a beautiful square, enclosed by big gilded wrought-iron fences and gates. We were put up in the same hotel. Nancy owed its few high points, of which this square with the hotel is one, to the Polish King . . . (?),[2] the father-in-law of Louis XV, who reigned there and in Luxembourg.

Our reception was very friendly. Everyone made efforts to be friendly

1. Erwin von Witzleben (1881–1944), one of the new field marshals; commander-in-chief of Army Group C in the campaign in France; took over the new Army Group D in October 1940; May 1941 C.-in-C. West, from March 1942 onward in the leadership reserve. In lively contact with opponents of the regime since before the war; played a prominent part on 20 July 1944; sentenced to death and executed 8 August 1944.
2. Stanislaw (I) Leszczynski (1677–1766).

to us. But overall the impression of the staff was quite different from that in Brussels. There the staff was filled with life and spirit and a feeling of collective responsibility; here it was the typical higher staff, where everyone has known everyone else too long, hasn't really anything more to say, and all look to the chief, try to please him and to do what meets with his approval. To make up for the lack of conversation they toast each other, they talk about hunting and leave, because they cannot think of anything else. Yet they are all nice enough, and W. himself is very friendly and not field-marshally; but the spirit is lacking.

What I could find out confirmed the picture one gets all over France: the population is apathetic and that is why grievances can drag on which otherwise would long since have led to considerable political difficulties. The food situation is very bad: "For the time being we are hoping to manage until the end of the month, then we must somehow get new supplies." Because the supply lines are not yet functioning, industry is mostly dead. The electric cables for energy supplies are destroyed, the canals have suffered lasting damage. Train connections with Paris, taking 8 hours, were restored only a few days ago; the bridges are all destroyed. The political situation is characterized by uncertainty about the future of the region. Inhabitants who have fled or joined the exodus to the South or West are not permitted to return. But Bürckel's[1] activity in the territories annexed to Germany will mean an influx of the expropriated, Jews and Frenchmen, who may be permitted to reside here, or may be pushed on farther.

Administration is impeded by lack of clarity about the jurisdictions of Bürckel and Streccius,[2] by the confusion of civilian and military offices. Its effects remain latent as long as the population remains apathetic. It will lead to very serious political crises as soon as the resistance of the population crystallizes in some way, either because of real famine or because of German failure or hesitation vis-à-vis Britain.

The following morning, Sunday the 11th, we departed at 8.30, again down the beautiful valley of the Moselle. It really presented an even better picture this morning: there had been rain in the night, and in the colourful morning sun it was all especially bright and glorious. After Pont-à-Mousson we drove along the right bank as far as Metz, went to get our permit to inspect the Maginot Line, and then drove inside the Maginot Line all the way from Diedenhofen to Saaralben. You can see the defence works marked on the map.

1. Gauleiter Josef Bürckel had become chief of military government in Lorraine.
2. General Alfred Streccius (1874–1943), chief of military government in France. Like Falkenhausen (cf. n. 1 (p. 88) to letter of 9 August), he had been military adviser in China for years.

The overall impression is of a gigantic defence system planned with extraordinary intelligence. The large installations are constructed with observation posts at the highest spots to direct the fire of the large gun emplacements, which lie totally concealed and are in turn protected tactically by installations of less fire power. One really can say this system affords absolute protection, since no tank can get past these deep ditches and steep walls, and no infantryman can brave the fire of the installations meant for close combat. That is why there was no fighting at all for these defence works: they are quite untouched, and one looks in vain for a shell crater in their vicinity.

Between these large installations and protected by their long-range fire power, a broad belt of tank and infantry defence emplacements stretches uninterrupted through the landscape. Even the roads are part of it. Carefully constructed barbed-wire defences, *chevaux de frise,* tank traps, minefields fill a belt 1 km wide on the average. To a depth of roughly 50 m around all woods on the French side the trees have been felled, without being removed, which makes any attacks through the woods practically impossible, too. This defence belt is further reinforced by flooding and artificial swamps in the lower-lying tracts of land. The defence from the heights is as follows: in front of a hill there is a machine-gun bunker with a direct field of fire across the defence belt, which also gives flanking protection to the neighbouring pillboxes, rarely more than 100 m distant, and in turn receives flanking protection from them. Behind the hill is an artillery bunker, which can prevent any penetration of the defence belt by direct fire, which is itself almost impossible to hit because it is protected by the elevated ground in front against direct fire, by its construction against indirect fire—with the exception of a direct hit on the firing slits from above. All the roads on which we drove had iron barriers, mines, tank traps, and similar devices affording protection.

The whole system is impressive to look at because the careful and methodical planning is so obvious and because one has to conclude from these preparations that the line is impregnable if it is seriously defended. At the same time the expense, the waste of money, and the waste of land, whereby thousands of square kilometres are taken out of useful cultivation, are depressing. In this entire region nothing grows but thistles and other weeds, and the wind just blowing across it was carrying whole consignments of mature thistle seed, to spread like a plague over German land perhaps 100 km away, where people will have no idea why there are so many thistles. In brief, such a defence system is inorganic and diseased. If we cannot manage without such things, in Europe, I mean, then we deserve no better. The whole thing, despite its admirable planning, is an unhealthy and infectious rash which must never be allowed to occur again.

Having seen all this, one asks oneself how the breakthrough was possible. We inspected the northern breakthrough area between Cappel and Püttlingen thoroughly, and had lunch on the same day with a battalion staff—for in this totally evacuated region there was no food to be had privately. The battalion's artillery had supported the breakthrough. Our question how such a thing is done was answered simply as follows: the emplacements are immune against attack in normal circumstances, and therefore, in all the many months they spent in positions around these bunkers, no attack was ever seriously considered. But in May, when the French, because of the low morale of their troops, evacuated their infantry field positions on the glacis, that is, positions needed for the defence of the fixed emplacements, there was a chance. It was possible to bring heavy anti-aircraft guns and field artillery up to the edges of woods that were still standing, without being seen or hindered in any way, because there was nobody left in the glacis to report or obstruct them. Thus, depending on local conditions, it was possible to approach within 1 km to 75 m of the front machine-gun pillboxes and to direct superior fire power at their firing slits. Only after these advance bunkers had been finished off did the infantry proceed against the artillery bunkers behind the hill, which without the bunkers in front of the hill were now without any means of observation. Once the infantry got right up to the bunkers, it was easy to finish them off with flamethrowers, because these bunkers, dependent on the support of the others, were not equipped for close combat. So it was possible to make a fighting advance. But even with this chance the Maginot Line would not have been overcome if the French occupants had really put up a fight. In fact they always evacuated the bunkers after the first hit, even if their fighting power was in no way impaired by it.

The evidence at the breakthrough point corroborates this description. The advance bunkers without exception have one or two hits, which scratched them. Very few bunkers are seriously damaged. In most of them, for instance, one still finds tables, chairs, bunks. The bunkers farther back all show signs of having been attacked with flamethrowers. The barbed-wire entanglements are almost all intact; in only a few places, perhaps 200 m apart, narrow passages have been cut. There are a few graves of German soldiers to be seen, and I have seen only two graves of French soldiers. The German soldiers were mostly killed singly, and only in a few places were several killed simultaneously, apparently by artillery. One cannot see any shell craters in the terrain, not even on the roads. The roadblocks were obviously removed by force. In the flooded or swampy places there are pontoons.

In the evening we reached Strasbourg, had the last good coffee and an excellent cheese sandwich. The town was still very empty, but no longer completely deserted, and life was beginning to look normal again. Only German was to be heard, not a word of French. We looked at the cathedral. It was black with soot inside and had no atmosphere because the pulpit had been boarded up and the windows removed. But even so it was a magnificent sight. At about 7 o'clock we crossed the Rhine on a pontoon bridge at Kehl and then spent the night at Karlsruhe.

There you have the story of a journey which was instructive for your husband.

Berlin, 20 August 1940

I have just seen in *The Times* that Eileen[1] died suddenly of a heart attack in Tottenham Court Road. I am very sad about it because she was a real friend and I was so sure that I could keep contact with her through this time. . . .

Berlin, 21 August 1940

The day is over. I thought I'd chew on Kant[2] a bit and write to you at leisure. Instead I spent the whole day fighting like a lion for a French officer's life which the Reich Marshal[3] wants to have at all costs. The fight is not over yet; but the result so far at least is that the execution will be put off. It was dramatic, and I not only fought here in Berlin but was also driven to the nearby Führer Headquarters—without Führer at the moment—to see what I could do on my own. Now I have just come from there—it is 7—and can only just change before going to Kirk's. . . .

I had a long talk today with Groos about the basic principles of naval warfare. I am, as you know, rather critical of our Naval Command and aghast at the AA, which always indulges in quite exaggerated notions of the potential effectiveness of our navy and air force in the war at sea. Their trees always grow into the sky. Again I've had considerable differences with them and have Groos entirely on my side—unfortunately rather too much so. It is unfortunate because he identified himself with

1. Eileen Edna le Poer Power (1889–1940), economic historian, professor at the London School of Economics.
2. He was reading the *Critique of Pure Reason.*
3. Hermann Göring (1893–1946), highly decorated fighter pilot in the First World War, early and leading National Socialist; 1933 Prussian Minister of the Interior, then Minister President; commander-in-chief of the Luftwaffe from its creation in 1935; from 1936 Plenipotentiary for the Four Year Plan. Sentenced to death at Nuremberg; committed suicide.

my proposals and is no longer seen by the AA as arbiter but as partisan. It is not a happy situation.

Here is the notice from *The Times* and a picture of Frau Doktor[1] which C. brought along. Please return both.

Berlin, 22 August 1940

. . . Today I fought once more for the life of that officer, like a lion: the matter received the attention of Göring, Keitel, and probably the Führer; but at 1.15 it turned out that this officer does not exist, that we had all got excited about a hypothetical case. That was really funny and rather typical. . . .

Berlin, 23 August 1940

. . . Today, at last, I finished a big piece of work. I have still to read and correct the proofs and then I'll be rid of it at last. I think I spent about 3 months on it. I'm fed up to the teeth with it.—I don't think I told you that we moved out of the Tirpitzufer and that our group has now taken up quarters in the Grossadmiral Prinz Heinrichstrasse: in the corner house at the Tiergartenstrasse, the house next door to the Bekkers'[2] former flat. Again Schmitz and I have a very nice room with a view on the Tiergarten. I have not yet sat there because during the move I preferred my quiet room in Bendlerstrasse. But tomorrow I must go there.

I had lunch with Reichwein.[3] I didn't say a word about Asta because we were so deeply involved in other questions that it simply did not happen. We made an appointment to continue our discussion Tuesday evening and I'll mention the Pearl[4] then. But it was a nice lunch. We ate the remainder of the chicken and peppers. . . .

Sunday night I cannot call you up because I'm going to see Kirk. It turned out to be impossible on Wednesday and I remained with Deuel. Perhaps I'll call you Sunday morning. I must see how I feel. Saturday evening has its merits too. But I don't know yet.

1. Eugenie Schwarzwald had died on 7 August 1940—see Introduction, pp. 6–7.
2. Willem Bekker was a Dutch client of M.'s.
3. Adolf Reichwein (1898–1944), educator and Social Democrat, known to M. since the days of the work camps; much travelled, wrote his doctoral dissertation on China and Europe, later published writings on other countries; 1929–30 worked for C. H. Becker, the Prussian Minister of Education; 1930 professor at Pedagogical Academy in Halle; after his dismissal in 1933 he taught in a rural elementary school; during the war he was a museum administrator in Berlin and active in political opposition; took part in two meetings at Kreisau; arrested 4 July 1944, executed 20 October 1944.
4. His sister, Asta.

Berlin, 24 August 1940

... Your letter of the day before yesterday, which arrived today, also sounded a bit sad. My love, times are too bad for that, we can't afford it. First of all, get more sleep.

The discussion with Gablentz last night was a great success. G. was nice, and he is very good and useful in a discussion.[1] The entire day yesterday was nice for me as a result of the two talks with Reichwein and Gablentz.—But, I, too, am a bit down; the weather and the cold get on my nerves.—Now, at half past three, I am sitting on the sofa with my legs wrapped in a rug and the electric heater directed towards my feet, and am writing in that position. But the immense importance this weather may have in the history of mankind[2] drowns out all nervousness.

Churchill's last speech was quite outstanding and one gets the feeling that inwardly the British may now have got past the critical period. The speech is more modest and certain, more confident. It emphasizes the need for all to give of their best and ends with a sentence that goes roughly: *and if we exert ourselves to the limit of our capacity, and after we have done all that is in our power, we can only pray that God may consider us worthy to give victory to our cause.*[3] It is a different tone of voice: God is no longer their own champion but it is left to him to decide whether the British deserve victory.

Militarily nobody can form a picture. Only a few weeks now separate us from the great decision, and a tremendous amount depends on it. Politically, the rapid preparations of the U.S.A. to come to complete union with the Empire are the most important factor. I have the impression that this union, however it may be disguised, will exist by the end of this year and will be the year's most decisive event. It therefore seems that changes of the greatest magnitude[4] are to be expected.

1. For the written preparation of this discussion see van Roon, *Resistance to Hitler*, pp. 299ff.; for the subsequent correspondence see ibid., pp. 301f, 304ff., 307ff.

2. A reference to German invasion plans and the air war over England. The Battle of Britain was far from decided until 15 September.

3. English in the original. It was Churchill's speech in the House of Commons of 20 August 1940, in which he said: "I hope—indeed I pray—that we shall not be found unworthy of our victory if after toil and tribulation it is granted us." It was in fact an allusion to the tasks of peace after the war.

4. The contrast of this vision with the facts is rather striking. Britain's inability to pay for American arms in dollars beyond 1940 was overcome by the Lend-Lease Act of March 1941, but even then the psychological gain was greater than the material. The United States preserved its benevolent neutrality until the Japanese attack on Pearl Harbor on 7 December 1941 and the subsequent German declaration of war on the U.S.—see letter of 10 December 1941.

Berlin, 25 August 1940

... First I worked a bit, then I read about 50 pages of Voltaire, then I thought for a while, laid a game of Patience, and glanced at Goethe's "Pedagogical Province."[1] Do you remember where he deals with education, and the children are brought up to three kinds of reverence: reverence for what is above us, reverence for what is below us, and reverence for what is equal to us. What a splendid formulation. N[ational] S[ocialism] has once more taught us reverence for what is below us, i.e., material things, blood, ancestry, our bodies. To that extent it is right, and we should not forget the lesson. But it has killed reverence for what is above us, that is, God or whatever you may wish to call it, and has tried to lower this under us by the deification of things of this world which fall under the rubric of the reverence due to that which is below us. Similarly N.S. has destroyed reverence for what is equal to us by trying to put at least some of those who are equal to us beneath us.—On the other hand liberalism of the degenerate kind teaches reverence for what is equal to us but neglects the other reverences. Yet wisdom lies precisely in the equilibrium, and this wisdom is really possible only for the liberal countryman, since all others have so little relation to what is most alive below us that they can hardly learn to revere it.

The more I think about it, the more I feel that "freedom" and "natural order" are the two necessary poles between which statecraft must move. And these two poles don't admit any further analysis and definition. Any attempt to scratch at them further is useless: they are concepts given us simply by intuition, not by the understanding. That is why all discussion about it is totally fruitless. A human being can be free only in the framework of the natural order and an order is natural only if it leaves man free. We won't be able to describe at what point this balance is achieved, but we will see and feel it; nobody can say how it is to be achieved, we have to try it. It is a process of *trial and error....*

Berlin, 26 August 1940

... So now we have had the first big air raid on Berlin, last night. I have no idea what happened, because I haven't talked to anybody, but it is no joke to lie awake from 12 to 4, especially as there is a hellish row in the area around Derfflingerstrasse, which is swarming with anti-aircraft guns. In between one hears the bombs exploding, which doesn't exactly cheer one up either. C.B., however, slept like an angel and said he was

1. See Johann Wolfgang von Goethe, *Wilhelm Meisters Wanderjahre* (*Wilhelm Meister's Journeyman Years*, or *Travels*), bk. 2, chaps. 1, 2.

used to this kind of thing. It was surprisingly prompt, for yesterday, no, during the night from Saturday to Sunday, we bombed London for the first time; the bill was presented at once.

I am already drawing up a programme of entertainment for you. Friday after supper we shall go to Reichwein's, on Sunday to see Kirk. In addition I want to invite Dohnanyi and Trott for you one day. . . .

Berlin, 6 September 1940

. . . I look forward very much to my leave—tremendously. I must get really and thoroughly fit for work again, because I may be facing a very important year. Before 31.12.41 a tremendous lot will happen, for the war will not outlast the new year unless it becomes a fight between the hemispheres, which I do not expect.

I spent the day in continual meetings, starting at 11. Emerging from one of them, I met Deuel again, and he was beaming. . . .

Berlin, 7 September 1940

Last night we had a fantastic air-raid alert. I had slept through the starting sirens again but woke when the heavy anti-aircraft artillery, which seems to have been reinforced further—especially around Keitel's house—began firing like mad. The windows were rattling and the explosion of the guns created lightning effects. Quite soon I was wide awake. At about half past one the area of the garage was brilliantly illuminated. I thought there was something on fire and was about to get up when I realized that it was only one of those clusters of flares which, as I could see from the shadows on the house next door, must have been almost directly above the garage. From time to time a little hail of shrapnel fell in the garden, some splinters so close to the window that they made a whistling noise. In sum, the whole thing, which lasted until 3.15, struck an entirely new note. . . .

Yorck is coming to lunch today and will probably stay till 5; he will then be off to Silesia on his way to Prague, where he goes on Monday. I shall therefore have a good early afternoon. Apart from that I am hoping for a peaceful, undisturbed Saturday and Sunday during which I can devote myself to Kant. On Sunday at 6 I am going to Gablentz's for supper. He lives in Frohnau—which means quite a trip. . . .

Berlin, 8 September 1940

The night was quiet. I got up at 11.45 and got dressed in expectation of our friends. But they didn't come, and so I undressed again at 1.45 and

slept. The damage of the night before was indeed so heavy that it is foolish to stay in bed if one cannot sleep. And sleep is made impossible by
the anti-aircraft guns that now surround the nearby house of our Field
Marshal Keitel. The window panes rattle and everything shivers and
shakes.

I already had a cold yesterday, and as I woke up with a headache today,
I decided to stay in bed. I had breakfast and am now having lunch and
also writing in bed. Telephone and doorbell have been switched off so
that nothing can disturb my peace. I spent the whole morning reading:
Voltaire, *The Times*, and a book Yorck put into my hand: Jünger, *Der
Arbeiter*—which, however, strikes me as romantic humbug. . . .[1]

My thoughts are constantly in England, where an essential part of our
future depends on the abilities of a few thousand men. I assume that by
Friday we shall have some notion whether or not the defence is weakening. So far nothing of the kind has been noticeable. In any case a major
operation has been in progress since the night before last; it is the second.

We can't go to the Yorcks' on the 29th. It is the birthday of his brother
who was killed in action, and he does not want to inflict visitors on his
mother on that day. We must therefore hold our budget discussions during the week or postpone them to the 29th. I want to tackle a certain piece
of work during the three weeks at Kreisau and therefore to start real work
without delay on Monday; at least in the morning. Please try to arrange
things so that we have breakfast early, about 7 or 7.30, and, if possible,
alone. Then I can work for 4 hours every day without interruption, from
8 to 12.

Berlin, 9 September 1940

. . . It was nice at Gablentz's. Einsiedel and he and I talked at length
and quite productively. Frohnau is a nice place, as you may remember,
and the weather was also nice in the afternoon, so that we sat outdoors
until 7.30. I was home by 11 and had a quiet night. At 11 the weather
was already bad, this morning it was quite overcast, and since 11 it has
been raining. I have heard nothing about the weather in England. If it is

1. It was a description of The Worker as the figure of the future: Ernst Jünger, *Der Arbeiter:
Herrschaft und Gestalt* (Hamburg, 1932). Jünger was a highly decorated young officer in the
First World War and a remarkable writer, mostly on the experience of war, after it. Consid-
ered a nationalist and a militarist, he was on an Allied "grey list." Yet his visionary tale *Auf
den Marmorklippen* (Hamburg, 1939; *On the Marble Cliffs*, trans. Stuart Hood [Hinsdale,
Ill., 1948]) was a thinly veiled and very vivid indictment of the Nazi regime. The typescript
of his essay *Der Friede* (1944) had much clandestine circulation in 1944 and 1945 (*The
Peace*, trans. Stuart O. Hood [Hinsdale, Ill., 1948]).

the same as here, our second air assault will probably be repelled, too, and the British will gain time to repair whatever may have been damaged in their defences, especially the airfields that we attacked—so that after a few days we would have to start again from the beginning. . . .

Berlin, 10 September 1940

. . . Furtwängler[1] came to see me last night. As always we had a good talk. He, too, is now working in the AA and seems very satisfied. I was a little disappointed with him in that the pressure of work seems to leave him too little chance to think. But he may simply have had a bad day. All the same it was profitable, only in another field.

Today I am having lunch with Brandenburg[2] & Körber.[3] It is a bit of a nuisance because just now I don't like to be distracted from the things I'm chewing on. But Brandenburg wanted it. Trott comes in the evening. Yesterday I had lunch in town with Reichwein. It was really quite productive.

We are having a cold, grey day.

This is where I stopped in the morning. Meanwhile the day is gone & I am already back at Derfflingerstrasse. The lunch with Brandenburg was rewarding after all. A good man. I am constantly surprised at the extent to which all these people have lost their orientation. It is just like a game of blind man's buff: they have been turned round and round blindfolded and no longer know what is left and right, front and back.

Both your Sunday and Monday letters were there when I got back. What a touching letter from Madame Fischbacher.[4] Yes, I'll write to her as soon as I have time. . . .

Berlin, 11 September 1940

. . . The air raid was heavy and damage at Siemensstadt and in the North is considerable. I hear that there is some damage on Unter der Linden as well, also at a few other places in the centre. I think 2 or 3 nights like this will make our Pearl lose her liking for Berlin.

1. Franz Josef Furtwängler (1894–1965), trade unionist and writer; during the war he worked for the AA. M. knew him from the latter days of the Weimar Republic.
2. Ernst Bruno Brandenburg (1883–1952), higher civil servant in the Ministry of Transport, prematurely retired in 1940. He had appeared as witness for Pastor Niemöller in the latter's trial in 1937.
3. Korvettenkapitän (Reserve) Normann Körber of the Abwehr.
4. Evidently the reaction of the mother of Pierre Fischbacher to a letter of condolence on the death of her son.

Today I have my first lunch discussion on the preparation of the peace negotiations. Schmitz is coming, and a representative of the FHQ,[1] a Major von Tippelskirch. After my return I want to extend this sytematically, to build an esprit de corps among these people. In the afternoon a man is coming for a long business discussion, and Deuel comes in the evening.—Yesterday Trott appeared with Bielenberg, less to exchange information, as I had expected, than to hear where one should steer now. It is the same thing: they have somewhat lost their bearings and allow themselves to be impressed by external events and expect answers from these events which they don't believe they can find in themselves. It is a kind of hoping for a miracle or gift from heaven.

The cold is icy and it is raining. Heating is forbidden. So far 13% of domestic fuel for this winter is available, and there is no improvement in sight. Even if this winter should be less cold than the last, more people are certain to suffer from the cold; then to have nothing to eat, and air raids—but these of course only if the landing in GB[2] fails—is a little too much.

Berlin, 7 October 1940

How lovely it was with you. I enjoyed it so much and I was so contented to be with you. I liked everything so much and I wish I could stay for a long time and for ever. . . .

I am sad about having to leave all the things on the farm, in the garden, on the Peile, the slope, the Kapellenberg that were begun. It is such a pleasant occupation. I'm already looking forward to the removal of the old and the erection of the new fence, to the shrubs and the cherry trees on the slope. I anticipate it all with eager expectation.

Berlin, 8 October 1940

. . . The war situation is unchanged and static. The co-belligerents[3] on both sides are getting ready to take part. Apart from that, preparations

1. Führer Headquarters.
2. On 3 September Hitler had envisaged the landing in Great Britain—code-named "Sea-Lion"—for 21 September; the Luftwaffe had been attacking London every night since 7 September. On 12 October Hitler postponed Operation Sea-Lion until spring 1941.
3. He probably meant chiefly the United States, where the presidential election was imminent and Roosevelt had to be wary of the isolationists. On 27 September 1940 Germany, Italy, and Japan concluded a tripartite treaty (*DGFP*, D, XI, no. 118). Hungary, Roumania, and Slovakia joined it on 20, 23, and 24 November. The question of a Spanish entry into

are being made that could possibly bring a virtual decision of the war. But we have to wait and see. Viewed as a whole the situation is a bit better for us now than it was when I started my leave. Probably thanks, in the main, to the abortive enterprise at Dakar . . .[1]

Berlin, 10 October 1940

. . . Deuel came last night. His successor has arrived and he leaves for Lisbon on the 11th of December. He is very relieved about that. Kirk departs tomorrow. Their absence will mean a great gap[2] for me. The situation in the U.S.A. seems unchanged: it is hardly a question any more of "whether" but, rather, of "when."[3]

I am a little ashamed of my vacillating views on the development of the war in May, about the end of that month and the beginning of June. I am embarrassed at having allowed myself to be so much impressed by events. Since about July my better insight has prevailed again, and today I see the interlude of uncertainty as simply ridiculous.

What a great clearance this war will bring about! It offers a really big chance of arriving at a time of real stability. It feels close enough for me to touch it, and I therefore have no patience and hate having to keep this vision to myself. But I must wait and join in the curious dance. Yet this prospect is threatened by dreadful dangers which may destroy it all. I think I see the dangers, I see them growing, but I cannot do anything in the crisis they raise but wait and watch.

My love, in a few days you'll be here, and who is looking forward to it? Your husband. If Herr Deichmann happens to be here, we could perhaps use Marchstrasse again?

I have a lot of work to do, and in the next few weeks it will be a very great deal. Basically I have only one goal: to form a staff of soldiers who recognize the problems of a peace treaty, and with whom one can work.

---

the war was also being discussed, with Canaris acting as a brake. The advantages of active participation at Germany's side were being presented to the Vichy government. See Hitler's Directive of 12 November 1940 in *DGFP*, D, XI, 1, no. 323.

1. From 23 to 25 September British naval forces had attacked the West African port of Dakar in order to facilitate a landing of troops under General de Gaulle, who continued the war for France at the side of Britain. Vichy French naval forces and coastal batteries defeated the attack.

2. "Kirk, when he left Germany in October 1940, turned over and entrusted personally to me the most delicate and valuable of his clandestine 'contacts' among the German oppositionists. This was Count Helmuth von Moltke. . . ." (Kennan, *Memoirs*, p. 119).

3. The question of America's entry into the war. It was to take another fourteen months.

It is not a question of high officers, but of people in my price range who sit in ante-rooms and have to do the real work. . . .

Berlin, 15 October 1940

. . . Trott was here for lunch. We mostly exchanged information on conditions in England. The result was unimpressive because nobody really knows anything definite. But I had just had a report from a neutral businessman who left London on 27 September. He reported in detail about what is smashed and what is not. The lasting impression is that on the whole little has been destroyed, but admittedly he did not see the docks. . . .

Berlin, 24 October 1940

The day is gone already. I was busy with a series of superfluous things. My love, it was so nice with you again, I am so much at home with you and nowhere else. But what's to be done? It's better to sacrifice the ring in time, like Polycrates.

The day was wearisome. I could still feel the inadequacy of the night in my bones, and everybody else was the same. I started by reading several *Times*es carefully, which was very rewarding.

Berlin, 28 October 1940

. . . So now Greece[1] is in the war. There was a delay—by 24 hours—and I can't find out why. Such things usually have a political, not a military or technical significance. We'll know in a week whether the Turks join in, and whether the British get the islands.[2] A lot depends on this week, for the war in the Mediterranean, and the strategic situation, can become much clearer. The curious thing, at which I am surprised myself, is that all this no longer excites me; it slips past, and no more affects the total picture than the shadow of a cloud crossing a landscape.

Berlin, 29 October 1940

This is the week I've looked forward to; we have to pass through one of the big crises that in themselves and in their resolution always open new vistas on the future. This week does seem to fulfil my expectations. The

1. Italy had attacked Greece in the early morning.
2. British forces landed in Crete on 31 October. Turkey stayed neutral.

presidential election a week from today will put an end to this crisis. Perhaps it won't change the situation, but it may have tremendous significance for the further course of the war; we'll have to wait and see. Such crises are so stimulating and agreeably heighten one's awareness of being alive. . . .

Berlin, 6 November 1940

The presidential election is over. I expected that Roosevelt would be elected again; but I don't know anything about the U.S.A., so I accepted my own estimate with reservations. But this result is overwhelming. The last figures I heard are 447:84 for R[oosevelt]. This election may be a milestone in world history: for the U.S.A., abandonment of the control of all important posts by the victorious party and formation of a permanent civil service; for the world, a free hand for a truly competent organizer and opponent of the dictatorships. If R. were to seize the opportunity he could enter history as one of the greatest men of all time, the man who reversed the War of Independence, carried out the fusion[1] of the Empire with the U.S.A., and thus re-established an uncontested and incontestable naval supremacy, which is the precondition for a stable peace. It is a really great day and I feel all the time like celebrating with myself. However long and hard and steep the way may be, as long as it is in the right direction all is well. There are still many difficulties ahead; but this day has not only cleared one obstacle but, by restoring the United States' freedom of action, also established the precondition for clearing future obstacles.

Yes, there was something else I wanted to tell you: Monday night from 11.30 till 1 a.m. I spent in the hall of Breslau station; because the waiting room was overcrowded, I sat on the counter of the luggage office, in a corner. For these 90 minutes I observed what passed: 90% soldiers; elderly people who looked tired and listless and were weighed down by bundles of all kinds; young fellows, particularly of the Luftwaffe, plainly proud and pleased with this kind of life; older regular soldiers; but mostly typical occupation troops. With the soldiers were girls who attached themselves to them or belonged to them, incidental appendages. The rest—about 5%—were travelling officials, who felt important, were badly dressed, and seemed deadened and indifferent. Among them were Poles coming to work in the Reich: all of them looked wretched, worse off than our Poles, and they were so dirty I could not have stood having one of them sit next to me.

1. Cf. letter of 24 August 1940.

But all the people who passed were types, not human beings. They were material for slaughter or for work, they were machines with a particular function in a process. Except for my very nice porter I literally did not see a single human being. The movement that has swept these creatures with it has torn their human bonds. In Africa it's called *detribalised* and is related to the idea that the Negroes have become ungovernable and incapable of governing. But we have the same process.

I must go, my love.

Berlin, 9 November 1940

. . . Today at 2.45 I had lunch at Derfflingerstrasse with Einsiedel and Gablentz. We had the chicken. Then we discussed my little memorandum until 6 o'clock; tomorrow I'll have lunch at Yorck's for the same purpose, and then I'll probably start to reformulate[1] it. I wonder whether the end result will be usable.

This evening, i.e., now, and tomorrow morning I want to write something more about post-war possibilities in foreign policy,[2] and tomorrow evening I want to go to the Waetjens' at Babelsberg. You see I have an enormous programme for the week-end. Besides, the discussion with those two at lunch was very strenuous.

Berlin, 10 November 1940

. . . Molotov's[3] forthcoming visit is announced in today's papers. It is due to the Führer's handwritten letter to Stalinchen.[4] Whether we'll succeed in keeping the Russians as favourably inclined as hitherto is a question of some interest. Relations with them have become less tense[5] again in the past weeks. I don't expect the visit to do more than confirm the fact. In particular, I do not expect it to lead to pressure on Turkey,[6] though that possibility can't be excluded.—It now seems to be certain that the British

1. See M.'s memorandum of 20 October 1940 in van Roon, *Resistance to Hitler*, pp. 310–17; cf. M.'s letter to Yorck and Gablentz of 16 November 1940 ibid., pp. 306–9.
2. Not preserved.
3. V. M. Molotov, Soviet Foreign Minister.
4. "Stalinchen"—"dear little Stalin"?—a diminutive equivalent, however ironical, of "Uncle Joe"? Ribbentrop had written to Stalin on 13 October, inviting Molotov to visit Berlin to discuss the further development of a common policy (*DGFP*, D, XI, 1, no. 176; Stalin's answer ibid., no. 211).
5. One of the points of conflict was the question of dissolution of the European Danube Commission—see *DGFP*, D, XI, 1, no. 310.
6. For the draft agreement between the tripartite powers and the Soviet Union with two secret protocols see *DGFP*, D, XI, 1, no. 309.

have landed on a number of islands: Crete, Lemnos, and others. I haven't been able to find anybody who could tell me how soon these islands can be transformed into usable navy and air-force bases. On the Greek main-land there seems to be only air force. For the last two days the Italians have been making some progress, though very slowly.

Berlin, 11 November 1940

... Yesterday I was at the Yorcks' for lunch. They were alone, because I wanted to discuss something[1] with him; the discussion, I hope, benefited us both. It was very nice, as always. I look forward to the time when I can live with you so peacefully. Perhaps it will come. But at Kreisau, not in the city . . .

My current work doesn't interest me at all at the moment. There's noth-ing useful I can do, and I'm dealing with minor rubbish. My thoughts are always occupied either with the settlement after the war or with Kreisau. I swing like a pendulum from one to the other. . . .

Berlin, 13 November 1940

... Mr. Molotov[2] is in Berlin, but to my disappointment I have not yet seen a flag with a hammer and sickle. I don't see that this visit will pro-duce anything but propaganda. I don't think one should expect anything else. But we've been wrong quite a few times on such questions. . . .

Berlin, 14 November 1940

... At Groos's yesterday afternoon it was quite nice. Apart from a few women there were Herr von Raumer—the little one you met with me at the Kieps'—and Carl Schmitt.[3] There was excellent looted coffee. . . .

Berlin, 25 November 1940

This is a day with an enormous amount of work and so I can only send you a very short greeting. My love, it was so very lovely with you and I

1. The discussion dealt with fundamental questions and prompted M.'s letter to Yorck of 16 November (cf. n. 1 to letter of 9 November) with its rejection of Hegel's "deification of the state" and anything that might lead to it.
2. Cf. letter of 10 November and Note by the Under-Secretary of State of 11 November (*DGFP*, D, XI, 1, no. 317); Note by the interpreter Schmidt on the talks between Ribbentrop and Molotov and Hitler and Molotov on 12 and 13 November (ibid., nos. 325, 326, 328).
3. Carl Schmitt (1888–1985), famous and from 1932 notorious constitutional lawyer, of whom M. did not think much.

was so contented by and with you. I am already looking forward to the time when we'll be able to live together again. My heart, do be well. I hope you had a good journey and find everything all right.

My love, I'll write nothing else today. Be well.

Berlin, 26 November 1940

. . . I'm already looking forward to the Sunday after next, when I'll be able to see everything. How nice it will be, in particular, to know how big the sugar-beet harvest really was, instead of being suspended between fear and hope. . . .

Farewell, my love, soon, soon I hope to come and would so much like to stay.

Berlin, 28 November 1940

. . . Yesterday Deuel and I were quite elegiacal about our last evening. I shall really miss him, because I like him and talking with him has always been a great help to me. Of all the men I see and with whom I talk intensively, he is the only one who doesn't want me to strengthen his faith, so to speak. Even Yorck, who is on the whole the most independent of them, wants that. That's why, for all the friendship, the others take it out of me more than Deuel. . . .

Berlin, 30 November 1940

. . . Your husband is really quite well. Because he has a lot of work now he realizes that he is more productive than a while ago.—He had lunch with the Willem Bekkers. She expects the baby on the 18th of December and seems to be in very good spirits. He has meanwhile become the great man in the NSB[1] and Mussert's[2] representative in Berlin. He wants to acquire a suitable house in Berlin for the NSB, one as appropriate to their importance as the one the Fascio have.[3] He has the Golden Party Badge with the number 3027 and his Party rank is one above Gauleiter, with a uniform covered in gold. It is all very comical.

My leave has been granted from 23 December to 9 January 1941. I

1. Nationaal Socialistische Beweging, the Dutch Nazis.
2. Anton Adriaan Mussert (1894–1946), founder of the NSB; collaborated closely with the German occupation regime in Holland from 1940 on, including the recruitment for the Dutch SS; advocated the merging of the Netherlands in a Greater Germanic Reich; 1942 nominated Führer of the Netherlands; 1946 sentenced to death.
3. The representatives of the Italian Fascist Party.

hope to be able to leave on the evening of the 20th; at any rate I have announced it to Tafel. It may turn out to be the 21st, but I'll certainly be there on the 22nd. In addition I hope to come home next Saturday/Sunday. That is not so certain, however, because there is such a dreadful lot of work. But I have just achieved 2 big successes for my chief, and a third one is imminent, so I expect all my wishes for leave to be granted without any trouble.

Today some Italians arrived, with whom we must negotiate tomorrow. It will go on till late at night, and I'll therefore not phone, but call Monday morning instead.—I'm already much looking forward to my Christmas leave, and the prospect of perhaps being able sometime to be at Kreisau for several consecutive months hovers before me like a mirage. I should add that this prospect has actually become much more agreeable and real since I can now hope that in the foreseeable future Kreisau will be free of debt, or at any rate virtually free of debt. That greatly improves our chances of overcoming economic crises. . . .

Berlin, 2 December 1940

. . . Another day without break to stop, and your husband is correspondingly exhausted. But an affair that looked very dangerous because our Hermann had committed himself strongly.[1] Your husband intrigued like mad and brought about a withdrawal by the Reich Marshal and one that moreover makes him look successful.—All this is meaningless, of course, but excellent practice in manoeuvring.

Unfortunately I have a touch of flu. Not bad, but bad enough to make me feel "that I have to reduce my speed," to stay in the jargon of Wehrmacht communiqués, or do they say "with reduced speed." But I am still upright. I'll take Infludo again tonight. Luckily there will be a quiet night because the weather makes British incursions practically impossible, as I heard.

After working for the Reich incessantly for three days with brief interruptions for sleep, I rang up Tafel just now and asked for home leave for Saturday/Sunday, giving the broken bridge as reason. So I'll arrive Friday night and really should come back Sunday night but hope to be able to travel as late as Monday at 7; but that is still uncertain.—Please ask Thomas on Saturday and finish the accounts; one or two figures were still missing. . . .

---

1. The sentence remained incomplete. Conflicts with Göring in the matter of Prize Law arose, inter alia, from Göring's function as Plenipotentiary for the Four Year Plan.

Berlin, 13 December 1940

. . . Tomorrow will be another full day. Yorck comes for lunch and then there is Sunday peace. I need it badly because I have an awful lot to clear up and finish. Kiep wanted me to come out, but I don't want to go. Also I hate the kind of sociability that brings together 2 dozen people.

Did our papers carry the news of Lothian's death? He is the third: Tweedsmuir,[1] Hichens,[2] Lothian.[3] I'm very sorry, although I didn't think too much of Lothian. . . .

Berlin, 14 December 1940

. . . Now for the tea at Rabenau's.[4] The guests were an uninteresting woman, General Glaise-Horstenau,[5] the Austrian Minister of War in 1938, a Dr. Chi with a German wife, and I. Chi is Chiang Kai-shek's private secretary and conducted all the negotiations with Falkenhausen and Seeckt;[6] that's why he was at Rabenau's. An enthusiastic young man, who as a student worked at the Ottmachau dam.

First the conversation wandered; then we got round to topical questions in China, the reason for his presence in Berlin, the situation in Chung King under bombardment, and finally our war. And lo and behold, this man was the first since Deuel whose basic strategic concept was similar to your husband's. I don't know to what extent it was his at the outset. But when I found that I was gaining ground with him, I was so delighted that I let myself go with a kind of lecture on the strategy of wars between world powers. The more I said, the more he agreed. Though the two land generals ventured a few interjections at the start, after 10 minutes only Chi and I were talking; we'd simply argued the two professional soldiers

1. Lord Tweedsmuir (1875–1940), writer (under his original name, John Buchan), politician, since 1935 Governor General of Canada; as a young lawyer he had worked under the High Commissioner Lord Milner in South Africa.
2. Lionel Hichens (1874–1940), another member of "Milner's Kindergarten" (1902–7); later businessman in England; killed in an air raid.
3. M. had disagreed with Lord Lothian's advocacy of appeasement in the thirties—cf. Introduction, p. 11. Lothian was the third man from "Milner's Kindergarten" to die in the war. He was succeeded by Lord Halifax, till then Foreign Secretary, as Ambassador in Washington.
4. General Friedrich von Rabenau (1884–1945), chief of Army Archives until 1943, was a member of the board of trustees of the Moltke Foundation. Executed April 1945.
5. Edmund von Glaise-Horstenau (1882–1946), Austrian historian and general; 1925–34 head of the War Archives in Vienna; 1936 "national" member in Schuschnigg's Cabinet; 1938 Vice Chancellor; 1941–44 German General Plenipotentiary in Croatia.
6. Colonel General Hans von Seeckt (1866–1936), creator of the "unpolitical" Reichswehr in the Weimar Republic.

to the wall. That went on for over an hour, during which the two generals hardly got a word in; they just sat there and listened and from time to time they said "I see," while the two of us sang the paean of naval supremacy as the one great force in the world. I was a bit embarrassed afterwards and wrote a letter of apology to Rabenau, in which I said I must have been a little forward but had been so delighted to find at last, after 14 months, a man who speaks my military language that I couldn't contain myself.

In any case I want to get permission to cultivate Chi's acquaintance.— His account of the situation in China was very optimistic. He reckons with a Japanese defeat in the foreseeable future and mentioned a period of from 2 to 24 months. All the information I have points in the same direction. My dear, perhaps we have only one task: to master the chaos here. If we succeed in that, there will be a period of peace, of secure peace, extending beyond our maximum lifetimes. I by no means underestimate the difficulties, but this war will really decide the burning issues and will not be followed by another war on the same issues. Today I feel the same as in 1930, when I saw a way out of chaos for Kreisau. Of course things can go wrong: but that's not the same as being in a position with no way out. . . .

Berlin, 16 December 1940

. . . There was a lot of work today. Lots of little things, but they had to be done. I suppose the dismissal of Laval[1] will be in our papers. That dots the "i" of my Christmas leave.

Last night we had two warnings. Result: *Stadtbahn* cut between Potsdam and Babelsberg, Halensee and Zehlendorf stations hit. Traffic at these three points is maintained by buses. Schmitz therefore arrived an hour late; Peters too, with whom I ate. In addition the underground has a hole at Tauentzienstrasse and isn't going either, and some of the trams don't go because the generating plant at Klingenberg was hit. It is a considerable achievement for the British, especially since none of them were shot down.—I slept through most of it.

I had lunch with Peters today. He was nice as always and has the Iron Cross. He has left his battery, and his new occupation, at Air Command, is ascertaining the effects of air raids on our region. He was still very new and not quite used to conditions in Berlin.

1. On 13 December Pétain had dismissed Laval and changed from Laval's policy of collaboration to one of *attentisme*. Cf. letter of 13 August, p. 98.

Eddy[1] will come about 8.30, and I have to discuss something with him. But then I want to go to bed early to get the better of my improving cold. Moreover I have to go to Schramm[2] in the morning. Raczynski,[3] whom I was once going to send to you at Kreisau from Bad Salzbrunn, will have lunch with me tomorrow, and Yorck comes in the evening. Wednesday lunch Trott and Bielenberg, evening George Kennan.[4] It is altogether a lively week.

1. Waetjen.
2. Dentist.
3. A client and art collector.
4. George Frost Kennan (born 1904), American diplomat and historian; before he joined the Berlin Embassy in 1939 he had served in the Baltic, in Moscow and Vienna, and, after the Munich Agreement of September 1938, in Prague; after the war Ambassador in Moscow 1952–53 and Belgrade 1961–63; permanent member of the Institute for Advanced Study at Princeton.

1941

Berlin, 20 January 1941

. . . I saw Suchantke's letter. I am to go to Hall, near Innsbruck. I said that I'll agree to do anything as long as I get a visa for Italy for both of us, so that I am not a prisoner at Hall. Otherwise I'd prefer Bolzano or Merano. Tafel will take it all in hand and will, I hope, deal with it all very well. I suggested the 15th of February as the date of travel, Tafel wants the 1st. Duration of leave 6 weeks, of which at least a fortnight in the sanatorium. Well, we'll see. . . .

Berlin, 23 January 1941

I did not write to you yesterday because my arm hurt so much. A man who was to take blood from me was so clumsy and poked around in my arm for half an hour—or so it seemed to me; he had to make several attempts. Result: 4 weeks. Perhaps I can still organize another week by hook or by crook. In that case I'd be for a fortnight at Cortina, 7 days in Rome, a fortnight at Kreisau.

I have a lot of work and am working badly and with effort. But I expect I'll get through it by the 14th of February and get everything in order slowly. There is nothing new to report from here. Time flows slowly and stubbornly. *I am marking time.*[1] Nichol[?] came last night and returned the 2 records I had given Deuel. D. had not been able to pack them. D. has written a series of articles,[2] which seem to have created quite a stir in the U.S.A. and here. . . .

Berlin, 24 January 1941

I am decidedly better today. It is 4 o'clock in the afternoon and I am still feeling fresh and lively, a thing that hasn't happened for a long time.—I had lunch with Hans Adolf, and Einsiedel is coming tonight. Yorck and Kessel to lunch tomorrow, and then begins a long and solitary Saturday/Sunday, which I badly need to finish the work for my office, which has suffered a good deal as a result of my reduced capacity for work. . . .

Berlin, 25 January 1941

Yorck and Kessel, who were here for lunch, have just left. Kessel is going to Geneva in a week's time; he's been posted there at least for a while. This morning I felt quite unwell again and accordingly have not done much. . . .

Yes, the cost of the convalescence. They only pay properly if I go to a soldiers' home and that doesn't appeal to me. They'll certainly pay *some-thing*, but only when I come back.—And I myself am to blame for my "illness." I am altogether dissatisfied with the way I ran my life in 1940; I made cardinal mistakes which I hope never to repeat; I lost my equilibrium scandalously and did not recover it any too gracefully; I'll always remember 1940 as a black year; I was really not up to it and I must be glad and thankful if a convalescence costing RM 1,000 puts me back where I was in April 1940 and I'll then have paid for the sins of the 6 months from May to the end of October. I hope I have learnt my lesson. Neither the soldiers nor the war are to blame, only I myself.

Farewell, my love. You may have missed the point that I owe it to you that I got the bad 6 months behind me; but if you don't know it, I can tell you so explicitly.

Berlin, 4 February 1941

What a nuisance all this business with the Schloss apartment is for you. You are bearing the brunt of it. How did you track me down at the

1. English in the original.
2. Cf. Wallace A. Deuel, *People Under Hitler* (New York, 1942).

Yorcks'? Did you write down their telephone number? For it isn't in the directory.

Haushofer,[1] the two Yorcks, and I talked last tonight till 12.30! Quite an achievement, don't you think? But it was nice and stimulating, and Yorck and I get on very well with each other, even if I am a good deal to the left of him.—And with Haushofer I found myself in greater agreement than ever before. So it was a pleasant and stimulating evening. . . .

Berlin, 24 March 1941

Just a little salutation from a hectic day. It was so lovely with you, as always. And the 5 weeks[2] have a lovely glow, like a sun in one's back. . . .

Berlin, 27 March 1941

There is nothing much to report. I just keep working by day at the Office, evenings in my own office, where a lot has to be finished and tidied up. In between I dream of flowering shrubs, fruit trees, deep digging, ploughing, fields, bees, manure, spreading, planting plans, and so on. When I think of these pleasurable activities, everything I do here appears unreal and ghostly and altogether unimportant. I have never felt compelled to stay in the city and therefore never realized how great my need for the country is. But now I know it. And I am convinced that the whole "illness" is due to that. Well, in wartime this is one of the lesser evils.

Berlin, 29 March 1941

The days pass slowly and everything seems to stand still. My notions of what would come have so far outrun events that I must now stand still and wait. I don't mind standing and watching. But my firm notions of the

1. Albrecht Haushofer (1903–45), son of the geopolitician Karl Haushofer; writer, geographer, historian, political scientist; taught at the Hochschule für Politik and the University of Berlin; temporarily did honorary work for the AA; friend of Yorck and Haeften (q.v.); was able to use contacts with Rudolf Hess, the Führer's Deputy, for peace feelers and help for persecuted persons; after Hess's flight to Scotland on 10 May 1941, under arrest for two months, subsequently under surveillance and rearrested 1944; shot by SS in April 1945, carrying the manuscript of his prison poems, *Moabiter Sonette* (Zurich, 1948; *Moabit Sonnets* [New York, 1978]).
2. M. had had the sick leave he had applied for during the previous summer, and they had spent the time together, in the Dolomites, in Taormina—where they met his brother Carl Bernd, who was stationed in Sicily—and at Kreisau.

course of events prejudice me. I see everything that happens as confirmation, every fact is fitted into the whole. Perhaps it does not fit? Perhaps everything looks different from the way I imagine it. I have become rigid and inflexible. Is that a sign of advancing age or was my long view correct? As far as I am concerned nothing has changed since my visit to France last August. I am surprised, but that is how it is. I look for new insights, changed points of view, improved plans. Yet all my thoughts begin not today but at a point still in the future. Why? Am I unable or unwilling to see reality or do I look at reality through the veil of appearance? An overall assessment that remains constant in every detail for 8 months during a time like this strikes me as suspect and uncanny. And yet I cannot change it.

I thought that after the 5 weeks I would see things differently and have new ideas. During the time just before, I found the defence of my own views rigid, unproductive, aggressive. But I have returned with the same eyes. I do not see a new reality. All I see, hear, experience leaves me cold, does not touch me. Today I can endure the sufferings of others with an equanimity I would have found execrable a year ago. My one reaction, perhaps, is to classify it and fit it into the framework of my preconceived notions, in some place where it seems to belong.

What am I to do if this continues? Will I not lose all power of persuasion, all my drive, all vitality? I cannot substitute understanding and experience, for mine are only modest.

I have only one urge and desire: to come to Kreisau to look after the farm, to do the digging and the hoeing myself, to plant and to prune, and to wait until events have caught up with my ideas. But that is the attitude of the Emperor Barbarossa, who waits until the ravens fly.—Never before—except in the last few months, when I blamed it on my illness— have I been so indifferent to events which everybody told me were important, decisive, tremendous, dramatic. I simply stand there, or, rather stand aside, and ask: why? Everything has already been decided, the drama is over. Can you explain that to me? Have I changed? . . .

Berlin, 1 April 1941

. . . The war has resumed its fast progress. The Italian military communiqué has admitted the loss of 3 cruisers and 2 destroyers in a naval engagement[1] and that will clarify the situation at sea in the Eastern Mediterranean, at any rate until land operations create a new situation with

1. These losses had been incurred in the Battle of Cape Matapan, 26–29 March.

regard to bases. Yesterday Anthony Eden[1] was in Belgrade with Sir John Dill[2] and that may well mean that we shall be faced by a regular Balkan front,[3] which will at the least mean occupation troops and may cause serious difficulties. The month which begins today will bring much suffering to large parts of Europe. . . .

Berlin, 14 April 1941

It is 10 o'clock and the church bells are ringing through the open window. They sound so peaceful, and I wonder whether you are sitting in Gräditz and listening to a nice liturgy and a bad sermon. How gladly I would hear the bad sermon. . . .

We had the news of the Russo-Japanese pact[4] at midday yesterday. I have the impression that it surprised everybody here, but I am completely uncertain about the interpretation of this event. Unfortunately we don't, however, know the text yet, but the fact as such is a sensation. Perhaps it is a big German victory, to which, however, we contributed nothing but the threat to Russia. Perhaps Russia wants to buy herself free from us; or conversely, she may want to protect her rear in case of complications in the West. In any case this could be quite a decisive event *one way or the other.*[5] I hope the text comes tomorrow, because today I don't want to be distracted by it from my work.

The fall of Bardia is very serious for the other side. The whole thing is a complete surprise for them as it is for us. Because of the limited strength of the troops at his disposal Rommel's[6] situation will continue to be a real cause for concern for quite a while even if he succeeds in holding the positions he has won or may yet win farther forward. Whether it is an

1. Anthony Eden (1897–1977), later Earl of Avon, was British Foreign Secretary 1935–38, 1940–45, and 1951–55; Dominion Secretary 1939–40, Secretary for War 1940, Prime Minister 1955–57.
2. Sir John Dill, Chief of Imperial General Staff 1940–41, British representative in the Joint Chiefs of Staff, Washington, 1941–44.
3. On 25 March Yugoslavia had joined the Tripartite Pact; on 27 March, after a coup d'état, Peter II acceded to the throne and there were anti-German demonstrations. Hitler decided to smash Yugoslavia and signed Directive 25 to that end. A German attack on Greece— after the Italian attack had run into trouble—was postponed. This meant the postponement of Operation Barbarossa, the attack on the Soviet Union, by several weeks. The German attack on Yugoslavia and Greece began on 6 April; an independent State of Croatia was proclaimed on 10 April.
4. Japan and the Soviet Union had concluded a neutrality pact on 13 April.
5. English in the original.
6. Erwin Rommel (1891–1944), General, later Field Marshal; since February 1941 commander of the German Africa Corps in Libya. Cf. n. 2 to letter of 25 November.

unmixed blessing for us to be there seems to me at least doubtful in the long run, because it means that we have to keep those positions supplied, and our supply lines will always be vulnerable as long as the British position in the Mediterranean has not been shaken. But of course this advance, if it can be continued, also contains the possibility of overthrowing this position. So this confirms once more what I have kept learning in this war: that every situation carries the seeds of its own destruction as well as of its successful development, and that in the last resort the vitality and morale of the individuals involved, but especially of the leaders, decide which seeds develop and which dry up.

Berlin, 15 April 1941

. . . There is nothing to report from here. The Russo-Japanese declaration is the chief sensation of the day. It is not quite clear what its effects or its consequences will be. The only thing that seems certain is that we did not know anything about it. Despite this the declaration seems to be agreeable to us, at least at the moment, and that is certainly how we will exploit it. Whether it means a great deal remains doubtful. . . .

Berlin, 17 April 1941

. . . Today there was a letter from the chief of the Army Personnel Office informing me that there will be 3 ceremonies[1] on the 24th: 1 at the OKW, 1 at the Moltke monument, and 1 at Kreisau, at 11 o'clock. I am to tell him who in the family wishes to participate where. I have therefore asked H.A.,[2] Bill,[3] and Aunt Leno[4] to inform me of the wishes of their respective brothers and sisters by Saturday. I assume that you two will take part at Kreisau, or does Asta want to break out? I'll put her down in any case.

Tomorrow Ulla[5] will be with me, and Trott will drop in towards the evening. I think that's all I have to report. I am already tremendously looking forward to being back in Kreisau soon. . . .

1. Official celebrations of the fiftieth anniversary of the death of Field Marshal Moltke on 24 April.
2. Hans Adolf von Moltke.
3. Wilhelm von Moltke, son of "Uncle Helmuth" (cf. n. 7 to letter of 22 August 1939).
4. See n. 2 (p. 30) to letter of 22 August 1939.
5. Ulla Oldenbourg, old friend of the family, prominent Christian Scientist.

Berlin, 19 April 1941

... The war in Greece proceeds slowly. I assume that we penetrated the Greek-British positions at Mt. Olympus yesterday. The British troops have been gradually disengaging for a few days now, and seem to want to take up defensive positions again stretching from Thermopylae across the entire country. There is thus the possibility of another big battle at Thermopylae. It would be a strange connection across the millennia.

Berlin, 20 April 1941

... Yes, I reckon with Peter and Marion Yorck coming. I also heard from Jowöchen yesterday that he expects to arrive at lunchtime on the 23rd. It will be a full house. I hope it won't be too much for you.

... Now it is 11 and I have spent the time till now with the letters of Freiherr vom Stein.[1] I want to finish them today, for I am reading far too many books at once and must tidy up a bit. These letters are very encouraging and such a clear proof that this man also didn't know how to carry out what he had come to see as right. . . .

[P.S.] Don't let's put up a flag.[2]

Berlin, 25 April 1941

... My love, the 3 days were so pleasant despite all the rush and toil. I am glad that everything my Pim had to do went off so splendidly and that Pim was well enough. . . .[3]

Berlin, 27 April 1941

... There is nothing to report. I do nothing but read. I find it very interesting because it extends my knowledge of the thoughts of our friends on the other side. It is astonishing how hard it is in wartime to escape intellectual isolation, even in a post as favoured, comparatively speaking, as mine. The lack of information, which in part we bring about ourselves as a necessary measure, but which in part is forced upon us by the blockade and the reduction of dealings with the outside world, does have devastating consequences, and it will take a big effort to get in step with developments in the world at large once this war is over. . . .

1. Karl Reichsfreiherr vom und zum Stein (1757–1831), Prussian statesman and reformer.
2. Cf. n. 1 to letter of 17 April.
3. Freya expected a child in the autumn.

Berlin, 29 April 1941

. . . Suddenly there is a big row here, on matters of principle, concerning Schmitz, who is in Belgrade. I must see to his defence as best I can. Fortunately I have played my way into the foreground and will therefore probably be told to report to Canaris tomorrow or the day after. I am very much interested in that, because the most fundamental principles are involved and Canaris can't avoid taking a decision on them. I certainly shall treat them exclusively as matters of principle and shall see what happens. I'll be alone with Canaris, so that his only possible reason for dissimulation would be one that lies in me. I can only hope that I'll have a good day. My basic theme is this: what is right and lawful is good for the people, what is international law is good for the conduct of the war. And that is how I'll formulate it. Perhaps I'll be thrown out. If not, my position will be firmer. . . .

Berlin, 30 April 1941

. . . The discussion with Canaris lasted an hour and was thoroughly satisfactory. I left no doubt concerning my views and he entirely agreed with me. Nothing has been decided, but I hope that this affair will move forward properly. In any case I was pleased to learn where C. stands. . . .

Berlin, 8 May 1941

. . . From 20 May onward there is a total prohibition on leave and that includes business leave and anything resembling it. Whether that is only intended to prevent a rush at Whitsun or whether it is because of new plans, one cannot yet be sure. I think that further reductions in passenger traffic will turn out to be necessary in the course of the summer.[1]

Berlin, 9 May 1941

. . . Yesterday I had lunch with Peters. It was nice as always. The interesting thing is that he is obviously living in a totally different environment in the Air Command from the one I am used to. There they are obviously dominated by Party pieties and jingoism to an extent I never encounter elsewhere. This goes so far that they interpret the remarks in the last

1. The German attack on the Soviet Union was to begin on 22 June.

speech[1] by the Führer on armament for the year 1942 as nothing but a
ruse to deceive the British, for in reality this year will, according to them,
see the end of the war. I also got him to instruct me on the bombs now
used by the British. I'll tell you about them some time when I see you.

I spent the evening by myself. C. was out. I finished the second volume
of the Soloviev; the end of that was rather interesting, especially if one
keeps in mind the fact that the book was written at the end of the last
century.[2] . . .

Berlin, 12 May 1941

. . . The wedding[3] requires a tailcoat! Horrible. Please send it or let
Asta or C.B. bring it. Unfortunately I'll need everything: suit, shirt, collar,
tie, several, please, for some of them are too long, patent-leather shoes.
How can one do a thing like that in the midst of war and at 4.30 in the
afternoon. It is dreadful.

I am very glad about C.B.'s leave. He mustn't go back to Africa, for
things there are getting nastier all the time. I am very much in favour of
his staying in Taormina. I hope he has good weather too, which would
add considerably to the attractions of a leave. . . .

Berlin, 13 May 1941

. . . In my thoughts I am always at Kreisau and wondering how everything looks and planning all that might be done. But above it all hovers
the dark cloud of the unsettled and uncertain political decision which lies
ahead. Nobody knows when it will come, nobody knows if he can do
anything about it. Let us hope that the decision comes soon.

1. In his Reichstag speech of 4 May Hitler had called for an extension and intensification
of female labour "even though we are now in a position to mobilize half of Europe for work
in this struggle."
2. Vladimir Soloviev, *Three Conversations on War, Progress, and the End of History, including
a short story of the Anti-Christ*, translated from the Russian by Alexander Bakshy (London,
1915; first published in Russian on Easter Day 1900).
3. See letter of 22 May.

Berlin, 15 May 1941

... The talks with Trott and Haeften[1] were very satisfactory. Haeften is a good man though very conservative and Trott[2] not quite reliable. At our last talk I had not quite succeeded in convincing them or winning them over to my line of thought. But last night I was in better form and easily penetrated Haeften's hard shell, and then Trott went along. It is a great effort to win such people over to the "big solution" because they know the routine too well. But once it is done, one has a reliable companion—I mean Haeften.

Berlin, 16 May 1941[3]

... In a fortnight I'll be with you. Thank God. I no longer have the slightest desire to be here. But what's the use. Only the fact that the worm is in the apple, as Churchill said on the occasion of the latest defection,[4] makes things here bearable.

---

1. Hans Bernd von Haeften (1905–44), Legation Councillor in the AA; nephew of Brauchitsch (q.v.); studied law and went to England as exchange student; active in international and ecumenical work; entered foreign service in 1933: Cultural Attaché in Copenhagen and Vienna 1934–37, Legation Secretary in Bucharest 1937–40, deputy head of Information Division 1942, deputy head of Cultural Division 1943. Active layman in the Confessing Church, friend of Martin Niemöller and Dietrich Bonhoeffer. His wife, Barbara, was the daughter of Julius Curtius, Reich Minister of Economic (1926–29) and Foreign Affairs (1923–31). Haeften, who had opposed the regime from the beginning and who took a lively part in the discussions of the Kreisauers, was arrested on 23 July and executed on 15 August 1944. His youngest daughter, Ulrike, born shortly before his arrest, later married Konrad von Moltke.
2. In a note contributed to the German edition (p. 244) Freya von Moltke pointed out that this letter could give rise to more misunderstandings about Trott, who has been the subject of much controversy. M. did not mean to impugn Trott's reliability as an opponent of the Nazis. What was at issue was M.'s post-war plans of a federalist and supra-national character. M. was never a nationalist and hardly even a patriot in the usual sense. Trott was a patriot, whom some of his former British friends considered a nationalist.
3. Erroneously dated 16.4.41.
4. On 10 May Rudolf Hess, the Deputy of the Führer, had flown to Scotland and landed by parachute near Glasgow, where he demanded to speak to the Duke of Hamilton. He wanted to make peace and mentioned the removal of the Churchill Cabinet as an essential prerequisite. In Germany this embarrassing incident was explained by "delusions" and "mental aberrations" of the Führer's Deputy; in England it was interpreted as a sign of German disunity. For Albrecht Haushofer—cf. letter and n. 1 of 4 February—the matter had unpleasant consequences, which he tried to allay by a report to Hitler: see *DGFP*, XII, 2, no. 500.

We've just had a lovely talk on the phone. I'm particularly pleased to hear that you're having good weather. Yes, I am very excited about the bees, especially your view that you can get No. 29 coming on far enough to lock out in time for the flowering of the rape. What are you doing about No. 18? Do you hang finished combs in there, so that they need not build, or do you make them sweat wax? I was wondering if you shouldn't take a comb with brood away from No. 29 and put it into No. 18, but as with all things, it is probably better to look after the best and strongest.—And, of course, the emphasis is on *things* as distinct from human beings.[1]

This morning, after a very good sleep, I woke up with a fright shortly before 6: I saw you on Zeumer's cart, and the horse was running away across the rough ground. Please be careful!—You ask about Haeften. He is a new acquisition. He has just come from Bucharest and is a very good man. I thought you were with me when I met him at the Yorcks'.—Yesterday I had lunch with Yorck, Kessel, and Haeften. It was very nice and rewarding. Haeften put up strong resistance before I convinced him, but now I count on him to remain firm as steel.

Today and tomorrow I am once more occupying myself with the Empire and its future. I hope to learn a lot.—It seems to me that the war will bring more surprises in the next 8 weeks than it did in the first 18 months. There are infinite possibilities for variations, and it is impossible to foresee their consequences. Yesterday someone suggested that the Russians should declare war on England in order to protect themselves from us. It would be really very funny!

[P.S.] Can you, please, send me the documents relating to the scare about the play-school?[2] Yorck and I want to go and see Backe[3] about it.

---

1. Probably a reference to the "euthanasia" campaign to kill inmates of institutions, ranging from imbeciles to light cases of epilepsy. It had been authorized by Hitler in a document backdated to the beginning of the war, to give the impression of a connection with the exigencies of war. It was supposed to be kept secret—indeed, the operation was surrounded by a barrage of misinformation, false death certificates, and the like. But word got out via the next of kin. See n. 1 (p. 157) to letter of 6 September.
2. The village kindergarten was threatened with Nazification.
3. Herbert Backe (1896–1947), member of the Party and the SA since 1923; June 1933 Commissar in the Food Ministry; October 1933 Under-Secretary; April 1944 Minister. April 1947 suicide in Nuremberg prison.

Berlin, 18 May 1941

... I am so depressed about the French. This plain treachery towards their former allies[1] lowers them to the level of the Italians and Spaniards. However this war ends, nobody can care about them any more and one can only despise them. It is good that Pierre[2] did not live to see this. It would have hurt him very much. I keep asking myself whether at least a few Frenchmen won't emerge who will endeavour to save at least a vestige of honour.[3] ...

Berlin, 19 May 1941

... On the whole yesterday was not as peaceful as I had expected. The cause was a somewhat troubled soul. C.B. worried me again, and the entire week before caught up with me. After all I lost 2 people I knew.— I still have a horror of Wednesday and still don't know if I won't cry off at the last moment, pleading a service trip. Really one can't marry in tails and a long dress. I feel quite sick when I think of it.

Berlin, 20 May 1941

... Yesterday was peaceful. I had lunch and supper by myself at home. In the afternoon I was in my office. My chief concern was the situation in the Middle East, that's to say in Syria and Iraq;[4] it is not at all nice for the British, almost unpleasant. No, *"unpleasant potentialities"*[5] would be the right expression. ...

---

1. On 17 May the French had shot at British planes attacking Damascus. Hitler had received Admiral Darlan, the French Foreign, Interior, and Naval Minister, on 11 May; on 25 May Halder mentioned negotiations with Darlan about French assistance in Syria, Iraq, and Africa. Protocols on cooperation were signed in Paris on 27 and 28 May (*DGFP*, D, XII, 2, no. 559). On 19 May the Germans announced the conditional release of up to 100,000 French prisoners of war.
2. Pierre Fischbacher—cf. letters of 3 and 13 August 1940.
3. General de Gaulle is never mentioned in the letters.
4. The pro-German Rashid Ali el Gailani had seized power in Iraq and constituted a threat to British supplies in the Middle East. The British base at Habbaniya had been attacked on 2 May. British forces from Palestine reached it on 18 May and Baghdad on 30 May. Rashid Ali fled to Persia, and on 31 May the Regent of Iraq was reinstated.
5. English in the original. Cf. Hitler's Directive No. 30 of 23 May on the Middle East in H. R. Trevor-Roper, ed., *Hitler's War Directives 1939–1945* ... (London, 1964), pp. 72–74.

Berlin, 22 May 1941

... This morning I woke up at 4, took Suchanaan's drops, and went back to sleep until shortly after 5. Then I woke up for good, from a dream in which I had tried to persuade Hans Adolf of the principles of the Fourth Reich. It was quite an interesting dream, for H.A. used quite proper arguments, which were not to be dismissed lightly. After I had liquidated that dream I turned once more to the Berghaus, its garden, and the bees, my favourite subject of meditation. . . .

The world situation is madly uncertain once more. It holds out the chance of a big success to the British as well as to us. But whether the British will be strong enough to seize this chance seems to me more than doubtful. At any rate the strongest group of Italians in Abyssinia has now surrendered, which frees forces there. Whatever happens, 8 very important weeks lie ahead of us and they will probably decide whether the war will last for years or can be concluded *within a reasonable time.*[1]

Berlin, 22 May 1941

We're in the last 10 days of the month and I'm glad I can get away at the end of them. I am greatly looking forward to that and only see with displeasure that it will be so brief.

The wedding is over, thank goodness. The service was in Russian and I did not understand a word. It was all liturgy, mostly in the form of antiphonal responses between the priest and a fairly good choir. The "church" was somewhat primitive but gave an idea of a Greek Orthodox church. The most striking thing to our eyes is the endless depiction of Christ in icons as risen and transfigured, and never as a man or a suffering human being. For us that is hardly Christianity any more because the logical consequence would not be keeping His commandments on earth, accepting the suffering implicit in that, but hoping for transfiguration by Him. . . .

In the morning I saw British newsreels with pictures of the destruction in London. Very interesting, almost all of it places I knew well: Oxford Street, Piccadilly Circus, Horse Guards Parade, Admiralty—undamaged, bank, zoo, etc. The pictures again very impressive and completely convincing. The rest of the pictures less interesting: inspections, weapons, aircraft, and so on, the naval battle of Matapan[2] with very beautiful pictures but not really interesting. But I love ships, and all pictures of ships in motion excite me. To me a ship is a symbol of freedom. . . .

1. English in the original.
2. See n. 1 to letter of 1 April.

A dull morning greeted me today, or, rather, I greeted it, because as usual I woke up at 4 and was unable to get back to sleep despite Suchantke's drops. But the excitement of these days is considerable, and insomnia therefore justified. Yesterday it was still impossible to get a clear picture of the fighting,[1] but I have the impression that we are getting the upper hand slowly and with heavy losses. On the other, and less sensational, but if anything more important front, it seems to be the other way round. The reports from Baghdad[2] at any rate sound a bit crestfallen. Apart from these engagements on land, an enormous naval battle[3] is in progress, i.e., air versus navy, with forces engaged on both sides which are unprecedented in this war, and this battle can decide a lot. In any case, a point has once more been reached where the roads to either a short or a long war may part, and in view of the significance this question has for the lives of all of us, sleeplessness on account of excitement seems justified.

Yesterday Schütte[4] came to lunch. He is one of my early working associates who changed over to National Socialism, somewhat like Raupach.[5] He is in charge of "cultural" relations with Russia and reported rather interestingly from an area that is unfamiliar to me.—In the afternoon there was a mediocre meeting under Gladisch, mediocre because the first team of Wehrmacht delegates was unable to come because of pressing events. And that immediately lowers the general level. This afternoon I have a meeting with Gramsch[6] where he and I will be the chief combatants. Because the topic is a major matter of principle concerning long-range planning, I am very pleased. There is nothing better than a good antagonist; for one such I'd even put up with poor allies, although it is better still to be alone, as today. . . .

1. On Crete.
2. On the developments in Iraq see n. 4 to letter of 20 May.
3. In the Battle in the Atlantic 18–27 May the British lost the battle cruiser *Hood* and the Germans the battleship *Bismarck*.
4. Ehrenfried Schütte (born 1910), participant in the Löwenberg work-camp movement during the late twenties and early thirties; 1936–41 Secretary General of the "Zentralstelle Osteuropa," which was merged with the Reich Ministry for the Eastern Territories; 1942–45 lieutenant in Amt Ausland, Abwehr II. In retrospect he wrote: "On 21 July 1944 I realized that for Moltke the encounter had been a recruiting talk, which disappointed him" (letter to me of 31 July 1987).
5. Hans Raupach (born 1903), economic historian specializing in Eastern Europe. Participant in Löwenberg work-camp movement; during the war in Abwehr II; after the war professor, finally in Munich; head of Osteuropainstitut in Munich 1963–75.
6. Friedrich Gramsch, Ministerialdirektor in the Four Year Plan.

Berlin, 24 May 1941

Gramsch wishes to be remembered. The talk with him was fruitful and interesting. It will be continued after Whitsun. But he also caused a lot of work for me this week.

Bill and Trude may have a basement flat[1] that's becoming vacant and Carl and I are thinking of taking it in order to have a safe place for air raids. I shall look around in any case, because Derfflingerstr. is too much endangered.

Oh, my love, how I am looking forward to next week. There's quite a while to wait yet, and then it will be over so quickly. But I'll have seen everything once more. . . .

Berlin, 27 May 1941

. . . There is nothing to report. The days creep along. Today I had lunch with 2 economists at Yorck's, on Thursday we intend to meet again for lunch and perhaps he'll come in the evening too.

Berlin, 3 June 1941

. . . There is a great deal of work here. It bothers me and I'd rather do less. The situation is unchanged. But the British have actually succeeded in getting 15,000 men out of Crete again. They are masterly in escape. But the overall Crete operation is an impressive affair. Yet one cannot draw far-reaching conclusions from it.—Iraq has been settled in favour of the British, apparently without much military effort on their part. That surprises me and indicates that I regarded the British position in the Arab countries as weaker than it is.—But in any case the whole enterprise in Iraq was only the first rumbling of a storm that is surely coming in the Middle East. . . .

Berlin, 5 June 1941

. . . I had a very agreeable afternoon yesterday. I had lunch with Haeften, as I wrote already, and had a very good conversation with him until 4. Then I went to Gramsch's where I spent 2 hours in a very lively and, on the whole, peaceful conversation. It got to the point where he said to me: For this job you have, ultimately, to answer the question whether life exists for the sake of war or war for the sake of life; today my directive is

1. In the house of Wilhelm and Gertrud von Moltke in Teutonenstrasse, Berlin-Nikolassee.

quite clear. I replied: Please assume, for the statement you have to make, that at the decisive moment the answer to this question will be that this war was for the sake of life.—Then I went to see Yorck, with whom I talked until 8, about the play-school[1] and similar things, and then Einsiedel came until 11 and reported quite interestingly from Switzerland. . . .

Berlin, 7 June 1941

. . . On 20 June all passenger traffic for which there is no special authorization will be stopped, and most trains still running then will be cancelled. You must therefore travel on the 19th. I'll try to get a sleeper for you because the last trains will be quite impossible. I propose the following programme for your visit: 1 meal with Trott and his wife and Stauffenberg, one meal with Haeften and his wife and Reichwein, then sometime Schmitz, perhaps together with Kiep. If you like that, Saturday 14th and Wednesday 18th would be the suitable days. But then you'd have to give meat coupons to Frl. Saager at the very outset, though after Carl's last meal; and perhaps bring pigeons for one of the meals. . . .

For lunch today I'm going to see Yorck, with whom I want to discuss some things the whole afternoon; in the evening I want to devour the rest of *The Times* at home. Tomorrow I want to visit the new flat in Nikolassee as early as possible and perhaps take it. . . .

Berlin, 8 June 1941

. . . The flat is stuffy but tidy. Furniture modern—awful—and ideal from the point of view of air-raid precautions; it could not be better. We agreed that you will look at it at the end of the week and that we'll decide then. Of course I want Carl to see it too.

At a quarter to 12 I was at the Sarres',[2] in pouring rain. I worked very agreeably in their garden before and after lunch. At 4.30 I went home. . . .

Berlin, 10 June 1941

. . . . Yesterday I had a very nice lunch with Trott at the Guards Cavalry Club and then we had coffee at Derfflingerstr. He is going to Switzerland

1. Cf. n. 2 (p. 135) to letter of 17 May.
2. Friedrich Carl Sarre, Berlin lawyer, brother-in-law and associate of Eduard Waetjen. M. had moved to their office in early 1940.

today but returning on Monday, and I have made a tentative appointment with him for the following Wednesday; but we shall discuss that when you come. . . .

Berlin, 20 June 1941

. . . My morning is still entirely dominated by the presentation I made yesterday. Schmitz and Widmann[1] congratulated me first thing in the morning and some of the others rang up to ask if they had understood this or that point correctly. In addition all have asked for the written notes by tomorrow, because they want to use the Sunday to study them, and that means that I have to dictate the transcript of the shorthand report and that some unhappy girl will put the written version on a stencil overnight. So you see it is a real hit and of course I am pleased about that. . . .

Berlin, 21 June 1941

I feel as though it were the 31st of December, it is as though a new year were beginning tomorrow. Tomorrow everything will look different, and many things will assail us which we must arm ourselves against.[2]

I have telephoned with Fräulein Greiner. She's accepted the outcome.[3] So that's that.—At 2 today Radowitz[4] and I are going to see Langbehn[5] in order to talk about Ulla with him. I wonder how that will go.—In the evening Yorck and I are going to see Haeften.

I have little to report, because I am excited about tomorrow. That is strange and it surprises me, but it is so. . . .

Berlin, 24 June 1941

. . . Fortunately this is my last letter but one. Tomorrow comes the last one and then Friday evening is coming along with big strides. Dohnanyi isn't available today; Peters + Gablentz were free to come instead; tomorrow I'm going to the Sarres' in the afternoon; on Thursday I'll have lunch by myself, because I have to give my report afterwards;

1. Regierungsrat Dr. Berthold Widmann, member of the International Law Group of the Abwehr and on the staff of Gladisch (q.v.).
2. The attack on the Soviet Union began on Sunday 22 June, at 3:00 a.m.
3. It concerned the letting of the apartment in the Schloss at Kreisau.
4. Friend of Ulla Oldenbourg.
5. Carl Langbehn, lawyer, anti-Nazi who as Himmler's lawyer had useful access to him. Arrested 1943 and executed after July 1944.

Mierendorff[1] is probably coming on Thursday evening, Dohnanyi to lunch on Friday, evening with the Yorcks, with whom I'll go to the train because they'll be travelling too.

There is nothing to report about myself except that I feel the urge to come to Kreisau for somewhat longer, and as soon as possible.

[Berlin] 25 June 1941

So this is the last letter, how nice. There was no letter from you yesterday, but I hope to find one at lunchtime today.

My lunch with Dohnanyi didn't come off yesterday because he was detained by official work. Gablentz came instead and afterwards Peters for coffee. Both were nice, but horrified at my disclosures about our envisaged conduct in Russia.[2] Odd to see the naïveté even of people who (a) have a critical mind and (b) are quite well informed in some areas. . . .

1. Carl (Carlo) Mierendorff (1897–1943), Social Democrat; volunteer and officer in the First World War; writer, editor, wrote his doctoral dissertation on the economic policy of the German Communist Party; 1926–28 Secretary of the parliamentary SPD; 1928–30 press chief of Wilhelm Leuschner (q.v.), the Hessian Minister of the Interior; 1930–33 Reichstag deputy; 1931 took a leading part in exposing the "Boxheim Documents," a Nazi blueprint (signed by Werner Best—q.v.—but disavowed by Hitler) for the seizure of power. Worked with the group of "religious socialists" around Paul Tillich and contributed to *Neue Blätter für den Sozialismus*. Re-elected to the Reichstag in 1933, but arrested, maltreated, imprisoned in various concentration camps 1933–38, then banished from Hesse and employed in the economy (by the firm Berliner Braunkohlen-Benzin-A.G.) under SS supervision. Still in contact with the opposition; very active in Kreisau Circle, though, for reasons of security, at none of the meetings at Kreisau. Killed in an air raid on Leipzig on 4 December 1943. In the letters he is usually called "Dr. Friedrich" or "Friedrich."

2. It is difficult to say how much M. himself knew. Officially Ausland/Abwehr had no part in the preparatory orders for "Barbarossa." Even a note of 27 June 1941 by Schmitz for the head of the division only mentions "certain orders" when it posed the question whether "certain orders that have been given are in conflict [*Widerspruch*] with the declaration that Germany was acting in accordance with the Convention of Prisoners of War [Geneva 1929] vis-à-vis the Soviet Union. If there is this conflict such a declaration can only be made if these orders are modified in the interest of the German prisoners of war in the Soviet Union." The argument of reciprocity and expedience was the only one that was likely to cut any ice. Later M. and his allies exerted themselves to get prisoner-of-war mail from the East through to the German next of kin; it was being held up in order to create the impression that the Russians took no prisoners. The orders in question demanded of the Wehrmacht cooperation with the SS Einsatzgruppen, especially regarding segregation and "special treatment" of politically undesirable prisoners. The chief documents were the so-called "Barbarossa Order" of 13 May 1941, the Commissar Order of 6 June 1941, and Instructions on Conduct for the Troops in Russia of May 1941. See Helmut Krausnick, Hans Buchheim, Martin Broszat, and Hans-Adolf Jacobsen, *Anatomy of the SS State*, trans. Richard Barry, Marian Jackson, and Dorothy Long, intro. Elizabeth Wiskemann (New York, 1968), pp.

In the evening Einsiedel and I were at the Yorcks'. They were nice as always and E. & Y. seemed to me to get on quite well. At 11.15 I had enough and wanted to go home alone, but E. insisted on coming with me. Chiefly, I think, because he wanted to hear what I thought of the conversation. I went to Nikolassee and was there much sooner than I would have been in Derfflingerstrasse. The apartment was clean and gleaming, washstand, bathtub, bed, kitchen, everything immaculate, much more so than it ever is at Derfflingerstrasse. I hope it continues.

This afternoon I want to go to the Sarres' and look forward to it. The last 2 weeks were rather strenuous and the coming 2 will be too. I want to go to bed early, which will be easy because again I'll only have to get to Nikolassee and thus can be in bed not much more than a half an hour after leaving the Sarres, as compared with an hour and a quarter otherwise.

The trip into town in the morning, by the way, isn't bad; for I take the train at 7.47, which is too early for the smart set. Therefore the train is empty and there is room. I always read decisions of the Reichsgericht on the train now, which is very necessary.

Otherwise, my love, I don't think I have anything to report. I am very eagerly waiting to see how everything looks at home. I hope the weather stays good till Sunday. The predictions are favourable, but we know how unreliable they have been.

Berlin W 35, Viktoriastrasse 33   *1 July 1941*

. . . Last night I visited Guttenberg.[1] I was terribly tired, because the whole day had been one strenuous meeting after another. With some effort he extracted from me what he needs to continue his activities and at 10.15 I took my leave. At 11 I was in bed and when I woke up it was

---

532ff. But even before these orders Hitler had on 30 March 1941 addressed about 250 higher officers on the coming war in Russia and the methods to be used there, and that information had not remained confined to those present—see *The Von Hassell Diaries 1938–1944: The Story of the Forces Against Hitler Inside Germany, as Recorded by Ambassador Ulrich von Hassell, a Leader of the Movement*, intro. Allen Welsh Dulles (Garden City, N.Y., 1947), 4 May, 16 June 1941. For a comprehensive account of the German treatment of Soviet prisoners of war see Christian Streit, *Keine Kameraden: Die Wehrmacht und die sowjetischen Kriegsgefangenen 1941–1945* (Stuttgart, 1975), in the present context especially pp. 33–50, 225, 339.

1. Karl Ludwig Freiherr von und zu Guttenberg (1902–45), conservative landowner and publisher of the oppositional *Weisse Blätter*. Served in the Abwehr during the war, knew M. before. Established contact between M. and the Bavarian Jesuits—cf. letter of 15 October. Shot by the SS in April 1945.

8.30. That's a thing that hasn't happened to me for years. I was blissful, for it meant that I could start this rather important day properly rested.

In the morning I talked mostly about yesterday's conversations, especially with Gramsch, and prepared for the afternoon meeting in other ways too. At 2 I went to eat and now I'm sitting peacefully in Derfflingerstr., reading the newspaper and writing to you, and shall only leave here at 3.40 to arrive just in time for the meeting. This evening, then, a big chapter in my work will be concluded and I hope successfully.— While I'm sitting here and writing, I'm eating strawberries from Kreisau, which are still splendid.

I find the military news none too edifying. In Russia we haven't even reached the main line of defence despite the fact that there has already been heavy fighting with very heavy losses. I assume nevertheless that all will go well, but there can be no question of a military walk-over supported by unrest in Russia. Also the fact that the Metropolitan of Moscow[1] supports the Russian war effort doesn't look like disintegration. —All this is serious, because at the least it means that this campaign will entail considerable losses. In addition it looks as if the Russians might succeed in withdrawing to the east intact. . . .

Berlin W 35, Viktoriastrasse 33   *3 July 1941*

. . . Yesterday I had lunch with Reichwein, who now intends to come to Kreisau. I think it will be nice to have him there, and Werner,[2] Hütter, & Reichwein will somewhat reinforce the masculine element. I hope it won't be too much for you. But I don't think so. R. doesn't look well.—In the evening I wanted to go to Nikolassee, but it rained so hard that I stayed and read *Times*es. But there was nothing new in them.

I still don't like the look of the Russian war; but today the big new attack begins, and perhaps it will have more decisive results than this first battle.—But the fighting morale and tactical leadership of the Russians far exceed all expectations and I'm coming to the conclusion that we were seriously misinformed about Russia; or at least I was. . . .

Today I had lunch with a friend of Lukaschek's,[3] in the evening I'm

1. On 22 June the acting Patriarch, Sergius, had issued a proclamation "to the church" condemning "the fascist bandits."

2. Werner Busch, a cousin of Freya's.

3. Hans Lukaschek (1885–1960), known to M. since the late twenties; Centre Party politician until 1933, co-founder of the CDU in 1945. 1922–27 German member of the Mixed Commission for Upper Silesia in Kattowitz; 1927–29 Mayor of Hindenburg; 1929–33 Oberpräsident of Upper Silesia and Regierungspräsident in Oppeln; after 1933 lawyer in Breslau. Arrested after 20 July 1944; acquitted by People's Court on 19 April 1945 on grounds of proven torture and lack of evidence. 1945–46 Minister for Agriculture and For-

going to the Yorcks', and to Nikolassee for the night. On Friday Yorck and Haeften are coming to Derfflingerstr. for lunch, Yorck and Einsiedel have tea with me at 3.30, and Mierendorff comes at 6. You see a typical major battle day. On Saturday I'll have lunch at the Trotts', Sunday with Üx, afternoon at the Kieps'—I declined 10 times and couldn't keep doing it. The two evenings I hope to spend peacefully and with *The Times*. There you have the programme of the week.

Otherwise, my dear, there is very little to report. There are 2 very decisive weeks ahead of us. We'll have to await the outcome.

Berlin W 35, Viktoriastrasse 33   *4 July 1941*

It's raining again, and I fear that it's raining again at Kreisau, too, or will soon rain. It's rather desolate.

Last night with Yorck + Abs[1] was tolerably productive. I think I like Abs better now that he's definitely established than I used to. He told quite nice stories. On Tuesday those two are coming to have lunch with me, and we'll get down to brass tacks. . . .

There is nothing new from the East. Again we have to wait, perhaps only for a few days, perhaps for 2 or 3 weeks, for anything more definite. The big and quite unanswered question is whether we have engaged a decisive body of the Russian army. Today's communiqué states explicitly that the Russians are also standing up to waves of dive-bombers. Only the British have been capable of that so far. And the fact that more than half of the forces engaged at Bialystock fought to the death and that only the rest surrendered is eloquent proof of the quality of that army.

Berlin W 35, Viktoriastrasse 33   *5 July 1941*

. . . Yesterday was satisfactory. Lunch with Haeften and Yorck was not as productive as I would have wished, but Haeften and his wife will be presented to you next time. There was no discussion with Einsiedel because Haeften was still there at 3.30 and in fact stayed until 5. But the discussion between the four of us was satisfactory. Mierendorff and

---

estry and Vice President of the Administration of Thuringia; after his dismissal by the Soviet Military Administration, lawyer in Berlin; 1945–49 Vice President for the (Western) Bizone in Cologne; 1949–53 Federal Minister for Refugees and Expellees in the first Adenauer Cabinet.

1. Hermann Josef Abs (born 1901), banker and financier, financial diplomat. From 1938 until the end of the war member of the board and director of the foreign department of the Deutsche Bank; continued his leading position in German banking. Contributed to some of the deliberations of the Kreisau Circle.

Reichwein came in the evening and the evening was very satisfactory. Both R. and M. were in great form and I think that a new and valuable avenue has opened up there. . . .

Berlin W 35, Viktoriastrasse 33   *6 July 1941*

. . . It was nice yesterday at the Trotts'. The apartment is particularly nice now, in the summer. There is a splendid view across lots of gardens from the balcony. I was home at 5.30, read *The Times*, and went to bed quite soon. I slept badly, because first I couldn't fall asleep and at 2 there was a preliminary air-raid warning from which the people returned at 3.

I had a client with me at Derfflingerstrasse the whole morning, from 9 on. So I'll have ample work in that area, next week. Now it is 12.30 and I'll be off to the Üxes' in 15 minutes. But I don't want to stay too long, because I'm expected at the Kieps' at 5. It bores me, but they are always so nice to me that I really must go. . . .

Berlin W 35 Viktoriastrasse 33   *7 July 1941*

. . . Yesterday morning I worked, as I wrote before, and for lunch I was at the Üxes'. Connie Üx,[1] the air-force major, was there. He was in charge of operations on the first day in Crete, because the general[2] had been killed at once. His descriptions of the first day were astonishing and it seems incomprehensible that the New Zealanders[3] didn't attack. They had neither ammunition nor food, but many wounded and dead.—I am sorry to say that his reports on the conduct of our own troops were most regrettable, almost frightening. He reported a lust for common murder and looting. I never thought it possible. If his reports are anything like representative, we are in very bad shape.

At the Kieps' it was rather boring. . . .

I still don't like the Russian war, i.e., not even from the purely technical point of view. All reports are the same: tough resistance, heavy fighting, slow advance. That means losses for us and the destruction of economic assets of all kinds: villages, harvests, factories, roads and rail. Then rain for a few days. We have had this war for two weeks now and have only penetrated into the Stalin Line in the far north, in all other places we haven't even reached it yet. Naturally even such a line is nothing without

1. Conrad von Uexküll.
2. Lieutenant General Süssmann.
3. The British and Greek forces commanded by the New Zealand general Bernard Freyberg.

people, but they'll have to change a lot if our work there is to be any easier.

Today I am having lunch with Stauffenberg. In the evening I want to work late at my office in order to get a lot done there and keep the Wednesday free for the Sarres. Tomorrow Abs and Yorck are having lunch with me. . . .

Berlin W 35, Viktoriastrasse 33   *8 July 1941*

. . . Yesterday I had lunch with Stauffenberg, supper with Willem Bekker, who had just come from Holland. He was much impressed by the famine there: 175 gr. meat per week, little bread, and no potatoes. Likewise Waetjen on France, where he'd just been. He says it is now unmistakable. The privation is quite obvious. 200 gr. of bad bread per week. It was beginning to affect the children.—In about a year it will be the same here if the situation continues to deteriorate.

Gramsch rang me up yesterday: he'd thought of our joint work every day and it did not let him rest; we'd have to stay in touch about it and take counsel about the possibilities there might be of expanding it. Gratifying, isn't it. He and his colleague Kadgien[1] will therefore have lunch with me on Friday. I am very pleased about that.

Yesterday a man came back from FHQ and stated that he had the impression that the people there were satisfied with our progress; they believe there will be a breakthrough and that they will then be able to roll up the whole front from behind. I cannot judge whether this diagnosis is correct, but it is certainly possible. Yet for a few days now there has been fighting on a totally immovable front which looks to me not like a breakthrough but, rather, like an orderly Russian withdrawal. But it is hard to judge. So much, however, is certain: if by the end of the month we are not considerably farther than now, or if the Russians succeed in taking back their front intact, to whatever point, the situation will look very bad indeed, because we shall then get neither grain nor oil nor locomotives or rolling stock. And without these things we can't go on very much longer.—I certainly never believed that the Russians could make this long a stand.

In Syria all will be over by the end of the week.[2]—The Americans have occupied Iceland and taken an enormous step in the direction of protecting shipping between the U.S. and Britain. For even if they only patrol

1. Civil servant in the Four Year Plan.
2. On 14 July General Wilson and General Dentz (for Vichy France) signed an armistice which left Syria to the British and Free French and granted free exit to the Vichy French.

the seas from Iceland and the U.S.A. and Greenland by air, they can hamper our conduct of the war at sea quite decisively. Wherever one looks, therefore, the situation is disagreeable for us.

Berlin W 35, Viktoriastrasse 33   *9 July 1941*

... Yesterday's lunch with Abs & Yorck was nice. Both of them were obviously pleased and the result of the conversation was satisfactory too. Abs had improved: he's so clearly "arrived" now that he no longer needs to be vain and ambitious. Among the German bankers he is now simply the *primus inter pares*. ...

Berlin W 35, Viktoriastrasse 33   *11 July 1941*

... There is a little movement in the Russian war again because breakthroughs have been achieved both in the middle, in the direction of Vitebsk–Smolensk, and the northern wing of the Southern Group, that is, the Northern Ukraine. If these breakthroughs can be consolidated, new progress on the whole front may well be possible. Tomorrow night will be the end of the third week of the Russian war.—The way the British have been attacking these last few days suggests that they want to attempt sporadic landings on the French Atlantic Coast; they systematically attack the tracks which are essential for supplies to the Channel and Atlantic Coast. I wonder if they will develop so much initiative. I can't imagine that, should such a landing succeed, we'd be able to offer much resistance to a serious tank attack behind the French coast. ...

Berlin W 35, Viktoriastrasse 33   *12 July 1941*

The chief event yesterday was the lunch with Gramsch and Kadgien. First of all the food was very good: rhubarb soup with dumplings, vegetable platter (cauliflower, peas, and carrots) with new potatoes, cucumber salad and lettuce, strawberries and iced coffee. Both of them were visibly pleased.—The strawberries had been given to me in the morning by a man from the Air Command who passes Werder on his way into town. They were not very good, but since there are none to be had in town, they were nice. And today yours are going to arrive.

Our conversation was largely a surprise for me, because it showed a degree of agreement that I had never expected in the diagnosis as also in the notions of what should happen *post festum*. And much more than that: they had, with my help, discovered a crack in the soldiers' front which had appeared solid to them[1] and now wanted to put their ideas about the situation and the possibilities of therapy into this crack. I imagine they were just as surprised when they discovered that I have been occupied with the same activity for some time now. In short, I have the impression that we three were all satisfied, and we resolved to carry this matter further after my return from leave.

In the evening I visited Furtwängler. We quarrelled about India, but I have the impression that he has come a bit closer to my position. At least he no longer demands complete independence for India but only dominion status.[2] That is a small concession. . . .

Berlin, 13 July 1941

. . . In the evening I was at the Yorcks' with Einsiedel. I had a few things to discuss with P.Y. and therefore arrived at 6.30. We had an excellent meal and afterwards turned to the more serious work and talked till 12. I had the impression that we got somewhere; the two others filled most of the evening and I sat there more as a critic and umpire, because I know less about those things than they do.—Einsiedel, who accompanied me to Nikolassee, was very satisfied too.

Geyr von Schweppenburg, the nice former military attaché in London, has been taken prisoner as general commanding an armoured corps, together with the staff of the corps; because of our orders, which have fallen into the hands of the Russians,[3] there is some concern about their well-being. Schmitz and I are in the happy position of being able to say: You see? We told you so.

We are now engaged in the breakthrough to Moscow. In my opinion that operation makes no sense. There seem to be doubts that it can be carried through successfully in view of the state of our tanks. But on one thing all agree: if it succeeds, all our tanks will have to go for repairs

1. Probably a reference to a—surprisingly late—realization that some of the military were against the regime.
2. The Indian Congress politician Subhas Chandra Bose had come to Berlin, via Moscow, early in the year. Trott had charge of him. Bose was disappointed by the attitude of the German government towards him. He had gone to Italy in May and returned to Berlin on 14 July. The Working Group (Arbeitskreis) India in the AA had meanwhile become the Special Section (Sonderreferat) India, to which Furtwängler, who had a long-standing interest in India, belonged too. Bose rejected dominion status and the Western type of democracy and aimed at a total victory over Britain, the dissolution of the British Empire, the independence of India, and an authoritarian-socialist regime in a free India. He opposed not only the British but also Gandhi and Nehru. The relationship between Furtwängler and Bose—whom Furtwängler had admired when he languished in British jails—cooled off.
3. Cf. n. 2 to letter of 25 June.

afterwards. And what is to happen then is a riddle to me, because the prize of this war isn't Moscow but the Ukraine and the Caucasus—and to reach those we shall have to employ every serviceable piece of equipment. In comparison Moscow is a sideshow and a liability, because with regard to food supplies it is a big deficit area, so that our troops won't be able to live on it for long.—In brief, this venture gives me the impression that people at HQ have lost their nerve. If so, then woe to us!

Berlin, 14 July 1941

. . . I told you how delicious the strawberries were for lunch. But a lot were left over, so that I had another big bowl for the evening. Then my conscience seized me and I found that I could really not eat these straw-berries alone. So I rang up Guttenberg, who was sitting at home, alone, and he came to supper at 8 and we polished the strawberries off together, with me thinking of you tenderly. While we were eating, Trott rang up and asked me to come because he had a Swiss friend there whom he could introduce to me or me to him. After due consultation both of us, Guttenberg and I, went to the Trotts', where we stayed until a quarter to 12, in pleasant conversation. The Swiss works in the Red Cross, visiting prisoner-of-war camps, and he told marvellous stories from British camps. I think the nicest is the following: a car mechanic writes to ask him for a German grammar: "*I am interested in languages; my French is quite good and my German fair. I would like to improve my German. Hav-ing the opportunity to stay in this country, I speak from time to time to the natives, but for further progress I will require a German grammar.*"[1] Nice, isn't it?

Because I had an appointment with Abs at 8 this morning, it was a short night. But tonight I want to go to bed early to make up for it. Today I am having lunch with a man from the Department for War Production, on official business, uninteresting, and in the afternoon I want to go briefly to my office and then home as soon as possible. . . .

Berlin, 15 July 1941

. . . Yesterday I had lunch and a quite satisfactory conversation with a man of good opinion and good will, quite intelligent, too, but unable to make any connection or transition between the human and economic spheres on the one hand to the social, and therefore to politics, on the other. Nowadays I am so surrounded by people whose interest lies in the

---

1. The italicized sentences are in English in the original.

latter direction that it was instructive and surprising for me to meet such a man again. There are bound to be lots of them.

At 3 I had a longish talk with Bürkner about my projects after my leave, and on the whole it seemed to me satisfactory. I only need his blessing to avoid collisions. For the time being we merely agreed that I'd make more concrete proposals in the middle of August.

At 4.30 I had an appointment with Yorck, to go for an hour's stroll in the Tiergarten. This we did, and I think we are mutually edified.—He may come to lunch on Sunday the 27th. I'd really also like to ask the Landrat and wife for Sunday the 27th. I wanted to discuss this with you; in case I don't see you before then, let me know, please, if that suits you. I'd like to discuss the Kapellenberg, Peile, & play-school with him.

Today Gablentz & Yorck are having lunch with me, in the evening I must go to my office again and shall probably have to work quite late there. Since you won't be here, I want to go to the Waetjens' on Wednesday.

There is nothing much to report about the war. I can't see the justification for the grandiose headlines in the newspapers—and I imagine the radio is proclaiming similar things. Progress is slow and tough. Of course big advances are made, but there continues to be serious fighting far to the rear and it is hard to see how that is to be cleared up. It is similar to the Japanese war in China, with this difference, that our superiority in weapons isn't as great as that of the Japanese.—A few days ago General Jeschonnek's[1] HQ, 250 km behind the front, was attacked by a Russian unit of the strength of about a battalion.

One of our people has just returned from Africa and gives terrible accounts. They sound as though things are so bad there that we have to retreat as soon as the British want it.—It is incomprehensible to me how one can issue any optimistic reports at all in the present situation.

Berlin, 16 July 1941

. . . Yesterday at lunch I had a very good conversation with Gablentz and Yorck. It lasted from 1.30 until 4.30, so you see it was extensive. G. was in good form. In the winter we'd got stuck, and quite apart from the fact that I, too, have learnt a few things in the meantime, he had regretted it and had occupied himself with the questions on which our opinions had differed and had also come to new results and was visibly relieved that I resumed the conversation. Yorck chiefly listened and was amused. . . .

1. Hans Jeschonnek (1899–1943), chief of General Staff of the Luftwaffe.

Optimistic views are being spread about the war in the East. I hope they are correct. The General Staff version is said to be that the Russians have no more reserves within reach and that as soon as the battle now in progress is concluded the way will be free. That would be something at least. But where next? To Moscow? It is an adventure with an unforesee-able end and I deeply regret that I approved of it in my heart of hearts. Misled by prejudice I believed that Russia would collapse from within and that we could then create an order in that region which would present no danger to us. But nothing of this is to be noticed: far behind the front Russian soldiers are fighting on and so are peasants and workers; it is exactly as in China. We have touched something terrible and it will cost many victims and certainly good people. Incidentally, it seems that Geyr was not taken prisoner. . . .

Berlin W 35, Viktoriastrasse 33   *17 July 1941*

. . . Today I'm having lunch at Schlichter's with Rantzau + Haeften, in the evening I'm going to the Yorcks' and then to Nikolassee.

Carl has arrived and we intend to have lunch together at Derfflingerstr. tomorrow. I am eager to hear what he'll report about Holland. The news about the food situation there is getting worse all the time. Now hunger has also come to Slovakia after we have eaten everything bare. Evacuees return from Bavaria with the news that there is nothing left to eat there and that the North German invasion has eaten everything up.—In Poland 25% of all workers in the armaments industry (who are getting special food) have been sick because of malnutrition during the last month, or have, at any rate, stayed away from work. TB is said to be tremendously on the increase. . . .

Berlin, 18 July 1941

. . . Last night at the Yorcks' it was nice and harmless. Apart from me there was a Professor Zastrow, who is a great champion of large estates. Nice and quite funny but beyond all serious discussion at times. At 11 I went to get a good night's sleep at Nikolassee.

Japan is the sensation of the day. There is enormous uncertainty here and nobody quite knows what will be the outcome of this government crisis. The coalition evidently broke up over the question whether Russia should be attacked now and Vladivostok and the northern half of Sakha-lin occupied. That is what the military party and the Foreign Minister, Matsuoka, want. But they are opposed by the majority of the Cabinet, who, however, have 2 different reasons: the maritime men want nothing to do with Russia, because they want to push south, and the others don't either, because they want to come to terms with England–U.S.A.; that is the financial group, with Shigemitsu[1] as its spokesman. It looks as though the maritime group cannot possibly prevail, while the chances of the army party and the financial group are about equal. The victory of one or the other will probably be manifest to the outside world by the appointment of Matsuoka or Shigemitsu as Foreign Minister. The result can't be favourable for our conduct of the war, and we may suffer a very serious blow if Japan changes sides.

The situation with the U.S.A. is getting more critical all the time. Here the opinion seems to prevail that their entry into the war can only be a question of another 2 to 4 weeks. . . .

Berlin, 19 July 1941

. . . The war is entering a new phase today, with Japanese occupying bases in Indochina and postponing an attack on Vladivostok. Presumably that means they are avoiding any move that would have political implications, because no-one objects to the incursion into Indochina[2] except the French, to whom nobody pays attention any more. The U.S.A. seems to have intimated to the Japanese that they'd do no more than protest in case of an attack on Indochina. For the Anglo-Saxons the matter has the following attractions: *a.* it occupies the Japanese in the only direction in which they can present no real danger to the Anglo-Saxons; *b.* it will cause the Japanese some digestive trouble and prevent them from reaching Vladivostok or Borneo in the next 12 or 18 months, which are critical for the war at sea; *c.* it will rouse the French against the policy of collaboration. We, on the other hand, will have to put a good face on it—though we'd rather see any other move—because under the Tripartite Pact Indochina belongs to the Japanese sphere of interest. So Japan will reap nothing but applause. . . .

Berlin, 21 July 1941

. . . The war in the East goes on slowly. A few things are being changed now, and they hope thereby to destroy some especially tough pockets of resistance. But I am increasingly doubtful about the military outcome.— Moscow is to be bombarded now; that seems to me a sign of weakness, for what would be the sense of such an attack if we were going to be there

1. Mamoru Shigemitsu, Japanese Ambassador in London.
2. The Japanese advance began on 21 July. There was no attack on Vladivostok.

soon. Today I have the impression that Kiev, Moscow, and Leningrad won't fall this week either. . . .

Berlin, 22 July 1941

. . . The Russians now seem to be using parachutists in tiny groups of 2 or 3 men who commit acts of sabotage deep inside Germany; thus they destroyed the Hindenburg Canal yesterday; it has no more water and it will not work again for 6 months. I still don't like the military situation in the East. According to the latest impressions (not reliable reports) the Russians are withdrawing systematically in the Ukraine, harvesting and moving the harvested grain to the East. If they succeed in this, we'll advance into a total void, and what is to happen then, heaven only knows. One thing seems certain to me in any case: between now and the 1st of April next year more people will perish miserably between the Urals and Portugal than ever before in the history of the world. And this seed will sprout. Who sows the wind reaps the whirlwind, but after such a wind as this what will the whirlwind be like?

Berlin, 23 July 1941

. . . Last night's "party" at the Yorcks' went on until 1.30 a.m. In Nikolassee I fell asleep promptly but woke up at 4, was awake until 5, and then my sleep was troubled and restless and I dreamt fantastic stuff. How fantastic you can see from the detail that Reichwein was sitting opposite me and declared that he had tickets in the Italian state lottery and would play until he had earned enough to settle in Malta or Cyprus with the money. How about that?

The conversation with Yorck + Gablentz was satisfactory. Except that Yorck and I are so well attuned to each other by now that a third party may easily feel like a victim and not a real partner; it struck me yesterday. But Gablentz was far superior to us in his knowledge of the concrete situation of the Protestant church and of theology. . . .

Berlin, 21 August 1941

Now you are gone. I wonder what kind of trip you had. After your departure I dressed, got the 7.45 train, and retired to Viktoriastrasse to continue the work I started yesterday. It went quite well and I wrote till 1.15, when it was finished. I've just read it; I don't like it yet but I want to discuss this version with Gramsch before I revise it.

I had lunch with Trott. He is going on leave and won't return until the middle of September. I had a few things to talk about with him, but more especially to set suitable assignments for him. I hope that this will work or, rather, has worked out.—Then I went to see Guttenberg. . . .

Berlin, 25 August 1941

. . . Churchill has made a really great speech.[1] Another one of the speeches that will enter world history as classics. It is less actual content than form and sovereign grasp that raise it to the heights. One feels, reading it, that the man is speaking past us, down on the low ground of history, to the great statesmen of the classical past.

Furthermore the Russians and the British have entered Persia. Whether the Persians will offer any kind of resistance is doubtful. Once they make contact, our dream of getting undestroyed Transcaucasian oil will be finished. . . .

Berlin, 26 August 1941

. . . The news from the East is terrible again. Our losses are obviously very, very heavy. But that could be borne if we were not burdened with hecatombs of corpses. Again and again one hears reports that in transports of prisoners or Jews only 20% arrive,[2] that there is starvation in the

1. On 24 August Churchill broadcast an account of his meeting with President Roosevelt which resulted in the Atlantic Charter. What Churchill had to say about Russia may have been of equal interest. He not only praised the bravery, dedication, and prowess of the Russians "in the defence of their hearths and homes" but he referred to the work of the SS Einsatzgruppen: "Scores of thousands—literally scores of thousands—of executions in cold blood are being perpetrated by the German Police-troops upon the Russian patriots who defend their native soil. . . . We are in the presence of a crime without a name." Churchill could not afford to reveal his source—the decrypts of Einsatzgruppen messages which had been intercepted since 18 July. Nor did he—at that stage—specifically mention the mass executions of "Jewish bolshevists," "Jewish plunderers," or simply "Jews" (see Martin Gilbert, *Winston S. Churchill*, vol. 6, *Finest Hour: 1939–1941* [Boston, 1983], fn. 1 to p. 1174; for full text see Robert Rhodes James, ed., *Winston S. Churchill: His Complete Speeches*, vol. 6 [New York, 1974], pp. 6472–78). Another factor Churchill naturally did not mention was his anxiety that Germany might "beat Russia to a standstill" before the United States came into the war (see Gilbert, *Churchill*, p. 1173). What may have caught M.'s particular attention was Churchill's stress on the differences between post-war planning in this war and in the First World War: the guilty nations were to be disarmed, but Germany's economy and trade were not to be put under restrictions (James, ed., *Speeches*, p. 6475). M.'s official position on world trade as preferable to Germany's policy of autarky—a view he had always held—in a report on the law relating to war at sea of 27 August 1941 may have been prompted by Churchill's speech. Hitler believed in autarky.
2. Cf. n. 2 to letter of 25 June, n. 1 above to letter of 25 August. The transports mentioned in the letter were an early sign of the "final solution of the Jewish question." On 31 July Göring (Plenipotentiary for the Four Year Plan) had charged Heydrich (Chief of Security

prisoner-of-war camps, that typhoid and all the other deficiency epidem-
ics have broken out, that our own people are breaking down from ex-
haustion. What will happen when the nation as a whole realizes that this
war is lost, and lost differently from the last one? With a blood-guilt that
cannot be atoned for in our lifetime and can never be forgotten, with an
economy that is completely ruined? Will men arise capable of distilling
contrition and penance from this punishment, and so, gradually, a new
strength to live? Or will everything go under in chaos? In 12 months we
shall know the answer to most of these questions. . . .

Berlin, 1 September 1941

. . . Tomorrow a new Stauffenberg[1] is having lunch with me, sent by
Guttenberg, who is on leave himself. Tomorrow night I must work in my
office; on Wednesday I want to go to the Sarres'.

There is nothing new to report, my love; everything is as ghastly as
before. . . .

Berlin, 2 September 1941

. . . Yesterday I had a long talk with Dohnanyi and have the impression
that my project will make progress. At least it advanced by a small
step. . . .

Berlin, 6 September 1941

. . . The afternoon with Preysing[2] yesterday was very satisfactory. I had
the impression that he, too, was satisfied. The 2½ hours passed quickly

---

Police and SD) with making all necessary preparations for such a solution. For the most
comprehensive account in English see Raul Hilberg, *The Destruction of the European Jews*
(Chicago, 1961). See also n. 4 to letter of 14 January 1942.
1. Probably Hans Christoph Freiherr von Stauffenberg, whom M. had met in England before the war. He, too, was working for the Abwehr.
2. Konrad Graf von Preysing-Lichtenegg-Moos (1880–1950), Catholic Bishop of Berlin
since 1935, Cardinal 1946. Before his transfer to Berlin he had been Bishop of Eichstätt,
where he was already known as an opponent of the regime. He soon came into conflict with
the aged, timid, and irenical Cardinal Bertram (1859–1945), whose archdiocese, Breslau,
included Berlin. In 1938 Preysing started an office in Berlin to help the persecuted (Hilfswerk beim Bischöflichen Ordinariat). He was one of ten members of a committee founded
in 1941 whose relatively innocuous title, Ausschuss für Ordensangelegenheiten, suggested
that it was devoted to matters connected with religious orders, but whose main task was the
overcoming of the paralysis caused in the annual gathering of the German Catholic bishops
in Fulda by Bertram, its chairman.

and in the end we had covered or at least touched upon a large area of human relations. In any case he urged me fervently to come again and I intend to do so at regular intervals of about three weeks.

It was nice with Ulla. The day after tomorrow she goes to Gastein. During supper we talked about things in general and afterwards I read her the three sermons by Galen.[1] I am having them copied now and shall send you a set for dissemination. They are wonderful to read aloud, because that brings out their great drive. Did I tell you that these sermons were read from all the pulpits in Westphalia last Sunday?—I asked P. about Galen. He assured me that he was a perfectly ordinary fellow, with quite a limited intellectual endowment, who therefore had not, until very recently, seen where things were going and who was therefore always inclined to come to terms. The more impressive, then, that the Holy Ghost has now illuminated and filled him. How much more significant is such a sign than it would be in the case of a highly intelligent man.

... I don't like the way the war is going at all. We have made some advances in the region of Petersburg, yet not at all expeditiously but, rather, slowly. In the centre the wedge in the area of Smolensk is under serious pressure from both sides because the Russians have succeeded in making considerable breaches in our line on both sides of this wedge, especially in the south. There is no progress in the south, on the contrary. Odessa is turning into another Tobruk and is getting stronger, not weaker.—The situation in Italy is obviously bad, in Africa likewise, in the Atlantic *very* bad. In short, the state of the war seems worse to me than even I had expected at this juncture. And if the situation continues to develop in our disfavour, we'll lose the ability to negotiate, which we need so badly.—Japan, too, seems to be finally in retreat now. Look at the map + see where Fuchau is, which the Chinese have reconquered: between Shanghai and Canton. Around F. the Chinese have gained about 50 km of ground to the north and south.

My love, I'll stop chatting. We must always realize that we are approaching very grey days whose cares and sufferings we cannot even imagine yet.

1. Clemens August Graf von Galen (1878–1946), Bishop of Münster since 1933, Cardinal 1946, a cousin of Preysing's. His sermons on 14 and 21 July and 3 August 1941 dealt with the perversion of justice in the Third Reich and the killing of incurables. Their text spread like wildfire at home—clandestinely, of course—and abroad, and brought about not the cessation but a considerable limitation on these categories of murders. Joseph Goebbels (1897–1945, Reich Propaganda Minister and Gauleiter of Berlin) convinced Hitler that it was inopportune to punish Galen during the war: he was too popular. For the text of the sermons see *The Bishop of Münster and the Nazis: The Documents in the Case*, trans. and annotated by Patrick Smith (London, 1942).

Berlin, 7 September 1941

. . . I read a *Times* after breakfast and now I write first. Curtis has written a new book on world federation[1] and I'll try to get it; that is at any rate *positive proof*[2] that he is alive.—Dorothy Thompson[3] has flown back to the U.S.A. . . .

Today I want to spend the whole day reading. The week is very full, and during it I won't have a chance to read one sensible word: Monday Kiep to lunch, Reichwein in the evening, Tuesday lunch Gablentz and C.D.s in the evening, Wednesday lunch Dohnanyi and Delbrück,[4] and in the afternoon and evening we're all going to the Cavalry School at Krampnitz for a riding show. It would be unfriendly not to go, though it is a real nuisance to me and takes away a precious day.

Berlin, 8 September 1941

. . . Last night I went to Nikolassee and the planes came at 11.30 and stayed till 3. Or was it 4? It was the first real attack on Berlin and such air raids will undoubtedly be more frequent now. Our airmen are full of praise of the British airmen and say their tactics are excellent. In lots of places buildings were damaged, among them the Hotel Eden. There must have been fires near Derfflingerstr., for at lunchtime there was a good deal of charred stuff in the street. About 12 hits on railway stations and trains, signal boxes, and so on, among them Halensee, Friedenau, and Tempelhof. A big fire in the south-east could still be seen in the morning.—Your husband slept reasonably well. Whenever the heavy firing got brisk I woke and usually went back to sleep after 10 minutes. But I must have woken 10 times. . . .

Kiep, with whom I had lunch today, is full of pessimism. Every day I wonder what people have been doing and thinking in the last few years. They must have been living in a dreamland.—Bad news is crowding in on us from all sides. Nothing special, but in Serbia a real front has been

1. Lionel Curtis, *Decision* (Oxford, 1941).
2. English in the original.
3. Dorothy Thompson (1893–1961), influential American journalist whom M. knew since his student days, when he had met her at the Schwarzwalds' and worked for her. Her weekly broadcasts to Europe in 1942 appeared as a book: *Listen, Hans* (Boston, 1942). If, as is said, she really meant Helmuth Moltke by "Hans," its call to action is another sign of the mutual isolation brought about by the war.
4. Justus Delbrück (1902–45), son of the historian Hans Delbrück, member (by marriage) of the Bonhoeffer clan. Civil servant until 1936, then in industry; since 1940 in the Abwehr; arrested 1944, but was able to get his trial postponed; free at the end of the war; died in Soviet captivity.

formed and a few hundred soldiers have been killed, important railway lines have been blown up, and so on. Aside from Russia the saddest part is the constant loss of supplies for the German Africa Corps. Hardly a day passes when we don't lose a ship there. In Malta there is a submarine station now, and there are bombers; Malta has thus become a real offensive base, not only a *point d'appui* for the defence of the sea approaches through the Mediterranean.

Berlin, 9 September 1941

... I don't want to be here at all. I'd so very much rather be at home. Everything strikes me as so utterly senseless, and yet one has to survive this time and wait. When it gets too awful I think of everything at Kreisau, of you, the Baron,[1] Asta, the apples & sheep, Herr Z[eumer], Schwester,[2] the milk, and the work in the fields. That improves the state of the soul.

Today I really wanted to write to Carl Viggo.[3] But it bothers me, because I feel that we are miles apart, since he is trying to hold fast to a fiction, which he must meanwhile know to be a fiction, that will dissolve to nothing. But perhaps it is easier for those at the front. They have got out of the habit of thinking and do only what the day requires of them. It must be closer to living like an animal. ...

Berlin, 11 September 1941

Imagine, my love, I didn't write yesterday. The day was so short, because I had meetings all morning, had lunch with Delbrück at 12.15, and the bus for the departmental excursion left at 2.10.

It was quite nice. While it was raining in the morning and pouring when we left, we had fine weather out there, not exactly sunny, but dry. I was the only civilian among hundreds of soldiers, and, of course, that in itself amused me. Then we were shown horses from 2 till 5.30. Remounts, finished horses, stallions, etc. Most of them very beautiful animals, among them a whole group of thoroughbred stallions. The riding was quite good too. Outside we were even treated to the spectacle of a departure for the hunt, with dogs and outriders in red coats, and a detachment of teams: a yoke of five Lippizaner, a sixsome of gigantic Holsteiners, a foursome of tiny Polish horses, a threesome, and one single horse. Well

1. Nickname for Caspar.
2. Cf. n. 2 to letter of 25 October 1939.
3. Carl Viggo von Moltke (born 1897) was the youngest brother of M.'s father; a judge in peacetime, an army officer in the war.

handled, and nice, well-harnessed horses.—Then in the hall there was jumping, dressage, and quadrille. Everything well done with fine horses. At the moment we are very well provided with horses, since we have stripped bare the studs and racing stables in all the countries we have conquered.

After the demonstrations there was a good meal in a new and very beautiful mess hall. Everything was splendid. The whole riding school—it is the old Hanover Riding School—was only finished in the war, an enormous luxury building with acres of barracks and stables, built very expensively with landscaping and so on. There we can at least see what's been done with our money. The commandant of the riding school was very nice, like most horse people, but not very bright. . . .

Berlin, 12 September 1941

. . . I have nothing new to report. I am leading a very restful life, don't do too much, and wait for my plans to ripen. Sometimes I get a bit impatient, but on the whole I have become quite serene about waiting. I think that on the whole I am patient, and that I have learnt by experience how important and productive it is to wait. People can be won only by waiting, pressure turns them off. . . .

The following landed on my desk yesterday: An officer reports that ammunition produced in violation of international law was found on Russians: dum-dum bullets. That they were such could be proved by the evidence of the Medical Officer, one Panning, who used the ammunition in a large-scale experimental execution of Jews. This produced the following results: such and such was the effect of the projectile when fired at the head, such when fired at the chest, such in abdominal shots, such when limbs were hit. The results were available in the form of a scientific study, so that the violation of international law could be proved without a doubt. That surely is the height of bestiality and depravity and there is nothing one can do. But I hope that one day it will be possible to get the reporting officer and Herr Panning before a court of law.[1]

There's no news about the war. It looks a bit better in the North and South, as if one could hope for some movement again sometime.—In the

1. It was not possible. Oberstabsarzt Dr. med. Gerhart Panning died in 1944. A copy of this letter was later used in the "Einsatzgruppen Trial." Panning, who was also the head of the Institute for Forensic Medicine and editor of the periodical *Der Deutsche Militärarzt*, formulated his article on the effects of Soviet explosive ammunition ("Wirkungsform und Nachweis der sowjetischen Sprengstoffmunition," ibid., vol. 7, 1942, pp. 20ff.) so carefully that there was no mention of these shooting experiments on human beings.

House of Commons Churchill gave his first optimistic speech.[1] Bad on the whole, but bursting with optimism. Roughly on your husband's level.

Berlin, 13 September 1941

. . . Yesterday Yorck and I had lunch at his place. Undoubtedly I can work better and faster and more usefully with him than with anyone else at the moment. In addition we are so completely equal—I mean on the same level. With Einsiedel, with whom I get on about equally well, there is, for some reason, a certain superiority on my side and that always bothers me. Yorck is really the only one with whom I can genuinely take counsel; with all the others it is really an apparent consultation that conceals an enquiry concerning the extent to which they are willing to be involved and what they want to do. That always leaves me with the responsibility or at least the central responsibility.

Kennan came in the evening. Very nice. These meetings are now more productive than the evenings with Deuel. He accepted a proposal of mine to do something specific, will quit the service at Christmas, go home, and devote himself to this task.[2] He is a good and a nice man and I hope that he really will prove to be an asset for us.—I am always astounded when told that one must give people a personal interest in any matter and demonstrate their own interest to them; I am incapable of that, because my own mind doesn't work like that; and my experience is the very opposite: most people want to be convinced that they are doing something without a personal interest—that is what they yearn for. *You know, my personal affairs are all in a muddle just now and I did not know how to get out of it; but this work will put me right again and I hope by that way to be able to repay my debt of gratitude to Europe for the most important 15 years of my existence.*[3] Those are Kennan's words. I don't know what he means by the first, I don't know his private life at all. But again and again what I find is gratitude for telling somebody: Do this, it is useful and brings you nothing, at best work, worry, and danger.—God knows I have no reason to think poorly of the people with whom I deal.

1. Text of Churchill's speech in the House of Commons on 9 September in James, ed., *Speeches*, pp. 6480–90.
2. Whatever the "task" referred to in the letter, nothing came of it; firstly, because Kennan was interned for months after the American entry into the war, secondly, because he did not trust American security and did not want to endanger M. and other German opponents of the regime. He thought the risk of leaks was smaller with the British, who also knew of M. and his endeavours. He may have overestimated that knowledge and its influence. Cf. Kennan's tribute to M. in his *Memoirs 1925–1950* (Boston, 1967), pp. 119–22.
3. The italicized lines are in English in the original letter.

It was 10.30 before we parted, but I was so stimulated that I could not have slept anyway and so I went to Nikolassee although it was rainy. . . .

Berlin, 16 September 1941

. . . There is nothing new about the war. On the whole the Eastern Front looks a bit better again: a gigantic pocket has been formed which will hold more or less and will improve matters somewhat for us. Also things are proceeding well by the Black Sea. The bad general situation along with the reaction to it in the occupied territories is bringing a wave of frightful measures intended to enforce obedience. The recognition has, at last, dawned that the death penalty has ceased to be effective. But instead of concluding that one must rule with people instead of against them, the conclusion has been drawn that something more horrible than death must be found. And for this the Führer personally has thought of some variations[1] quite worthy of note.—Everything will fall on us, and rightly so.—All these are signs of weakness and disintegration which can only trouble us. . . .

Berlin, 17 September 1941

. . . Today I am having lunch with Steltzer,[2] the man from Norway, and then go to the Sarres' to work peacefully in the garden.

From here there is nothing to report but rapidly increasing decay. I can

1. These included Keitel's directive of 16 September 1941 from Führer Headquarters concerning "communist insurgent movements in the occupied countries." It claimed that all resistance was part of a mass movement directed uniformly from Moscow, even if nationalist and other groups joined it. The Führer had now ordered that the most severe measures were to be taken everywhere. All resistance against the occupying power had to be taken as due to communist origin. In general the death penalty for fifty to a hundred communists was to be regarded as appropriate for one German soldier's life. The manner of execution was to heighten the deterrent effect.

2. Theodor Steltzer (1885–1967), professional officer until after the First World War; then Landrat (District Administrator) of Rendsburg in Schleswig until 1933; briefly imprisoned; increasingly active in church and ecumenical work, Secretary of the Protestant Michaelsbruderschaft; called up in 1939, met M. before he was sent to Norway in 1940. As lieutenant colonel and transport officer on the staff of the Wehrmacht commander-in-chief in Norway he maintained connections between the German and Norwegian resistance, which he was able to help greatly and which in turn helped him to escape the death sentence passed on him on 15 January 1945 (cf. n. 5 [p. 398] to letter of 10 January 1945). Active participant in the work of the Kreisau Circle. Co-founder of the CDU in Berlin; once more Landrat in Rendsburg, later Minister President in Schleswig-Holstein until 1947; 1950–55 head of the Institute for Public Affairs, 1955–60 of the Deutsche Gesellschaft für Auswärtige Politik; 1956–60 President of the German UNESCO Commission.

hardly believe that we'll last till next spring. But experience shows that such things always look worse from above than they really are down below.

My love, I don't feel like writing any more, because I am now really coming soon.

Berlin, 23 September 1941

... Einsiedel and Poelchau[1] are coming tonight, tomorrow I'm having lunch alone at home and shall then go to Babelsberg; Gladisch, Yorck, and Steltzer are coming on Thursday at 1 for the filet of beef and I do hope it will be nice. In any case I'll tell Frl. Saager that she must make a special effort. Thursday evening I want to work at my office, Friday evening I'm going to the C.D.s, and Reichwein and Mierendorff are coming Saturday night. There you have the whole week.

Yesterday we had glorious weather here but today it is overcast. Not a lot, but enough to hide the sun. I hope the weather at Kreisau holds up for at least another week; for then the hay will be in and the most important work done.—I've written to the Landschaft about the mortgage; the money can stay in your account for the time being.

There is nothing much to report about the war. The victory in the South is considerable, though again not as great as I'd expected. Also it doesn't strike me as decisive, because there are no indications that we'll get as far as the Caucasus and the best Russian army, in the centre, is commanded by Timoshenko. Until that army is beaten we've achieved nothing. At sea and in the Petersburg area there is nothing new. In the air it seems to me that the British attacks on us will abate, because evidently they want to send considerable quantities of planes to Russia, the Near East, and the Mediterranean; the latter obviously to cover the Italians somewhat, of whose staying power they don't think too highly, and rightly so. Nothing new in Japan and America; it seems to me that the Japanese

---

1. Harald Poelchau (1903–72) studied with Paul Tillich; belonged to a group known as Religious Socialists, contributor to *Neue Blätter für den Sozialismus*—one article describing the infiltration of National Socialists into bodies of the Protestant church. His dissertation was concerned with welfare law. From 1933 prison chaplain in Berlin-Tegel, an office in which he was able to help many who were persecuted and imprisoned, including his friends of the Kreisau Circle and many foreigners. After a brief post-war interlude as Secretary General of the Evangelisches Hilfwerk in Stuttgart, he returned to Berlin, where he worked for penal reform in the Central Administration of Justice in the Soviet Zone of Occupation and taught criminology at the university. 1949–51 prison chaplain once more; 1951–72 industrial chaplain of the Protestant church in Berlin-Brandenburg. Honored by Yad Vashem in 1972.

have already missed the moment for acting with some prospect of success. . . .

Berlin, 24 September 1941

It is good that all is over; I hope that you will make a quick recovery and that your little son[1] will thrive like your "big" one. I wonder what attitude Casparchen will take to the newcomer. Do look after yourself, my love.

I am enclosing a letter from Carl, which probably belongs in your files.—Last night I had a very interesting conversation with Einsiedel and Poelchau. I liked P. very much: young, open-minded, prepared to commit himself. How a man who attends many executions week after week can keep his soul impressionable and keep his nerve and even be in good spirits is a mystery to me.—His accounts were rather illuminating and I learnt much that was new to me about the mood of the workers, with whom he is obviously in close touch.

The night was quite peaceful again and once more I slept very well. We are having another glorious autumn day, warm and sunny, and I'm looking forward to the afternoon at Babelsberg. Tonight I'll sleep at Nikolassee.

Otherwise there is nothing new. In the U.S.A. the Neutrality Act is likely to be repealed[2] and the road will be clear for the use of American ships in traffic to England and Murmansk and Archangel.—Here the soldiers are drunk with triumph. This time it seems to me not genuine but exaggerated, because every one of them wants to enjoy that feeling once more before avenging Nemesis seizes him.—But again it is striking to see how these people forget the final goal, winning the war, in thinking of single battles.

Farewell, my love, be well, look after yourself, give my love to your little sons, and your house.

Berlin, 25 September 1941

. . . Things are working with Dohnanyi[3] at last. He is going to have lunch with me on Friday to discuss the next steps. I hope it works out, for Canaris comes back on Friday and may well invite D. to a meal. . . .

1. Konrad von Moltke was born on 23 September.
2. It did not happen until 13 November.
3. Cf. letter of 27 September.

Berlin, 26 September 1941

There was no letter from you yesterday but today's chances are very good, and I hope to find one when I come home to have lunch with Dohnanyi and Guttenberg.

Yesterday's lunch with Gladisch, Yorck, and Steltzer was very nice. They each had 4 slices of beef. The conversation was good and brutally frank, which surprised me a bit in Gladisch. I had the impression that all were satisfied. . . .

Saturday night I'm eating at the Yorcks' with Beck.[1] I wonder what kind of an impression he will make. Sunday afternoon Yorck and I are going to see Abs. So we have an animated life. On Saturday Waetjen is coming to lunch at Derfflingerstrasse. . . .

Berlin, 27 September 1941

. . . Yesterday's lunch with Dohnanyi & Guttenberg was very nice. Both were fresh and lively. Especially D. in such high gear as I'd never seen before. As regards the matters to be discussed, the talk was good, especially because D. had at last done and delivered his part of the work,[2] and matters can soon be taken further; we made some progress, too, and also laughed quite a lot, mostly at Guttenberg's expense.—The evening I spent with C.D.s, from a quarter to 7 to a quarter to 11. Very nice and encouraging. Both of them well and more capable of action than before. We delved into questions of economic policy, where C.D.'s views and mine were rather divergent, and I hope we learnt something in the process. Today I'm having lunch with Waetjen, in the evening it's Beck & Yorck, tomorrow Mierendorff & Reichwein to lunch, Abs in the evening. As you see, a big programme and no Sunday idyll at all. In addition I have an awful lot of work to do, which I'd really saved for Sunday. Well, it can't be done. . . .

My love, how are you? I'm already greatly looking forward to next week-end and perhaps the weather will be fine. The only awkward thing is that it's Harvest Thanksgiving and that I really ought to go to church.[3]

1. Ludwig Beck (1880–1944), colonel general, chief of General Staff 1935–38, when he resigned in protest against Hitler's plan to take military action against Czechoslovakia. Leading opposition figure from then on. Died 20 July 1944.
2. Evidently a paper on the military oath—since August 1934 pledging allegiance to Hitler personally—and the right to resist (cf. Ger van Roon, *German Resistance to Hitler: Count von Moltke and the Kreisau Circle*, trans. Peter Ludlow [London, 1971], p. 169).
3. He was patron of the local church.

Berlin, 28 September 1941

... There is no question of leave before the end of October, for first the iron that has been heated so laboriously must be struck.

Lunch with Waetjen was nice and without much result. From 3 to 5 I read *War and Peace*, slept a little, played Patience, and had tea. I badly needed to be a little lazy. At 5 I went to Yorck's. First I had things to discuss with him for about an hour and a half and then the guest[1] of the evening came and was very encouraging. It was a successful evening and we can only hope that it will contribute to the forging of the iron.[2] I then went to Nikolassee, because that enabled me to accompany him for a bit, and despite the quantities of coffee I slept at once. As I was half awake at 5.30 I pulled myself together soon and by 7 was at Derfflingerstrasse for Sunday breakfast. Then I Tolstoyed a bit more and now am sitting at my desk, first to write to you and then to go on working till Reichwein and Mierendorff turn up at 11. They'll stay to lunch, then Yorck will come and we'll go to Abs together. There you have the past and the immediate future. ...

The days are rushing ahead. It seems so fast to me because I see the deterioration and every day that passes without a halt being called to this misery and murder is like a year that's been missed. Every day costs 6,000 German and 15,000 Russian dead and wounded. Every hour costs 250 Germans and 625 Russians, every minute 4 Germans and 10 Russians. That is a terrible price which must now be paid for inactivity and hesitation.[3]—Thanks to the resistance at Kiev, the Russians have got hold of themselves once more. They have rallied in a new line: true, it has hardly any tanks and fewer guns, but we, too, have many fewer tanks and guns, and the others have certainly as many planes as before. Where from no-one knows, but there they are. And the Russian news bulletins reveal such absolute confidence: "We have lost many men, we have lost so much material, but the Germans forgot that if we fight in our own country our army is merely our vanguard and every Russian is a fighter." Those are big words, very big words; if they are true, Russia is invincible. And these words appear to be true, and what the Russians lacked in will our measures[4] have instilled in them.

---

1. Beck.
2. The connection between the Kreisau group and its plans with other military and civilian opponents with a view to a coup d'état.
3. On the part of the generals who saw the need to remove Hitler.
4. Cf. M.'s use of this argument in one attempt to fight the inhuman treatment of Soviet prisoners and civilians—Introduction, p. 16; Jacobsen, "The Kommissarbefehl" in Krausnick et al., *SS State*, p. 526.

Berlin, 29 September 1941

... Yesterday was hectic. The conversation,[1] which began at 11, was nice and produced results, but lasted till 3.30. About that time I had to leave and go to Abs's with Yorck. Fewer results there, but it was nice. Then I went home to eat with Yorck. We had things to talk about there till roughly 9.30 and then I went to Babelsberg. There you have the whole day. . . .

My love, I can imagine so well how you hear and watch the sounds of the house while you are in bed and all the others busy. Can you read or are you not strong enough?

[Berlin] 30 September 1941

I slept at Derfflingerstrasse and thus got your long Sunday letter in the morning. There was such a lot in it. Z[eumer], too, had written me a business letter and a letter of congratulations;[2] I am enclosing the latter. So I was very well informed and since there have meanwhile been 2 more fine days I feel that things have now made real progress.

No, my love, I don't expect you to be a giant, but it is surely good that you are already up. I thought we might perhaps drive across the fields on Sunday, or do you think that won't be possible? Otherwise I mainly want to have a look at the building activities and try to ascertain how and when work can begin on the shepherd's place in Wierischau.—Esther[3] has phoned. She doesn't want the apartment. It's annoying. I rang Frau von Rintelen and told her that we'd also be prepared to let for a shorter period. She wants to think it over until tomorrow, but I don't think that anything will come of it. But let's discuss that, too, on Sunday.

This is a peaceful week on the whole. And very necessary too, to allow me to catch up again with my work, which suffered a bit last week. This evening I'm visiting Peters, Trott comes for lunch tomorrow, and in the afternoon I want to visit the Sarres. Thursday and Friday are still quite free; except that Yorck & Guttenberg are having lunch with me on Friday.

It is another cold, fine day today. When I look out I always wonder whether the weather will hold till Sunday. That would be very nice, though it isn't what really matters.—So Asta is leaving today, and that will be quite a change for you. It would be nice if she were to return in the spring.—I wonder how the apples are? Still on the trees? And are the tomatoes getting ripe? Well, I'll soon see for myself.

1. With Mierendorff and Reichwein.
2. On the birth of Konrad.
3. Esther von Oppen, a friend of Asta's.

Otherwise I really have nothing to report. The days follow each other, the most dreadful things are happening, and all Europe has a ghastly winter ahead of it; it will bring misery and want in a measure unprecedented in the area between the Urals and Spain. And in this misery there are only very few islands and even these cannot expect to be spared in the long run.

Berlin, 1 October 1941

A new month begins today, a very important one, for it decides whether we'll really succeed in largely eliminating the Russians. If we don't succeed this month, we'll never succeed.—One gets the impression that Timoshenko really is a quite outstanding general and a match for our people; at any rate everyone is waiting in vain for him to make a mistake we can exploit.

What a nice telephone conversation we had yesterday, my resurrected one. You sounded quite chipper. I hope getting up was good for you and leads to further progress. Well, I hope to see for myself the day after tomorrow, and this is the last letter.

Last night I visited Peters, with whom I talked well and, as it seems to me, to good purpose. At the moment he is a liaison officer of the Air Force Command Staff for the defence of Berlin, and it was quite funny to be able to watch the approach of the British as reflected in the reports coming in. As early as 9.30 P. was able to tell me from their directions of flight that there would not be a concerted attack on Berlin, and at 10.20, when they were near Lüneburg, he told me that there might be a little swing to Berlin. So I went off to Nikolassee and indeed there was a warning at about 11.30. But I was only awake for a short time and no longer heard the All Clear. Something must have come down in our vicinity, though, for I heard the familiar whistling.

This afternoon I'm visiting the Sarres again. Before, at 1.30, I am having lunch with Trott. Reichwein is coming to lunch tomorrow and Guttenberg & Yorck on Friday. And then I leave. . . .

Berlin, 9 October 1941

. . . The news from the East is excellent. Contrary to everyone's expectations Timoshenko's army seems to be the weakest of the three. For the first time their resistance is not thought to be very serious or very concentrated and it is hard to avoid the impression that it might be possible after all to force a total collapse of the Russian Front before the winter. Objectively it would change nothing, but at home it would mean a tremendous boost to morale, perhaps abroad too, i.e., in neutral countries and occupied territories. But we'll have to wait and see. . . .

Yesterday was not really fruitful, although I kept extending it in repeated attempts to draw some sparks from the man before me. But to no avail. To make up for it, Poelchau was very nice again and instructive for me.

It was impressive in that he had just learned that 5 of his charges were to be told at 7 p.m. that they would be executed at 5 in the morning. He normally sits with them from 7 till 5, but he had a substitute for this night. I made him describe such a night; it is horrible and yet, somehow, sublime. But he said that no-one is so well prepared to face death as these people; and he said that in the 8 years of his work there was not one— with the exception of hysterical women—who did not go to the scaffold calmly. What an accomplishment such a night means! It is gruesome and frightful; but such a night poses questions which are not put otherwise so starkly, so nakedly and absolutely. He never offers Communion, but 50% of the people he looks after ask for it spontaneously. . . .

Berlin, 10 October 1941

I am writing early in the morning because the day looks as though it won't afford any later opportunity to write. At 10 I'm going to a meeting of the Academy for German Law, and it will last until evening, with a break for lunch. I want to listen to some lectures on questions of international law being given by some quite good people, among them especially a man[1] who works in the military administration in Belgium and who always supported our positions. . . .

I'll spend Sunday at the Borsigs'.[2] I don't know anything beyond that. It is said to be an estate near Berlin and the father of the present owner was a big tree specialist. Yorck told me that and has arranged this visit.

1. Carlo Schmid (1896–1979), son of a French mother; worked at the Kaiser Wilhelm Institute and taught international law at Tübingen; no appointment or preferment after 1933; during the war worked as Kriegsoberverwaltungsrat, or administrator, in Lille for the German Military Government. After 1945 leading Social Democrat, Minister of Education and Justice in Württemberg-Hohenzollern; 1948–49 member of Parliamentary Council and chairman of its main committee; from 1949 on, member and first chairman of the Bundestag; 1966–69 Minister for Federal Affairs. Professor of public law in Tübingen 1946, professor of political science in Frankfurt 1953. In his memoirs (*Erinnerungen* [Munich, 1981], pp. 199ff.) he mentions numerous later meetings with M., about every two months, in Lille, but gives no dates. M.'s letters only mention him again on 8 June 1943. But there are no letters for one trip to Belgium—see n. 5 (p. 210) to letter of 23–26 March 1942.
2. Ernst and Barbara von Borsig, whose estate at Gross-Behnitz also was the venue of further meetings in March and June 1942 and February 1943.

I'm chiefly interested in seeing how the older Borsig planted young trees under old ones, and how these have developed.

Berlin, 11 October 1941

... At yesterday's meeting of the Academy for German Law one speaker was a Kriegsoberverwaltungsrat Schmid, by trade a professor at Tübingen, who now runs the economic administration in the part of Northern France under Falkenhausen's command. I liked his report so much that I asked him to come to lunch at Derfflingerstr. We talked for 2 hours and it was very rewarding. Schmid made a superb impression. As always with people who really incline to my way of thinking, we reached the question of religion within 10 minutes and I can remember few conversations so concentrated and satisfying. He is a bit too much of a mystic for my taste, but the kind of work he is engaged in prevents him from getting submerged in mysticism, and that is a good thing.

We then returned, together, to the conference, where we were regaled with a very insipid lecture by Weizsäcker,[1] and then I made myself scarce because I could not stand the chatter of the assembled crowd and the threat of the "social gathering" to follow; I worked at my office for 2 more hours, had supper with Einsiedel, and retired to Derfflingerstr. and an hour of *War and Peace.* So the day was more peaceful and agreeable than I had expected. At 4 I woke up and thought about Kreisau, my family, and the war, an activity which didn't torment me, but led me agreeably into the new day. I became aware of a change that has taken place in me during the war, which I can only ascribe to a deeper insight into Christian principles. I don't think that I am less pessimistic than I used to be, I don't think that now it has assumed coarse materialistic forms, I feel the suffering of mankind less than before, I still think that the murderer is to be pitied more than his victim, and yet I find it easier to bear; it is less of an impediment to me than before. The realization that what I do is senseless does not stop my doing it, because I am much more firmly convinced than before that only what is done in the full recognition of the senselessness of all action makes any sense at all. There are times when I quarrel with

---

1. Ernst Freiherr von Weizsäcker (1882–1951), Minister in Oslo and Berne 1931–36, Under-Secretary of State 1938–43, Ambassador to the Vatican 1943–45. Protector and helper of opponents of the regime in the AA; 1949 sentenced to five years' imprisonment in the "Wilhelmstrasse" or "Ministries Case" (see *Trials of War Criminals Before the Nuernberg Military Tribunals Under Control Council Law No. 10* [Nuernberg, 1946–49]) but released in 1950. Father of the later President of the Federal Republic. M. knew him from 1935, when he met him in Berne while looking for work in Switzerland at the League of Nations.

myself and accuse myself of having made up this theory for my own comfort; it may be so; and yet I cannot give it up.

Forgive the outburst.[1] It is the outcome of the night or morning watch.—The weather seems to be clearing up; that would be nice because then there would be the pleasant walks ahead.

Today at lunch Yorck & Guttenberg will eat the duck and Yorck & I will then depart at 3.

Gross-Behnitz, 12 October 1941

. . . Your husband is in the first-floor room—the ground floor is closed—which is on the extreme right, seen from the lake. You see the window on both postcards. The position of my bed is such that, when the window is open, I see the plane tree, which also appears on the third postcard. Yesterday it poured and I slept very well till shortly after 6, and when I woke up I could see the stars in the night sky, not yet the plane tree. A few minutes later there was a narrow strip of clear sky above the wood, a few minutes after that I heard the swans rising from the lake, and after half an hour the sky was swept clean; the first I saw of the sun was its reflection on the leaves of the plane tree. I read something Yorck had given me, looking up from time to time and admiring the fine day that announced its coming in the plane tree. At 8.30 I got up at last, and had breakfast from 9 till 10.

Borsig is a mild farmer who has had the farm since '33, with its intensive cultivation of potatoes and vegetables. He is intelligent and open-minded, a little bit too much the farmer. She is a nice fair-haired woman whose father was killed as an officer in the last war and who, though she grew up in Berlin, seems to have taken to the land. They have a son aged 5.

Apart from the Yorcks, the Wussows[2] and the Trotts are here. I am the only one without a wife, my love, which is sad. But all the others clearly envy you your second son. . . .

Berlin, 13 October 1941

. . . While the girls[3] walked round the lake in spite of rain, a serious disputation started. It was opened by Wussow and Borsig, but within 10

1. For a "sober" version see M.'s letter to Lionel Curtis of April 1942 in Michael Balfour and Julian Frisby, *Helmuth von Moltke: A Leader Against Hitler* (London, 1972), pp. 184ff.
2. Botho von Wussow (1901–71), landowner, at times in the foreign service, and his English wife.
3. Marion Yorck, Mary Wussow, and Clarita Trott, who were all there with their husbands.

minutes was transformed into a duel between Trott and myself on the question of whether one is justified in thinking about the constitutional structure, with me maintaining that the justification for it lies in the heart of every human being and does not require an external occasion. Trott, on the other hand, thought that there would at least have to be a promise and probability of concrete realization. I had the impression that on the whole I got the better of the argument, especially since I was in good form and had Yorck's support—as in general agreement between us two was conspicuous in this disputation and in the rest of the conversations. . . .

The walk took us through some fields but mainly through the wood, which was one of the chief purposes of my visit. It is a beautiful wood with tremendous variety: there are hardly any uniform areas. There are as good as no complete clearings: the worst is taken out, and as soon as the density permits it new trees are sown and planted below, rejuvenating the forest. I learnt a lot and was greatly encouraged to try the experiment I'd had in mind for Kreisau. I'll tell you the details when we come to put it all into practice.

I walked with Borsig for all of the 3 hours, and when I wasn't questioning him about the forest and his experiments, we talked about agricultural policy. He defended quite liberal positions: "Bankruptcy as the way to the better farmer," "free play of forces," etc.; I, on the other hand, defended the thesis that one had first to form a picture of the kind of life one wanted on the land, how many people should live there, and what kind of people, and that one would then have to employ the means calculated to reach this goal regardless of whether these means fit very well in the overall concept, because it was a question of curing a diseased condition. But B. was madly tenacious and I was probably not in my best form either, and so the conversation came to nothing. I reported it to Y. and he was amused but claimed to have expected as much: B. was a hard-boiled liberal on grounds of tradition and would need repeated assaults. . . .

Berlin, 15 October 1941

I must continue with Monday evening. Guttenberg came with the top Jesuit of the Jesuit Province of Munich,[1] which includes Württemberg,

1. Augustin Rösch (1893–1961), 1935–44 Provincial of the Upper German Province of the Society of Jesus, in constant conflict with the regime, driving power in the Committee for Religious Orders (cf. n. 2 to letter of 6 September) founded in 1941. A warrant for his arrest went out after 20 July 1944, but he was not discovered until 11 January 1945 (cf. letters of 10 and 11 January 1945). Imprisoned by the Gestapo until April. 1945–47 priest; from

Baden, and Allgäu. As far as I can make out he has only the top Jesuit in Rome[1] above him. A peasant's son with an outstanding head, skilful, educated, sound. I liked him very much. We also talked about concrete questions of pastoral care, education, and an arrangement with the Protestants; and the man seemed reasonable, factual, and prepared to make considerable concessions. . . .

Reichwein came to lunch on Tuesday, in good form; he'd had a few ideas. I questioned him a bit more, and I hope that something will come of it. I asked him to think about the question of religious education and tell us what we must do. He thinks, too, that one should start in the 5th year, and he will select some books for you.

Now, my love, I have caught up with everything and want to stop for the moment. Dohnanyi + Oster[2] are coming to lunch and then I'm going to Babelsberg.

Berlin, 16 October 1941

This letter is likely to arrive on the 18th. Much as I try, I can't remember having been married to you for 10 years. At any rate, I find it very surprising when I think of it. The 10 years are so small, so very small, in retrospect. My love, and yet it was so lovely with you, every day, every hour, every morning, and every evening. I only hope that you'll remain content, enjoy your sons, and continue to love your husband. . . .

Berlin, 17 October 1941

. . . There is little to report of the war. The weather at the front is very bad: − 20 degrees and fog up north, in the centre and at Leningrad snow and wind, down in the south snow and rain. I can't shake off the impression that once more the victory hasn't been decisive, even in the limited sense I'd imagined.

Peters & Yorck had lunch with me today. This evening I must work at my office, tomorrow I'll have lunch with Widmann, who invited me, and I'm hoping to spend Saturday/Sunday working peacefully.

December 1946 on, member of the Bavarian Senate; also, from March 1949 on, director of Caritas, the Catholic charity organization, in Bavaria.

1. Vladimir Ledochowski (1866–1942), general of the Society of Jesus.

2. Major General Hans Oster (1888–1945), son of a parson, opponent of the regime since 1934; from 1938 on, after the Fritsch and Sudeten crises, in close cooperation with Beck. It was he who had brought Dohnanyi into the Abwehr. Friend of Canaris's since the early thirties; suspended from office 1943; hanged, with Canaris, in April 1945 at Flossenbürg.

Berlin, 19 October 1941

I found your jubilee letter[1] last night when I returned, at about 10.30, from the Yorcks', where I had been all day. Many thanks, my love. Let us see what we make of each day, taking strength and confidence from the past for the dark and uncertain future. Yesterday Yorck, Gablentz, & I discussed church questions. We had lunch about 2.15 and Gablentz left at 6.15. He and I bore the brunt of the conversation, while Yorck listened and only contributed from time to time. The 4 hours were frightfully strenuous for me, but I believe that we have made considerable progress and got Gablentz down to tackling new questions and problems of detail. He now has work for at least 1 or 2 months.—Afterwards Yorck and I discussed questions of agricultural policy. We want to have a week-end on agricultural policy at the Borsigs' and that has to be planned. First Y. is to work out the questions. Borsig is to do the main report and someone else the preliminary report. When all that is ready about 10 people are to be invited who represent different regions, types of farms, and approaches to agricultural policy. In short, we are still at the very beginning, and we started by discussing the way the assignments should be set.—The Schwerins[2] and Wussows turned up at 7.30, I stayed for supper but went home at 10. And I was dog tired. . . .

Berlin, 21 October 1941

The day is so full of gruesome news that I cannot write in peace, although I retired at 5 and have just had some tea. But my head aches all the same. What affects me most at the moment is the inadequacy of the reactions of the military. Falkenhausen and Stülpnagel[3] have returned to their posts instead of resigning after the latest incidents,[4] dreadful new

1. It was the tenth anniversary of their wedding. They had married on 18 October 1931.
2. Ulrich Wilhelm Graf Schwerin von Schwanenfeld (1902–44) and his wife, Marianne (née Sahm, daughter of the Mayor of Berlin), landowner and farmer; cousin of F.-D. von der Schulenburg (q.v.). Took part in Polish campaign as reserve lieutenant, then Orderly Officer of the First Army under Witzleben (q.v.) in the French campaign; 1941–42 on the staff of C.-in-C. West (Witzleben, then Rundstedt); active participant in the planned plots of Witzleben and the Beck-Goerdeler group; 1942, on staff of Brandenburg Division, which was under the Abwehr; 1944 in Quartermaster General's office in Berlin. Always active as liaison between civilian and military resisters; arrested at plot headquarters at Bendlerstrasse on 20 July 1944, executed 8 September 1944.
3. General Otto von Stülpnagel (1878–1948), commander-in-chief in France until February 1942, when he was succeeded by his cousin Karl-Heinrich von Stülpnagel (see letter of 8 June 1943).
4. The escalation of the hostage shootings from 3 September 1941 led to Stülpnagel's final request to be relieved of his post on 15 February 1942. He had threatened resignation from September onward.

orders are being issued, and nobody seems to see anything wrong in it all. How is one to bear the burden of complicity?

In one area in Serbia two villages have been reduced to ashes, 1,700 men and 240 women from among the inhabitants have been executed. That is the "punishment" for an attack on three German soldiers. In Greece 220 men of one village have been shot. The village was burnt down, women and children were left there to weep for their husbands and fathers and homes. In France there are extensive shootings while I write. Certainly more than a thousand people are murdered in this way every day and another thousand German men are habituated to murder. And all this is child's play compared with what is happening in Poland and Russia. May I know this and yet sit at my table in my heated flat and have tea? Don't I thereby become guilty too? What shall I say when I am asked: And what did you do during that time?

Since Saturday the Berlin Jews are being rounded up.[1] They are picked up at 9.15 in the evening and locked into a synagogue overnight. Then they are sent off, with what they can carry, to Litzmannstadt[2] and Smolensk. We are to be spared the sight of them being simply left to perish in hunger and cold, and that is why it is done in Litzmannstadt and Smolensk. A woman Kiep knows saw a Jew collapse on the street; when she wanted to help him up, a policeman stepped in, stopped her, and kicked the body on the ground so that it rolled into the gutter; then he turned to the lady with a vestige of shame and said: "Those are our orders."

How can anyone know these things and still walk around free? With what right? Is it not inevitable that his turn will come too one day, and that he too will be rolled into the gutter?—All this is only summer-lightning, for the storm is still ahead.—If only I could get rid of the terrible feeling that I have let myself be corrupted, that I do not react keenly enough to such things, that they torment me without producing a spontaneous reaction. I have mistrained myself, for in such things, too, I react with my head. I think about a possible reaction instead of acting.

Berlin, 22 October 1941

My letter of last night was written so much under the impression of ghastly news that I hasten to write another to you this morning although there is nothing new to report. Last night at the Hülsens' was quite peaceful, even though the events of the day encircled me like ghosts. There was

---

1. It was the beginning of the deportations from Berlin. Kurt Daluege, as head of the Ordnungspolizei, had signed the first deportation order for the German Jews on 14 October. Emigration from the (Old) Reich was prohibited on 23 October.
2. Lodz.

only a little trouble when Hans Carl said that all this was the fault of the British and the French, and I protested energetically. This thinking in clichés is too sickening. . . .

Today I am having lunch with Hans Adolf. I wonder how it will go. For my present frame of mind I am not prepared *"to stand any nonsense."*[1]— in the evening I am going to visit Peters and look forward to talking with him and Gramsch.

Well, my love, I've just remembered that this is already the last letter. How pleasant. I hadn't realized it. There are only two more nights between me and my bed at Kreisau. I'll stop quickly at this pleasant prospect before less agreeable ones intrude.

Berlin, 3 November 1941

The light has gone out in the office because we are using 4 electric heaters. So I'll write a line by candlelight and then go home.

My love, it was lovely with you as always. I hope the little island can be preserved, where one can at least put down one foot in peace. I do so like it, and I'm already looking forward to my return.

Berlin, 4 November 1941

I just have another 20 minutes before I go to see Gramsch, with whom I'm having lunch today. I am looking forward to it because I expect it will be nice. Then we'll have the coffee-and-cake party. I wonder how it will be.

Last night I met Herr Kohn[2] in the cellar by the furnace; he told me that he works in the synagogue where the Jews are rounded up before they are deported. What he reports from there is horrible. Carl was listening. We were somewhat downcast at supper, especially as the new red wine, the first bottle of which we opened, is no good at all. Your spouse, more accustomed to atrocities, slept sweetly, while Herr Deichmann hardly slept at all. . . .

Berlin, 5 November 1941[3]

One grey day succeeds another: there is drizzle, there is snow, then thaw, and then it freezes again. It probably is the same at Kreisau. It is

1. English in the original.
2. Herr Cohn's (or Kohn's) presumably non-Jewish—i.e., "Aryan"—wife later replaced Fräulein Saager as housekeeper in the apartment. Evidently it was she who protected him from deportation.
3. Erroneously dated 5.10.41.

really nasty. At the front it is exactly the same: not a severe frost, which might be tolerable, but cold which does not reduce the dirt but only makes the mud cold. And the progress of the war is correspondingly slow and, I presume, wears out men and materiel accordingly: many men who return will never be the same again as a result of this crazy overexertion.

Lunch at the Gramsches' was nice. It started with grace being said, a rare thing these days. A man who serves in the Baltic told stories, partly interesting, partly atrocities, true no doubt. When he was in full spate I could stand it no longer and said that we were hardly the people to talk, but had to hold our tongues since we were behaving as badly. That brought me enthusiastic support from Frau Gramsch, who was obviously relieved that someone had said it. That settled the man, and we returned to more technical questions: agriculture, the new rubber plant, and the like. We had a good duck, well carved by Frau Gramsch, and afterwards beautiful fruit from Tyrol.

Later we held our group meeting with your poppyseed cake, which was received with universal applause; it really was especially good. I packed up what was left over and shall give it to Unger[1] today. I asked Steinke[2] yesterday whether I might give Unger some food because he had so visibly lost weight, and he thought U. would not refuse it. He is, after all, the last Jew I know, and I somehow regard this as the purchase of indulgences and am convinced that you approve. I shall take him what is left of the cake today and some bacon, and in a few days 3 or 5 eggs and apples.

The saying of grace at the Gramsches' prompts me to raise the question with you whether we should not reintroduce it via the children. It has become increasingly clear to me in these past years that the existence of each and every one of us depends on maintaining the fundamental moral laws laid down in the 10 commandments: freedom and preservation from bodily harm, but also food and drink, housing, clothing, and heating. But because one cannot think of this connection when entering one's home, firing the stove, etc., or express this awareness then, the common meal is the only remaining occasion to draw attention to it. And that seems to me to be, apart from any religious basis, the primary function of saying grace.

I have pondered this question for quite a while now and thought that it would surely be good for the boys[3] if they got used to saying grace, and

1. Dr. Walther Unger was a member of the family and firm of Kempinski. M. was looking after the "Aryanization" of the restaurant as the Kempinskis' lawyer. The rest of the family had emigrated in time.

2. Werner Steinke, manager of the firm of Kempinski—probably Berlin's most famous restaurant.

3. Caspar, who was four years old, and his playmate Adrian von Steengracht, son of Gustav Adolf and "Illemie" von Steengracht (q.v.).

we could bring it back via the boys without seeming ridiculous or starting a debate. They would have to take turns and say grace on alternate days, if possible differently.—I think it would also improve table manners.

We must, it seems to me, do all we can to instil into their very flesh and blood the principle that there must be an accounting for every action and that all men are equal before God, so that whatever happens to one human being concerns all others too, and that no-one can hide behind some notion that any human being is in a different category.

I don't know how clear or unclear all this is. These are only fragments of thoughts, whose connection is clear to me because I have brooded on them for a long time. Perhaps the connection is not yet clear to you, because I have only expressed it in fragments. Then ask me, please. I, for my part, think that we should return to saying grace. . . .

Berlin, 6 November 1941

Last night, when I got home, I found 2 letters from you waiting for me, which pleased me very much. It all sounded quite satisfactory.—On Carl Viggo's attitude I have to say the following: it is characterized by fear of responsibility for anything beyond the vision of his own two eyes. The whole question of physical courage, which seems to be connected with it, is nothing but camouflage. No doubt it is more comfortable to feel responsible for a few people only and deliberately wear blinkers that prevent one from seeing the evil done in the discharge of this responsibility—to be unwilling to see that one is defending murder and robbery. In reality it is these people who are the crux of the evil, not the criminals. There are and have been criminals everywhere; but it is the inescapable duty of all the righteous to keep crime within bounds, and whoever evades this task is more guilty than the criminal himself.

Lunch with Yorck was nice; he had made some progress during the week and we discussed further plans. Tonight he is on firewatcher duty at his office and Einsiedel & I will join him at 9 and work a bit. He & Guttenberg are coming to lunch at Derfflingerstr. tomorrow. . . .

It is grey and cold again, but no moisture comes down. How is it with you? Oh, how much I'd prefer to be at home.

There is nothing new to report about the war. There are directives from Headquarters[1] that make one doubt the sanity of the people there. Taken all in all, it is really funny. Suddenly there is to be large-scale employment of Russian prisoners throughout the economy, and a subsidiary clause

1. For Hitler's Order of 31 October 1941, signed by Keitel, see Streit, *Keine Kameraden*, p. 204.

states that "adequate nutrition is, of course, a precondition." They behave as though they knew nothing about their earlier orders.

As for the rest, there is heavy fighting everywhere except in the North. A new drive on Moscow is in progress; I wonder if this will lead to the conquest of the city. Things are continuing in the Crimea, we are approaching the isthmus of Kerch, where the decision when and how we can push on to the Caucasus will fall.

Berlin, 7 November 1941

Today it is 8.30 p.m. before I get to write to you. It was quite impossible during the day. Last night I suddenly got a toothache and made an appointment with Schramm for the morning; it took three-quarters of an hour. In addition I was already a bit late because I had stayed at Yorck's with Einsiedel until 11.30.—At 12 I had to go to the Ministry of Food to discuss our tax question. It took over an hour. At a quarter to 2 I got home, where I had to discuss things with Yorck & Guttenberg until half past 3. At 4 a man came for a preliminary talk about a conference on Jews in the Foreign Ministry, which followed at 5 and lasted till 7.30. Then I went to my office, dictated for an hour, and want to go home now. . . .

Berlin, 8 November 1941

There were two letters today. The last one dating from yesterday. So I feel splendidly informed.—Let me return to the subject of C.V. once more. I am so bitter, not to say ready to explode, about this type, because nobody causes me so many difficulties as do these lazy men. It is this kind of man who gets us the reputation in the world of not being able even to govern ourselves, let alone others. These people have a restricted horizon, they do not see that every action takes its place in the universe, that all things are interrelated, that a murder in Warsaw has repercussions in Calcutta and Sydney, at the North Pole, and in Kurdistan, not political but moral repercussions. I only accept the argument of self-surrender to a very limited extent. It is a form of self-gratification, a cloak put on after the event. Fredchen's[1] saying is nonsense, because one does not fight for but against something. Hatred, not love, is the dominant element of war. War breeds cowardice, servility, and mass-psychosis. Take this example: yesterday I was at a meeting in the Foreign Ministry about the persecution of the Jews.[2] It was my first official contact with this question. Against

1. Frede-Ilse, wife of Carl Viggo von Moltke.
2. Cf. Introduction, p. 15.

24 men, and quite inflexibly I attacked a decree[1] which already had the approval of all ministers and the Chief of the OKW, and for the moment have halted its course. And when I returned, the OKW official in whose competence it really fell asked me: Why did you do it? You can't change a thing, although of course these measures are catastrophic. He was a typical C.V. H.A. is another. I quite appreciate the charm and the qualities of these men, but their actions are dictated by expediency and have no moral basis. They are like chameleons: in a healthy society they look healthy, in a sick one, like ours, they look sick. And really they are neither one nor the other. They are mere filler. There has to be filler too. But it is intolerable for the filler that extends the diseased part to pretend to a moral *raison d'être*. I know I am being dreadfully severe, and I am getting more and more severe. But it is necessary, because otherwise, without being aware of it, one falls into dubious company.

Now to grace before meals. You must be able to take it seriously, otherwise it makes no sense. It depends 90% on you. Of course one's attitude is important and is more decisive than form. But if it is possible to develop symbols, forms, and exercises corresponding to the attitude, it will add much strength.[2] A man once said to me in criticism of another: "What do you expect of a man who grew up in a home where daily necessities were the only subject of talk at table?" Therefore the old rules—(a) grace, (b) no talk about food at meals—made sense.—After all, we are producers of food, and if the saying of grace at table makes sense anywhere, it is natural on the land, where salad and apples, jam and spinach, potatoes and stewed fruit can be ruined by a sudden change of weather. If it were possible to send the boys into the world feeling instinctively that in the absence of grace something is missing, that would already be valuable. Whether it is possible only you can decide, and I only intended it as a suggestion. . . .[3]

1. The Eleventh Decree under the Reich Citizenship Law—i.e., one of the Nuremberg Laws of September 1935—came into force on 25 November 1941. It made German Jews abroad stateless—and this included Jews who were deported—and dealt with the penal and property consequences of this expatriation: confiscation and expropriation. This decree and its supplementary decrees, especially a regulation—not for publication—of the Reich Ministry of the Interior which also applied to Jews deported to German-administered areas, especially the Government General, and the Reichskommissariate East (Ostland) and Ukraine, did not mention the word "deportation." The language was laundered with a cynicism exceptional even by Nazi standards, the suggestion being that people moved east of their own volition.

2. Cf. letter of 11 January 1944.

3. F.M. decided against it.

Berlin, 9 November 1941

. . . I spent the morning with some Jewish people whose affairs had to be settled before their deportation. During the last 3 days another 10,000 have been notified to hold themselves in readiness. The bearing of these people was good to see, and I can only hope that ours will be no worse when our turn comes. . . .

Berlin, 10 November 1941

Just a little line. It was a big day. From 8 in the morning until now, 9.30 at night, no respite, not even for a minute. I am preparing for a major fight in the Jewish affair[1] and have been looking for allies today. I expect the entire week to be under this star. I had lunch with Guttenberg & a Countess Ansembourg; Mierendorff turned up at 6 and has just left.

Count and Countess Ansembourg: very rich[2] people from Luxembourg, she a Belgian, he the former Luxembourg Minister in Brussels. He prisoner of the Gestapo for 3 months, now free but banished to Liegnitz. She joins him tomorrow. They live at the Forsthaushotel. I said you'd ring them up sometime and would be in touch with them when you are mobile. Gave them Ilona's[3] address, but perhaps you can urge her to get in touch with the A's too.

I'm tired and hope for a better time for writing tomorrow.

Berlin, 11 November 1941

. . . The day was strenuous. In fighting the latest decree[4] against Jews I have, however, succeeded in getting the 3 most important generals[5] of the OKW to write to the 4th that he must immediately withdraw the approval he gave on behalf of the chief of the OKW. The next stage is therefore to see whether he does so. Only after that will the real battle be joined. Wouldn't it be splendid to be thrown out of this club on such an issue?

At lunch I had a long discussion with Steltzer and Yorck. The former is to make one presentation at Kreisau[6] at Whitsun and he seems to like

1. See letter of 8 November.
2. "Very" added later.
3. Ilona Gräfin Schweinitz, who lived in Liegnitz.
4. Cf. letter of 8 November.
5. General Georg Thomas (1890–1946) of the Economic and Armaments Division (Wehrwirtschafts- und Rüstungs, or WiRü-Amt) of the OKW, an opponent of the regime, was one of them; a representative of his office had attended the meeting at the AA on 7 November.
6. Steltzer was to speak on the relationship of church and state.

that prospect quite a lot.—He had just come from Petsamo, which he left in a temperature of 22 degrees below zero. Dusk falls from 2 p.m. onward. Dreadful, isn't it? . . .

Berlin, 12 November 1941

My love, I have made such astonishing progress in the fight for Jews and Russians, or against the degeneration of military thinking, that I seem to rush from one open door to the next—therefore no letter. Report tomorrow.

The C.V. letter[1] was not intended to be severe towards you.

In haste my love.

Berlin, 13 November 1941

Today I'll write in the morning, before I do anything else or before anyone else can want something from me. The last days have been madly strenuous—less because anything substantial can be achieved than because I had to try to achieve agreement among the decent people on the line to be taken. That is why I slept very little for two nights, because I woke up at 3 and thought about Jews and Russians.

To return to C.V. once more. My patience with these people is totally at an end and yet I must not show it; it is hardly bearable. For instance Hans Adolf yesterday; he is a C.V. in a somewhat more advanced stage. He was quite broken. But do you think he now feels any obligation to do something to clean up the mess that has been accumulated with his help? Far from it! I only had to say that one must write off a lot in good time for him to reply with obvious indignation: Never can this be written off. And in 12 months he will give his blessing once more to a Free Corps operating against the enemy occupation forces trying to maintain order. And if I were by any chance to remind him that what he now sees is precisely what I predicted in the first months of the war and before the outbreak of the war, and that he retorted: "Then you must stimulate a more optimistic outlook in your circles," he would still regard my diagnosis as something no patriotic man might think, let alone say. I'll say nothing any more. I've written off these people, don't want anything of them any more, and only want to beware of getting their backs up against me before it is necessary. But you will, I expect, understand that in my heart there is no patience left for them and no patience for their defence. Their motto is the hope to save themselves:

1. See letter of 8 November.

if together we cling
singing God save the King
and throw men overboard to the sharks.[1]

Well, what actually happened? I find it hard to remember these two days. Russian prisoners, evacuated Jews, evacuated Jews, Russian prisoners, hostages shot, gradual encroachment in the Reich itself of measures "tried and proved" in occupied territories, again evacuated Jews, Russian prisoners, a Mental Home for SS men who broke down "executing" women and children.[2] That was the world of these two days. Yesterday I said goodbye to a once famous Jewish lawyer who has the Iron Cross First and Second Class, the Order of the House of Hohenzollern, the Golden Badge for the Wounded, and who will kill himself with his wife today because he is to be picked up tonight. He has a nice daughter of about 19 who wants to live and is determined to endure what is ahead. I gave her my "permanent" address, in case we and she survive the deluge and our address is still the same. It did not seem very likely to any of us.

And yet I was actually able to throw a spanner in the works, obstructing a bit, at least, of the persecution of the Jews. My self-appointed representation of the interests of the Wehrmacht has been endorsed by Canaris and by Thomas.[3] I dictated letters and both were visibly pleased when they signed them. Which proves the general rule that as soon as one man takes a stand, a surprising number of others will stand, too. But there always has to be one to go first; otherwise it does not work. And apart from the unpleasantness and strain of going first: how rarely do I have an opportunity to do it. I am pleased, of course, if I succeed. Thus it was nice to see an old colonel suddenly get red in the face, a visible sign of his joy that something was being done for once.

Steltzer + Yorck came for lunch on Tuesday. It was nice and got us a good deal further. Tuesday evening I worked with Einsiedel from 7 till 9, at 9.30 I ate with Guttenberg, and was in bed at 11.30, but awake again at 3 unfortunately. Hans Adolf came for lunch yesterday; we talked about further steps in the tax affair. I had an awful lot of work in the afternoon and was at Waetjen's in the evening, where it was nice and harmless. Then I slept at Nikolassee. Today I'm having lunch by myself, go to Preysing's in the afternoon, and shall telephone with you in the evening.

1. English in the original.
2. Preysing later recalled an incident M. told him about: a nurse he had met worked in an SS hospital for such cases.
3. Cf. n. 5 to letter of 11 November.

Berlin, 14 November 1941

You were probably somewhat dissatisfied when we telephoned yesterday, because your husband was not very communicative. But he had slept badly for nights on end, tortured his brain day and night for solutions, and was quite simply tired and preoccupied. A few things made progress this week: in the Jewish affair[1] I have, for the moment, secured a veto by the OKW. In the matter of the prisoners of war my chief opponent, General Reinecke,[2] has at last found himself forced to suggest that the Red Cross should try to look after German soldiers who have been taken prisoner. It must follow that we, too, admit the Red Cross and therefore change our methods.—I was able to get Preysing yesterday to file suit in the matter of the confiscation of St. Clement's Church,[3] and tomorrow I travel to Stettin in order to try and win over General Föhrenbach[4] for my plans. But all that requires a lot of thought and consideration, and it is this that occupies me completely.

The afternoon with Preysing was very nice. Peters had written an opus on the church question which satisfied neither of us altogether. That was the one subject of discussion, the complaint about St. Clement's the second, the persecution of the Jews the third. In the morning he had just been confirming Jews who were to be transported to Litzmannstadt in the evening. He said it was possibly his most beautiful confirmation. Once arrived there, they get ¼ of our food ration.[5] The Dean of his cathedral[6] had been indicted for malicious defamation, because he prayed for the Jews,[7] and the news of his interrogation came through while I was there:

1. See letters of 8–13 November.
2. General Hermann Reinecke (1888–1973), head of the General Wehrmacht Office (Allgemeines Wehrmachtsamt, or AWA), which dealt with prisoners of war; 1943 chief of National Socialist Guidance Staff in the OKW; later instrumental in the defeat of the plot of 20 July 1944 and the punishment of those involved in it. Sentenced to life imprisonment by a U.S. Military Tribunal in 1948, released 1957.
3. Like much other church property at that time it had been confiscated, and Preysing's protests had been unavailing. He finally made the matter public in a pastoral letter—cf. n. 3 (p. 217) to letter of 9 May 1942.
4. Max Föhrenbach (1872–1942), deputy commander, then commander of II Corps, Wehrkreis II, Stettin. Retired in 1942.
5. This information probably came from Margarete Sommer (1893–1965), who ran the Hilfswerk (cf. n. 2 to letter of 6 September) after the arrest of Bernhard Lichtenberg—see n. 6 below.
6. Bernhard Lichtenberg (1875–1943), priest since 1899, at St. Hedwig's Cathedral since 1931, Dean since 1938, the year Preysing started the Hilfswerk, which Lichtenberg headed until his arrest.
7. He had been denounced by two visiting, sightseeing women students who had heard him pray for the Jews at a cathedral service, as was his habit. He was sentenced to two years'

"What is your attitude to the racial question?" "The only distinction I make is between Christians and non-Christians; the former I include as brothers in my prayers, for the latter I pray for illumination."

"What is your attitude to the state?" "Be subject to the higher powers put over you, says the Apostle Paul." [1]

"What is your attitude to the Führer?" "He is not my Führer, for that he is only for Party members in his capacity as head of the Party. But I am not a member and know only one leader, Jesus Christ. My attitude to Hitler as head of state is based on my attitude to the state."

"If you don't change your attitude, we shall send you to join your dear Jews in Litzmannstadt." "That is the very thing I was going to ask: for what more beautiful task could there be for an old clergyman than to assist these Jewish Christians who are destined to die."

And all that from a former Centre functionary. [2]

I spent the evening with the Yorcks. Schulenburg was there. We worked to recruit him for us and I must now endeavour to bring about the pre-conditions we discussed. We went on till 12.10, and it was after 1 when I got to bed. But it was necessary.

This morning I had to put a great deal of effort into making my trip to Stettin possible. Now it is all arranged. Whether anything will come of it remains to be seen; if nothing comes of it, we are as far as before. If something does come of it, it will mean a big step taken. I can really go forward with my work then.

While all this is being tried, the chaos is rising around me. I see it coming, and this brings the critical moment, which must not be missed, closer and closer.

My love, I have told Schulenburg that he could perhaps come to Kreisau on Sunday. I am sorry, of course, but it is necessary.

I have to go to see Kennan.

Stettin, 16 November 1941

Yesterday I didn't write, because time was too short in Berlin, and in Stettin I didn't have an opportunity either, because I was, unfortunately, met. When I went home at 10.30 I was tired and there seemed to be no point in it.

Meanwhile, I have seen General Föhrenbach, who is a very good man.

---

imprisonment for misuse of the pulpit and for malicious defamation of the government. After serving his sentence, he was to be taken to Dachau concentration camp, but died on the way there.

1. Letter to the Romans 13:1.
2. Before 1933 Lichtenberg had been a Centre Party member of the Berlin City Parliament.

He is an old general, the best imaginable: intelligent, prudent, capable of commitment, modest. I did not achieve a complete success with him; rather, he asked for time to think it over, and then the discussion is to continue. That may be expected to take place immediately before Christmas.

Now it is 12.15. I want to have lunch and then take a train to Berlin at 2. There I'll try to talk to Oster and Dohnanyi, and it will probably be late before I get home. . . .

Yesterday was a morning when lots of details had to be seen to that had been left during the stormy week. I had lunch with the Trotts, and then we had a lot to talk about, which fully occupied the time until the departure of my train. How gigantic the problems confronting us are, and what giant is to solve them? Is it possible that a group of average men will succeed in it? Or is it not actually more probable that such a group will succeed than a giant?

I look forward to the telephone call and the news from Kreisau.

Berlin, 17 November 1941

When I got home this evening I found 2 letters after already collecting one yesterday on the way from the station to Dohnanyi. How good it all sounds. I hope it won't be too much for you.

I left Stettin in the early afternoon, under the strong impression of the excellent old man. He is a little as I imagine the Field Marshal must have been. The most striking thing is really his power of decision. My presentation of the rather complicated proposal lasted 15 minutes, then he replied for 10 minutes, and then we examined the arguments in an exchange lasting another 15 minutes, and with that we had properly exhausted the subject. He took his leave with these words: "It is a very good cause. I don't know a better way, but I am not good enough for it." That is impressive. Daddy could have spoken like that, and the old Field Marshal. But F. is going to discuss the whole question once more, in Berlin on 18 Dec., with me and Beck, and I am convinced that we'll get him then. On Wednesday afternoon I am going to see Beck, to discuss it with him.

In preparation for this discussion and one with Halder, I have just been to see Dohnanyi and, as he had to be at peace for that, I invaded him Sunday evening, especially since he was flying to Warsaw today. It had the desired effect, and I hope it will now be possible to take 2 or 3 big steps forward before Christmas. I hope that I can still get this done.

I spent the whole day on the Jews[1] again and have actually managed

1. See letters of 8–14 November.

to get all departments of the OKW behind me on this question. Tonight a colonel is travelling to see Keitel in order to propose to him tomorrow that an objection against the intended decree should be registered. So in 2 or 3 days I should know whether I have really won a victory[1] on this limited issue.

Meanwhile hunger, disease, and fear are spreading under our rule. Nobody knows what the consequences will be or how soon they will set in. But one thing is quite certain: the Apocalyptic Horsemen are beginners compared with what is ahead of us: *certus an, incertus quando.* Every day brings new insights into the depths to which human beings can sink. But in many respects the bottom has been reached: the lunatic asylums are slowly filling with men who broke down[2] during or after the executions they were told to carry out.

Berlin, 18 November 1941

. . . On the poultry list I have this first comment. I think it would be wise to keep a pair of ducks over the winter, for it strikes me as more than doubtful that you'll be able to buy duck eggs next year. Everything that's humanly possible will have to be done to limit poultry keeping, and if I had anything to say I'd forbid ducks and geese altogether, in any case prohibit all trading in eggs and ducklings, so as to make sure that no farmer would have more eggs hatched than he has food for raising ducks. The same goes for geese. How about chickens? Couldn't we have chickens instead for Aunts and Edith, or perhaps chickens and eggs? Or apples? Pension Annie's goose I wouldn't take away; that's too personal. Among the three names with question marks I would like to give Unger something, and I'd much rather take it with me next time, for he'll certainly not live to see Christmas, and there is no knowing how much longer he's got. But a chicken would be very nice for him too, though a duck would be nicer. I would not cut ourselves down, because, after all, we are feeding the greatest number, and you have to bridge the time when there is no fresh meat. I am returning the list.

The war looks bad. There is a joke going round here: "Eastern campaign extended by a month owing to great success." A bitter remark. I don't think that we can still make significant progress before the New Year; perhaps in the South; an advance near Maikop may still succeed; I don't believe that either, but it is possible. The unfortunate millions of troops who now freeze out there, are wet, and die! A comparison with the

---

1. It was only a brief delay. The Eleventh Decree (see n. 1 [p. 180] to letter of 8 November) was published on 25 November 1941.
2. Cf. letter of 13 November.

World War '14/'18 is impossible, for then fewer people were involved, and could therefore be better looked after, and there were houses in which they could stay. The present situation is different in both respects. What will the army that we meet again in March be like? With no leave worth mentioning, insufficient supplies, no quarters, no adequate clothing, no military success?

And the domestic situation is far worse than I had imagined. The persecution of the Jews and the attack on the churches have caused intense disquiet. The promises of military successes, of leave for soldiers or their return are not being kept and cannot be kept. Everyone can see hunger approaching, and there is nothing else to buy either, there is nobody for the most necessary work.

Who is to master such conditions, one asks oneself every day.

Berlin, 25 November 1941

. . . A very laborious week still lies ahead of me, because I'll be distinctly busy at both my offices, but it is doubtful that it will mean any progress.—The mood here is depressed, for the series of strange deaths[1] of the last few days seem to everybody like the rumbling of the approaching storm.

In North Africa Rommel[2] has once more assumed his command and appears to get everything possible out of a bad situation. The British seem to have undertaken rather a lot all at once and will probably lose a lot of feathers; but on the whole one gets the impression that they will grind the unfortunate Africa Corps to pieces slowly but surely. Rommel has extricated himself with his armour from the threatening encirclement and is now south-west of Tobruk. The British have not yet succeeded in establishing a link between their offensive group and the garrison of To-

1. On 17 November Ernst Udet (1896–1941), an air ace of the First World War and Air Inspector General in the Second, had committed suicide. According to the official version, he had crashed while testing an aircraft. A state funeral was ordered. On 22 November it was reported that the highly decorated air-force colonel Werner Mölders had crashed in a courier plane. He, too, was given a state funeral. He had been known as a devout Catholic and his death, as well as that of Udet and the crash of General Huntziger, the French Minister of Defence, gave rise to rumours.

2. Since February 1941 chief of the German Africa Corps, later commander of an army group in Italy, and from December 1943 on of Army Group B in Northern France. He became the most popular German general of the Second World War. Slowly convinced of the harmfulness of Hitler, he yet opposed assassination but not an attempt to arrest him. But first he wanted to have a frank discussion with Hitler. Severely wounded on 18 July 1944, he was, when barely recovered, presented, on Hitler's orders, with the "choice" between a discreet suicide and a treason trial. He chose the former and was given a state funeral. See n. 6 to letter of 14 April.

bruk. But this week will largely clarify this. In Russia there is slow progress in the vicinity of Moscow, in the South there is a standstill with slight
tendencies to a backward motion. . . .

Berlin, 26 November 1941

. . . The war in Africa is rapidly developing in Rommel's favour and one
gets the impression that despite their superiority the British will be
beaten off. The main armoured attack aimed at effecting a link with Tobruk has miscarried, at any rate, Rommel's tanks have their hands free
and can now turn east to set upon the British, who penetrated Bardia and
Capuzzo, and to encircle them. It appears that our chief difficulty is the
water supply. It would certainly be an astonishing victory for the Africa
Corps and one that could considerably affect the whole situation, if it
brought the French over to our side. But we must wait a few days before
we know more.

This afternoon I must work in my office again, where there is another
high tide at the moment, by my standards, at least. It will probably get
late. Today's lunch will be devoted to the preparation of our projects in
February, at Easter, and Whitsun.[1]

Today my Christmas leave has been granted, from the 22nd to the 3rd.
I really want to get a lot done before. Will I succeed? The days pass, and
one regrets every day, for one is squandering one's time. And if one realizes that the greater part of all humanity is doing that, one feels quite
sick. The exception is my Pim, who plants trees and shrubs, looks after
the boys and the house.

Berlin, 27 November 1941

A very nice lunch with Yorck has helped us both considerably. We discussed the subjects for the week-end in February and for Easter. We have
now got far enough to be able to formulate things in writing so as to
prepare the participants for their subjects. Sunday night we'll continue
the talks at Yorck's with Abs, Mierendorff, and Einsiedel.—Then we'll
have to devote ourselves to the Whitsun discussion at Kreisau, for which
a first preparation is to take place on Sunday afternoon in a meeting
with Reinhold Schneider[2] at Luckner's[3] place. But that will be more of
a social function than a working discussion.

1. The planned first gathering at Kreisau.
2. Reinhold Schneider (1903–58), Catholic poet and writer. He was forbidden to publish,
but illegally his writings were circulated widely.
3. Heinrich-Alexander Graf von Luckner (1891–1973), painter, friend of the Yorcks'.

Yesterday afternoon I worked for Kempinski[1] again; they are once more threatened by measures which we want to escape if possible. It took till after 10 o'clock, and I was correspondingly exhausted, but nonetheless didn't sleep well, without being able to think of a reason. . . .

Berlin, 28 November 1941

The tide is high at the moment. Everything has to be done immediately and simultaneously. Yesterday I worked till 11.30, today I started at 8; now I'm waiting for a man from Norway who wants to give me information on various matters, Trott is coming at 2.15, and at 3 there is a big meeting on Kempinski, at 6.30 a party of Groos's staff. I spent the first part of this morning working on news of the resignation of Halder and Brauchitsch,[2] which may turn out to be very significant. In addition prisoner-of-war matters have to be attended to, and so the day spills over.

Kennan came last night, nice and harmless. He talked rather interestingly about the American-Japanese negotiations; the U.S.A. has handed the Japanese a note in which they demand the evacuation of China and withdrawal of recognition of the government in Nanking. That will probably lead to a breakdown of the talks, and it is then left to the Japanese to make war and get themselves finished off quickly or let themselves be ground up slowly. . . .

Berlin, 29 November 1941

. . . Yesterday's staff party with ladies was funny, but nothing for me. It was an affair for the smart social set and everybody boasted about what they could get on the quiet and how it was still possible to live well. None of this was to my taste, and I only hope that nobody noticed that. But to make up for it I ate very well. . . .

Berlin, 30 November 1941

. . . Before I forget I must ask you to tell Z[eumer] the following—but with express instructions not to pass it on at any price: The Russian prisoners will probably all be withdrawn again and sent back to the occupied Eastern Territories because we cannot feed them and people prefer to let

---

1. Cf. n. 1 to letter of 5 November.
2. Brauchitsch offered his resignation repeatedly, for the last time on 17 December; it was granted on 19 December, when Hitler himself became commander-in-chief of the army. Halder stayed on until replaced by Zeitzler in September 1942.

them starve to death there rather than here. For *us* this means: *a.* he should take every Russian he gets for the work planned, better more than 20, as many as he can use, and *b.* he should do everything to get a full contingent of Poles for next year, even more than we need. He is in any case to try and get more workers than he needs, for they will be in short supply.

For your and Schwester's information: a wave of typhus has come to the Old Reich via the Eastern Territories. So far this wave was halted roughly at the Oder. But last week 2 localities where prisoners were employed west of the Oder were hit.—All this is rumour, and I have no time at present to check it; but the reports come from sources likely to know. Please get detailed instructions about the disease. I am told that it is caused by deficiencies and dirt, and is transferred by lice. It would therefore be necessary to instruct everyone who has dealings with the Russians. We can discuss it on Sunday.

Yesterday's party at Luckner's was nice and quite useful, too. Schneider said little, but I liked him on the whole. He does, however, strike one as a sick man; I'd say TB. Luckner is a very nice man; but in all such discussions one sees the difficulties that stand in the way of getting beyond generalities and picturing things concretely. This is hard but necessary. . . .

Berlin, 3 December 1941

. . . Tomorrow I'll have lunch with Kiep, Schlieffen, and Woermann, to see Schlieffen's photographs of the trip.[1] Kiep pressed me into that.

The Jesuit Provincial Rösch,[2] whom I want to win for Whitsun at Kreisau, is coming tomorrow afternoon and in the evening I'm going to Kennan's. On Friday Yorck, Mierendorff, Abs, and Einsiedel are coming to Derfflingerstr. for lunch, in the afternoon I'm going to see Preysing with Steltzer, and in the evening I take my train to Vienna. As you see, it is a lively programme. Also, Canaris is coming back today, and that should give a strong new impetus to my main project. . . .

Berlin, 10 December 1941

. . . The journey was good. Until about Sagan I read Reichsgericht decisions and from then on *Vanity Fair*. That was a delightful occupation.

1. The tour of the newly occupied territories in the West in August 1940—see letters of 7–15 August 1940.
2. First mention by name—cf. letters of 13 and 15 October. Rösch took part in the first of the three week-end meetings at Kreisau.

It teems with wonderful sayings. Take, for instance, the concept of the *"mature spinster"*—isn't it beautiful? We were 1½ hours late in Berlin, which totally upset my programmes. Frl. B. was at the station with a taxi, I went straight to the Office, where I telephoned for an hour, and then went to see the departmental chief, who is sick in the military hospital and wanted to talk with me about the prisoner-of-war matter.

On the phone I found out first of all that the meeting I had arranged for Steltzer and Rösch on Saturday was a success. They were to prepare for Whitsun at Kreisau with the aid of Yorck and Guttenberg. That will therefore be all right. We'll meet again on 10 January. In addition Steltzer and I had been summoned to Preysing at 4.30 and I had to put it off till 5.30 because I had to go to see Bürkner before. So we were at P.'s at 5.30. But unfortunately P. & St. did not get on as well as I had expected. Both had, perhaps influenced by my descriptions, expected more of each other than they could find in the first conversation. At 9 Erich Kaufmann's[1] brother came to see me, wanting me to talk to Hans Adolf about intervening for Erich K., who has now lost his citizenship and pension on the basis of a new decree.[2]

Then Tuesday's main theme began, namely, whether and how one could prevent a German declaration of war on the U.S.A. In my opinion this offered a quite unique opportunity to achieve a compromise with the Anglo-Saxons with a change of crew, and to leave the Japanese to their fate, and thereby extend our hand to the Anglo-Saxons. Unfortunately all the people who ought to have gone into action quite automatically on this question failed to function, and when I got into the affair it was already too late. Today the declaration of war will be proclaimed.[3]

On Tuesday at 8 I visited Hans Adolf in the matter of Kaufmann and he was very nice and satisfactory, which was a pleasant surprise for me. I told him from the beginning that the matter was hopeless, but that I thought that must not be a reason for inaction, and he agreed with me and was at once prepared to see the Kaufmann brother, who after all is a full Jew, though without a star[4] because he has children by an Aryan wife. You must know that K. accomplished a great deal for the Germans in Poland in the years before 1933 and worked with H.A. a lot when H.A. was head of the Eastern Department.

---

1. Famous jurist, born 1880, who had emigrated to Holland. After the war professor of public law and legal adviser of the Federal Chancellor and the AA.
2. See n. 1 (p. 180) to letter of 8 November.
3. After the Japanese attack on Pearl Harbor on 7 December, President Roosevelt did not mention Germany when speaking of the state of war with Japan on 8 December. Germany declared war on the U.S. on 11 December (*DGFP*, D, XIII, nos. 572, 577).
4. On 1 September 1941 an order had been issued forcing Jews to wear a yellow star of David on their clothes.

Yesterday was a crazy day. At 10 I had a discussion at the Ministry of Economics, at 12 a long discussion at the Kammergericht, unfortunately on matters of burning urgency that I couldn't put off, at 5.30 I had another urgent talk with Mother Dippe[1] and Dörnberg,[2] and at 6.30 another urgent one with Herr Steinke, a client. Finally Steltzer came at 7.30. The attempt to stall the declaration of war had to be squeezed into this already very crowded programme. Thus the day really was without a break except for the 30-minute lunch at Derfflingerstrasse, when I wrote my brief note to you.

Today is not very different. I now want to try to draw the consequences from the failure of the apparatus vis-à-vis the question of the declaration of war and to establish new connections. This will take a lot of time now and in the next few days.

Today Haushofer and Yorck are having lunch with me at 1.30, at 3 Yorck & I see Haeften, Einsiedel is coming in the afternoon, and Guttenberg with an Austrian in the evening.

My love, I wonder how you are and whether you have open weather and can plant. How may the milk be doing and the sheep? My thoughts are always at home when I am not actually busy, for that is where my roots are.

Berlin, 11 December 1941

. . . I am returning Schmidt-Rottluff's[3] and C.V.'s letters. C.V.'s[4] is so full of incoherent nonsense that one wonders how an intelligent man can get into such mental confusion. It is a sign of his indolence: since he takes his lot as it comes, he paints himself a picture of the world around this lot. Everything in this picture, however, is askew. The overestimation of material things and of power, the overrating of war in relation to all the other factors of politics, the disrespect for the individual, the ignorance of the first foundations of all European civilization, namely that every human being is an independent thought of the Creator, this regress to the Old Testament and Asiatic notions.—Well, the future will probably change his ideas. . . .

Yesterday's lunch with Yorck and Haushofer was nice and perhaps useful too. Afterwards we all were with Haeften, and at 5 I was in my office,

1. Mother-in-law of his brother Joachim Wolfgang.
2. Dr. Freiherr von Dörnberg, chief of Protocol in the AA.
3. Karl Schmidt-Rottluff (1884–1976), painter and graphic artist. A prominent member of the avant-garde before 1933, he was then ostracized and forbidden to paint; 638 of his pictures were removed from German museums. Now he was to paint Kreisau, whose loss M. foresaw.
4. Cf. letter of 6 November.

where I worked till rather late into the night. Today I'm having lunch with Edith,[1] and Trott is coming in the afternoon, before going to Switzerland in the evening, and in the evening I want to work.

Berlin, 12 December 1941

. . . The days hurry along. It is 12 days to Christmas Eve, and I wonder how everything will look then. There is constant bad news from Russia. Not only that we are retiring along the whole front, but also that there are signs of disintegration among the troops, which bode ill. There are reports that north of Moscow tank units blew up their armoured vehicles and went home, or, rather, started home, by bicycle. The whole Eastern Front may offer a very surprising picture in a few days.

Berlin, 14 December 1941

. . . Yesterday was a terribly hard day. After a rather lively morning I went with Guttenberg to lunch at Yorck's. There ensued a vehement battle over the significance of the monarchy[2] (a) as a goal and (b) as first measure as soon as may be possible. G. left at 6 but came back later. Y. and I were quite exhausted, lay down for a quarter of an hour, and then had to discuss other business. Haeften came after supper and Guttenberg returned at 9. Then we went on until nearly 12, and at 12.30 I was home. Fortunately we finally achieved what we wanted, but it was very hard work. . . .

Berlin, 15 December 1941[3]

. . . The crowded days won't stop now. In the morning there was a great deal to be done. Waetjen came at 12, at 1.30 Yorck & Leuschner,[4] the

1. Edith Henssel—cf. n. 2 to letter of 16 June 1940.
2. *Von Hassell Diaries*, 21 December 1941, mentions many conversations in the preceding weeks on basic questions connected with a change in the system—i.e., a coup d'état. A return to the monarchy was discussed, but neither the former Crown Prince nor his son Louis Ferdinand seemed right. Hassell mentions a suggestion by Trott, who was passionately concerned to avoid any suspicion of reaction and militarism, to make Martin Niemöller Reich Chancellor.
3. Erroneously dated 5.12.21.
4. Wilhelm Leuschner (1888/90?–1944), wood carver, trade-union leader, Social Democrat. 1928–33 Minister of the Interior in Hesse, where Mierendorff was his press chief 1928–30; in January 1933 deputy chairman of the German Trade Union Federation; repeatedly held in concentration camps; then started a non-ferrous metal firm which gave him some security and freedom of movement. Cooperated with Goerdeler and other opponents of the regime outside the socialist orbit. Proponent of a single united trade union after the war. Executed 29 September 1944.

former chairman of the General German Trade Union Federation, had lunch with me. I talked with both of them until 4 and then I had a few things to discuss with Yorck. At 5 I had appointments at my office, now it is 7 and Einsiedel is coming, and afterwards I still have to draft a contract. Tomorrow there is a discussion at 10, at 1.30 I want to have lunch with Reichwein, there are more discussions in the afternoon, one of them with Beck, and in the evening I shall be visiting Peters, together with Harnack,[1] whom you may remember from times past. . . .

Berlin, 16 December 1941

Last night I worked till 10 in my office, went home and to bed, but read another chapter of *Vanity Fair* and probably didn't put the light out till after 11.30. So I was late this morning and met the postman with your Sunday letter.

My remark expressing satisfaction at the approaching end of your nursing is due to my apprehension about the general situation. It seems to me that in the not too distant future it may be desirable for you to regain your mobility, and that is why I am in favour of terminating your personal nursing.

It keeps getting warmer outside, and it is pleasant, after all. For we'll still have enough cold and rain. Once Christmas is over, one can stand the unpleasantness better, because at least the days get longer.

Today at 10 there is a great war council at my place with Y., Guttenberg, and Haeften. At 12 I have to go to the Kammergericht and Mierendorff is coming at 1.30.—Every day is crowded, and it always strikes me as a miracle when one has got through safe and sound and without having to let too many things lie.

My cold seems to be gone.—The general situation is deteriorating from day to day.

---

1. Ernst von Harnack (1888–1945), son of the church historian Adolf von Harnack. Social Democrat; former Regierungspräsident of Merseburg; connected with the opposition to the regime, Goerdeler and Beck on the one hand, Mierendorff and Leber (q.v.) on the other. Sentenced to death and executed January 1945.

1942

How satisfying and lovely it was with you. How pleasant these peaceful pauses are. Now I am back in that end-of-the-world atmosphere which, fully envisaging the approaching catastrophe, yet sees no means of averting it. The coming months will be unimaginably terrible. I think the military situation can only be restored by a miracle. A.H. has issued an order forbidding all withdrawals[1] and so we enable the Russians to smash our front by degrees without incurring the supply difficulties they would have if we retreated. The result will be that the Russians, without making any real territorial gains, will simply annihilate our Eastern army where it stands. And the soldiers still fail to see that. That's because they aren't commanders but technicians, military technicians, and the whole thing is a gigantic crime.

Berlin, 7 January 1942

. . . Yesterday I had a peaceful lunch with Peters, saw Kessel briefly in the evening, and then sat with Friedrich[2] from 8 till 12. A very fruitful

1. Hitler's order had been issued on 26 December 1941.
2. The name he used for Mierendorff from then on.

and encouraging evening. I keep being surprised at how good the man is, and very much hope that you'll like him when you come to Berlin. . . .

Ah yes, Serpuchoff.[1] On the basis of his information Friedrich thinks that to receive S. at the Berghaus is sheer suicide and won't benefit anybody. I was much impressed by what he told me, and today I incline to the view that one should move towards Nora Bergen's[2] neighbourhood via the Radermachers[3] & Poldi Feigl,[4] for there it is likely that only Serpuchoff's friends[5] will appear but not S. himself. . . .

Berlin, 8 January 1942

This morning, when I emerged from the basement at Nikolassee, the world presented a fairy-tale picture. It was probably shortly before sunrise and illuminated—though not quite light—by that, partly by the moon, which was still shining. Everything looked a bit bigger and more magnificent because it couldn't be seen quite distinctly. The sky was quite clear and dark blue with the cold. In this light the pines and other trees, mainly linden trees and birches, stood adorned by heavy hoarfrost. It really looked splendid.

Yesterday I had lunch with Kessel; it was rather annoying because he has lost all contact with reality as a result of his long stay in Switzerland and simply erects dream landscapes. The discussion was friendly in form, but the distance could not be bridged.

In the evening I went to the Waetjens' with him; it was very nice, as always. The Christmas tree was still there; it is a blue fir with a few candles, about 10 fine apples, a star at the top, and a comet's tail from the top to the manger which stands in a gap of the branches at the foot of the tree. The manger is surrounded by a number of Italian figures from the 18th century, about 15 of them, about 20 cm tall, all wood-carvings. Two days ago the 3 Magi had come to the front, Caspar, in a red sash, was kneeling at the manger, the others stood a bit farther away. To the left there was a crowd of faithful shepherds, some of whose faces had marvellous carving, and above this scene the heavenly host hung on little strings, about 20 angels or more in different sizes, from about 15 cm to 5

---

1. The imaginary Russian occupier of Kreisau after the German defeat.
2. A friend who had moved to Italy.
3. Viennese friends from Schwarzwald days. Ludwig Radermacher (1867–1952) was a classical philologist.
4. A Viennese friend.
5. The Western Allies.

or 3 cm. But actually I think our tree is more beautiful, though I'm always interested in seeing other people's.

Now, my love, I must hurry away.

Berlin, 9 January 1942

. . . Yesterday's lunch with Gablentz was very nice. Our relations, which used to be difficult, are quite relaxed now and he's pulling his full weight. But again and again I'm surprised to see how long it takes to win over good people. Dr. Friedrich is another case. After months of preparation, things are not only going well, but obviously so well that he feels the need himself to discuss his thoughts and plans with me. Finally I had an encouraging tea with Preysing, for 2½ hours. You'll like him too. From the human point of view there is therefore much that is encouraging, but it is hard to see how this can still be capitalized.

Yesterday I was reading *The Times* and among the deaths there was a Frisby, "on active service." But fortunately it was another one. . . .

Berlin, 10 January 1942

. . . At lunch yesterday I had a very satisfactory conversation with Haeften. For months it didn't go well at all, but now it is going very well and we have reached a stage in which we can communicate quickly. In the evening I and Üx and a few other people were with a man called Schneider, a big steel industrialist, who had magnificent silver and china and fed us well. We ate off very beautiful 18th-century Meissen, and the table decorations were also Meissen of that time. I'd been at Schneider's once before, some time ago, with Hans Adolf. From my point of view it was a superfluous evening, but once more it was instructive to see how many people are still blind to the true causes and still don't look for mistakes in themselves but in others. "It's all the fault of the British." "This isn't what we wanted." Üx and I joined forces in attempting to explain to these people that with this attitude they deserve exactly what they're getting.

The war goes worse every day. Perhaps there will be a miracle; but it would have to be soon.

Berlin, 11 January 1942

I cannot shake off the question: how can the German people be told what is happening now and what will be happening in the coming weeks, and how will people react to it? Failing a miracle, even the Cassandra cries I have uttered since the beginning of the war will be far surpassed by reality. Will there be anyone then who can master the chaos? Will each individual recognize his own guilt? Will Eastern Germany, that is to say Prussia, then suddenly be missionized and Christianized? Or will everything sink in the maelstrom of pagan materialism? For better or for worse, the battle that began at Christmas has opened a new epoch, an epoch that means a bigger change than the Cannonade of Valmy.[1] Perhaps this is the final end of the Holy Roman Empire, perhaps it is its resurrection.

Yesterday's lunch with Steltzer, Guttenberg, & Yorck was very satisfactory. At the outset St. was a bit exhausted, then got going and did very well. Steltzer has departed for Frankfurt a.M., will return on Wednesday, and we want to continue on Thursday evening. Making these plans is so agreeable, stabilizing mind and soul, that that in itself makes them fruitful; for when one emerges from them and realizes that we still expect to see Whitsun at Kreisau, one rubs one's eyes. In the evening I ate with Steltzer alone, and he left for Frankfurt at 9.

If it is granted to me, I want to spend today by myself and in peace at Derfflingerstrasse. I have to read some *Times*es and want to tidy up and work a bit. But on the whole I don't want to do much. Oh, how nice it would be to be at home now and going to look at the sheep with you.

Berlin, 12 January 1942

What a charming week you have ahead of you. I hope it isn't all too strenuous for you. Please take care; better stay in bed for half a day sometime. The year will bring enough exertion and you must not get exhausted during the first month.

Here it is cold and clear; $-9°$ and no clouds; not a trace of snow. The sensation one gets is of cold increasing daily until it is deep winter. My God, how will the part of the world that interests us look when it thaws again! Beside this thought there is no room at the moment in my imagination and in my head for anything else.

There wasn't much peace yesterday at all. Friedrich turned up at 2 with new information & plans. By the time we had worked through the field it was 5; I then went to see Guttenberg & at 7.30 I was at Peter's with Haeften. When we had finished it was 10.30 and I wasn't in bed until 11.30, where my sleep was like a Swiss cheese, full of holes.

This week's programme is gigantic. Lunch today with Reichwein, Einsiedel in the evening, tomorrow lunch with Kadgien & Gramsch, supper

1. The bombardment and battle of Valmy on 20 September 1792 was the first decisive victory of the French revolutionary army.

with some man at Mangoldt's,[1] Wednesday lunch with Trott, evening probably Ulla or aunts, Thursday lunch Hans Adolf, afternoon at Prey-sing's with Steltzer, evening Steltzer, Rösch, Gablentz, Yorck. Friday lunch Yorck, Haeften, Guttenberg, Schulenburg at my place, evening Friedrich and associates. In between quite a number of individual talks will have to be fitted in and there is quite a bit of work at my own office too. So I'll be rather the worse for wear, too, when my Pim arrives.

There is actually nothing to report, my love. The surface is still calm; there are still 3 meals a day and all *"conveniences"* as if the world were still standing; it strikes me as quite uncanny every morning. Farewell, my love, keep well, look after yourself during the short time you can still look after yourself.

Berlin, 13 January 1942

. . . Yorck's brother Bia[2] is wounded: in at the armpit and out at his back. The wound itself is harmless, especially since he was taken straight from the field dressing station to East Prussia by plane with Kluge, where he landed at the Dönhoffs'.[3] But there he had a nervous collapse with high fever, so that Peter went there today. Since he had already written him off, so to speak, because he was in the very worst spot, it is a relief on the whole. But it is very awkward that Peter had to drop out just now.

Yesterday I had lunch with Reichwein, who was somewhat worn out by several trips but had rather valiantly done something at least. . . .

Berlin, 14 January 1942

It is − 14°, that is one degree colder than yesterday.—Yesterday's lunch with Kadgien and Gramsch was nice, as always, but its content very sur-prising, for those two had apparently resigned themselves to an impend-ing era of rule by Heydrich[4] and based their thinking on this assumption.

1. A businessman and client of M.'s.
2. Paul Graf Yorck von Wartenburg (born 1902), owner of the estate Klein-Oels in Silesia.
3. The family had estates in East Prussia. Marion Gräfin Dönhoff looked after them during the war. She was a friend of the Yorcks'. After the war she became editor-in-chief of the Hamburg weekly *Die Zeit.*
4. SS Obergruppenführer and General of Police Reinhard Heydrich (1904–42), chief of Security Police and SD (Security Service), since autumn 1941 also Deputy Reich Protector of Bohemia and Moravia. On 31 July 1941 charged by Göring with the preparation of a "final solution of the Jewish question" (cf. n. 2 to letter of 26 August 1941), he was now, on 20 January, about to hold the interdepartmental conference at Berlin-Wannsee which had had to be postponed from December. At it he laid out the plans for ridding Europe of its Jews (text in *DGFP,* E, I, no. 150). He died in early June 1942 of wounds sustained in an attempt on his life near Prague.

One detail worth mentioning is that there are plans to conscript women for the labour force to make up for men called up after our losses in the East; and geese will be forbidden entirely for the new year. Ducks and chickens will probably still be allowed for people's own use. . . .

Berlin, 15 January 1942

What sad news that was today. How very awkward for you and how sad for the poor Baron. These illnesses that last months are really bad, because they set him back every time. I hope that at least he'll get over it quickly so that he can go to Switzerland; for that seems even more necessary now than it did before. And poor you, what nasty times if little C. is always ill.

I had not intended to write today but will, because it now seems possible that you won't come. But I am very much concerned that you should come as soon as possible; only we have to be sure that nothing can happen to the little Baron meanwhile.

Yesterday Trott was here for lunch; considerably got down by the situation and without much drive. In the afternoon I was at my own office and in the evening with Ulla. Ulla was quite cheerful and contented. . . .

The war goes badly, though less distinctly so than a week ago; but the internal situation is the most worrisome. . . .

Berlin, 16 January 1942

. . . Yesterday we had a discussion in preparation for Whitsun, which I think went very well. Unfortunately, Yorck wasn't back yet and Rösch not yet here, but Steltzer, Gablentz, Guttenberg, & I made, I think, considerable progress. It went on until 12, but then I slept well until 6 and feel quite rested.

I had a memorable lunch with Hans Adolf.[1] At last his views are 100% the same as ours; even 110% now. But when I objected that nothing had really changed, he protested vigorously. I was relieved, for better late than never. But his assessment of the military situation is even gloomier than mine; this little nuance, 10% overreaction, makes up for earlier deficiencies. . . .

Berlin, 20 January 1942

It was lovely that you were here, and I think it was the right thing to do. Quite a bit can now be fitted into the normal course of action that would

1. Cf. letter of 13 November 1941.

have looked hurried in 2 or 3 weeks' time. You could, if necessary, drop a remark about Daddy's letters, that they were being taken away to be put in order. . . .

The search for C.B. has so far been without result.[1] It seems, however, that the British broadcast names by wireless telegraphy; one military station, at any rate, already had names of men killed on December 30th and buried by the British. The chief danger is that he may not have been found and died of thirst somewhere. This waiting is ghastly. . . .

Berlin, 21 January 1942

. . . The cold here continues unabated; always around −13°; it doesn't get much warmer at midday either. All the poor people without heat, not to mention the Jews! I hear that recruits are now very often trained far to the east, that is to say roughly where the old demarcation line with Russia was, and that it is not only freezing cold there but also unimaginably primitive and unhygienic. Luchter must therefore take enough warm things straightaway.—In the Luftwaffe an order has been issued that under all circumstances officers reporting to the Reich Marshal must be free from lice. A sign of the times.

I've been thinking and come to the conclusion that we should give Caspar and Konrad an envelope each to take with them, to be opened if we perish or can't be found, containing the addresses of people to whom they can turn and the names of those who are to be their guardians *a.* if they are in Germany, *b.* if they are outside Germany. Please think it over. . . .

Berlin, 23 January 1942

. . . Immediately after lunch I had to prepare for a big tea of the Comrades.[2] 8 turned up at 3.30. We had your poppyseed cake, gingerbread, little gingerbread sandwiches with butter, and white bread, schnapps, & cigars. Conversation went on until a quarter to seven. At 7 I was already at the Venetia with a somewhat different cast: Guttenberg, Delbrück, 2 Bonhoeffers (one a lawyer for the Lufthansa[3] and one a pastor[4] in the

1. His brother Carl Bernd had been missing in action since 30 December 1941. This was later assumed to be the date of his death—cf. letter of 20 March 1942.
2. An ironic use of the German word *Genossen*, customary among socialists.
3. Klaus Bonhoeffer (1901–45), active opponent of the regime; executed February 1945. Brother of Dietrich Bonhoeffer.
4. Dietrich Bonhoeffer (1906–45), Protestant minister, teacher, theologian, long since under prohibition to teach, preach, or write, and banished to Bavaria, where he worked for the Abwehr, chiefly in conjunction with his brother-in-law, Hans von Dohnanyi. He used the

Confessing Church). Talk, on roughly the same subject, lasted until 1 a.m. So every minute was full and you were simply short-changed.

Today I am lunching with Borsig at the Yorcks'. We want to prepare for the Ides of March.[1] I wonder whether we'll make sufficient progress. In the afternoon I have a lot to do at my own office and at 7.30 I'll be with Reichwein. That, too, will last a long time. Tomorrow I've kept lunch free to have at least one peaceful hour; Friedrich is coming at 5, at 8 I'll be at Yorck's with Schulenburg. Sunday morning the Jowos are coming to breakfast, will then go to Nikolassee, and return for lunch; in the evening I'll put them all out and go to bed early.

My love, I hope you'll see a silver lining in the dark clouds. My love, you have to stay cheerful now, you'll have to be prepared for the worst but work for the less bad. If we keep our nerve and strength, we'll get through somehow.

I hope all your children[2] stay well.

Berlin, 24 January 1942

. . . First of all I must [tell] you a fantastic advertisement from issue 41 of Mathilde Ludendorff's[3] Hefte: "German woman, pure of race and clean of blood, with effervescent womanhood, sexually aware and happy to give birth, seeks companion for the work for Germany's future." Also I wanted to ask you to tell Zeumer it now looks as if German agriculture will get the necessary fuel after all. The main reason is that no-one expects big offensive operations, because we are short of many other basic requirements; but you needn't tell Z. this. . . .

There has been a fearful row in our Office. The Führer charged all and sundry with knowing too much; it wasn't necessary for the Office or even a number of people in the Office to have a comprehensive view of the

mobility conferred by his Abwehr connection to maintain relations with the ecumenical world abroad—cf. n. 6 to letter of 9 April, and letter and nn. of 15–17 April. Arrested in early April 1943 and hanged—with Canaris and Oster—on 9 April 1945 at Flossenbürg. See Eberhard Bethge, *Dietrich Bonhoeffer, Man of Vision, Man of Courage*, trans. Eric Mosbacher et al., ed. Edwin Robertson (New York and Evanston, 1970); this is a somewhat abridged version of Eberhard Bethge, *Dietrich Bonhoeffer: Theologe, Christ, Zeitgenosse* (Munich, 1967).

1. A discussion at the Borsigs' estate on agricultural policy after the war.
2. Hans and Dickie Deichmann's children, Josefa, Maria, and Thomas, were also at Kreisau.
3. Dr. Mathilde Ludendorff (1877–1966), physician and "religious philosopher"; second wife of Erich Ludendorff (1865–1937), the general of the First World War, on whom she had a strong influence and with whom she founded the "Tannenbergbund," an association dedicated to the struggle against "supra-national powers": Jews, Jesuits, Free Masons, and Marxists; she was strongly anti-Christian and favoured a Nordic religion.

whole situation, everyone should know only as much as he needed to know for his limited task. From Russia we are therefore to get from now on only the Russian army communiqué and no enemy broadcasts at all. What a sign of weakness!

Yesterday's lunch with Borsig and Yorck was very nice and reasonably successful. But really B. is largely an agricultural industrialist.—The evening I spent with Reichwein; I was very tired, but he felt he was getting what he wanted, and that is what matters to me; it makes possible an identity of direction of a quite considerable circle of people. At 11.30 I was in bed, dead tired, and slept deliciously until 6.45. Tonight there will be another strenuous evening and during the night from Sunday to Monday I want to catch up with everything.

Do not be *downcast*,[1] my love. There is no point in that at all. We will have to bear very much very bad news without allowing it to rob us of our freedom of action. Churchill once ended a speech with the sentence: *"and so we can state, that Great Britain is still the sole master of its destiny."*[2] That's a very fine saying.

Berlin, *26 January 1942*

. . . Our security regulations have been further tightened up. Under the new rule it is forbidden to make a report on the military situation, the so-called presentation on the situation is discontinued, and only Canaris himself may now see the report on the situation made outside. This speaks volumes about A.H.'s assessment of the external and domestic situation. . . .

Berlin, *27 January 1942*

. . . My love, yes, I'm glad that your spirits are rising again. Nothing can be done without courage. One must simply resolve to let nothing get one down or turn one from the proper path. Whether one then has the strength to persevere and is able always to recognize the right path is not in one's own hands alone; the will is enough.

I had a very nice letter from M[other] D[eichmann] on Daddy's death[3] and C.B.'s being missing in action. . . .

---

1. English in the original.
2. A free paraphrase (English in the original) of the end of Churchill's speech of 9 September 1941: "We are still masters of our fate. We are still captains of our souls"—Churchill's version of the poem "Invictus" by William Ernest Henley.
3. Sir James Rose Innes, his grandfather, had died on 15 January.

Berlin, 2 February 1942

How lovely were the two days we had. How much I'd like to stay with you, and how much luckier I am than all that mass of humanity pushing through the railway station at Breslau last night.—There's been a big pause here. Colonel Oxé[1] appeared, then Frl. Breslauer, and now it is nearly 1, and Trott is coming to lunch at Derfflingerstrasse at 1; I therefore have to be brief.

Schmitz's funeral[2] is tomorrow afternoon in Bonn; we're taking the sleeper tonight, I've cancelled the return sleeper and want to travel by day, as I hope to spend a peaceful afternoon with Mütterchen. . . .

Incidentally, Schulenburg had breakfast with me today and we had a nice and useful talk. . . .

HOTEL KÖNIGSHOF

BONN AM RHEIN

3 February 1942

Your husband is seated beneath a picture of the Führer with the Rhine and the Siebengebirge behind him. Magnificent. Oxé & I arrived safely in Cologne today and then went by car to Eichholz, where we had breakfast. By 12 we were in Bonn, where we arrived at the Königshof after dealing with all the formalities. Here we'll now have lunch with Gladisch & Stauffenberg, who've been here since yesterday, and the funeral begins at 3.30. The weather is icy. Much colder than Berlin.

Friedrich came last night and wanted to accompany me to the tram when we were finished. I fell very badly on my face in Derfflingerstrasse on the ice that had a little snow on it and broke off two front teeth and tore a gash in my lip. It isn't bad, but a nuisance, particularly the feeling that I can no longer speak, only lisp.—Friedrich brought me to the tram and I got to Potsdamer Bahnhof just in time.

It was nice at the Joests'.[3] Karl-August J. is wounded, with a shot in the calf; so far so good; but of course there is fear that the journey back will really take it out of him. He is said, however, to have got to an airfield, and that would of course be a good thing.—Bad news about C.B. has come via the Faulhabers; the British airman who shot down the plane is reported to have said that 2 airmen bailed out but that one of them was caught by the falling plane and died. This story doesn't quite fit into the picture given by other reports.

1. Colonel Werner Oxé, who succeeded Tafel as head of Group VI/VIa in the Abwehr.
2. Schmitz had had a fatal skiing accident.
3. Relatives of Freya's.

Godesberg, 4 February 1942[1]

. . . The funeral yesterday was quite awful. A man in a gown, at the very most a "German Christian,"[2] spoke in a little cemetery chapel. There wasn't a single word from the Bible, instead poems of all kinds and German sayings, also proverbs. The word "Christ" didn't occur, the word "God" in a subordinate clause at the end; to make up for it there was a reference to "The Horst Wessel[3] Regiment in Valhalla"; no hymn was sung. At the graveside the Lord's Prayer was said, with a few changes in wording: in the chapel a "prayer" was said, a meaningless series of fragments of thought based on the notion of "Death as the Source of New Life," i.e., nothing related to something above man, everything related back to other human beings and therefore abandoning the principle that every man is a special thought of the Creator's mind. I could have been sick on the floor. Schmitz certainly wasn't a believer, but he was a precise thinker, and then to offer this rubbish was really incredible. The speakers at the graveside were Oxé, a man from the Oberprisenhof, Blau from the Institute, and Gladisch, all mediocre, Gladisch too, I'm sorry to say. And the "parson" saluted the coffin on all suitable and unsuitable occasions by raising his right arm. Not one sign of the cross . . .

It is remarkable how much worse things are here than with us: every place is badly heated and many people are said to be completely out of coal; train connections are simply dreadful, for instance only 3 express trains along the Rhine and hardly any passenger trains to Cologne. The local train along the Rhine only goes once an hour, and then only to the city boundary of Cologne, where one takes the tram. And that's how everything here seems to be.

Berlin, 6 February 1942

That was a distressing outburst yesterday. I keep telling you that you should look after yourself and not do too much. What are all those people for. Lenchen could have gone to Liegnitz just as well as you, and Lenchen can also bring the two sons to Berlin with Sister Clara if you are not ready. There isn't the slightest reason for you to drive yourself so much. It seems to me that you make your life more and more strenuous the less you are restricted by shortage of money. Time was when you had time for every-

---

1. Erroneously dated 4.2.41.
2. Adherent of the Nazified part of the Protestant church.
3. Horst Wessel (1907–30), martyr of the National Socialist movement, killed in a brawl; author of the text of the anthem of the movement, which became the second national anthem in 1933.

thing—and now you haven't been involved in the farm operation for months and still don't have any time for yourself. I simply can't understand it. You do too much menial work. Last night I woke up because I dreamt that Asta rang you up from Breslau to ask you to darn a pair of stockings for her and send them to her quickly and that you promptly did it. I was so cross that I couldn't go back to sleep, although it was only 3.45.—I must plead once more for the removal of the telephone. If you didn't have a telephone, it simply wouldn't happen that your plans changed, because there would be too many constants that couldn't be changed. But this devilish instrument saves you the trouble of planning ahead, and that's the reason you don't carry out your plans but accommodate yourself to the plans of everybody else. I am firmly convinced that the removal of the telephone would save you many hours of work every day.

Now to the Baron: I wouldn't let him leave Kreisau as long as he has a positive reaction unless the doctor approved of the possibility discussed below—not Weigand but the pediatrician.—One cannot take the responsibility of letting someone who spreads germs circulate among other people. . . .

About myself there is nothing to report. There is a lot I should be doing but don't do. Over the week-end I must do a fairly big piece of work for my office. Tonight I want to go to bed early again because I have slept badly for two nights now.—My love, I hope you slept well last night and I hope you have a nice day in Breslau. I hope you'll feel better than last night, look after yourself, give my love to your sons. . . .

Berlin, 7 February 1942

I am somewhat *"tottery"*[1] because Schramm drilled my teeth for all of 3 hours, with a new set of injections after every hour and in between times special injections to stop the bleeding. It wasn't bad at all, only I feel a bit the worse for wear. I'm writing now all the same because it isn't certain that I won't have some pain later, when the effect of the last injections wears off. Also it is already 12.20, and at 1.20 I want to go to lunch at Peter's with Guttenberg.

My love, I have a bad conscience about my last letter. I now remember it as schoolmasterish and not at all kind; I didn't want to be like a schoolmaster but only to help my Pim in his misery and woe. But of course for that the letter comes much too late. Forgive your thoughtless husband, my love. . . .

1. English in the original.

Berlin, 8 February 1942

... Yesterday's lunch at the Yorcks' was nice and peaceful. I was a bit under the weather after my 3 hours with Schramm, although I had no more pain, and therefore mainly listened to the others. All I heard was mostly negative and that was sad. Everybody is in the grip of a strange paralysis of the will, and instead of "It's too early," as they were telling me before Christmas, I now hear "It's too late." It is sad to see how right Peter and I were in our diagnosis that the 18th of December 1941 was the "right" day.[1]

Afterwards P. & I visited Friedrich. I like the man so much, he is sober and imaginative, doesn't deceive himself, and has ideas. He's coming to supper on Monday the 16th and then you'll meet him. But there was no really positive result yesterday either. . . .

20 March 1942[2]

Yesterday I was simply unable to write. I had an incessant stream of visitors. In between I had to write a long opinion for an appeal and I left the house together with the last visitor in order to spend the evening with Peter. Then the evening went on till 12.30. At 5.15 I was wide awake, got up, and have been sitting firmly at my desk since before 8, except for lunch with Hans.

The evening yesterday was very nice. Fritzi[3] was still there and we talked in an atmosphere which was soothing and peaceful but noticeably more hushed after the loss of our brothers[4]. . . .

23 March 1942[5]

... I had another vision at Kreisau as I was coming from the Kapellenberg, where I'd helped bury old Hoffmann; then I'd walked around up

1. Cf. n. 2 to letter of 28 November 1941.
2. No place is given. The letter had to pass censorship—the original has pencil ciphers in the upper-left-hand corner. F.M. was in Switzerland. Participants in the discussions of future agricultural policy at the Borsig estate Gross-Behnitz from 13 to 16 March included Nora von zur Mühlen (the widow of Karl Ohle, the Social Democrat Landrat of Waldenburg in Silesia), Fritz Christiansen-Weniger (another friend from the days of the work camps), Friedrich von Zitzewitz-Muttrin (a Pomeranian landowner), and Hans von Galli, S.J., whom Rösch had chosen to attend.
3. Schulenburg.
4. Carl Bernd von Moltke was presumed killed on 30 December 1941 (cf. letter of 20 January 1942) and Yorck's youngest brother, Heinrich (born 1915), was killed on 10 March 1942.
5. No place given—see n. 2 to letter of 20 March.

there, past Mami's grave,[1] to the chapel, past the new family cemetery, and to the village road. I was walking to the farm; there was nobody on the road, for it was 3.10 on Sunday and the mourners had already dispersed. The sun was shining, quite nice and warm. It began by the mill and stopped at teacher Reetz's. This was its content:

I was a very old man and had outlived you all. I was walking slowly but steadily. It was the anniversary of your death and I was coming from your grave. You'd been dead 20 years. Caspar and Konrad didn't occur. The people living with Anders and Batke hadn't known me in my youth or as a man. They regarded me with some shyness but on the whole reverently.

Walking along—as an old man—I thought of the day when I had put a memorial stone for C.B. in the new cemetery and how painful it had been then, how painful had been the deaths of Granny[2] and Schwester,[3] how Mami had died before, and how we had all lived together. But now I was quite alone.

I had achieved all I wanted; the world looked the way I'd wanted it but it had cost a terrible effort, and you had not lived to see the result. That was the worst pain: I had not been able to tell you that all the sacrifice and renunciation and effort were rewarded. I thought of all these sacrifices and strains and wondered whether the result was worth it. And then I thought, although it hurt: even if it meant that I tormented myself and that you didn't have what you were entitled to, if I had no more family or friends, because I ignored the first and outlived the others, even if it meant that I didn't even have a comfortable old age but lived here alone with a housekeeper—I had to act as I did and would do it again.

And at that moment I was at Reetz's and was 60 years younger. Strange, don't you think? It is the legend of the Field Marshal and it is Daddy without Granny and without Mami. While I write this I recognize every one of those feelings. . . .

[continued] Cologne, 26 March 1942

. . . The three days in Berlin were simply one big rush. On Monday and Wednesday afternoons I had to make a report for Gladisch, which had to be given final form. Even if it was now only a question of dictating, verifying figures, and correcting vocabulary and syntax, it still took a lot of time. Then there was work in connection with the previous week's hitch

1. His mother had died on 11 June 1935, while visiting relatives.
2. His grandmother died before the year was out.
3. Ida Hübner did not die till long after the war.

about the Norwegian ships in Sweden.[1] The AA was trying to make us partly responsible for the hitch, and that had to be prevented. Then there were heaps of current work just at this moment. Tomorrow I must have lunch with a man from a department hostile to us. I now meet him regularly to forestall incidents. Willem Bekker came with a fairly big job. Schlitter,[2] Graf Goltz,[3] Sarre, all wanted something from me. As though all that weren't enough, an emissary arrived from Steltzer calling for help in a certain matter[4] which I wanted to give him at all costs. How it will go I still don't know, but it seems to be going in the right direction.— Then there were difficulties with Friedrich, and Tuesday evening Guttenberg, Schulenburg, Peter, & I had a long talk lasting till 1 a.m., on the basis of which I advised you to come alone. The discussion had to be detailed and exhaustive, for otherwise we'd have had to do everything all over again.—I've surely seen some piling up of work in my day, but I have never before experienced anything like the mad pace of these last few days. Thus I departed with all papers in disorder and will have to sort them out in Brussels;[5] I only hope I've left nothing behind. . . .

Berlin, 9 April 1942

. . . If my plans[6] work out, I want to leave tomorrow morning, be in Oslo Saturday lunchtime, and travel from Oslo to Stockholm on Tuesday

---

1. On 19 March the British government had succeeded in getting the Swedish Supreme Court to release 12 Norwegian ships in Gotenburg. Sweden had refused to surrender them to Germany or to their former Norwegian owners after the Norwegian government in exile had transferred ownership to the British government. Only two of the ships that left on 31 March, with valuable cargo, reached England.

2. Oskar Schlitter of the AA.

3. Probably Rüdiger Graf von der Goltz, the lawyer who defended Fritsch in 1938.

4. The escalation of the church struggle in Norway, which endangered Bishop Berggrav—cf. n. 6, below.

5. There is no letter from this trip.

6. The trip to Scandinavia had been arranged very suddenly—cf. n. 1, above. Eivind Berggrav, the Bishop of Oslo, was the central figure in the Norwegian church struggle, which was closely linked to the patriotic resistance. After the installation of Vidkun Quisling as Prime Minister in February, troubles were exacerbated. Over a thousand teachers resigned when a kind of Hitler Youth was to be started. The Lutheran bishops laid down their offices in the state church, the pastors followed suit on 5 April, Easter Day. On 2 April Berggrav was put under house arrest, on 8 April he was put in prison, and it looked as though there would be a trial for giving aid and comfort to the enemy. Instead he returned to house arrest (on 16 April), from which he managed to get away occasionally in various guises, e.g., dressed up as a policeman. This was made possible by the cooperation between the Norwegian resistance and Germans who sympathized with it, notably Theodor Steltzer. The Abwehr, too, was among the sympathizers and quickly organized the intervention by M. and Bonhoeffer.

morning. Wednesday night from Stockholm to Copenhagen, and Friday morning from Copenhagen to Berlin. That is the programme. That would mean that I'd be back in Berlin on Friday evening; perhaps everything will be put back a day. In any case I don't want to arrive in Berlin later than Saturday evening.

Today is a frantic day. It is 8 o'clock, Gablentz comes at 8.30, at 9.30 I must go to a meeting at the Tirpitzufer, at 11 first meeting under Gladisch, at 12 Frl. Breslauer comes, at 12.45 Eddy,[1] at 1.30 Peters is having lunch with me, from 3 to 5 I must put my things at the Office in order, at 5 big meeting under Gladisch, certainly until 7, possibly until 7.30. Then I'll go to my own office, where I must stay until I've finished. On Friday morning Dohnanyi & Bonhoeffer are coming at 8.15 and the train leaves at 10. That's why I don't know if you'll get a letter.

Sassnitz, 10 April 1942

We missed the ferry, and the next departure probably won't be till early the day after tomorrow. It got stuck in the ice repeatedly and now goes without schedule. This morning it left with the help of an icebreaker and took 12 hours to Trelleborg. It can't go at night and therefore won't come back until tomorrow. If all goes well it may be here by midday, and we may get to Trelleborg by evening, but that is very unlikely because there is a stiff east wind blowing, driving the ice of the Northern Baltic this way. Around Sassnitz there is a pile-up of quite substantial ice floes. So if the ferry isn't here by midday tomorrow it can't go back the same day but only on Sunday. That means a really nasty delay, for instead of Sunday midday we'll be in Oslo only at midday on Monday. That may mean missing Stockholm. Well, I'll have to be patient.

Your phone call this morning came through just before I left. That is really very annoying, but we should make an attempt in any case. The chance that it will succeed is very small.—Backe is reported to have said that even a good harvest can't help us any more, that it isn't worth holding people for agriculture and everything must be staked on a purely military victory this year.

My love, I'll continue tomorrow. Now we are going to eat and then to the cinema! I've given in, because I didn't want to let the good Bonhoeffer down. Good night, my love, my hard-working one. . . .

They helped the Norwegian Lutherans and—using the well-known arguments of the "interests of the Wehrmacht"—persuaded the German authorities that repressive measures against the church caused needless unrest among the people and trouble for the occupying power. See Bethge, *Bonhoeffer*, pp. 656–59.

1. Waetjen.

GRAND HOTEL

OSLO

15 April 1942

I've been here now for 3 whole days and didn't write in the rush because the letter wouldn't have reached you anyway.

On Saturday[1] morning we woke up at Sassnitz and since the day was
not too bad, though very misty, we decided to take a walk. My chief concern was to work out with Bonhoeffer our respective roles and it seemed
easier to do it during a walk than in a room. We walked from 9 until 1.30,
about 6 km to the chalk cliffs of Stubbenkammer and about the same
distance back, always in the beech wood high above the sea. It was a
beautiful trail. But apart from some liverwort quite wintry. In the summer
and even more in the autumn, when the leaves fall, it must really be quite
enchanting there. Apart from a woodman we didn't meet a soul and had
plenty of time to discuss everything. The results, so far at least, have been
satisfactory.

When we got back to the hotel at 12.30 [sic] there was no news from
the ferry and people in the know said we'd only leave on Sunday morning. So we had lunch and while eating our dessert (!) suddenly we saw
through the window the ferry coming out of the fog. It was really marvellous. So we dashed to the harbour, where we were told the ship was
leaving in 2 hours and we should hurry; they'd try to catch the connection
to Oslo at Trelleborg.

We did indeed sail at 4.30. The ship was comfortable, the company
simply embarrassing and awful. I'd have preferred to speak nothing but
English so as to put a distance between myself and this gang of thieves
and clods. Apart from one or two bearable people and the stewards and
some German foremen travelling third class, the ship contained only the
scum of the German middle class. Employees of firms working in Oslo
whose talk concerned nothing but shady deals and how to eat and drink
and smoke and stock up as much as possible on the ship. They instantly
formed queues in front of the cigarette counter. Luckily the meals were
very modest and the clods cursed a lot about that. I'd stayed away from
the 4 o'clock lunch because I couldn't face sitting in the same room with
those people for an hour; I would have been too embarrassed in front of
the stewards. I ate later and as good as alone. Only the captain and the
first officer and perhaps 5 others ate at that time.

Our train was due to leave at 9.26 p.m. and we sighted Trelleborg at 9.
But it took another 2 hours to get in, because we got stuck on an ice floe

---

1. 11 April. The original has "Sunday" crossed out, then "Saturday" inserted.

and had to extricate ourselves. This was done by shoving backwards and forwards, with bright searchlights shining on the ice. It was a wonderful sight because the ice looked so imposing: it piled up in great mountains and plateaux, it moved apart and flowed together again, closing the channel of navigable water. And just when I thought we were stuck for good, the big floes parted and opened a channel for us, and 10 minutes later we landed at Trelleborg.

The train had left meanwhile. But we got a special train to Malmö and stayed the night at the Savoy Hotel. There was a big dance there with the men in tails and white ties and the women in long dresses. It struck me as very odd. But at 12.15 I went to sleep quickly, as our train was leaving at 8 next morning.

The journey through Sweden was rather uninteresting. The country is flat, the architecture mediocre, the fields looked good but it was still winter: nothing was being done in the fields. All the clods from the ship were there again, but luckily we sat with tolerable people in our compartment, so that the clods were out of sight and I only heard them from time to time. Something very funny happened in the train: a very nice-looking young Swedish soldier must have noticed that the clods, my countrymen in the corridor, were a source of great embarrassment to me. At any rate, he stood outside and, whenever these gentlemen passed by, looked at me pityingly. And when he got off, shortly before the frontier, he looked at me as if to say goodbye and then saluted. I saluted back and thus we parted in complete understanding without having exchanged a word, although there had been a closed door—with a pane of glass—between us.

The journey from shortly before the frontier to the interior of Norway had a magical beauty: across mountains and valleys, past frozen lakes and along fjords, with a setting sun and beautiful light. It made me see what a beautiful country this is and how shut off from one another people live here. It is a country where individualism must flourish.

So, now I'll stop before I start a new chapter. At 12 we were in Oslo, where Steltzer met us at the station and took us to the hotel. I've been put up in an enormous, princely apartment, half salon, half bedroom, with bath etc., on the *belle étage*, while my companion, as they call him here, lives on the 3rd floor.

[continued] 17 April 1942[1]

Monday morning 9.30 was the time of the first official visit and from then on the series was uninterrupted until 8 p.m. Then, at 8.30, came our

1. It must have been the 16th, which was a Thursday. Bonhoeffer's diary also mentions Thursday the 16th as the day of the journey to Stockholm and Friday the 17th as the day in

first visit to three quite outstanding Norwegians,[1] who received Steltzer, Bonhoeffer, and me like princes; fortunately with a lot of coffee, so that I got over my tiredness. The conversation went on till 1.30, which was really somewhat long. Monday evening was the high point of our stay. There were more official talks on Tuesday morning, and in the afternoon from 3.30 until 8 a meeting with one of the previous evening's three Norwegians to fill in details. B. was busy with another Norwegian. The evening I spent alone with Steltzer. On Wednesday, I first had a lot of writing[2] to do, and at 10.30 I saw Falkenhorst's[3] chief of staff for a final talk, at 12 the colonel general and his immediate staff. Our final talks went on in the afternoon, at 7 I was finished, and at 8.30 Bonhoeffer and I were with Steltzer. Today, Thursday morning, we left for Stockholm at 7 and at the moment we have stopped for a little while at the frontier station.

On Monday and Tuesday I felt well though a bit limp, on Wednesday I had a very bad throat, so that I could hardly speak; this morning I had a temperature as well, but now it is almost cured, with the efficacious help of the yellow scarf. I expect that by tonight everything will be all right.— Oslo looks like this: enchanting, really fairy-tale landscape, with very ugly architecture. In the scale of the town one still senses former affluence, but it makes a more threadbare impression now than Brussels. However, we had fine weather, which makes everything look better. I didn't get out of the city at all, because I had just one meeting after another.

B. and I always had breakfast together in my room, because that gave us the best opportunity to harmonize our plans for the day. On Monday I had lunch with the head of the local Abwehr office, supper with Steltzer, Tuesday lunch with Falkenhorst's chief of staff, Tuesday evening with Steltzer, Wednesday lunch with Falkenhorst, and on Wednesday evening I ate nothing because I felt rotten and didn't want to put the additional burden of digesting on my body.—Except for the meal with Steltzer, the other gatherings all really left something to be desired, because the people had too little substance. Relatively the best of them was the chief of staff, a Colonel von Lossberg, but the colonel general really is a shock-

---

Stockholm, with flight to Malmö in the evening, Saturday the 18th flight to Copenhagen and return to Berlin—see Bethge, *Bonhoeffer*, p. 658, fn. 214.

1. Probably the pastors Alex Johnson and C. B. Svendsen and Professor H. Ordring or the painter H. Sørensen, a friend of Berggrav's and Steltzer's.

2. He used the occasion of his sojourn in Sweden to write a letter to Lionel Curtis in England, in which he described the situation in Germany—see n. 1 (p. 171) to letter of 11 October 1941.

3. Colonel General Nikolaus von Falkenhorst (1885–1968), C.-in-C. Norway until 1944. Sentenced to death in 1946, but reprieved and released in 1953.

ing fellow. He is unable to listen, delivers monologues, tells silly stories, and is extraordinarily foolish. What a contrast to Falkenhausen! At table I did a number of things contrary to all military protocol, mainly to amuse Steltzer and the Ic,[1] Major [Müller?], and I succeeded all too well, so that [Müller?], who was sitting opposite F., was unable to keep a straight face. That at least was fun.

As regards the object of the trip, I have the impression that it was a success, in its official aspect as well as in its covert part. I've agreed with all the soldiers concerned—except the colonel general—on the contents and recommendations of my report for Admiral Canaris and that was, of course, very important.—The train is moving.—

[P.S.] Mailed in Berlin, unfinished. Good night, my love. J.

Schöningen, 19 April 1942

. . . The day here will be strenuous, but it is worthwhile. Just now—9 o'clock—I woke up from a 90-minute slumber in bed. I needed it. I like the Schlanges[2]—father and son. He is madly progressive, which surprised me since I'd imagined him much more reactionary. Total break-up of the Reich, division into separate big regions, etc., are expressions he uses as a matter of course. Agriculture here is fully mechanized; all work in the fields, including planting and cultivating, is done by tractors which have been thought out to the last detail and, skilfully deployed, are capable of much more than ours. I'd like to send Z[eumer] here sometime. . . .

Berlin, 28 April 1942

. . . My love, it was so lovely with you—as always; only there was so much to do, and you had all that drudgery. This morning the opus went off to Bonhoeffer, and he'll come back with it tomorrow morning. I hope I can then finish it and send it off during the day.

I hope today will be peaceful. Last week's storm has subsided and it looks as if everything may now return to a fairly calm pace. I, at any rate, have now finished off everything and the next move is up to the others.

Meanwhile it is afternoon. Einsiedel came. He can't come next Monday and is asking about the time from the 13th to the 27th of June. I agreed to it, subject to your consent. Please let's talk about it.

1. Intelligence Officer.
2. Dr. Hans Schlange-Schöningen, farmer, November 1931–May 1932 Reich Commissioner for Osthilfe (Aid to East German Farmers) under Brüning; after the war Food Commissioner in the British Zone, then first German consular representative in London; and his son, Dr. E. S. Schlange-Schöningen, whom M. had met in England in the thirties.

The lunch was satisfactory. Poelchau & Gablentz are enormously different; and that will lead to a good discussion. The food was good too.—So Peter talked to Fischböck[1] today and is practically out of it.[2]

Otherwise, as you can imagine, nothing new has happened so far.

Berlin, 6 May 1942

. . . Peter had lunch with me yesterday, in the evening there was the mess dinner which lasted till 11, and in between I was with Preysing and in my office, where Wense[3] came to see me. He was appalled at conditions in Holland, where people apparently are being killed en masse, some after court-martial sentences, some as hostages. He does not feel at all comfortable and said he was constantly trying to stage a row and issuing ultimatum after ultimatum, but, so far, without success.

Hans Adolf is coming to lunch today; tonight I'm going to visit Preysing and afterwards probably to my office for quite a while.

It's beginning to get warm. I hope at Kreisau too.

Berlin, 7 May 1942

. . . Imagine, one of Davy's children has diphtheria, another scarlet fever, they went down on the same day with these charming diseases. Isn't it awful. Poor Davy!—H. A. is leaving the AA,[4] thank God. It was high time.

Last night I was at a meeting till about 9 and then went to bed at once and slept pleasantly well. But I was terribly tired.—Today Waetjen is coming to lunch with me with a man by name of Knipphausen[5] from Stettin; in the afternoon there are more meetings, and Friedrich is coming in the evening. Today Steltzer came to breakfast; tomorrow he's coming once more, to lunch. He looked up Merete[6] in Copenhagen, which I was glad to hear. Tomorrow afternoon we're both going to see Preysing to discuss my Norwegian report with him. . . .

Berlin, 8 May 1942

. . . Last night Friedrich & Reichwein turned up. F. had been fortified by 3 weeks in France, Belgium, and Holland and was full of new ideas

1. Hans Fischböck was Josef Wagner's successor as Reich Price Commissar.
2. Yorck left the Price Commissariat and joined the Wirtschaftsstab Ost (Eastern Economics Staff) in the OKW.
3. Agricultural adviser for Kreisau.
4. H. A. von Moltke did not leave the AA—see letter and n. 6 of 12 January 1943.
5. Possibly Knyphausen—M. usually wrote names by ear.
6. Merete Bonnesen, journalist working for the newspaper *Politiken;* friend from the Schwarzwald circle.

arising from what he had seen and heard. Again I liked him very much. He returned the day before yesterday. Furthermore, Uncle[1] has expressed an urgent desire to see me. He'll therefore come on Sunday with Friedrich, who'll appear once more. Reichwein had a raging cold and could hardly speak, which pleased Friedrich & me since it gave us a chance. . . .

Berlin, 9 May 1942

Yesterday really was a Major Battle Day. I worked at the Office until 10.30 and from then until 1 a.m. there were constant discussions, without a break. First a man[2] came from Rösch who wanted to know various things and furthermore came from talks at the Vatican [*beim Papst*] and wanted something in that connection too. He sat with me until 1.15 and then went with me to Derfflingerstrasse. There Steltzer was waiting for me and he, too, had a lot to report and talk about. From Norway there really was little new: the affair runs its course, and many people will die because of it. But there is no sign of the opposing front weakening in any sense, and in the long run we'll all have to draw in our horns a bit.

Steltzer left at 4 and I went back to the Office for a few minutes, and at 4.30 I was at Herr Becker's for a haircut. There wasn't enough time left to have it washed, as I had to be at Preysing's at 5. We discussed the significance of pastoral letters and of sermons and the possible content of pastoral letters[3] and their language. I had the impression that we made quite a lot of progress. P. was obviously satisfied, and so was I. He's going

1. Leuschner—cf. n. 4 to letter of 15 December 1941.
2. Possibly Alfred Delp—see n. 1 (p. 236) to letter of 31 July—but probably Lothar König, S.J. (1906–46), Rösch's secretary; theologian, geographer, cosmologist; member and courier of the Committee for Religious Orders (cf. n. 2 to letter of 6 September 1941) and often the liaison between Munich and the Kreisauers in Berlin.
3. Sermons and pastoral letters were open to charges of "malice," political "misuse of the pulpit," or treason, while written memoranda, as long as they were not published, could be more open, but rarely had any effect. Preysing's pastoral letter on the confiscation of church property—cf. n. 3 to letter of 14 November 1941—angered Goebbels, who was not only Minister of Propaganda but also Gauleiter of Berlin. He considered Preysing an agitator against the German leadership and conduct of the war—see Louis P. Lochner, ed., *The Goebbels Diaries 1942–1943* (Garden City, N.Y., 1948), p. 96 (entry for 21 February 1942). On 11 March 1942, however, he blamed the injudiciousness of party radicals, too, when he wrote: "As a result of a pastoral letter by Bishop Preysing concerning the religious question, we find ourselves in a somewhat precarious situation in Berlin. Unfortunately a number of church buildings were requisitioned by the party and the Gestapo without my knowledge. Although I had forbidden this in the strongest terms, a couple of smart-alecks . . . have been at work, with the result that we have now conjured up a church conflict in Berlin which I did not desire at all but tried under all circumstances to avoid." He was going to try to postpone the showdown with the church till after the war (ibid., pp. 120f.).

to write a new one now and I'll be curious to see whether the result of this conversation will be detectable in it.[1]

At 7.30 Rösch's man came to Derfflingerstrasse to learn about the conversation with Preysing, so that I had to hurry to get home. C.D. & Einsiedel came at 9 and since one of the main questions from Rome was: "What ought to be said on the question of the economic order?" I decided to keep the stranger there and to give him some grounding. And that's what the three of us did until 12; then he left and C.D. and Einsiedel stayed until 1.

Yesterday was of course a bit exhausting but also encouraging. Today I want to go to bed early because Sunday will be another Major Battle Day: the former Staatssekretär Krüger[2] is coming in the morning, Friedrich and Uncle are coming in the afternoon. Today I'm having lunch with Illemie,[3] and Reichwein is coming at 3. . . .

You're coming on Tuesday, my love. Look after yourself, don't do too much these days when you have to cook. Take care of yourself.

Berlin, 10 May 1942

. . . I'm going to see Schmidt-Rottluff in a quarter of an hour and shall take the letter with me. So I'll try to make him come, but warn him that you won't be there and that it won't be so comfortable. I hope I'll succeed. I expect we'll talk about it on the phone tonight. It's such a beautiful season just now and it seems to me that that should show in the pictures.—Poor you, all the things your husband has burdened you with.

I liked Krüger, yesterday. He is actually even better than I remembered him. He is going to take over Point 2 of our programme and will come on 12 July. I'm very pleased about that. Today it is like a veritable dovecote here and I can only get away now because it is lunchtime, and I suppose that nobody will come in the next 90 minutes.—Reichwein and Guttenberg turned up this morning, Friedrich and Uncle will come in the afternoon, at different times. R. is in good form and is obviously looking forward to Whitsun; Guttenberg can't come. His birthday is on the 22nd,

1. On 28 June 1942 Preysing preached a sermon on the Christian view of justice, on 15 November 1942 another on the right of all human beings to life and love. His Advent pastoral, which was also intended for the West German dioceses, did indeed reflect what had been discussed. It stated clearly that law and justice were not founded on the particularity of a people (*völkische Eigenart*) and that rights were not the privilege of a single people (*Volk*), but belonged to all humanity and could not be denied to people of other races.

2. Hans Krüger, Social Democrat, former Under-Secretary of State in the Ministry of Agriculture. He took part in discussions on agricultural policy.

3. Ilse-Marie, wife of Gustav Adolf Freiherr von Steengracht (q.v.).

and it's his 40th, and his whole family have decided, because it is so near to Whitsun, to make one big celebration out of both and he doesn't think he can get out of it. The air here is full of rumours about German and Italian peace feelers. It seems that there may be something in the Italian one, as if a crack in the Axis started at Salzburg.[1] Musso seems under strong pressure from his home front, and it looks as though at least one of the highest Italian Party chiefs, who stakes all on unconditional cooperation with Germany, has been arrested. It is hard to say what's in it. But it is rather striking that the King is giving so many audiences to Grandi[2] & Badoglio,[3] who are both anti-German.

Oh, how I'd like to be at home and I'll hardly be able to wait for next Sunday. These are the most exciting days, when everything suddenly starts. . . .

Berlin, 1 June 1942[4]

It was lovely with you as always. My dear one, it's only with you I am at home, and I like it so very much. It will only be a few days before I'm back again;[5] they'll unfortunately be very stormy days for me and will surely pass quickly.

Your husband had a good trip; he sat the whole time on the seat he'd captured and read Somerset Maugham; it filled up in Guben, and as a very unhappy woman who'd just seen her husband off to Russia was standing outside the door, I got up and stood for the rest of the way to Berlin, but went on reading and could actually stand quite comfortably because the compartment was in the middle of the carriage and it wasn't so crowded there.

The problems began in Derfflingerstrasse because I had no house

1. Hitler and Mussolini had met at Schloss Klessheim on 29 and 30 April—see *DGFP*, E, II, nos. 165, 178, 182, 183.

2. Conte Dino Grandi, former Italian Ambassador in London, then Foreign Minister; chairman of the Fascist Grand Council, in which capacity he brought about the fall of Mussolini on 24 July 1943.

3. Marshal Pietro Badoglio (1871–1956) assumed the leadership of the Italian government after the fall of Mussolini.

4. During the Whitsun week-end, 22–25 May, the Kreisauers had met at Kreisau for the first time. The agenda included the relationship of church and state (with presentations from Steltzer and Rösch for the Protestants and Catholics and Hans Peters on the Reich Concordat of 1933); education (Reichwein on schools, M. on university reform). Other participants were Freya and Asta von Moltke, Peter and Marion Yorck, Yorck's sister Irene Yorck, and Harald Poelchau. For documents see Ger van Roon, *German Resistance to Hitler: Count von Moltke and the Kreisau Circle*, trans. Peter Ludlow (London, 1971), pp. 329–32.

5. For Asta's wedding.

key[1]—we'd stupidly forgotten about that. I woke up Frau Cohn, who came looking pale as death because she thought her husband was being taken to be shot—500 Jews are said to have been shot yesterday and the day before[2]—and was very relieved when she saw me. She then helped me find a ladder, and I climbed in through the bathroom window; and found my key in the apartment so that I could open the door and bring up my suitcase. . . .

The general situation has developed apace. Last night there was a big raid on Cologne:[3] all railway stations were hit, very severe damage to war production, after 24 hours still no water, electricity, and gas. 10,000 bombed out. We seem to be approaching the time of big air raids. . . .

Berlin, 3 June 1942

. . . Yesterday Steltzer arrived immediately after lunch, looked well, and was obviously still very much taken with Whitsun. We discussed our future plans in broad outline and then adjourned until the evening. At 4 I went to my office to deal with the most urgent things and at 6 I visited Friedrich, who was in good form again and had done his homework. So it was a useful hour. He then left for The Hague, Brussels, and Paris. I went on to Peter's, where I met Steltzer and where we had marvellous asparagus from Cauern. Haeften came after supper and we were well occupied until midnight. Haeften, too, was in good form. Today we want to continue at 5, and then I'm hoping for a peaceful, albeit late, evening at Derfflingerstrasse, where I have to read a lot of *Times*es.

Otherwise your husband is well. He slept splendidly for two nights and woke agreeably at 6.15 both times. About military events I've heard nothing new. Probably the most important thing at the moment, apart from the fizzling out of the offensive in Africa, is the fact of the big British air raids with more than 1,000 planes each night. I haven't heard anything about the last raids, but the number of planes alone is enough to make it clear that there must be considerable damage. It will be interesting to see the balance sheet after they've kept up these raids for a month. . . .

1. F.M. had been in Berlin during his absence.
2. After an arson attack on an anticommunist exhibition on "The Soviet Paradise" on 18 May in which five young Jews took an active part, 500 Berlin Jews had been arrested; 250 of them were shot and the other 250 sent to a camp, where they were killed later. Further measures were threatened in case of further sabotage. After the Czech attempt on Heydrich's life on 25 May (he died on 2 June) Goebbels mentioned the arrest of 500—more?—Jews and threatened that after every assassination or Jewish attempt at revolt 100–150 Jews would be shot.
3. It was the first raid by the RAF with over a thousand bombers.

Berlin, 4 June 1942

. . . There is nothing to report. Yesterday's lunch was cancelled because I had too much to do. At 5 Steltzer, Peter, Haeften, and Wurm's representative[1] in Berlin came to Derfflingerstrasse, and in the discussion, which lasted 3 hours, we tried to clarify the conditions of Wurm joining in, an attempt which seems to have had a positive result. Now Wurm[2] is to come in the middle of the month. This would mean that an essential point[3] of the Kreisau programme would be put to the test of feasibility. . . .

Berlin, 9 June 1942

This is another first letter after a few lovely days[4] with my Pim. You arranged everything splendidly, my love, so well that there were even a few idyllic moments. Now you have the big clean-up, which of course is a bother. I am eager to know what impression you will get of your battlefield: money, stores, etc. I hope you won't be on short commons now. . . .

Berlin, 10 June 1942

Another cool, half-sunny, half-overcast day is beginning. It is only 8 and I'm sitting very contentedly at my desk above the trees of the Tier-

---

1. Eugen Gerstenmaier (1906–86), Protestant theologian and church official (Konsistorialrat); after the war, CDU politician. Suspect among some segments of the Confessing Church because of his work in the Church Office for Foreign Relations (Kirchliches Aussenamt) under (the Protestant) Bishop Theodor Heckel, whose task was the official connection with the churches abroad. Gerstenmaier was, however, also viewed with suspicion by the SD and the strongly Nazi Deutschlandabteilung (German Division) in the AA. Yet the Cultural and Information divisions of the AA used him for special tasks. Trott and Haeften belonged to the Information Division. Gerstenmaier soon became an important member of the Kreisau Circle. He continued to work with its other members after M.'s arrest, and was himself arrested at the conspiratorial headquarters at Bendlerstrasse on 20 July; sentenced to seven years' hard labour (the public prosecutor had asked for a death sentence—see letter of 10 January 1945). After the war he founded the Protestant Aid Association (Evangelisches Hilfswerk); 1949–69 CDU member of the Bundestag, 1953–54 chairman of the Foreign Affairs Committee, 1954–69 President of the Bundestag.
2. Theophil Wurm (1868–1953), since 1929 President of the Protestant Church in Württemberg, 1933–49 with the title Landesbischof. Since the outbreak of the war, and especially since the summer of 1941 and his protest against the "euthanasia" campaign, increasingly recognized as leader of the part of the Protestant church that had not been Nazified. Earlier there had been disagreements between him and the Confessing Church.
3. The agreement of the Protestant and Catholic representatives on church-state relations and education after the war—see van Roon, *Resistance to Hitler*, pp. 329f.
4. Asta's wedding.

garten. When one realizes that it must have been some city's turn last night, that certainly last night many people died or were bombed out, one is amazed at the peace in which one is living oneself, and thinks that it will end soon. It is a curious feeling, these hours before the eruption of the volcano.

Yesterday I had lunch with Harnack, whom I won as a recruit. Again I didn't like him altogether, but I'm confident that he will take his place and pull his weight. Otherwise there is not much to report about him.— I saw C.D. briefly; he was also eating at Reich's.

In the afternoon I visited Preysing and we talked until 7.30 about the Kreisau programme. The going was not altogether smooth, and he made some objections, which have to be considered. Unfortunately I am still not certain whether the objections are to substance or form. Next Wednesday the battle is to continue. I must settle things with him and we'll simply keep at it until they are settled. . . .

Berlin, 11 June 1942

So here we have another 11th of June. It is 7 years ago now, and to me it seems as though it were yesterday, that you told me in the flat in Frie-denau when I came to lunch with Carl that Mami had died. And on the other hand it is as though worlds separated me from those days. On the 11th of June '35 I was going to England for the first time to see what I could do there, and now I feel so much at home there that even the three-year separation makes no difference. And how different everything else is too. . . .

The Ministry of Food is in complete dissolution:[1] Main Division I of the Reich Food Estate—"Man" [*Der Mensch*][2]—goes to Ley,[3] soil im-provements go to Speer,[4] machine technology etc., to the Ministry of Economics, the rest of the ministry will be put under SS supervision, and Ministerialrat Harmering [?], who is responsible for our *Erbhof* affair, will

1. Hitler had dismissed the Reich Food Minister, Walter Darré, on 23 May. The business of the ministry was carried on by Under-Secretary of State (Staatssekretär) Herbert Backe— cf. n. 3 (p. 135) to letter of 17 May 1941.
2. "Human Resources"?
3. Dr. Robert Ley (1890–1945), Reich Organization Leader of the NSDAP, leader of the German Labour Front (Deutsche Arbeitsfront, or DAF—see n. 3 to letter of 6 January 1940). Among the accused in the International Military Tribunal at Nuremberg. Committed suicide.
4. Albert Speer (1905–81), architect, Reich Minister of Armaments February 1942. Sen-tenced to twenty years' imprisonment at Nuremberg for his participation in the slave labour programme.

be replaced by an SS Gruppenführer Lorenz.[1] I assume therefore that we've missed the bus.—I have an appointment for lunch with Hans Adolf today, to discuss the changed situation. This afternoon & evening I must go to my own office, where I haven't been for a week.

Berlin, 12 June 1942

. . . I can still make no plans, because I haven't heard from Munich yet. Friedrich is returning next week, Wurm is coming the week after, and by the end of the month I hope to be able to get a clear picture of the battle-field.

There are rumours here that Hermann[2] has been deposed as Heir Presumptive and that Himmler[3] has taken his place, with the immediate right to take part in all military discussions. If this is true[4] it is an event of great symptomatic importance and wouldn't surprise me at all. It is not to be made public. Of course this rumour can also have been put about to undermine Hermann by a whispering campaign.

Berlin, 14 June 1942

. . . Yesterday I ate with Father Hahn[5] at Illemie's. A witty and nice man. From there I went on to Schiffer's.[6] He is in brilliant form; it is really impressive to see how he manages to keep his composure and to occupy

1. Werner Lorenz, head of the SS Central Race and Resettlement Office (Rasse und Sied-lungshauptamt, or RuSHA), head of the resettlement staff of the Reich Commissar for the Consolidation of German Nationhood (Reichskommissar für die Festigung des deutschen Volkstums, RKF, Himmler—cf. n. 3 to letter of 12 June), head of the Volksdeutsche Mit-telstelle, a "resettlement" organization. Eventually Kreisau *was* made into an entailed es-tate, despite the fact that the decision was now under SS-RuSHA jurisdiction.
2. Hermann Göring.
3. Heinrich Himmler (1900–1945), Reichsführer SS (RFSS) and chief of German Police, Reich Commissar for the Consolidation of German Nationhood (Reichskommissar für die Festigung des deutschen Volkstums, RKF); August 1943 also Reich and Prussian Minister of the Interior, after 20 July 1944 also commander-in-chief of the Replacement Army; Feb-ruary 1945 commander of Army Group Vistula. Committed suicide after capture by the British.
4. It was not true, despite the rapid growth of Himmler's power with the war in the East and the radicalization of the regime. On 12 June Himmler as RKF endorsed the "Generalplan Ost" for the Germanization of conquered territories.
5. Baron Hahn, the father of Baroness Steengracht.
6. Eugen Schiffer (1860–1954), co-founder of the German Democratic Party, former Reichstag deputy, Minister of Finance and Minister of Justice. In the thirties, centre of a discussion group, the so-called "Schifferkreis," which included Hans Krüger (cf. n. 2 [p. 218] to letter of 9 May) and had M. as one of its speakers at least once in 1937.

his head with general concerns and not even to mention the specifically Jewish ones. His pleasure at my visit was obvious.—From there I went to a party at the Kieps'. I had to go sometime. It was the same as always. Actually they are very nice, and it's only the "society" around that is hard to take. I was through there at 8 and, being in the Grunewald, I went to visit Ulla, where I stayed till 9.30. She is only moderately well. On 4 July she wants to go to Gastein and intends to turn up in Silesia in early August.

Steltzer was with me yesterday morning, for nearly 2 hours. I have such a pleasant, warm feeling for him and feel so safe with him. When I consider what good men and women I've already had the good fortune to meet in my life, I truly can't complain. Would I have met this tremendous variety at any other time? In less turbulent times, wouldn't I have been born into, or after a short time found myself in, a set group, and wouldn't my circle have been automatically limited? . . .

Berlin, 15 June 1942

. . . Lukaschek turned up at 12.45, stayed for lunch, and then went with me to Harnack's. I've just come from there. Now I'll stay on at home and at 8 I'm going to see Husen,[1] with whom L. is staying, for a brief evening talk. It is a bit hard for me today but L. & H. both rather wanted it. . . .

Berlin, 16 June 1942

. . . Last night I visited Husen. It was nice but not productive because there was a dreadful talker present. L. was in good form.

C.D. is coming to Derfflingerstrasse for lunch today. I am curious to hear what he has to report, for he is now in a position where he can observe the general process of disintegration rather well.—My arbitration court sits this afternoon. I wonder how it will turn out.—Einsiedel intends to come in the evening if my court has finished.

---

1. Paulus van Husen (1891–1971), jurist, longtime friend and colleague of Lukaschek's, as Landrat in Rybnik and as German member of the mixed commission for Upper Silesia 1927–34; specialist on minority questions, Catholic, member of Centre Party; during the war served as reserve captain in the OKW/Wehrmachtführungsstab. Specialist for legal questions in the Kreisau Circle, took part in the third Kreisau meeting, wrote the draft papers on the punishment of Nazi criminals—see text in van Roon, *Resistance to Hitler*, pp. 340–47. Arrested in August 1944, sentenced to three years' hard labour in April 1945. Co-founder of the CDU in Berlin—together with Lukaschek, Steltzer, and Gablentz; 1945–48 legal consultant of U.S. Military Government in Berlin; 1948–49 judge at Bizonal Court in Cologne; 1949–59 President of the Supreme Administrative Court and of the Constitutional Court in North Rhine Westphalia (cf. van Roon, *Resistance to Hitler*, pp. 70–73).

Guttenberg rang me up; he has returned. There is nothing new of any kind. Only that the British and Americans have publicly promised the Russians to open the Second Front[1] in Europe in 1942. That is interesting. Altogether the conviction seems to be forming abroad and among wide circles of our own officer corps that the war is going to end this year. . . .

Berlin, 17 June 1942

. . . Today I'm going out to lunch with Trott and will then go to Derfflingerstrasse. I wonder if he'll take the plunge now.[2] At 5 I'll be at Behrenstrasse. It will be a difficult discussion today, and it is likely to be long, certainly until 7 and probably until 8. Much depends on the course of this conversation. I'm inclined to put it like this: if it goes well it will be a real success, if it doesn't go well we'll have to think about detours to change Conrad's[3] mind, and that will take time. Moreover, I am uneasy about not hearing from R.[4] The reason may simply be that he doesn't have a suitable channel of communication at the moment, but it may also mean that he is encountering difficulties like mine. . . .

So, now, my dear heart, I must do a little work. First I have to go to the Institute and reshelve some books which I secretly removed for yesterday's arbitration meeting. Incidentally, I was asked if I wanted to become a professor. I have the impression that it was Bruns who hit on the notion, but I'm not sure; in any case, I declined unambiguously.

1. Delays about relieving the pressure on Russia by setting up a second front in the West were a moot point in inter-Allied policy and strategy—see John Lewis Gaddis, *The United States and the Origins of the Cold War 1941–1947* (New York, 1972), pp. 66–72. In 1942 America was not yet ready to contribute sufficient forces for a second front in Europe. Nevertheless, the communiqué released at the end of Roosevelt's talks with Molotov on 11 June mentioned complete agreement concerning the urgent task to create such a second front in 1942. The British government remained firm in its refusal to undertake a suicidal operation. A British-Canadian landing at Dieppe on 19 August collapsed the same day. In November 1942 the Allies landed in North Africa.
2. The letter of 18 June gives no clue to the precise nature of the plunge; the letter of 20 June mentions Trott's forthcoming trip to Switzerland. As regards Trott's special "Indian Section," Hitler had at last, on 25 May 1942, granted the audience Bose had sought since arriving in Berlin on 3 April 1941. But Hitler was unforthcoming and did not favour Indian independence, let alone the recognition of Bose as head of an Indian government in exile; he had merely been given a radio station "Free India" for broadcasts to his countrymen. A small "Indian Legion" formed from among Indian prisoners of war was offered to Rommel, who declined the offer. Bose left Germany in February 1943 and went to Japan.
3. Preysing.
4. Rösch.

Berlin, 19 June 1942

Another grey & icy day today. And wind, to boot. I don't think it is more than 10 degrees. This weather can embitter one, and I keep thinking sadly of our bees. What may they be up to? They can't build up a stock.

We've just received a regulation giving farmers harvest leave again. I've asked for two weeks starting 27 July. I can't get away earlier because of work. . . .

My talk with Conrad on Wednesday again lasted 2½ hours but produced a big step forward. The larger part of the difficulties has been overcome and we'll manage to remove the rest too. But it was a real Major Engagement; fortunately I was in good form.—Reichwein wanted to come last night but brought Friedrich with him, who had just returned from Paris and wanted to see me at once. F. was in excellent shape, had done some useful thinking about our proposals and practically endorsed them. He had all kinds of new ideas and suggestions. We sat until 12.30 after Reichwein had left about 11. Continuation Saturday night or Tuesday night. In the afternoon there was, in addition, a man from Wurm;[1] it looks promising. The Main Battle is to take place at 14.30 on Wednesday and will probably take up the whole afternoon. The Sunday I want to spend quietly at home and read my *Times*es in peace. With all the present intense activity I am very receptive for peace. . . .

Berlin, 20 June 1942

. . . What is there I can tell you about myself? Yesterday I had lunch with Guttenberg. He does have great charm, but unfortunately he is simply lazy and doesn't have the energy for a sustained effort. He had some quite interesting details about Suñer's[2] visit to Rome:[3] S. has dissociated himself from us completely: he wants to reintroduce the monarchy, to reconcile the Italians and French, and bring about a Romance or Latin Alliance between Spain, France, and Italy. That is a severe blow for us.

I went to my office in the afternoon, finished the arbitration judgment, and had a lot else to do, too. Trott turned up there at 7 for a brief talk before his departure for Switzerland. . . .

1. Probably Oberkirchenrat Dr. Wilhelm Pressel, an adviser of Wurm's on matters of church policy.
2. Ramón Serrano Suñer, Spanish Foreign Minister.
3. See *DGFP*, E, III, nos. 37, 55.

Berlin, 22 June 1942

. . . Today I'll have lunch with a man from the Institute, Wengler.[1] He is an extraordinarily intelligent man, a bit too much so; he has written the fundamental works on problems of double taxation and is a specialist in African native law. A man with a Jewish type of brain, but of the best kind. In the evening I want to go to my office.

The fall of Tobruk is a great event, and completely unexpected, for here we had the impression that we'd got stuck since about the 10th, then came the fall of Bir Hakeim, and then the tidal wave broke. It was known that the British didn't want to hold on to Tobruk, but that they didn't even try to evacuate the encircled troops is astonishing. It will cause a political landslide in the whole Mediterranean area, in Ankara, Vichy, Madrid, Lisbon, and French Africa, and perhaps the military events aren't over, perhaps Rommel will now go on and reach his goal, Suez,[2] after all. It isn't likely, but the way the armoured resistance of the British has been eliminated brings even that into the realm of the possible. Much will depend on the question of whether we can now reinforce Rommel. . . .

Berlin, 23 June 1942

. . . Yesterday I had long talks with Haeften and with Gablentz to prepare myself for the conversation with Wurm. For lunch today I am free, which is unusual, and in the evening I'm going to visit Friedrich. . . .

Berlin, 24 June 1942

. . . I was with Friedrich from 8.30 until nearly 12. He has performed all his commissions satisfactorily, though not without conflict. He has got about as far with his people as I have got with Preysing. But on the whole I am surprised at how well it has gone, and yesterday it came out that he, too, was worried before his talks.

So Wurm is coming this afternoon. He spent yesterday in preparation, and all kinds of people rang me up to ask what should be discussed with him. I hope therefore that some spadework will have been done. I'm expecting Gablentz at any moment, and he'll tell me about the preliminary talks. I very much wonder how that will go.

1. Wilhelm Wengler, after the war professor in Berlin. In 1948 he published an article about M. and their work in the Abwehr: "H. J. Graf von Moltke (1907–1945)," *Die Friedenswarte*, vol. 48, pp. 297–305.
2. In the course of June, Rommel crossed the Egyptian border with his German-Italian panzer army and was made Field Marshal on 26 June. He intended to reach the Suez Canal, but was stopped at El Alamein, a hundred kilometres west of Alexandria.

Otherwise, my love, I have nothing to report. I won't have to wait long now before I come. I'm so much looking forward to you, to the children, and to Kreisau in general. Yesterday I saw the first open linden flower!

Berlin, 24 June 1942, evening

I'm writing once more today because I won't be able to get a letter home tomorrow morning and because I feel the urge to write. The conversation with Wurm went well. But now I'm so exhausted from the effort of these 2½ hours that I can no longer think. I'd like to walk for 2 hours, but in this stinking city it is impossible. I feel so empty—as if there were nothing left in me. And yet there was no resistance, and the whole thing went so smoothly that it was rather uncanny. But I had to put a lot of effort into it.[1]

So now a really big step has been taken. I still have to go to Munich and Freiburg[2] soon. It seems that there will be no progress in Munich without me. It is annoying, because frankly it is a nuisance for me. I only hope that tomorrow will be a day when I can rest my head. For I am tired but, unfortunately, not yet sleepy by a long way. Perhaps I'll bicycle a bit, to get sleepy.

Berlin, 30 June 1942

The lovely days are over again. They stand like precious green islands in the roaring river: before one gets to them one can see them ahead for a time, enticing and green; after losing them again, one looks back at them. What would the river be without the islands? But, then, would the islands be quite so beautiful without the river? . . .

I could only say hello at the Office, then talked for about an hour with Rösch and his secretary, König, and I made an appointment with them for 2. Then I chased through all kinds of offices and had not yet read my incoming papers by a quarter to 1, when I had to hurry home to see to lunch. There was potato soup with an onion—in the absence of other vegetables—and afterwards half a pigeon, and finally, with Rösch and König, strawberries and coffee. A princely meal, R. & K. stayed till 4.30 and went on from me to Preysing, and then came to fetch me from my office. I briefed them carefully for the difficulties with Conrad. Their

---

1. While M. was concerned to bring the Protestants represented by Wurm together with the Catholics (represented by Preysing), Wurm was also working for agreement among the disunited Protestants themselves—see Bethge, *Bonhoeffer,* pp. 592f.
2. To see Cardinal Faulhaber and Archbishop Gröber—cf. letter of 30 June.

man[1] had done everything he was supposed to, but they had not yet talked to Gröber[2] because they first wanted to have Conrad's blessing for it.

At 4.30 Haeften & Trott came, the latter just back from Switzerland with the first British and American reactions to our efforts. Not uninteresting and fairly hopeful.[3]—At 6 I was at my office, where I had lots to do, and it was 8 before R. & K. turned up. They had wrestled the whole time, that is, about 3 hours, with C., and had found him, as I had, a hard nut to crack but not unconvertible. Conrad was particularly relieved to hear that he wasn't to play the main role. I had asked R. to make that quite unambiguously clear. Asked who might be eligible for the role that was envisaged, C. had named Gröber, and that settles it.

Further programme: R. travels to Freiburg at once, and K. comes here on the 8th or 9th to inform me of the result. If it turns out to be satisfactory, as we expect, I am to meet Gröber on the 12th. On the 14th we have the talks with Wurm's people, here in Berlin, and on the 19th I travel to see Wurm. This means that there is only one Sunday this month, the 5th. We'll telephone about it the day after tomorrow.

This week is frantic: tomorrow morning Peter is coming, who is terribly out of it all, tomorrow afternoon Friedrich is coming to me with his Austrian,[4] the day after tomorrow in the evening there will be a discussion

---

1. The Archbishop of Munich, Cardinal Michael von Faulhaber (1869–1952); 1903–10 professor of Old Testament exegesis and Biblical theology in Strasbourg; 1910–17 Bishop of Speyer; 1917–52 Archbishop of Munich and Freising, from 1951 Cardinal. He had made a great stir in 1933 with his Advent and New Year's Eve sermons—see Michael Kardinal Faulhaber, *Judaism, Christianity and Germany*, trans. George D. Smith (London, 1934).

2. Conrad Gröber (1872–1948), Archbishop of Freiburg since 1932. Called "Brown Conrad" in the early days of the Third Reich, he was even a "Promoting Member" (Förderndes Mitglied) of the SS briefly, then became a staunch opponent of the regime and correspondingly suspect (cf. letter of 9 July). Member of the Ausschuss für Ordensangelegenheiten (cf. n. 2 to letter of 6 September 1941). Did much to help the persecuted, including Jews; his chief agent in this was Gertrud Luckner (born 1900), who was sent to Ravensbrück concentration camp from 1943 to 1945 after she was caught.

3. But see the description of Trott's disappointment, verging on despair, when the Secretary General of the Provisional World Council of Churches brought him the British reaction to his memorandum (A. W. Visser 't Hooft, *Memoirs* [Philadelphia, 1973], p. 158). The attempt of Hans Schönfeld and Dietrich Bonhoeffer to secure a helpful response for the German opposition from the British government was equally unsuccessful. They had, independently of each other, met George Bell, the Anglican Bishop of Chichester, in Sweden. Bell's efforts to get a favourable response from Eden or from the American Ambassador in London were fruitless—see Bethge, *Bonhoeffer*, pp. 662–71.

4. Heinrich Gleissner, until the Anschluss Landeshauptmann (Commissioner) of Upper Austria; after detention in concentration camps employed in the Braunkohlen-Benzin-A.G. under Gestapo supervision, like Mierendorff; returned to his former post after the war.

between Friedrich, the man he is putting forward for constitutional questions, and myself. Christiansen[1] is coming on Friday, and Trott wants an evening, and Jowo has asked me to eat with him and General Köstring,[2] former military attaché in Moscow. Borsig, too, is on the programme. Frau Cohn is having difficulties, and there is all hell let loose.

Berlin, 1 July 1942

It is 10.45 at night and I'm only just finding time to write. It was another mad day. To start with I woke up too late, that is, not before 6.30. Then I wrote my letter to Granny. At 9 I went to an office for Frau Cohn, who is threatened with the loss of her livelihood and living quarters. There I found a very nice and understanding Oberregierungsrat who only does what he must to keep his job; therefore Frau Cohn will probably be all right for some time. At 10 I was at the Office, where I had to do some telephoning, Peter came at 11, and at 11.30 I had a meeting, at 1 a short one at Derfflingerstrasse, at 3 another one at the Office, and in between I cooked: vegetable soup from nothing, pigeon with barley. I was given a very urgent job at the Office at 5, Peter & Friedrich came to Derfflingerstrasse with an Austrian[3] of Friedrich's at 5.30, the Office job had to be done in between, Peter left at 7.15, the Austrian at 7.30, then Friedrich and I talked on till 10.30, and during that time I cooked a really marvellous pea soup, which we ate. So far I've cooked every meal by myself and eaten at home, not always alone, and have not used a single egg! . . .

Talk with Friedrich good, as always. No particularly new perspectives. Only that we talked at length about restitution for workers, Jews, Poles, etc. The main fight on the trade-union question[4] comes next week. I wonder how it will end. Tomorrow he, Peter, & I will work on his man for constitutional questions. Before, at 5.30, I'll go to Peter's and will have supper there.

Further programme: Rösch is with Gröber today, after getting Faulhaber's & Preysing's blessing. I'll hear on the 9th whether I'm to see Gröber

---

1. Friedrich Christiansen-Weniger, agricultural expert, head of the agricultural experimental institute at Pulawy—see letter of 4 May 1943.
2. General Ernst August Köstring, persona non grata for his warnings about the Red Army's capacity to resist and recover, from 1 September 1942 on concerned with Caucasian questions in Army Group A.
3. See n. 4 to letter of 30 June.
4. The question whether there were to be industry-wide unions or even a unitary, single trade union, which Leuschner aimed at but which conflicted with the general aim of the Kreisauers to decentralize and to activate the individual and small communities; yet they favoured the deprivatization and nationalization of key industries.

on the 12th. On the 19th I'm travelling to see Wurm. On the 10th and 13th of August talks with W.G.F.[1] Therefore you must, please, come next Sunday. It is the only free Sunday in the foreseeable future.

Berlin, 7 July 1942

It is 8.15. I wonder if you're sitting peacefully at home having breakfast or have already had your breakfast. I very much hope so, for, after all, you left on time. My love, it was so lovely with you, as lovely as always. I was glad, too, that you were there for one of the talks with Friedrich, which have been so frequent lately. When we are alone it is a lot more concentrated and quite a bit faster, but essentially it is the same. Last night was really quite typical. . . .

Today I'm having lunch with the Stauffenberg I met in London[2] and to whom I recommended Little Wolff[3] as teacher. Afterwards I may lie down for an hour to gather strength for the evening. From the Office I'll go to my own office and from there to Peter's.

Berlin, 8 July 1942

. . . Yesterday evening was terribly strenuous. There was a Big Battle and we only got to the point of discovering the reason for the Uncle's abysmal mistrust. The result was that at least we got him to the point of admitting: yes, if these factors really come into play, there will be a completely new situation, and in such a situation we, too, may draw new conclusions.—My impression is that we achieved the decisive breakthrough, but not until midnight, and therefore one must wait and see whether everything will get rigid again or the victory is final. We continue next Tuesday. . . .

Berlin, 9 July 1942

. . . Yesterday I had lunch with Kiep, then had coffee with him and Jowo and Inge in Derfflingerstrasse. Peter came at 5 to fetch me from the Office and stayed till 7. König, Rösch's secretary, came at 7.15; he brought the news on Friday that our friend in Freiburg[4] has a constant shadow, so that

1. Wurm, Gröber, Faulhaber.
2. Hans Christoph Freiherr von Stauffenberg—cf. letters and nn. of 1 September 1941 and 20 and 21 September 1943.
3. Viktor Wolff, son of F.M.'s law professor Martin Wolff.
4. Archbishop Gröber—cf. n. 2 to letter of 30 June.

I can't see him on Sunday. This set us new problems, we discussed these until about 9 o'clock while we had a very good supper, and Frau Pick[1] was quite up to the unexpected visitor and in good humour into the bargain; and then we went on to Peter's. I wanted to inform him of the outcome of our discussions and moreover to ask him to keep an appointment Rösch made for me today. So the peaceful evening I had planned didn't happen and it was 11.30 before I was in bed.—I shall travel to Freiburg on Saturday but shall only see Rösch and settle everything through him on the spot.

Today—in 10 minutes—I'm going to lunch with Gramsch, and I wonder what I'll hear there. Tonight I'm going to visit Einsiedel in order to take counsel there with him and C.D. I want to set them a joint task which proved to be necessary after the talks with Friedrich and Company.

Just now Borsig was here, to talk about something. This morning I talked to Hans Adolf and it seems as if the matter[2] will move ahead once more.

Berlin, 10 July 1942

Yesterday's lunch at the Gramsches' was nice. I find her a particularly nice woman, and I was the only guest, so that we were able to talk in peace. He looked tired and has had considerable setbacks in his job because of Speer's rise, and, after 7 years of real power, sees himself more or less shelved and living on his past greatness. But he was in good spirits all the same. Both of them are very religious, and they were obviously impressed by the possibilities I saw there. After all, I have been living so much in this way of thinking that I am always surprised when somebody tells me that this is new and interesting. . . .

At 8 I went to Einsiedel's, where C.D. was, too. We talked till 12 and I think we made clearly discernible progress.[3] Luckily Einsiedel had made coffee and it sustained me. At 1 I was at Nikolassee, dead tired, and slept well till 6.

Today I'm having lunch with Trott, and then we'll both go to Peter's, from where I want to go to my own office and then early to bed; I must get a good night's sleep once this week. Yet I feel well and cheerful and it is only my reason that drives me to bed early. . . .

---

1. New housekeeper at Derfflingerstrasse.
2. Making Kreisau and Wernersdorf into entailed estates (*Erbhöfe*). Cf. letter of 11 June.
3. In the preparation of the discussion of questions of economic policy at the next Kreisau meeting.

Berlin, 11 July 1942

... Yesterday I had lunch at Trott's and afterwards A.T. & I went out to Peter's to discuss further plans. Nothing particularly new came of it, except that we decided, following my preliminary discussion with C.D. & Einsiedel on Thursday evening, to organize a week-end at Behnitz July 19 without me for these two, Peter, & Schmölders,[1] because we have to make further progress with the subject we got stuck on at Easter before the October days. ...

Berlin, 13 July 1942

Yesterday I didn't write because it was simply impossible. I left here at 9.11 and at 7.30 R.[2] met me at Karlsruhe; the train was an hour late. The night was not very productive, for at first I hadn't been able to sleep, and after I'd taken a pill the train shook so badly that I woke up several times and woke up for good at 5.30.

R. took me to breakfast at one of the branches they[3] have there and again I had a splendid breakfast. In particular there was delicious apple jelly. The talks showed in three hours that there were quite a number of difficulties with Gröber, partly psychological, partly only technical. The technical ones, of course, don't matter, because they can be overcome; the important ones are psychological. R. may have made a mistake, it seems to me, in his presentation to G.; G. felt taken by surprise and retreated behind the technical difficulties. It was therefore very necessary that I clear up this matter. We have, I think, found a way out that will bring us back to the right path, albeit with difficulty.

Meeting such an obstacle is always an important moment and gives one an opportunity to clarify one's own opinions and methods, which one doesn't get when things run smoothly. But the main thing is that one must always be able to overcome the difficulties. Unfortunately we haven't got that far yet, and the tension will continue for some time.

At any rate, by 11 we'd got to the point where we were quite clear how to proceed and, as I had a train at 12, they quickly gave me something to eat—again quite excellent, with currant ice cream at the end and coffee and cake, and R.'s secretary went off to Munich to carry out our agree-

1. Günter Schmölders, economist, friend of Yorck's. He took part in several discussions of the Kreisauers in 1942–43 and contributed a memorandum on post-war economic policy in a European bloc.
2. Rösch.
3. The Jesuits.

ment, and I went off to Berlin. As you see, there wasn't a minute the entire day when I could have written. . . .

Gerstenmaier & Peter are coming tonight to prepare for the talks with Wurm. Tomorrow Poelchau is having lunch with me, in the evening Friedrich & Uncle at Peter's to continue the Big Battle. Steltzer is coming on Wednesday; he just phoned from Helsinki; Zitzewitz is also supposed to come on Wednesday. So the week will be very lively. . . .

In the *Parliamentary Debates* of 8 May, I think, Henry Brooke[1] occurs. Also a poem is quoted which was sent to an M.P. by an unknown soldier. I'll copy it for you:

> Costers have died that culture shall remain,
> And country lads for freedom on the seas,
> Who saw no ships before they went to fight,
> And derelicts have died for decencies,
> And outcast men have perished to maintain
> The Christian faith against the powers of might.
>
> Oh, that the nation with one voice could say,
> "This time the land you save shall be your own,
> This time, at last, the good rich English soil
> Shall yield to those whose hands have made it pay,
> Yourselves shall profit by what you have grown
> And harvests shall belong to those who toil."

Berlin, 14 July 1942

. . . So last night we had our conversation with Wurm's man, Gersten-maier. It showed that he thought it was not good to have preliminary talks with Wurm so long before the main conversation; we should make it easy for W. and hold the meetings no more than 10 days apart. Result: we want the first meeting between W. and me between 7 & 10 August and the meeting of the three between 10 & 15 August. Gröber is to come between these two. In these circumstances it seems to me that I should change my leave, officially start it on 11 August, make myself scarce in the evening of the 6th, and come back on the 25th or 30th. I must wait till Oxé is back, and then I want to talk it over with him.

Poelchau is coming to lunch today. He is to familiarize himself with the

---

1. Henry Brooke (born 1903), cousin of Michael Balfour; conservative Member of Parliament 1938–45 and 1950–66, Minister of Housing 1957–61, Home Secretary 1962–64, Life Peer 1966.

question of restitution[1] and I want to see him in that connection. But quite apart from that I want to hear what he's been doing. . . .

Berlin, 15 July 1942

. . . Yesterday's lunchtime conversation with Poelchau was satisfactory. He asked if we could come together to visit him and his wife when you are here. The boy he wants to send us is called Loebell and will probably not come before the end of the month, because he is still at Wolfgang-see.—The evening with the Uncle lasted until midnight again, but yielded quite considerable progress. We have got as far as we wanted, namely that the Uncle will send us a delegate[2] for October. We skated across a few things still, but a broad basis for further work has been gained. And that means a quite important step forward. . . .

Berlin, 31 July 1942

. . . The other things you told me didn't sound too bad. The worst is the loss of fodder in the silos and the poor yield of milk. With clover and Landsberg Mix it should be possible to improve it. I can't quite see the reason for Zeumer's money worries. He must have got the money for the pigs, that was roughly RM 5,000; he must be able now to raise money from early potatoes, and the peak period for wages for sugar-beet hoeing must be past. In any case he should buy the horses if he can get them. I am prepared to give him the money for that separately. How far have the men in the cowshed got? Oh, I'd like to come as soon as possible and to see everything for myself. How do the beets look? In this humidity the lice can't have made much progress. And are the potatoes reasonably clean?

Yesterday, then, there was the big discussion with Maass & me at Friedrich's. Peter, unfortunately, wasn't able to come with us. The result was satisfactory. Maass is pedantic, somewhat like a schoolmaster,[3] a difficult partner in conversation, outstandingly knowledgeable in his own special

1. Cf. letter of 1 July.
2. Hermann Maass (1897–1944), Social Democrat; 1924–33 General Secretary of the Reich Committee of German Youth Associations and editor-in-chief of the monthly *Das Junge Deutschland*; then ran a small aluminium works with Leuschner and cooperated with him politically; like Leuschner in contact with the military opposition. Took part in the second meeting at Kreisau. Arrested August 1944, sentenced to death 20 October 1944. Cf. van Roon, *Resistance to Hitler*, pp. 121–24.
3. Maass had indeed studied philosophy, psychology, and sociology after serving in the First World War, then qualified as a teacher before qualifying as a social worker.

field, imbued with great seriousness & sense of responsibility, well prepared. He fits in well with the general political line and at Kreisau he will
be the ideal representative of Uncle. This evening Friedrich & Delp[1]
came to a meeting at my place, tomorrow lunchtime it will be Delp &
Maass at Peter's. . . .

Berlin, 1 August 1942

. . . Yesterday I had lunch with Hans Adolf. It all seems to be going
quite well and H.A. thinks that all changes in the register will be com-
pleted by the 1st of October.[2] Well, I am very curious.

In the evening Delp & König came from Munich, in fact directly from
seeing the Bishop of Fulda.[3] First I explained the overall concept for an
hour, and at 7 Friedrich & Peter joined us. We had an excellent meal:
soup, gorgeous mixed vegetables and potatoes, fruit, and coffee. At about
8.30 the serious work began, at 9.30 we got into our serious difficulties,
and after another hour the deadlock was broken, and when we parted at
12 we had achieved a great success. I think that the necessary basis for
confidence has been created between these people, so that progress can
be made, which is all the more necessary as Delp came charged by the
three Bishops, Faulhaber, Pr.,[4] and Dietz, to invite Friedrich & me to the
meeting. The technical aspect: we postponed everything to the end of
the month because it seemed better to us after hearing the reasons related
to us. Thus I don't need to travel at all now but hope to arrive home at the
end of this week. Friedrich, too, is departing on Wednesday, so that we
get a breathing space and the others, that is, Delp & Maass & C.D., have
to work. I am a bit fed up, too, and my head is spinning. Now that the
essential thing, namely that meetings will be held, has been settled, I feel
tired and am pushing for the stable.

At lunchtime today we are meeting at Peter's. Maass will also be there,
and we'll talk chiefly—rather, only—about the preparation for Kreisau.

1. Alfred Delp, S.J. (1907–45), contributed work on social questions to the Kreisau Circle.
He had taught at Jesuit colleges and published, inter alia, on Martin Heidegger. Priest 1937,
worked on the Jesuit monthly *Stimmen der Zeit* until its suppression in 1941, especially on
social questions; since 1940 also engaged in the Mission to Men. Rector of St. Georg in
Munich-Bogenhausen. Took part in the second and third meetings at Kreisau. Arrested 28
July 1944, took his last vows in prison despite Gestapo threats, tried with M. (see letter of
10 January 1945), executed 2 February 1945. See van Roon, *Resistance to Hitler*, pp. 75–81.
2. To make Kreisau and Wernersdorf into *Erbhöfe* (cf. n. 2 [p. 232] to letter of 9 July).
3. Johannes Baptista Dietz (1879–1959), Bishop of Fulda 1939–59; chairman of the Committee for Religious Orders (see n. 2 to letter of 6 September 1941).
4. Preysing.

There will be a pause in the evening. Tomorrow morning at 10 there is a meeting Delp & Trott on the foreign-policy section, tomorrow at 2 it will once more be the turn of Friedrich & Delp & Peter & me to concert the war plan in the higher spheres and to fix it finally. Sunday evening Trott & Friedrich & I on the foreign-policy part. Then in the coming week there is still a plan to have meetings C.D. & Maass and C.D. & Delp. And then I'm coming home.

Berlin, 2 August 1942

... Yesterday there was another one of those dramatic discussions which are intended to weld together the gentlemen from Munich and Uncle's men. At 2 we had lunch at Peter's, and things started at 3. The good Maass again regaled us with professorial disquisitions lasting 90 minutes: dry, humourless, full of banalities. The rest of us slept through long stretches of the lecture, Peter and I quite shamelessly, and Friedrich kept losing his cigar, which had gone cold, from his mouth; this woke him up every time, he'd look at me, laugh, pick it up, sleep again until he lost it anew. But in those 90 minutes we nevertheless came to realize that here a man was speaking who really had something to say about the condition of the workers; and during the 90 minutes there were high points when we all listened, with close attention, and many a pearl was hidden among the banalities. But, anyway, I won't let him get away with such discourses at Kreisau.

Then for an hour nothing seemed to move at all, and suddenly, around 6, everything went at a gallop; the point we agreed to regard as the test of mutual good faith had been found, for 10 minutes Delp & Maass spoke the same language even if the content differed; and then Delp suggested writing down the respective theses quite briefly and exchanging them before going on. Then we stopped. Both parties are to consult their chiefs and on 22/23 August we are to have the exchange of theses here.

I believe it could not have gone better and I am convinced that there will be agreement on the 22/23rd. But the conflict, the antithesis is right and necessary.

This now determines further procedure. The Bxxxx[1] have been postponed to the 24th and 26th of August. This means the following schedule: I'll come home now as soon as possible, how soon I can come I don't know yet. In the evening of the 21st we are unfortunately meeting here again, on the 22nd and 23rd we have meetings here: Uncle & Maass & Friedrich versus Rösch & Delp & König. On the evening of the 23rd Delp

1. First "bishops," then except for the "B" made virtually illegible.

& Friedrich and I will travel to Bamberg to the Bxxxx, on the 25th Friedrich and I to Heidelberg. You, too, will travel to Heidelberg on the 25th, on the 26th there is the meeting with W.[1] in Heilbronn,[2] then you and I do the tour of the fruit farms, and in the evening of the 28th we'll be in Godesberg, from where I'll return to Berlin during the night of 30/31st. We still need the approval of the Bxxxx for this programme and then everything will be set. That will give me about two weeks at Kreisau, after all.

This morning there is a pause and at 2 we'll continue without Peter, to prepare for the meetings at Bamberg with Delp + Friedrich. I must therefore settle down to work at once and prepare drafts of texts. That will take until about 7, then F. is eating with me and we'll bicycle at 8 to Trott's; he at last wants to discuss his foreign-policy questions.

Well, now I've had enough of dramatic discussions. I can't hear about all that stuff any more. The point of departure I was looking for at Whitsun[3] has now been found, after much to and fro, and I must put it all out of my head for a while. I'll look forward all the more to Kreisau.

Berlin, 3 August 1942

I wasn't quite finished with my work yesterday when the people came at 2. We worked until about 7, then the out-of-towners had to catch their train. Friedrich still had some rendezvous; I had supper and got my bike ready, and at 7.45 Friedrich & I met at Olivaer Platz to bicycle out to Trott's. It was an enjoyable ride; the streets were empty, the asphalt is marvellously easy to ride on, it was a little close, but to make up for it the air still had the fragrance of the flowering late-summer linden trees. At 8 we were there, had a talk which I thought very satisfactory, and departed again at 12; at 12.30 I was home. The ride back was really even more beautiful, for it was cooler, and yet warm, an enchanting summer night. I thought how much nicer it would be at home now. . . .

Berlin, 6 September 1942

Hans rang up yesterday at 5 and said he'd just arrived from Rome by plane and was going to travel on the same night to U[pper] S[ilesia] and asked if he could eat with me. We made an appointment for 8 o'clock. At 8.15 he turned up, quite distraught. He'd had a telegram from Holzinger

---

1. Wurm.
2. First "Stuttgart," crossed out.
3. At the first Kreisau meeting.

that Josefa[1] had had an accident and might not live; he had telephoned Jack[2] and then Frau Holzinger, who told him what I told you this morning. He asked for another call to this number; it came about 9 and Frau Holzinger thought he should come because today would decide whether the child was going to live. So he left for Frankfurt at 10.30. I hope it won't affect his work in Rome[3] badly for he had an appointment in U[pper] S[ilesia] with a very important man from Genoa, who has to travel back on Wednesday.

Yesterday at midday I worked till 2 and then went to Herr Becker's for a haircut and didn't have to wait long. By 2.45 I was back at home, thanks to lucky connections, and made myself something to eat. Frau Cohn had not done anything more: Cohn's parents (76 & 72 years old) and his brother and sister-in-law, as well as the (82-year-old) proprietress of the house next door, where the Führer's Adjutant, Schmundt, lives, will be deported tomorrow, and that had understandably plunged the Cohns into total dismay. It was too much misfortune at once. . . .

From among the fruits of my reading I enclose a cutting from *The Times*. We call the stuff Cyankali.[4] . . .

Berlin, 7 September 1942

. . . Reichwein was rather tired. They have been without a maid for 4 months and his wife, with her 4 children, is at the end of her strength.— Otherwise the conversation was quite productive and he has been put in harness again.—This evening I'm going to visit Gerstenmaier.

Josefa's death should be considered only from the point of view of Hans and Dick. I am very worried that Dick may not stand up to it, may blame herself, and be seriously harmed. There is a war on, and one must digest and forget such accidents as quickly as possible, because one needs one's strength for other things. I'm also worried, of course, that Hans may now devote himself too much to his family and won't understand the point of view of the people who are waiting for his work.

Granny's letter is splendid. I'm getting it copied and shall send it to Jowo.

1. Hans and Dick Deichmann's little daughter had scalded herself and died.
2. Dick Deichmann's sister, Jackie Vlielander-Hein, another old friend of the Schwarzwald days, who lived in Holland. She later spent some months in jail for helping Jews.
3. His work with the Italian resistance.
4. Potassium cyanide; presumably a report about deportations, perhaps on mass killings by gas—cf. letter of 10 October—or about suicides.

Berlin, 8 September 1942

Today is the Angel's[1] birthday.—Last night was very nice and also productive. One has to take trouble with Gerstenmaier, who does not easily fit into a convenient category; but it is worth the effort, and if it were possible to integrate him fully, it would be a considerable step forward. He is newly married and has a nice wife[2] of Baltic origin. I took the opportunity to learn something about various questions of dogmatic theology and church history, as, for instance, the present significance of the Council of Trent and the Augsburg Confession, the position of Karl Barth,[3] and so on. It was certainly instructive. . . .

Peters has just been to see me. As ever an innocent angel above the waters. Curious how he manages that. His reports from the Air Command and of a telephone conversation with Hermann[4] were shocking as always. But otherwise there was nothing special. . . .

Berlin, 9 September 1942

. . . About me there is nothing important to report. I slept very badly last night and don't know why. I thought about Michael[5] for hours. I fell asleep after 5 and only woke up at 8. That cramped my day. I had lunch with Haeften, who was very nice again. He is an engagingly intelligent man, calm and upright. The atmosphere around him is so clear.

Now it is 4.20. Konrad[6] expects me at 5. I am quite keyed up about this first conversation after an interval of 2 months. He always gives me good tea and after my poor night I look forward to that too. In the evening I want to stay at home by myself. There is a silly job I have to do, and I must finish it before my departure, and tonight is the only chance. I hope nothing interferes. . . .

1. His youngest brother, often nicknamed "Engel," would have been twenty-nine.
2. Brigitte, née von Schmidt.
3. Karl Barth (1886–1968), Swiss theologian, important figure in the first phase of the German church struggle and the formation of the Confessing Church; relinquished his professorship in Bonn and returned to Basel, where he taught from 1935 on.
4. Göring.
5. He had taken the opportunity of his earlier Scandinavian trip to send a letter to Michael Balfour from Sweden, proposing a later meeting in Stockholm. Balfour did not get the necessary permission—see Michael Balfour and Julian Frisby, *Helmuth von Moltke: A Leader Against Hitler* (London, 1972), p. 186.
6. Preysing.

Berlin, 10 September 1942

. . . Regarding your plans, please think of the following: I would suggest that you don't depart from Kreisau until the 24th. I'll return to Berlin
on the 24th, so that we would meet here. Above all that gives you a whole
week with Schmidt-Rottluff and, despite the accident,[1] it would be rather
unfriendly to leave immediately after his arrival. It won't make such a
great difference to Dick,[2] because knowing you are coming will
strengthen her in any case, and a week sooner or later can't make a real
difference.—But, even then, leave yourself a margin of several days, because I'm considering cancelling the week-end 25/26 September altogether. I'll tell you the reasons later.[3] Then I wanted to come to Kreisau
that week-end and then I'd be in favour of your only coming with me
on the 27th. I'll talk about it to Hans and you can then talk about it at
Heydebreck.[4]

Yesterday was very satisfactory. I told you about the nice lunch with
Haeften. In the afternoon I was at Behrenstrasse. It was very satisfactory
and edifying, although the poor man[5] is so badly affected by the misery
of the times that he is seriously ill once more. But we had spent 2 stimulating and useful hours when I left him at 7.

. . . Fritzi[6] turned up at 8, in excellent form. I've never had such a stimulating talk with him, so without dispute. We went over the whole terrain,
discussed the reasons for my measures, and on the whole he was not only
satisfied, but even convinced of the necessity of certain things he had
originally disliked. We then talked about Russia; he fully agreed with me
and even went further and, for instance, said spontaneously that "the
relationship between officers and men in the Red Army is really exemplary and almost impossible to achieve." In all other respects, too, we
were in agreement concerning the outcome, even if at times we differed
in our diagnoses. Thus he attributed much that I considered the result of
education to the innate good qualities of the Russians. Before we had
finished there was an air-raid alert and he stayed with me for the night
and slept in Carl's bed. I don't think that's so terrible. . . .

1. Cf. letter of 6 September.
2. Hans Deichmann's wife (who had also belonged to the Schwarzwald circle).
3. The planned second meeting at Kreisau was postponed to October.
4. Polish Kandrczin, terminus of the Kreisau rail line and an I. G. Farben installation.
5. Preysing.
6. Schulenburg.

Berlin, 11 September 1942

As I'm sending this letter by Hans, I'll write briefly about the week-end 26/27 September. I'm not satisfied with the preparation; it is not good enough or ripe enough, and I don't want to risk a flop. The whole thing is too dangerous for that. Moreover, since there will be no meeting at Kleinöls[1] now, I want to suggest to Peter that we cancel September and postpone the subject to October and deal with both then. That must be possible. Special security considerations argue for concentration. That frees the week-end, and since I had reserved this week-end, I really want to come home. I did, after all, ask to be free that Friday and Saturday. . . .

There is nothing new. North Africa is rather worrying and in the East there seems to be a standstill—at Stalingrad as well as in the Caucasus. But I still assume that Stalingrad will probably fall, because tactically the position of the Russians—having to supply a big army across rivers where they can be attacked by artillery and from the air—is frightfully difficult. In the Pacific the American preponderance becomes clearer all the time, in the Mediterranean as well, and in the Arctic that of the British.—The Russian planes which keep favouring us with visits mainly put down agents. . . .

Berlin, 14 September 1942

. . . It is 11 at night. First Trott & Haeften came, at 7.30 Frl. Breslauer for some dictation, and at 8 Hofmann, who has just left. We had a good evening and were able to see that some progress had been made.

Today was incredible. Nothing went right with my travel papers, and I had to pursue the matter all day long. But what was much worse was that I had to get some quite critical affairs to the point where nothing can go wrong with them while I am away. So I worked like mad today. In between there were talks with Guttenberg, Kiep, & Gerstenmaier. I don't care for such days. . . .

I keep thinking of the farm and about all the potential for improvement and reorganization. How pleasant it would be if I could occupy myself with that rather than this rubbish I have to do. . . .

Oslo, 17 September 1942

. . . We could still see the estuary of Oslo Fjord, but then it began to pour. We saw the water close below us, then a house, a garden, a few

1. The planned meeting at the Yorck estate.

trees, beside us houses and gardens close enough to touch and to the right and left above us through shreds of cloud bits of rocks and woods. That wasn't exactly cosy. But then came the landing, and it was horrid. Just before the airfield the machine suddenly dropped into a hole, the pilot had to rev up the engines again to get as far as the airfield, and that made us overshoot; after the wheels were already rolling he decided to take off again, and the landing only succeeded the second time and even then only with difficulty. The airport is very small for these big machines, and we suddenly found ourselves on the edge of it. But all went well. Naturally I was the only one with an umbrella and therefore the only one who arrived dry. The others, headed by a Waffen-SS general who was being met by another one, were nicely drenched before they reached their cars.

After I had unpacked and eaten, St[eltzer] and I visited our friends,[1] with whom we talked for 2 hours; we staked out the field and made a plan of campaign for the week. Once again I was impressed by these men: good, determined, sound. At 6 I was back at my base, changed, read a little, ate at 7.30 at the table of the C.-in-C.,[2] who disappeared to the cinema with all his people after the meal, while St. & I talked until about 10. I was tired and went to bed very soon, but only slept moderately well.

St. is much better. He has picked up again, has red cheeks, and is in good spirits. He has meanwhile had news from his son who was taken prisoner in Africa & is now in Canada. He will come to Kreisau on 15 October. With me the C.-in-C. is very friendly; I eat entirely at his table, which is otherwise shared only by gentlemen with red stripes on their trousers. That is very welcome to me, because it automatically legitimates my presence & facilitates my entrée to various people I have to see. I'll ask him for an official appointment for tomorrow afternoon and hope that it will go so well that I can reappear here in 6 months' time without much ado. The most important man for me, the Ic,[3] Lt. Col. Worgitzki, is very nice, obliging, curiously unmilitary for a hard-boiled General Staffer. He has assigned an orderly officer to me, a Herr von Löbbecke, as a bear-leader and guide, and since I make no use of him, everything is very friendly, even cordial. Otherwise these people are very isolated here and learn very little of the rest of the world, so that they are quite pleased to hear something.—The Ia,[4] Herr von Lossberg, I know well enough for relations to be easy. We haven't had a talk about official business yet. This

1. Cf. n. 1 (p. 214) to letter of 17 April.
2. Falkenhorst.
3. Intelligence Officer.
4. First Staff Officer (Operations).

time the greatest effort has gone into winning over the new chief of staff, General Bamler.[1] He is ice-cold and not altogether pleasant, but very intelligent, at any rate the most intelligent man at the whole table. I want to establish myself here in such a way that my occasional appearances are regarded as natural events needing no explanation.

Wednesday morning I started on the real work and collected material from all those less important people with whom one has to be on good terms. It kept me on the move until lunchtime. Lunch took such a long time that I only just managed to be ready for an appointment with our friends at 3.30, and I went alone. It was in a new flat with beautiful furniture. Most of it French, but in excellent taste. The conversation lasted till 7.15; it was really the first working session of the young people among themselves. Then I had supper with one of St.'s closest collaborators, Herr Schauer,[2] and talked with him until 10. The next big meeting with the older men was at 10.30, with St. on my side vis-à-vis the others. It went on till 2 a.m. and was strenuous and fruitful. It showed that the documents we drew up for discussion in August[3] were considered a sensation of the first order here, which naturally pleased me very much. We were back home at 2.30.

This morning at 9 there was a long meeting at the Reich Commissar's Office, and from 11 on I joined in the general amusements. There are two Swedish officers here and the German military attaché in Stockholm, General von Utzmann. They have to be entertained and I joined the entertainment, because all the red-trouser types I needed were also taking part. At 11 we drove up the Holmenkollen, a mountain above Oslo Fjord; there we walked briskly for an hour. At 1 there was a good lunch with these people and then a motor tour along fjords and lakes. It was an enchanting drive: an autumn sun shone in the glass-clear air, some clouds animated the sky, the fjords lay motionless at our feet, the woods had their first autumn colour. Then we had coffee in a requisitioned villa with a fantastic view. The house was well built with very beautiful rooms, an enchanting view of a part of Oslo Fjord full of steamers, sailing ships, boats, fishing vessels, warships. The one disgusting thing was the feeling

---

1. Rudolf Bamler, early Nazi and friend of Heydrich; 1933–39 head of Abwehr Group III for espionage and counter-espionage; during the attack on Russia, chief of General Staff of the 47th Army Corps; 1942–44 chief of General Staff of Army Command Norway. June 1944 taken prisoner in Russia as commander of an infantry division; 22 July 1944 signed the appeal of the generals and commanders of Army Group Centre to cease fighting and to terminate Hitler's regime and the war. After the war Bamler had a successful career in East Germany as, e.g., Inspector General of the People's Police.
2. Dr. Friedrich Schauer, a parson in civilian life.
3. Cf. letters of 14 July and 1 and 2 August.

of having entered a stranger's house, to sit there like thieves, while the owner, as I knew, sat in a concentration camp. I thought of Herr Serpuchov[1] and this put the whole affair under a cloud. Now it was 6. After an hour's talk with St. I changed, am now writing, as you see, and shall then eat with 2 nice people who work under Worgitzki, the afore-mentioned Löbbecke and a Major Hammersen.[2] So I'm deserting my distinguished table. In the evening I absolutely have to get some work done. . . .

Stockholm, 22 September 1942

I have been here since yesterday morning and am quite enchanted by this city. I'll enclose lots of picture postcards and, if I get a large enough envelope, a map of the city too. It is just a wonderful, beautiful, charming, lively, and hypermodern big city. As soon as you look at the map you can see how elaborately formed the city is by all the water. There is water everywhere and everywhere there are ships, bridges, piers, everywhere there is the life of a port. If, in addition, you imagine that all the terrain is rolling, and rocky, that therefore the city is built on rising terraces, you can picture the possibilities such a city offers. Here one recovers the sense that man's function is to beautify the world, that nature is to be brought to life and full effect by his hand. Steep cliffs tower amid the skyscrapers, the water is framed by woods of deciduous trees in the full glory of au-tumnal colour, and among the houses, none of them bad or ugly, one sees such gems as the Town Hall. Because it was built near the heart of the city in such a way that it is surrounded on three sides by water, one sees it everywhere: whether you arrive by train, or ride to the suburbs across the big bridge, or walk beside the Palace, or climb up and down the steep lanes of the Old City, you'll see the Town Hall or a part of it. It is truly a symbol. But the Palace is beautiful too, the Knights' Hall is simply splen-did, the church beside the Knights' Hall is magnificent, with green cu-polas large and small and a curious tower. The flower market in the square with the Orpheus Fountain is a sight worth seeing; of course the square can't compare with the Grand Plaza in Brussels, but it is a nice detail—I can't remember a city that, as city, ever pleased me as much, except, perhaps, for London, though in another way.

The city is curiously open and wild. There is something untamed about it, it may be because of the rock which protrudes always and everywhere. Large rock surfaces in which paths have been cut laboriously, separate

1. Cf. letter of 7 January.
2. Fridjof Hammersen of the Ic (Intelligence) Section.

the parts of the city from each other. The water is not surrounded by houses; no, in many places the rocks rise steeply by the water or a bit of wood survives that is inaccessible between rock and water and has therefore not been built on. This brought so much air into the city.

I also like what I see of the people. I believe they are wicked, I don't think them good-natured. But they also have something of this wildness, this original freshness. Of course I know nothing about them. I only see them as they bicycle through the city, in thousands, by the tens of thousands: boys and men and old men, children, girls, women and ladies and old women; all ride bicycles and ride them well. There are bicycle stands all over the city, and thousands of bicycles stand beside the roads. It is hard to imagine. The girls are surprisingly nice to look at. There are also ugly ones, but very few who are not well groomed. I have my doubts about the women and girls here; from the outside, however, they are really nice to look at. There is odd colouring here: fair-haired with brown eyes, fair with black eyes, red with blue eyes. One gets the impression that "the fight for a man" is rather severe here and makes high demands.

There are wonderful schools here. When one sees them one asks oneself how one can send a child to a less good school. Of course I know nothing of the spirit of the schools, though the children make a particularly nice impression. I repeatedly pass two big schools. The athletic field and playground of the one is situated on a rock 10 m above a main traffic intersection where some 8 roads converge. One sees children playing there—girls and boys together—and yet the playground is separated from the town by a 10 m elevation. Occasionally I have time to watch because I have had to change and wait for connections. And how the schools are equipped: wonderful windows, beautiful workrooms, also craft rooms, ingenious arrangements for ventilation, carefully built according to the sun, gym halls built entirely of glass and protected against the cold by there always being two panes of glass with an insulating vacuum between them. You can recognize that glass. The entrances to the schools have been planned carefully so as to avoid accidents as far as possible. In short, you see, I walk about in amazement. I'm bold enough to say that nobody who has not seen this city can judge what a modern big city is and what it can offer. Every minute one comes upon so many details that one may not remember them, such as the regulation of traffic, the interior design of the buses, the general cleanliness, the good lifts, the installations for automatic waste disposal in all the houses—they don't have anything like garbage collection here—and so forth.

But enough of Stockholm. I now go on where I stopped, namely Tuesday evening. Friday morning I read files like one possessed. Nothing particularly new, but I had to read them. For lunch Steltzer tried to seduce me to eat with him and the Swedish officers at the villa in the outskirts;

but luckily I remained firm, so I ate alone with the Generaloberst,[1] General Bamler, and Lossberg, the Ia; and Bamler invited me to drive with him after lunch to the villa, where Steltzer had meanwhile gone for a motor-boat cruise. So, for two hours we simply made conversation there, and that was very useful from my point of view. Perhaps I brought something or other home to him, but most importantly he asked me to be sure to come again from time to time, as such a talk was so stimulating. Thus I hope the man most dangerous to me up there is now mildly disposed to me. I still don't like him, but he is an intelligent man, with whom one can work. After my return I talked with Worgitzki and all the other Ic people from 4 till 6.30, gave and explained my assessments, got their approval, and also got their assurance that they'd be glad to see me back here occasionally and to hear something from the other commands. In the evening we all sat together, the others then went to a film, and I went with Steltzer, who had meanwhile returned from his motor-boat cruise, to see our friends. Pleasant surprises awaited us there: some personal,[2] but above all a material one: namely a downright princely dinner with a main dish of white grouse,[3] which I felt to be very tactful towards myself. On this occasion I learnt that white grouse and Scottish grouse are identical—a thing I never knew before. The evening went on till 2 a.m. and in conclusion St. and I had a short final talk, because he had to leave for Bergen the next morning.

I was thoroughly tired, but all the same got up at 7 and by 8.30 I had packed and breakfasted. This proved to be very necessary, for on this Saturday morning, which was really only meant for tidying up, there was so much to do that I only got through with my tongue hanging out. The core was an hour-long conversation with the Generaloberst, for whom I now really feel some warmth. He is truly stupid, but to make up for it he is free of so many faults that usually adorn his colleagues that I silently beg his forgiveness for much that I thought about him before.—I got to the airport at the last minute, everyone was already seated in the plane, including, again, the SS general who had provoked me so on the trip out—incidentally, by nothing more than his face and the back of his neck—when your husband, with open umbrella, avoiding the puddles, walked slowly past a guard of higher SS officers and climbed into the plane. Off we went again, through this fjord in the rain, but gradually the weather cleared, and when we crossed the Danish coast it was very fine.

By 5 I was in town at last; first I registered at a hotel and did my official

1. Falkenhorst.
2. The company included Bishop Berggrav, who was officially under house arrest.
3. The moorhen, closely related to the white grouse, was the heraldic animal of the Moltke family crest.

business, then I looked for Merete,[1] who was not in Copenhagen. I finally reached Kim[2] and learnt that she [Merete] was ½ hour away in the country. That's where I went on Sunday. She was there with her mother, holidaying in the house of a tenant of a Count Holstein. We took a very nice walk through Lederborg Park, which is very beautiful and surrounds a really magnificent house. The fields looked sad because masses of totally wet grain were still standing outside, ruined by the rain. What was interesting was that all the animals were kept in paddocks surrounded by electric fences. There were even little paddocks made on harvested fields. Merete was nice as ever but had nothing special. At 3 I went back to town, had tea with Kim and his wife, and at 6.45 left for Stockholm via Helsingör and arrived next morning, Monday, at 8.15 after a well-spent night in a splendid sleeper.

So, my love, enough for today; I must go.

Berlin, 28 September 1942

Again it was lovely with you, my heart, and everything in the three days gave me such joy and happiness. But I am especially glad to know that you and the two sons are well and I can only hope that it will continue. I was especially glad, too, that Schmidt-Rottluff's visit had been a success and that you liked not only the man but also the pictures of Kreisau. I do think that only a good picture is worth owning, because one gets tired of any other.

After your departure I went back to bed to do some thinking, because it seemed to me so cold and inhospitable outside. Then I got up, finished the tea, and went to the Office in my winter coat. At the Office it was freezing cold. . . .

Berlin, 29 September 1942

. . . My lumbago is much better. I hope it will soon be gone. I was just saying to Peter, whose sciatica is now starting up, what an imposing pair we'll make on the 18th of October.[3] We agreed on the reduction in numbers and tomorrow I'll write to Uncle Cle,[4] definitely calling him off. Meanwhile I've talked with Friedrich. He claims that, after the progress

1. Merete Bonnesen.
2. Merete Bonnesen's brother, civil servant in the Ministry for Social Affairs; he had also been a member of the Schwarzwald circle.
3. At the second Kreisau meeting.
4. Clemens Busch, uncle of F.M.

of the last 10 days, he could manage without Reichwein. All this will be clearer by the time you come through here.

F. had a little cold, had stayed in bed yesterday, and came to me in the evening. Otherwise he was better off. He's got used to the new situation and has come to terms with it. For the first time he was satisfied with his people's progress. They seem to have had heavy fighting but the keystone is to be put in place Wednesday night. F. & Uncle are to appear here Thursday or Friday. I am very curious. . . .

Berlin, 30 September 1942

. . . I was able to spend the whole morning on my report on the talks in Stockholm and get it behind me. It will be typed tomorrow, then covering letters have to be written, and that will be all for this part. The report on Oslo will be much more difficult. I want to do it over the week-end, for it cannot be done in half a day and I won't have a whole day. At my office there is only one more big job. . . .

Today Guttenberg is having lunch with me, I am with Conrad at 4.30, C.D. & Einsiedel are coming to me at 8 and seem to have done their work very well. Kiep is coming to lunch tomorrow, Steltzer at 5, he will probably stay for the evening, when Friedrich & Uncle will probably come. Perhaps we'll have the party at Hortensienstrasse. . . .

Berlin, 1 October 1942

. . . In the afternoon I visited Conrad for 2½ hours. He was in reasonably good spirits though rather worn out by the times. He listened to my report with great interest and seemed quite satisfied. There was not much tangible result, but that was not intended. When is All Saints? I expect I'll go there again either next week or immediately after Kreisau. Poelchau was also there yesterday afternoon. He said that Löbell liked Kreisau very much although the work had taken it out of him. I was glad to hear it. Otherwise Poelchau had unpleasant news: police, school, and the Jewish question. In the next few days 14 Norwegians are to be shot; saving them would have been rather important. . . .

Berlin, 2 October 1942

. . . Yesterday I had lunch with Kiep. He was nice and amiable but it didn't lead to anything in particular. In fact the general pessimism is astonishingly deep-seated and seems to have a grip now on the working class. Only the bourgeoisie seems to close its eyes resolutely to the facts.

Reichwein turned up at 3 p.m. to tell me about an internal discussion of their own on Wednesday evening, with renewed setbacks, but finally leading after all to the desired result. After him came Peter, who had had other things to attend to all week, so that I had to bring him up to date. Because he really must do a little work with Einsiedel & C.D. during the coming week.

In the evening Steltzer came, at 7, well & rested. He had to deliver some things to me and wanted to collect news, especially about Stockholm. Friedrich then appeared at 9 and we had a very good plum tart which Frau Pick had made, and tea. F. reported fully on Wednesday evening, which must have been very funny, because he groaned terribly about M.[1] It seemed to be quite entertaining for St. too. Then we assigned jobs and dispersed at midnight. St. I'll now see only on the train on the 15th. F. not until the 21st . . .

Berlin, 3 October 1942

. . . My days feel curiously light. I feel and see and hear progress, and that makes the days easy as they've never been before for me. And I'm not at all impatient and don't expect anything around the next corner. It is only the certainty of being on the right path and on a path that leads somewhere.

Yesterday I wrote a letter of admonition to Konrad.[2] Funny that something like that, which would still have frightened me a few months ago, should now be quite a matter of course. By a lucky coincidence our friend from Munich[3] came last night; I showed it to him and he broke into a storm of approval. Now Karl Ludwig[4] will deliver it today. I wonder if it will have an effect.

Reichwein was here for lunch. Not very well but in good spirits; he had rather interesting things to tell from the Warthegau,[5] where he has to spend a lot of time now. His wife has now got a Ukrainian girl, and I hope that that will lighten her load a little. He says one notable thing is the incredible cleanliness of this girl of only 15. She doesn't touch a saucepan, fruit, loaf of bread, etc., without first washing her hands.

Topf arrived at 6. He was at Stalingrad until 23 August and had been in the advance across the Don. His reports were rather interesting, optimistic on the whole, but he was at a total loss for an explanation of the

1. Maass.
2. Preysing.
3. Rösch or König.
4. Guttenberg.
5. Part of Poland attached to Germany and made the field of advanced experiments in National Socialist policy, especially anti-church policy.

lack of real progress. He said that, in view of the situation on 23 August and his assessment of it at the time, developments in the month of September were incomprehensible. At 7 Trott arrived; I was to have supper with him, but Keppler[1] had ordered him to a supper with some Indians. So he stayed with me till 8. At 8 our friend from Munich arrived, animated, animating, and in good spirits. One of his people is now in the military hospital in Schweidnitz. He says that the damage done in the air raid on Munich was middling, but the psychological effect tremendous.

There is peace here this morning. I must write the report on Norway and have therefore got out of everything else.—Outside it is beautiful and autumnal. From my window I can see the foliage of the Tiergarten changing colour. . . .

Berlin, 6 October 1942

I'm writing this to Kreisau although you are coming here tomorrow. Firstly because I'll see you only very briefly, and then because you'll have a letter on your first day home.

Yesterday Kadgien came to lunch and conveyed a rather pessimistic prognosis of our armaments production and that of the other side. The others, without Russia, now produce three times as much. And that includes everything on our side, i.e., occupied territories, Japan, Italy. And while for the others the trend is upward, ours has already turned down. This had been reported to Göring just before his speech.[2]

Guttenberg came after lunch to tell me that Konrad wanted me to know he'd taken my admonitions to heart. It was a load off my mind, because I'd been afraid he might take offence. . . .

In the evening I visited Gerstenmaier, who had just returned from Switzerland[3] and brought some things of interest. But we talked chiefly about the preparation for Kreisau. . . .

Berlin, 7 October 1942

Although I've only just put you on your train, I want to write at once, for who knows what the day will bring. I hope you'll have a good journey

1. Wilhelm Karl Keppler, Staatssekretär (Under-Secretary of State) for Special Tasks in the AA, among them supervision of the special Indian Section—see n. 2 to letter of 17 June.
2. At the Harvest Thanksgiving rally at the Sportpalast in Berlin on 4 October.
3. Because of his work at the Church Office for External Affairs, Gerstenmaier was able, without attracting too much attention, to see Hans Schönfeld, who worked at the Provisional World Council of Churches in Geneva—cf. n. 3 to letter of 30 June. Gerstenmaier had lost his AA employment in the early summer and had been taken under the wing of the Abwehr.

and no dangers to surmount. I was glad to see that you had a decent seat and that the children[1] were able to look out of the window.

My dear, what a lovely, if brief, visit it was; the only silly thing was that I didn't meet you properly. Well, it didn't make that much difference. You looked well to me and I hope this will continue. You have a massive week ahead of you, making arrangements for everything in a way that will allow you peace of mind for the occasion itself.[2] I hope everything works out again as well as at Whitsun. . . .

Berlin, 10 October 1942

. . . Yesterday's lunch was interesting in that the man I ate with had just come from the Government[3] and gave an authentic report on the "SS blast-furnace."[4] So far I had not believed it,[5] but he assured me that it was true: 6000 people a day are "processed" in this furnace. He was in a prison camp 6 km away, and the officers there reported it to him as absolute fact. They also told some quite fantastic stories about some of the gentlemen employed there.

In the afternoon there were meetings, so that I got no peace, and in the evening I was with Dohnanyi & Peters. Nice but without result. Dy. has become terribly sterile, and despite all one's liking for Peters, one has to rate his critical faculties higher than his faculties of synthesis. Still, it was necessary, and quite nice. Only the night was awfully short again. . . .

Berlin 11 October 1942

I'm sitting at the Office, unfortunately. It is a great nuisance, but another bad piece of nonsense has happened and now I want to prevent a

1. Maria and Thomas Deichmann.
2. The second meeting at Kreisau—cf. letter of 21 October.
3. Government General, the German-administered part of Poland, called Generalgouvernement Polen, set up by Hitler's Decree of 12 October 1939 and enlarged on 1 August 1941. Hans Frank, the Governor General, was sentenced to death at Nuremberg.
4. The Government General had three big death camps: Treblinka, Sobibor, and Belzec. After the installation of bigger gassing units in early October, Treblinka doubled its daily killing capacity to six thousand.
5. He had obviously heard unsubstantiated stories before—e.g., from his brother-in-law. Hans Deichmann had heard about the concentration (or labour) camp Auschwitz very early in a family (I. G. Farben) setting; in 1942 he visited it several times and saw emaciated prisoners, many of them wearing the Jewish star, and heard about a crematorium (Hans Deichmann, "Briefbericht," a privately circulated set of reports in the form of letters, 1977, and a letter to me of 18 December 1987).

complete collapse of my chiefs, who should attempt to extricate us once more from an impossible situation. It will cost the greater part of Sunday.

Yesterday I got to Peter's late; but then we had a profitable and useful conversation. It was very necessary, because so far this subject of the organization of the economy had been inadequately prepared. I now face this question more confidently and feel better about it.

Steltzer is coming tomorrow morning. I am very glad of that, for this way he will see Wurm, which is very important to me. So Monday and Tuesday will still be heavy days of preparation and then there will be an end of it. I am very curious how it will go. . . .

Berlin, 12 October 1942

. . . A violent storm has broken over a matter concerning prisoners of war.[1] After first doing all sorts of things without consulting us, they have to pull back, and now they consult us. I am glad of it, but it meant a stormy day and now I am in a great hurry and under great pressure.

This is the last letter, my love, and then I'm coming. I only wonder how it will all work out, because I am really afraid that the prisoner-of-war affair may detain me.

Today Hartenstein had lunch with me. He is a nice man, really. He's a bit recovered too and not as exhausted as he was two years ago.

Now I must hurry to my office, at 7 I have a course in air-raid precautions, and Trott comes at 9.15. Tomorrow morning we start with Canaris at 8.30 and there is quite a lot in the offing tomorrow otherwise. Tomorrow night I'm going to see Wurm with Steltzer and Friedrich.

Berlin, 21 October 1942

Your husband travelled splendidly. First I was alone in my compartment, then came a family with two boys aged about 3 & 6, who played in the compartment. But since I had a window seat, it didn't disturb me.

---

1. It may have been the shackling of prisoners of war—cf. n. 3 to letter of 10 December. In the British-Canadian attack on Dieppe on 19 August, German prisoners had been shackled. The Germans announced on 7 October that because of this, and because prisoners were also shackled in a raid on the Island of Sark on 4 October, all British soldiers taken prisoner at Dieppe would be shackled. The British protest pointed to Article 2 of the Geneva Convention. Nevertheless 1,376 British prisoners were shackled, whereupon the Canadian government ordered the shackling of the same number of German prisoners on 11 October. On 13 October Churchill told the House of Commons that the government had asked the Swiss as protecting power to protest against the violation of the Geneva Convention and to offer reciprocity if the Germans stopped their measures.

Approaching Berlin we had 30 minutes' delay but I was home by 2 and at the Office at 2.30, having eaten.

Ansembourg met me at the station and we went to the Reichshof, where we sat in a room alone and talked a bit. He chiefly wanted to unburden his soul. They cannot come to Kreisau. On the contrary, now Countess A. and her girl have been forbidden to go outside the town limits of Liegnitz. I offered to help him but he said they had everything except heat and hot water. He felt he was comparatively lucky, as all his acquaintances have now been deported and are in the camps Grüssau and Leubus with their families; I further told him to ask his wife whether you shouldn't some day pick up the children on your way through and take them to Kreisau for a few days.

The 7 o'clock train was not yet in when we parted; it was therefore a good thing that I had taken the earlier train.

Otherwise, my love, there is nothing at all to report yet, because I've only just arrived. With you it was, as always, lovely and you managed the 3 days[1] brilliantly. Our jubilee[2] was, to be sure, rather tumultuous, but it was memorable to make up for it.

Berlin, 22 October 1942

. . . Last night Friedrich was here and was very satisfied with the result. He and I have now arranged for him to try to get himself accepted without reservations by Uncle. He is to see Uncle on Sunday and is to tell me the upshot Monday night. Unfortunately F. will probably be transferred to Magdeburg, and that will badly hamper cooperation. . . .

Berlin, 23 October 1942

. . . Generally I would now be comfortably occupied without my work in the Office but that, unfortunately, also makes some demands on me. There are some more wild Orders[3] in the works and I must see to it that my dear chiefs remain firm and don't cave in, so that at least no responsibility falls on us.

Otherwise there is nothing to report.

1. The second meeting at Kreisau, 18–20 October, dealt mainly with constitutional, economic, social, and trade-union questions. For agreed texts see van Roon, *Resistance to Hitler*, pp. 332–37. The participants were M., F. M., Peter and Marion Yorck and Peter Yorck's sister, Irene, Einsiedel, Gerstenmaier, Delp, Maass, Peters, Steltzer, and Haubach (see n. 1 to letter of 26 October).
2. Their eleventh wedding anniversary.
3. Cf. n. 1 to letter of 3 November.

Berlin, 24 October 1942

. . . Gablentz came yesterday afternoon. The attempt to draw him in has, however, miscarried totally. He is a terribly stubborn man and set in some simple absurd theories. The trouble is that he then supports them with theological arguments, which is really more than one can bear. I repeated the lunchtime conversation to Steltzer; he nearly died of laughter. . . .

Munich, 25 October 1942

This is the end of a long day. I've had supper with our friends[1] and asked them to let me be alone for 10 minutes to write to you. Yesterday I had a long and satisfactory conversation with Gerstenmaier, who gave me a hostess present for you, a book that has something to do with astrology. He was clearly still under the *spell*[2] of the three days at Kreisau and of course I was very pleased by that. I had to discuss all kinds of questions about continuing practical work with him, and he was in good form.

In Munich, too, there had been an air-raid warning, and I walked through empty streets. After a good breakfast and a long conversation I went to see C.B.'s friend[3] at 11 and stayed till after 1 o'clock. I thought that rather long, but she apparently did not, and that's the main thing. I had lunch at Delp's, where there was a state banquet: bouillon with egg, venison with macaroni and dumplings, fruit tart, fruit and biscuits, and coffee. From there I went to the lawyer's[4] at 5, had no success, and then came here for supper. My train goes in an hour.

Delp, too, was obviously impressed by last week-end and had recovered, though he still had a boil. You, by the way, had left an especially good impression, you and Marion.[5] In the meantime he has had some success with our product and was full of confidence. . . .

1. The Jesuits.
2. English in the original.
3. Carl Bernd von Moltke's friend Irene Faulhaber.
4. Probably Josef Müller, whom M. met repeatedly. He, too, was protected by his Abwehr connection. It was he who had brought about the mediation between the Pope and the British, whereby the German opponents of the regime hoped to avert the German Western offensive and to arrive at a peace agreement (see n. 1 to letter of 17 November 1939). He was arrested in April 1943, but survived.
5. Marion Yorck.

Berlin, 26 October 1942

... I am returning Casparchen's works and Haubach's[1] letter. The cutting out and pasting is not badly done, but cries for discipline and instruction.

I had a good journey last night, arrived a little late, had the sandwiches I'd taken in my sleeper, and went straight from the station to the Office. I cleared up until 11 and then went out to do some reconnaissance. For the British started their offensive in Libya[2] on Friday and simultaneously bombed Italy heavily, and with that a very important juncture has been reached; the balance may shift and this may in turn have consequences. The British tactics seem to be entirely based on caution: a gigantic war of materiel in the desert, to wear down the whole front, and apparently not a blitzkrieg with wide outflanking movements. . . .

Berlin, 27 October 1942

The trees I see from my window have changed colour completely now. In three weeks the leaves will be gone and winter beginning. I wonder if this winter will bring the decision. Once more it very much looks like it.

The British seem to have attacked in Africa with different tactics: first an artillery barrage in the manner of the First World War in the West, and then infantry attacks without tanks.—They made considerable progress with this in the South, while we held our position in the North with counter-attacks. In any case this is developing into a war of materiel and

1. Theodor Haubach (1897–1945), Social Democrat; friend of Carlo Mierendorff since their schooldays; volunteer and officer—wounded and decorated—in the First World War. Took part with Mierendorff in literary and artistic ventures during and after the war. In 1923 took his doctorate under Karl Jaspers; 1923–26 active Young Socialists, with Mierendorff; 1924 co-founder of Reichsbanner Schwarz-Rot-Gold, the Republican paramilitary organization formed to counter those of the right and the Nazis; 1924–29 foreign editor of *Hamburger Echo*; 1927–28 SPD deputy in Hamburg City Parliament and member of the (national) Defence Committee of the SPD; 1929–32 press officer first in the Reich Ministry of the Interior, then of the Berlin police. 1930–33 worked with the circle of "religious socialists" around Paul Tillich and contributed to *Neue Blätter für den Sozialismus*. Continued in leading position of Reichsbanner and as political editor of its paper. After 1933 repeatedly arrested; 1934–36 in Esterwegen concentration camp; finally found work in the paper firm of a friend from student days. Briefly rearrested August 1939. M. mentioned him in a letter of 30 November 1938 as "a former Reichsbanner leader Haubach" he had met at the Borsigs'. They may have met as early as 1927—see Carl Zuckmayer, *A Part of Myself*, trans. Richard and Clara Winston (New York, 1970), pp. 42f. Joined Kreisau Circle 1942, attended the second meeting at Kreisau. Arrested 9 August 1944, executed 15 January 1945.
2. The offensive of the British Eighth Army under General Montgomery began at El Alamein on 23 October.

I doubt that we are capable of that down there. It seems that they are in earnest about beating Italy out of the war.

Last night I visited Friedrich, who had mostly good news: Uncle looks like approving of everything, broadly speaking; but the poor man was still badly affected by the times, especially by the risks of his own position. He obviously finds it all rather upsetting. . . .

Today I had lunch in town with Jaenicke to discuss the question of a successor for him. He'll have to go in the foreseeable future, because he was born in 1914. Tonight I'll be at Peter's with Maass, Einsiedel, & C.D. Listen, I'd rather like to return the flour to Marion if you can spare it. I borrowed it, after all, and I think I should give it back. If it can't be done, it can't.—In an hour I'm going to visit Conrad, who is to speak on Sunday.

Berlin, 28 October 1942

. . . I spent 3 hours yesterday afternoon with Conrad. He is in brilliant form, and I have every hope that his latest product[1] will be a masterpiece. Anyway I am full of hope. How encouraging that would be. From there I went to Peter's, where E.[2] and C.D.[3] and I stayed until 12. It was more a cleaning-up operation than anything leading further. Maass was only there long enough to deliver a lecture on Uncle's attitude, that is, his normal time of 90 minutes. His wife had suddenly been taken to a hospital, he didn't know why, and he therefore understandably wanted to get home.

Today and tomorrow are still stormy days. Fritzi[4] & Peter are coming to lunch and in the evening I must work in my office. Unfortunately there is a lot of work there. Tomorrow Gerstenmaier is coming and in the evening I'm going to visit Schlitter.[5] Then I'm hoping for a quiet week-end so that, if I can't come to Kreisau, I'll at least get my work up to date once more.

Berlin, 3 November 1942

. . . In the evening Gerstenmaier & I were at Peter's. Not only was it very nice, but we made considerable progress. In any case, it is really good to see what an addition Gerstenmaier represents. . . .

1. Cf. n. 3 (p. 217) to letter of 9 May.
2. Einsiedel.
3. Carl Dietrich von Trotha.
4. Schulenburg.
5. Oskar Schlitter, since August Legation Councillor in the Political Division of the AA.

Yesterday evening I had a decisive exchange with Bürkner. He didn't want to sign something that mattered a great deal to me and argued with me about the justification for an undiluted murder Order by the Führer.[1] I thereupon said to him: You see, Herr Admiral, the difference between us is that I can't argue about such questions. As long as I recognize imperatives that cannot be repealed by any Führer Order and that must be followed against a Führer Order, I cannot let such things pass, because for me the difference between good and evil, justice and injustice exists *a priori*. It is not subject to considerations of expediency or argument.— Whereupon he signed without demur. It is interesting to see again how such people can be swayed to the right side by a resolute stand.

Berlin, 4 November 1942

... Yesterday at lunch I had a rather informative conversation with Jaenicke and a man from another department about the use of courts martial. Odd to see what delusions such people sometimes have. In the afternoon there was one meeting after another, and at 7 I was at Peter's with Fritzi and a man from Paris.[2] I was terribly tired, so tired that towards 10 I repeatedly fell asleep and kept waking with a start. But then it became obvious that I simply had to weigh in and so, from 11 till 12 p.m., I did most of the talking in the discussion of European cooperation with England.[3] I was wide awake again but dead tired. . . .

Berlin, 5 November 1942

... Gerstenmaier & Trott came to lunch today. T. was very obstinate but he was tamed with G.'s help in a discussion lasting 3 hours. He is surprisingly intelligent but is rather burdened by it. It is always funny.

---

1. Almost certainly the so-called "Commando Order of 18 October 1942," which had meanwhile come to the notice of the Abwehr. Hitler ordered, in view of the Allied commando and sabotage operations, which were now more frequent in the West and in Africa as well, that all participants were to be killed and not to be taken prisoner. If one or two were to be interrogated first, they too were then to be shot.

2. Lieutenant Colonel Caesar von Hofacker (1896–1944), cousin of the Stauffenbergs and Yorcks. Till autumn 1943 in the economic division of the Military Administration in France; then staff officer on the personal staff of General Karl-Heinrich von Stülpnagel (see n. 4 [p. 310] to letter of 8 June 1943); prominently involved in the successful operation against the SS and SD in Paris on 20 July 1944, which was, however, stopped and cancelled after the failure in Berlin. Sentenced to death 30 August 1944, executed 20 December 1944.

3. The relationship between the envisaged European federation and Britain, or Britain's membership—and her position vis-à-vis the United States—was a problem M. had considered as early as 1941.

Moreover, he has, for some inexplicable reason, an inferiority complex towards me which leads him again and again to very aggressive attitudes and expressions. That is all very strange, but yesterday it would have been difficult if G. hadn't been present. So all went well. . . .

The development in the South is running its expected course and everything suggests that it will cause a short-circuit which will soon re-unite all.[1] In any case it has been dramatic so far and I can remember nothing like it since June 40. But it is still too early for a proper assessment. Yet, if things develop as I expect, the 8 weeks ahead of us will be filled with tension as seldom, perhaps never before in our lives. . . .

Berlin, 7 November 1942

I have the feeling that I have nothing to report, because the news from Africa and its consequences occupy me completely. I find it really difficult to concentrate on other things, for I keep noticing that my thoughts are there, while I'm reading something here. A great deal is being decided in these days, and the daring and success of the operations undertaken by the British today[2] will influence their prestige as world power more decisively and for a much longer time than any operation so far. Strange how infinitely many things suddenly depend on a single decision. Those are the few moments when one man can suddenly really count in the history of the world. Everything before, everything that follows is based on mass, anonymous forces and men. And then suddenly one feels that all these forces are holding their breath, that the gigantic orchestra that has played so far has fallen silent for one or two bars, to let a soloist set the tone for the next movement. It is only one heartbeat of time, but the one note, which will sound out alone and solitary, will establish the next movement for the whole orchestra. And all await that tone. One hears a possible melody in one's ear, one can imagine several variations, but one doesn't know what is coming. Thus one heartbeat becomes indescribably long. While I sit here, the decision that matters has long since been made, but I listen eagerly out into the world, to catch the note. Until now there has been only one such moment in this war: after Dunkirk. . . .

1. The German-Italian capitulation in North Africa did not come till May 1943, the fall of Mussolini in July 1943. But the Anglo-American landings in North-West Africa were imminent.

2. During the night of 7–8 November the Anglo-American forces under the command of General Eisenhower landed in Morocco and Algeria, in Rommel's rear. The British Eighth Army had continued its offensive after the Battle of El Alamein—see n. 2 to letter of 26 October—and had taken thirty thousand prisoners. On 20 November a Soviet offensive began, south of Stalingrad.

Berlin, 8 November 1942

I hear that the landing in French North Africa has taken place. *Alea iacta sunt.* How will it go? The reaction in France will also depend on the *"efficiency"*[1] with which the landing is carried out. I'll go to the Office in a minute to hear whether any reaction has been reported. Perhaps Pétain[2] will form a new government and join the British; perhaps he'll try to continue his balancing act. In 4 weeks, in any case, unless something quite surprising happens, the Mediterranean will be an English lake where nobody else has a say any more. The fleet that left Gibraltar on Friday evening consisted of 4 battleships, 4 aircraft carriers, 45 cruisers, 50 destroyers, and 390,000 tons of transport ships. That must mean at least 4 divisions. This is Ohm Jannie's[3] decisive hour, for this plan is surely his. . . .

Berlin, 9 November 1942

We've only just talked on the telephone but I'm writing because the day looks like being turbulent, if only because I must go news-gathering. It will still be very confused and entangled, but all the same may give a picture. The main question, after all, is whether the French put up with Laval's[4] policy, of entering the war on our side, and if so how we respond. The minimum would be to release all prisoners of war, for otherwise the affair really has no popular appeal. . . .

Berlin, 10 November 1942

. . . I am very well; I can't remember ever feeling so well and fit in November. The sense of approaching crisis and danger gives me an enormous stimulus, I can't deny. I wonder if things will now proceed apace or

1. English in the original.
2. Philippe Pétain (cf. n. 1 [p. 102] to letter of 15 August 1940) called on the French commanders in Algeria, Morocco, and Tunis to resist, but refused to declare war on the Allies. Admiral Darlan helped them in Algeria. He was assassinated on 24 December.
3. Jan Christiaan Smuts (1870–1950), general leading Boer forces in the Boer War, after which he worked for the integration of South Africa into the British Commonwealth and for the League of Nations. During the Second World War, South African Prime Minister and Minister of Foreign Affairs and Defence. Friend of the Rose Innes family. Churchill greatly prized the advice and assistance of the statesman and strategist he had fought as a young man and called him "a fount of wisdom" who helped "to fortify my own judgment" when he consulted with him in Cairo in August—see Winston S. Churchill, *The Second World War*, vol, 4, *The Hinge of Fate* (New York, 1962), pp. 397, 400.
4. The French Prime Minister saw Hitler in Munich the next day at the behest of Pétain.

if there will be a standstill. Either is possible. But Mussolini seems to have been summoned to Munich and to have declined to come.

It is enormously impressive to see how sea power prevails. It advances like a colossus. If one considers that in the entire Mediterranean—the Eastern Mediterranean is irrelevant in this context—the British only had Gibraltar, Malta, and Alexandria, only a few square kilometres surrounded by enemies, one sees how well the Empire is constructed. On those strategic key points the gigantic edifice rests. As long as Britain has a navy all is well. Why don't people here see that? Still don't see it? Does one need Anglo-Saxon blood to recognize it? What kind of people are leading us? What generals, who throw troops into Africa and leave Malta untouched? It is simply not understandable.

And I'm convinced that most Germans don't see what has happened in the Mediterranean area even now. The Battle of El Alamein probably brought the formal decision of the war. But the effect at the very least is that there can be no more question of an offensive. I wonder whether contemporaries understood the Battle of Trafalgar no better. . . .

Berlin, 11 November 1942

. . . Yesterday evening was fairly productive. It is taking a long time to integrate Fritzi completely, but he is well on the way now and I very much hope for complete success soon. He had a lot of *constructive criticism*[1] to offer on the Kreisau texts, but it concerned details, was sometimes based on misunderstanding, and partly referred to things we never liked either. . . .

The most important question at the moment is whether France will let us devour her. Since this morning, we and the Italians have been marching in,[2] the Italians in Corsica & Nice. It is obviously the price Mussolini exacted for his continued perseverance. I wonder if it will be enough. If it is, the decline will be halted, and we'll see a little pause, unless the French reaction is so strong that it cancels out the other. . . .

Berlin, 12 November 1942

Your Tuesday letter came at lunchtime today. So we are back to normal. First, Merian.[3] His news is essentially correct, at least as concerns the 50%ers. The first 50%ers have already been expedited [*abstransportiert*].

1. English in the original.
2. Entering the hitherto unoccupied part of France.
3. Agricultural and livestock adviser.

I don't know about the people who are 3/8.[1] In no case should one touch the matter, but keep still and only defend oneself if or when something happens. To negotiate in advance I consider quite mistaken.

That's as far as I got when Steltzer came; meanwhile I've taken him to his hotel and from there came straight to Derfflingerstrasse, where I have an appointment with Carl shortly after 6. At 6.45 I'll eat a little here and at 7.30 I'm going to the Gerstenmaiers'. On Monday I'm having lunch at the Yorcks' with Steltzer; at 4.30 I see Conrad[2] to give him the final prop before Sunday, and at 8 I'll get my train to Karlsruhe to see Rösch. You see, all the time remaining has been allotted.

My love, on the phone and in your letter you seemed somewhat exhausted. My poor dear, what a shame that you are poorly and yet have such a lot to do. I hope when Lenchen comes you really can shift some of the burden, for now you must gather strength! There are bad times ahead. If only all the children stay well.

Fattening the pigs: Merian should let me have the result of his examination in writing, so that we can have exact information when we discuss it on the 29th. I'm against fattening, not for financial reasons, but simply because of the fodder. We have to economize on fodder and can't always be short.

In a week's time you are coming, my love. Then we must go to church on the first Sunday in Advent. That will work too. Have you ordered the wreaths for Totensonntag? If only the shepherd doesn't stop the grazing too soon. I hope Z. won't allow it.—Another thing occurs to me: I'll write to Merian myself; why should you have to write to him again when it is no trouble at all for me. So don't do it.

In Africa there will probably still be a little resistance in Tunis and Tripoli, and that should be the end. What will Italy do then? Will they go on and rejoice in Corsica & Nice? It seems very doubtful.

Otherwise there is really nothing new, my love; the days race past; it feels quite improbable to me that only 11 days should have passed since 1 November. And yet I am impatient for the next 11 days, which will bring another great decision.

1. It was obviously the question of the deportation of so-called "*Mischlinge*," those with two Jewish grandparents and those with three great-grandparents of one "race" and five of the other. In the matter of the enforced divorce of "mixed marriages" and the deportation of the Jewish partners, church protests had some inhibiting effect.

2. Preysing was to preach a sermon on 15 November to prepare and support his pastoral letter, which was to be read on 20 December—cf. n. 2 (p. 264) to letter of 17 November. Secret surveillance reports of the SD (Security Service) called the latter an open attack on the ideological foundations of National Socialist views on law and quoted from it at length to substantiate the charge.

Berlin, 13 November 1942

It is snowing. According to the old saw that snow on the leaves brings back warm weather, we'd have a welcome relapse.

Yesterday evening at Gerstenmaier's was very nice. We had a number of things to discuss and the crystal-clear quality of Gerstenmaier's intellectual apparatus is a great help in every conversation. Trott & Peter were there, too. G. & Peter are coming to Derfflingerstrasse on Thursday, and if you're there you'll see them.

Today there is exceptionally little to do at the Office. That is nice, because I have to finish and tidy up quite a lot, and from about 1.30 on I'm occupied elsewhere.

My love, how are you? I am always afraid that I overburden you and give you too much to do. I'd like so much for you to have your head high enough above the waters and yet it seems to me that just now you have difficulty keeping your head above water at all. What can one do?

And at once I have another request. If you can spare some bacon and sausage, I have a very needy aspirant whom I'd like to give something. He can probably make good use of peas, too.[1] . . .

Baden-Baden,[2] 15 November 1942

. . . We made an excursion into town with Henry.[3] He really walks along very nicely and is altogether a sweet child. In the evening we sat until 10 and then sank contentedly into our beds, where I slept well but had two rather strenuous dreams: I had been sunk in a U-boat with C.B.[4] and we couldn't agree who should get out first; he said that I had a wife and children, and I said that of course the younger, with the greater expectation of life, must go first. . . .

Berlin, 17 November 1942

. . . Goerschen[5] came to lunch yesterday. He impressed me quite favourably, and it seems to me that good use can be made of him. The

1. Cf. letters of 5 and 18 November 1941; Poelchau, too, was helping to feed people in hiding.
2. On his way to visit his brother, Jowo, he had met Rösch at Karlsruhe.
3. Henry von Moltke, the son of Joachim Wolfgang and Inge von Moltke.
4. M.'s youngest brother, Carl Bernd, who had been missing in action since 30 December 1941 and was presumed dead.
5. Hans Wolf von Goerschen, business associate of Carl Deichmann's, who had emigrated to Holland before the war, had become a naturalized Dutch citizen, and was to establish connections with the Dutch resistance.

development of the war has made him so ready to do something that he'll probably cooperate. He has asked for time to think it over and will contact me when he comes again.—In the evening Steltzer, Gerstenmaier, Trott, and I were at Peter's to get on with the question of translation to the European plane.[1] We had quite a good conversation but made no progress. It was 1 before I was in bed.

Today at 11—in half an hour—I'm seeing Steltzer for a final review. He flies to Stockholm at 2. At 5 Hartner is coming to see me, and at 7 Friedrich & Peter. I have a business lunch in town. So the day has a heavy schedule. But all days now are like this.

Once more there is nothing to do at the Office. That suits me very well because I have an awful lot of reading to do.—Conrad's Sunday product is good but not very good and not very emphatic. It is aimed at those who can hear, not at the deaf.[2] . . .

Berlin, 23 November 1942

It was lovely, as always. My love, if only you don't overdo things. The bad times are still ahead of us. They will be bad in every respect, and moreover we'll be very poor. Therefore please spare yourself. . . .

Nothing seems to have changed in Africa, i.e., both sides are bringing up supplies they need for the decisive blow. But in the East[3] there seems to have been quite a nasty surprise. . . .

Berlin, 24 November 1942

. . . Yesterday I went to Ulla's on my bike, had a very nice supper there, and at 8.30 I moved on to Husen, with whom I stayed till 11.30. He too has made gratifying progress in his willingness to commit himself to action, and I'll try to integrate him. In any case he was much less apathetic than when I saw him last, two months ago. I got home on my velo by moonlight at 12, dead tired but satisfied. . . .

1. Cf. n. 2 to letter of 4 November.
2. Among those with ears to hear were the watchdogs of the regime—see n. 2 (p. 262) to letter of 12 November. The Security Service objected to "humanitarian" passages in the sermon that condemned racism, such as: "Every human being has a right to life and love. . . . It is never permitted to take away human rights from members of alien races: the right to freedom, the right to property, the right to an indissoluble marriage."
3. The Russian offensive south of Stalingrad had begun on 19 and 20 November. By the 22nd a quarter of a million German soldiers were encircled at Stalingrad. On the 23rd General Paulus asked Hitler for freedom of action, but Hitler insisted on the defence of position.

The situation is very bad. It's the East that's bad. I assume that somehow, somewhere it can still be stabilized, but almost certainly not without heavy losses.

Berlin, 25 November 1942

... The three of us toiled from 7 till 11.20 and it was really quite satisfactory. The slight distance there has always been between Fritzi and us had visibly shrunk and seems on the way to disappearing altogether. As usual, there were some quite amusing moments and everything was very satisfactory. . . .

Berlin, 26 November 1942

... The evening yesterday with Delp & Gerstenmaier was fruitful on the whole, even if it was only a kind of preliminary examination. But they are now sufficiently in line for us to have a final discussion in plenary session on the 17th. I wonder whether it will come off and whether it will actually be possible to finish the personnel plan[1] before Christmas. That would be a considerable step forward. I want to ask Steltzer, too, to come on the 17th.

Berlin, 27 November 1942

... In our Office there is unusual nervousness, not, as you might suppose, because of the war situation, but because General von Unruh[2] is coming and wants to comb out the department.

Today was uneventful, if you like. But abroad there was a plethora of sensations: the disarming of the French army,[3] the scuttling of the French navy,[4] the advance of the British between Bizerta and Tunis, the end of

1. The list of Landesverweser, or regional commissioners, men who were willing and able to assume regional responsibility and to act as liaison to the centre in case of a coup d'état or collapse, the latter probably combined with Allied occupation of at least part of the country.
2. Lieutenant General Walter von Unruh, who was charged with a manpower survey aimed at intensifying the war effort.
3. After the armistice of 1940 France had been left with an army of 100,000. It was disarmed and dissolved on 27 November. On the 16th French units had begun to fight at the side of the Allies.
4. The French fleet scuttled itself and five submarines escaped after SS tank units had occupied Toulon.

the first attempt of the army encircled at Stalingrad to break out to the west: probably poor Hans Clemens[1] is there, too. . . .

Berlin, 8 December 1942

You have only just left. But I think I'll write at once all the same, so that you have a first letter soon. The day is bound to be so filled that unless I write at once I won't get round to it until evening. Ah, my love, it was again so lovely and peaceful with you. To be sure the days flew by like the wind, but they shimmer so beautifully and not far away Christmas is shimmering. So this month is already over, so to speak, and the new, the important new year, is in sight.

You know what goes on here and how everything looks. Today will be full: one man has just gone, Einsiedel must turn up in 15 minutes, and all morning there will be a circus of men. The afternoon will be quieter, except for the threat of Uncle, but there is a lot of work waiting that was neglected in the last week. . . .

Berlin, 9 December 1942

How awful that Maria and Thomas[2] are seriously ill. That is a considerable burden for you at an inopportune moment; for you have your hands full with washing and slaughtering, Caspar's rash, and Christmas. How are you to deal with it all? Asta asked whether in the circumstances she shouldn't come to Kreisau. But I discouraged her because I can't imagine that she would be enough help to you, particularly in looking after the sick, to warrant it. It would be a sacrifice, after all, and it seems to me wiser to spare her for the time being. Do you agree?

. . . Last night I sat peacefully at home. I was tired and did not feel very well. I spent the evening looking through the letters of the Field Marshal. Some of them are really moving, especially the two written immediately after Marie's[3] death. But various letters to his mother, too, are equally beautiful, charming documents. . . .

Asta, Inge & Jowo came for lunch and we had your splendid chicken with white caper sauce. The whole thing gave great satisfaction and all were evidently contented if somewhat elegiacal, for Jowöchen now looks like departing definitely. They were very enthusiastic about the pictures,[4]

1. Hans Clemens Busch, cousin of F.M.
2. The Deichmann children.
3. Marie von Moltke, née Burt, died in 1868 at the age of forty-two.
4. Schmidt-Rottluff's pictures of Kreisau.

even more so, really, than I had expected. Asta chose a pastel drawing, because the water-colours, which she actually thinks more beautiful, are too big for her living quarters in the foreseeable future. Jowo had the same misgivings, but Inge wanted a water-colour, the view from the Berghaus hill through the "Park." We discussed this for most of the lunch and Jowo and Inge haven't yet made a final decision. I am very glad, however, that the undertaking as a whole is such a success.

Berlin, 10 December 1942

... The evening was otherwise very satisfactory. It didn't go 100% as I wanted, but the essential part was achieved, and the road is clear. In the time ahead this wound[1] will be forgotten, and for me the whole thing was an important *test of confidence.*[2]

Of the war I can report that Switzerland has now made a proposal that both sides should unshackle[3] their prisoners again. I hope we'll now succeed in burying the nasty affair.—Stalingrad looks a bit more hopeful.—In Africa the 8th Army is said to have started its attack on the El Agheila position today. That signals the approach of a very important decision. . . .

Berlin, 11 December 1942

... This morning Einsiedel & C.D. turned up; their work has already suffered from the Uncle-Delp row,[4] and they thought they were telling me news when they said that some disagreement seemed to have arisen. All the more agreeable for me to be able to reassure them. Still, it was interesting to see how fast the effects appear.

In the prisoner-of-war affair the British have done at last what I'd have done in their place 6 weeks ago: they have unshackled our prisoners of war unilaterally without waiting for our reaction to the recent appeal by

1. Difficulties with Leuschner, who was closely connected with the Goerdeler group? Cf. letters of 11 December 1942 and 9 January 1943.
2. English in the original.
3. Cf. n. 1 to letter of 12 October. Wengler later described M.'s fight against these measures, even after Keitel had forbidden further discussion of the matter. By patience and perseverance M. caused Hitler to rescind his order after an exchange of prisoners in which the international lawyers of the Abwehr had been instrumental (cf. n. 1 to letter of 22 June).
4. Leuschner had heard of Delp's efforts to keep Catholic trade unionists away from the Goerdeler group by describing it, including its trade-union sympathizers Leuschner and Jakob Kaiser, as reactionary and the Moltke group as more open-minded.

Switzerland. We have now set everything in motion for our side to follow suit.[1] I hope it does. Otherwise there is nothing new about the war. . . .

Berlin, 15 December 1942

. . . Willem Bekker came to the Office this morning. He is the Berlin chief of the Dutch state corporation that conducts the resettlement of Dutchmen in the Eastern Territories.[2] I don't understand how he can take part in such an operation, but was very interested in what he told me about it. Of the 130 Dutch farmers who have so far arrived in the East— the whole operation only started in September—19 have already been shot. . . .

Berlin, 16 December 1942

This is a last letter and therefore I don't much feel like writing. I frittered away the whole morning today because I was examined for my fitness for active duty. I don't know the result. In any case I was examined extraordinarily thoroughly, which surprised me very much.—Today I was to have lunch with Hans Adolf; but he wasn't able to manage it, and I didn't mind at all because I'm very short of time and Schlange is coming at 4, Friedrich at 5, and the Office party is at 6.30. So I took sandwiches.

Yesterday evening in my office was still stormy, as Peter, Eddy,[3] and Adam[4] appeared at short intervals. I then worked at my office until 9, had supper, and worked for another hour at home. . . .

I had a nice letter from Schmidt-Rottluff. He is giving me the picture of the Kapellenberg as a present. That is nice, although I would have found it even nicer if he'd given you your Zobten.[5] I hope the pictures arrive safely and are there by Christmas. Too bad that one can't get mounts, because they are more difficult to enjoy without the white margin. . . .

1. The matter was not resolved until there were enough eligible German prisoners in British hands.
2. This was part of the German plan to resettle the conquered East with Germanic stock.
3. Waetjen.
4. Trott.
5. The mountain which characterized the view from Kreisau.

1943

Now you are gone, but perhaps it won't be too long before I come to Kreisau or you to Berlin. I hope you had a good journey, my love, and I hope you come through the next days well. My poor dear, all this was frightful and exhausting once more. And you simply don't want to see what a bad husband you have.—But it was very lovely and satisfying with you. Thank you so much for coming.

The day was stormy. Fritzi appeared in the morning, Trott towards 11.30, Gerstenmaier & Peter at 12, staying till 2.30, at 3 Körber. Then there was lots of work. I didn't have lunch today, but Peter, Eugen, and I had the rest of the bread with butter and sausage that I had with me. The party[2] is to be on Friday after all, even if only as foretaste and without the major fireworks. . . .

Berlin, 7 January 1943

Your husband has just decided on a lazy afternoon. He's got his feet up and is looking after his throat, which has been nasty since yesterday eve-

1. Erroneously dated 6 January 1942.
2. The meeting with the Goerdeler group—see letter of 9 January.

ning but is on the way to improving. I only came back from the office at 9.30 after all, hadn't felt too well all day, and after supper I noticed that the trouble had definitely settled in the throat. I therefore slept with my scarf on, but woke up late and none too well, went to the Office in the morning, had lunch with Herr Deichmann, and since then I've been gargling, making compresses, etc., in order to restore myself to combat fitness. Of course it isn't worth mentioning, but since I am to appear as *"Leader of His Majesty's Opposition"*[1] I must keep as well as possible.

This morning at the Office was like a better circus again, it was swarming with all kinds of people. Oxé is back and that is very nice for me. It frees me of part of my responsibility and also means that I can stay at my desk and don't have to be always running to one of the chiefs. . . .

Berlin, 8 January 1943

. . . The most irritating part is that I consider all the work being done now as having no chance. But it has to be done with all due care all the same, so that others, and we ourselves, can't blame ourselves for having missed any chance. . . .

I am glad that you intend to stay in bed tomorrow. You should think of your own strength first now, because everything will depend on your strength. You must please not forget that easy and pleasant times are gradually coming to an end and that bad times will probably start before this year is out. . . .

Berlin, 9 January 1943

. . . My evening lasted till 1 a.m. It was odd, because we didn't really clash until 11; instead every attempt to push through to fundamentals was deflected into facile civilities. At last there was a chance, and on the subject[2] of our night session at Kreisau in October. After a few preliminary skirmishes on our side a really incredible statement emerged: flat, unimaginative, etc. I seized the opportunity and declared it made no sense to reply at 11.35 with the real discussion just beginning.[3] We would therefore not reply today. Then I shot off a poisoned arrow, "Kerensky

1. Leader of his group vis-à-vis the Goerdeler group, also referred to as "Their Excellencies." English in the original.
2. Economic and social policy.
3. Cf. Hassell's diary entry of 22 January 1943 which bears out this description and calls Goerdeler "really something of a reactionary" (*The Von Hassell Diaries 1938–1944: The Story of the Forces Against Hitler Inside Germany, as Recorded by Ambassador Ulrich von Hassell*, intro. Allen Welsh Dulles [Garden City, N.Y., 1947], p. 283).

solution,"[1] which I'd kept in my quiver for a long time: it hit home quite firmly and visibly—and with that the affair had a dramatic end and, I'm glad to say, not a flat one. We then ate pea soup and sandwiches. The others[2] were gone by 12, and Trott, Eugen,[3] Peter, and I then held a critical review.

Pape[4] came for lunch—yesterday. Sad, resigned, and looking poorly, shrunken. I am very sorry for him, especially since I can't help him at all. There he sits for the second winter now in a very forward bunker. They have nothing sensible to do, build bunkers, shovel snow, repair streets, and he is a clerk in the office. A case similar to Wend's,[5] only worse.— Then Friedrich[6] came. Well, chubby, contented. His assessment fully supports my blackest theses. I found that rather interesting. He went from me to Uncle[7] and will come to my place with Uncle for lunch today.

Berlin, 11 January 1943

... Yesterday[8] was very satisfactory. R[ösch] is really one of our best people. He wasn't very well yet, but his spirits were lively. First I talked with him alone from 9 till 2 o'clock, then I went to see a lawyer[9] I always visit, talked with him from 2.30 till 4, and then at 4.30 I was at Delp's, together with R. & König; there we had things to talk about till 9.20. Thus a madly strenuous day. I therefore went to sleep at once in my bed, although my companion declared he'd not been able to sleep a wink because of the rattling of the train.

1. Allusion to Alexander Kerensky, who in 1917 became so moderate a provisional Premier that the Bolsheviks overthrew his government before the year was out.
2. Among them Schulenburg, the mediator between the two groups. The "elders" were led by Dr. Carl Goerdeler (1884–1945), Mayor of Leipzig 1930–37 (when he resigned in protest against the removal of the statue of Felix Mendelssohn); Price Commissioner 1934–35; from 1938 on, active in economic life and in opposition to the regime; he soon became the civilian head of successive plots. Executed 2 February 1945. Ludwig Beck was present, but very ill, and soon after had a cancer operation. Ulrich von Hassell (1881–1944) had been German Ambassador in Italy until 1937 and since then active in the opposition, as was Johannes Popitz (1884–1945), former Under-Secretary of State in the Reich Ministry of Finance, then Prussian Finance Minister and professor at the University of Berlin. Another participant was Jens Jessen (1895–1944), professor of economics, early National Socialist, then strong opponent, executed November 1944.
3. Gerstenmaier.
4. Hans-W. Pape, Berlin lawyer.
5. M.'s brother-in-law, Wend Wendland.
6. Mierendorff.
7. Leuschner.
8. In Munich.
9. Josef Müller? Cf. n. 1 to letter of 17 November 1939.

We had a large field to survey: the frictions with Uncle, the discussions Friday evening,[1] my visit to Cracow,[2] Delp's character, the *"outstanding personality"*[3] we envisage, and so on, but the talks were very satisfactory both in quality and content. I also carried away the Pope's Allocution of 24 December[4] and it is really very beautiful. I'll bring it to show you.

I found a letter from you when I returned. Many thanks, my love. You know, I'd really like to come next Sunday. It would please me so much to be at Kreisau quite alone with my family for once, and that would fit into next Sunday. When will there be another such opportunity? Well, we'll telephone about it tomorrow.

Berlin, 12 January 1943

. . . Our Office[5] is moving today, to the House of Tourism at the Potsdam Bridge. For transport that has considerable advantages, since now all trams and the No. 28 bus stop at the door. Otherwise the location is much less beautiful. . . .

Hans Adolf has flown off to Madrid.[6] He is said to be utterly distraught. The last weeks have been ghastly for him. Scheliha,[7] his worries about the manager, his dying mother, and then the assignment as Ambassador. Poor man. Weizsäcker is reported to have said that, although he didn't want to go to Madrid,[8] great pressure was brought to bear on him, and his only real choice finally was between the Madrid Embassy and concentration camp.

Berlin, 13 January 1943

Today we moved into our new quarters at the Potsdam Bridge: House of Tourism. It is cold and draughty, the rooms are small and noisy, and

1. See letter of 9 January.
2. It seems unlikely that the intended visit to Archbishop Sapieha took place—cf. letters of 18 April and 1 and 4 May.
3. As head of state or government. Cf. letter and n. 2 of 14 December 1941; *Von Hassell Diaries*, 21 December 1941, 22 January 1943. English in the original.
4. Abridged text of the broadcast address in *Actes et documents du Saint Siège relatifs à la seconde guerre mondiale*, vol. 7 (Città del Vaticano, 1973), pp. 161–67. It dealt with human rights, the dignity and rights of labour, with the state, war, and the necessary renewal of society. It was remarkably open in its reference to the injustice being done to hundreds of thousands of innocents who were punished solely because of their nationality or descent. Full text in *Acta Apostolicae Sedis*, vol. 35 (1943), pp. 4–24.
5. The Abwehr's International Law Group.
6. He became Ambassador in Madrid, but died there in March.
7. Rudolf von Scheliha, before the war Legation Counsellor (Gesandtschaftsrat) in Warsaw; after promotion in the AA, among the accused in the proceedings against the Rote Kapelle, a communist espionage-and-resistance organization (to which he did not belong) in December 1942 and sentenced to death and executed.
8. First "Paris," deleted.

the only gain lies in connections. In bad weather or when I am in a hurry I can take the tram, and I'm now a stone's throw from my own office.— Everything is in place, and in a few days it may even be clean. . . .

Berlin, 20 January 1943

. . . I only hope you'll get well now. My love, think how important that can be. I have never so far considered the possibility that we might have to leave something necessary undone because you weren't up to it. And I am very grateful to you for that, but I also very much hope that it may continue, for just now, in the time immediately ahead, this freedom of movement may be very necessary. Look after yourself! . . .

Berlin, 21 January 1943

. . . My love, I'd like so much to be with you at home[1] and have no desire at all to be here. For I can do nothing but wait. I am too firmly convinced that there is nothing else to be done to have any faith in the busyness of the others.[2] Waiting is, of course, much more difficult than action and therefore trying to persuade others to wait is a thankless task. Fundamentally only Friedrich and Steltzer are really in agreement with me on this; the others follow me reluctantly. . . .

Berlin, 22 January 1943

. . . Today I had a lot to do till 10.30. I went out to gather information. The result is sad, much more sad than I could have expected as recently as 3 days ago. The Russians are practically at the outskirts of the city of Rostov and the whole thing looks like a rout.—There are to be big celebrations on the 30th, going on for 3 days. It will be a great public festivity.[3]

1. He had been at Kreisau the preceding week-end.
2. The preparation of the assassination and coup d'état, of which he disapproved and which failed in March. The Goerdeler group, with Beck, Oster, and Dohnanyi, was involved. The most notable attempt was that of Lieutenant Fabian von Schlabrendorff, who had done and who continued to do much, together with his cousin, Lieutenant Colonel (later Major General) Henning von Tresckow, Staff Officer (Ia) of the Army Group Centre, to get the military to act against Hitler and to maintain liaison with the civilian opposition. Schlabrendorff placed a bomb on Hitler's plane on 13 March 1943. It failed to explode. See Fabian von Schlabrendorff, *The Secret War Against Hitler*, trans. Hilda Simon, foreword by John J. McCloy (New York-Toronto-London, 1965), pp. 231–39. Cf. letters of 22, 24, and 26 January and 4 March 1943; Peter Hoffmann, *The History of the German Resistance 1933–45*, trans. Richard Barry, (Cambridge, Mass., 1977), pp. 280–83.
3. To celebrate the tenth anniversary of the Nazi seizure of power.

My plans have become a bit firmer. I intend to take a train from Berlin to Paris in the evening of February 7, shall be in Paris in the evening of the 8th, and reckon with 2 days' time. The evening of the 10th or 11th I shall travel to Brussels, where I shall probably have to stay over the week-end, so that I expect to be in Cologne at midday on the 16th and in Berlin early on the 17th. . . .

Today Haeften, Peter, and Gerstenmaier came to lunch and ate the hare with me. Frau Pick had prepared it splendidly and all found it delectable. Nothing new emerged; but the three of them are much more positive than I am in their assessment of our chances and that does lead to considerable difference in practice. I intend to tell them it's better they dance this special round[1] without me.

Berlin, 23 January 1943

. . . Oppen[2] was here for lunch; the one who used to be in the Ministry of Education. I had quite a nice and encouraging conversation with him. Even if he went astray for a while, he is a good man after all.—Tomorrow I'm going to see Peter at 11, then to lunch with him & Trott, in the evening to Gerstenmaier's. I hope I'll succeed in getting the whole club in line with me. Peter at least seems ready for that on the whole. He came to see me this morning, and I am glad and relieved that we are of one mind again.

At the Office I had pleasanter work for Gladisch today, which went well and smoothly. On Monday we'll probably get another period of pressure. In any case I am to try to summarize the interests of the Wehrmacht in a certain question, and it will mean a lot of work. . . .

Berlin, 24 January 1943

. . . At 10.30 I went to see Peter for a preparatory talk, then we both went to lunch with Trott, where Gerstenmaier was as well. Discussion of the right form and the right formula lasted from 2.30 till 6.30. I am glad that as a result of giving in over the New Year and subsequently trying to achieve a compromise with Their Excellencies[3] I now have Peter, who was much less negative than I, on my side. Today our positions are almost

1. Cf. letters of 21 and 24 January
2. Hans-Werner von Oppen (1902–83), joined the Party 1932; 1933–37 cultural officer in the Prussian Ministry of Education; in the war served in anti-aircraft units of the Luftwaffe; 1957–64 Director of the Academy of Fine Arts (Hochschule für Bildende Künste) in Hamburg.
3. The Goerdeler group—cf. n. 1 to letter of 7 January, and letters of 21, 22, and 26 January.

identical. I am afraid, however, that we won't yet get our way and that further demonstrations of the impossibility of their way will be required.

... The discussions of the past month have been a great strain. I feel so drained by them. The reason is probably that from the beginning I took a solitary line, and had to keep fighting for it, and that I felt responsible for maintaining the readiness and unity of our troop. To hold the right line was hard for me, and I may not always have succeeded. We will continue at my place on Wednesday.

Berlin, 26 January 1943

... Yesterday morning my door at the Office opened suddenly and in came a non-commissioned officer of the Luftwaffe, Walter Schneider.[1] In good health if still very slim, wiser and less clever; I liked him very much. He is a highly intelligent version of the real soldier Schweigk.[2] It is the Schweigk temperament with education and training. He isn't an officer cadet, for until 6 weeks ago the age limit excluded him. Unlike any of our people, he has been immersed in the rank and file at the front and, in his stories, everything, from heroism and comradeliness to sadism and executions, becomes human. He said, for instance, "I'm agreeably disillusioned by the war." Or "Heroism and comradeship are picture-book conventions, for nobody has the courage to act in accordance with his natural cowardice with the whole company looking on." "The soldier doesn't want the Knight's Cross to gratify his self-importance, but as a mark of Fortune's favour; for 999/1000th is luck and one-thousandth is accomplishment. Once a man has the Knight's Cross he feels like a commanding star of strategy. He doesn't behave any differently from the stars of the stage." And so on. You see what pearls he dropped. He goes to Vienna in a few days, and I told him that if he can manage it he should break his journey and visit you.

I met Peter in the evening and discussed the new situation.[3] I'm happy to say we are in full agreement again, and today I had a letter from Steltzer confirming me in my relative intransigence. And I think we'll pull it through. We'll try on Wednesday and therefore I can't have Mütterchen then.

Your telephone call interrupted the last sentence. What a relief that he

1. Old friend from the Schwarzwald circle.

2. (Anti-) hero of the satire on the Austrian military bureaucracy by Jaroslav Hasek, *The Good Soldier Svejk and His Fortunes in the World War*, first published in 1920–23.

3. After the discussion with the "Excellencies" on 8 January and the proclamation of the demand for "unconditional surrender" by Roosevelt and Churchill at their meeting at Casablanca on 24 January. Cf. letters of 21, 22, and 24 January.

was killed[1] before the whole enterprise became an agonizing slaughter. The poor man had been weighing on my soul day after day. Poor Maria. I only hope that nothing happens to Uli.[2] But now she'll worry all the more.

Yesterday afternoon I was with Konrad.[3] Again I liked him tremendously. He was reticent and sure in his judgments, careful not to say more than lay in his competence, but saying that confidently, unambiguously, and decisively. . . .

Berlin, 4 March 1943[4]

Immediately after breakfast I retired to the sofa and started reading *The Times*, interrupted by a game of Patience and a sad letter from Wiebke which I enclose. Unfortunately there was no letter from you. . . . König turned up at 12.30, risen from his 6 weeks' sickbed and in quite good spirits. The news was less good, actually bad. The matter has fizzled out and has been intercepted.[5] Well, it doesn't matter. I had not expected anything tremendous, but of course every extension is precious. I was not really prepared for his visit and so I have forgotten some things. But he'll come again tomorrow night before catching his train.—We then sat together a bit quite pleasantly, and at 2.30 he left and I returned to my *Times*, on which I worked, interrupted by another game of Patience, until 4.30. Then I had some delicious tea, read another one, and now you see what I'm doing. I hope Friedrich comes tonight. Reichwein was to make the appointment with him, and I'm always a bit sceptical of that, but it may work.[6] Husen is coming tomorrow morning; Hammersen, a major from Oslo whom I want to use as a courier, is having lunch with me; in the afternoon I have a meeting on prisoners of war at 3, Steinke is coming at 5, and König at 7. You see the programme is quite ample. And on top of it I still have quite a lot to do at the Office. I'm thinking of going to the Office tonight if Friedrich doesn't come and doing a little night shift.— Well, first I must read the office papers I have here.

I am constantly occupied with everything at Kreisau. If only I could stay home for a few days at Easter . . .

1. F.M.'s cousin Hans Clemens Busch was killed at Stalingrad.
2. Ulrich Busch survived the war.
3. Preysing.
4. This is the first extant letter after that of 1 February. It sounds like a Sunday letter—but Sunday was the 7th.
5. Probably an action of the bishops and probably blocked by Bertram—see n. 2 (p. 156) to letter of 6 September 1941.
6. Mierendorff was much on the move and had to be circumspect about his contacts.

Why can't people have patience? It seems to be the virtue hardest to acquire. I, too, prefer everything to go quickly, but I am relatively patient. Even König & Delp, who really should have learnt, from their discipline, to wait, are incapable of it, and when an action is followed by an inevitable setback, they become restless and don't see that beyond the valley there will be another height. Adam,[1] whom I left overconfident, was overtimid when I saw him again. All these changes of feeling seem to me so uneconomical: they must use up so much energy. . . .

Oslo, 17 March 1943

The whole train was already packed when I got to Stettiner Bahnhof; fortunately I remembered that I have a courier pass and had the courier compartment, which was still empty, unlocked for me. So I travelled in style. I read *Reports of the House of Lords* all the way, with great interest and not without profit.[2]

Furthermore, this line crosses much attractive country, so that there was always something nice to be seen when one looked out of the window. I first met the throng of my fellow travellers at Warnemünde: apart from soldiers, who were nice, an awful collection of slave-traders and slaves and some second- and third-rate profiteers.—I felt sick and was embarrassed for the first time in front of the few, themselves also not very high-grade, Danes who travelled with us. The qualitatively best human material was provided by the Danish customs officials.—Your husband was handled quickly and comfortably, thanks to his courier pass. On board ship everyone rushed to the dining tables and sat there in expectation of the ship's departure. I descended into the belly of the ship and retired to a cabin to continue reading *Parliamentary Debates* and

1. Trott—see letter and n. 2 of 21 January.
2. This may be a reference to the renewed plea of the Bishop of Chichester in the House of Lords on 11 February and 10 March for a differentiation between the Nazi regime and the German people, such as Stalin had made in a speech of 19 November 1942 and which the Casablanca formula of unconditional surrender called in question (cf. n. 3 to letter of 26 January). On 11 February Bishop Bell had countered Lord Vansittart's proposals for responses with his own: "The remedy is to tell those inside Germany who are anti-Fascist that we want their help in getting rid of the common enemy, and that we intend that a Germany delivered from Hitlerism shall have fair play and a proper place in the family of Europe." Bell returned to the subject on 10 March and elicited a clear reply from the Lord Chancellor: "I now say in plain terms, on behalf of His Majesty's Government, that we agree with Premier Stalin, first that the Hitlerite state should be destroyed, and, secondly, that the whole German people is not (as Dr. Goebbels had been trying to persuade them) thereby doomed to destruction." (Ronald C. D. Jasper, *George Bell, Bishop of Chichester* [London-New York-Toronto, 1967], pp. 274f.)

Round Table. At Gedser all went smoothly and we reached Copenhagen punctually.

I went first to my hotel and then to eat with Merete: good and simple. We had a very good conversation, but it became too long when there was an air-raid warning at 10.15, just as I was about to go, which kept me with Merete until 12.15. That was too much by my standards. As always I liked Merete very much. She's had a telegram from Esther & Rolf[1] at Christmas, via Sweden. Moreover she'd had a letter from Lotte Leonhard,[2] who made it to the U.S.A. and gives singing lessons there. Also Ljena was said to have arrived there with her husband. The two sons are married, one in Palestine, the other in England.

The next morning—Monday—I woke up with a cold which has not left me yet. That was very unpleasant. I tried to treat it a bit but failed. Then I sulked and read in bed until 9, had a quick and uninteresting breakfast, because I was out of sorts, and had my hair cut. At 11 Merete picked me up for a walk. Copenhagen is indeed a charming and beautiful city— with a harbour everywhere.

[*continued*] *18 March 1943*[3]

So, I got as far as Copenhagen. The British in a daylight raid destroyed a dockyard which forms a semicircle around a church, without hitting the church. A really astonishing achievement. One can see it distinctly, because at each end of the destroyed area a bridge leads across an inlet. It was a low-flying attack, after which, as Merete's sister Beatrice said, "they went home through my street." In the evening I travelled on after a good meal and as soon as I was on the ferry between Helsingborg and Helsingör I found myself among frightful compatriots. I didn't know where to crawl for cover, where to hide. My embarrassment was so obvious that the Swedish sleeping-car attendant had pity and removed the man above me, saying there had been a mistake. He had to take a berth in a car that came from Malmö an hour later and was added to the train. So I had a compartment to myself and travelled very agreeably and comfortably as far as Halden, where I had to change. By 1.30 I was in the hotel in Oslo.

Here everything was very nice. By 3.30 in the afternoon our discussion with our friends had got going and something had also been arranged for the evening, and so we made fairly quick progress. Yesterday and today I

1. Merete Bonnesen's sister and brother-in-law, the graphic artist Rolf Brand, who lived in England.
2. Singer, also an old friend from Schwarzwald days.
3. Erroneously dated 18.10.43.

attended to my business during the day, discussions continued last night, and the most important discussion[1] begins at 10.30 tonight. With my cold these nightly enterprises—it has so far been after 1 every night—are an irritating strain. But they are necessary, and so they'll have to be. For my cold I gargle and wear your black scarf faithfully day and night.

When I arrived in Oslo the weather was glorious, but since yesterday it has been grey. I have a very nice room on the 6th floor with a wide-ranging view over Oslo Fjord. It's a pity that the city is so ugly, the country is so beautiful that much could be made of it.—The domestic situation here is much less tense than 6 months ago. Actually one has the impression that the Quisling government[2] is resigned to having no say and no influence. It has lost the church-and-school struggle and is simply ignored now. This is the basis on which calm has been restored.

The recent sabotage operations were tremendously expert jobs, done in all probability by people who had connections with the inhabitants of the country but are hardly inhabitants themselves. The importance of these acts of sabotage and their expert execution have justified them in the eyes of the German offices here, and the fact that they were not supported by local inhabitants has dissuaded them from taking reprisals. So, in this respect, too, I am quite reassured. It seems to me that in proportion to the improvement of the enemy position, the desire of the Norwegians

1. It was the night he talked with Bishop Berggrav, who stated after the war that the conversation concerned the question of assassination or tyrannicide—which M. opposed on several grounds. Berggrav also mentioned an earlier talk, when M. gave a report of the student unrest in Munich and asked him to inform the world press about it. That must, however, have been during this visit. Hans and Sophie Scholl had been arrested on 18 February 1943 and executed four days later, together with their friend Christoph Probst. Professor Huber (see letter and n. 2 [p. 404] of 10 January 1945), Alexander Schmorell, and Willi Graf followed later. M. brought the text of one of the leaflets of the White Rose with him and arranged for it to reach England. It then returned to Germany in BBC broadcasts and RAF leaflets. He also wrote a long report on the affair, which reached the Foreign Office in London. He was concerned that the events should be registered there not just as a sign of crumbling morale in Germany, but as a sign that there were forces there with whom the British could and should cooperate. M. also used the occasion to write a long and detailed letter, in English, to Lionel Curtis on conditions in Germany. He left it with Dr. Harry Johansson, the director of the Nordic Ecumenical Institute in Sigtuna, for transmission to England. But Johansson considered it too dangerous to send. It never reached Curtis. Decades later it was found in Sweden and was then published—in an article on Trott's wartime travels. It is a key document on wartime Germany. For the full text see pp. 281–290. For the foreshortened and inaccurate version conveyed to Curtis via the Bishop of Chichester by Tracy Strong, the American General Secretary of the YMCA, who had memorized the document at Johansson's request, see Ger van Roon, *German Resistance to Hitler: Count von Moltke and the Kreisau Circle*, trans. Peter Ludlow (London, 1971), pp. 364–67.

2. The puppet government of Vidkun Quisling.

to engage in sabotage decreases, because they say to themselves, Why should we risk our heads now, at the last moment, to give a shove to what is falling of its own accord. On the whole, therefore, the danger of a big bloodbath here is not too great.

St[eltzer] is in good shape. We have reached an understanding on the various questions still open between us. I have the impression that he, also, is satisfied. Our Norwegian friends are obviously impressed by what I can offer them this time, and for me, too, it is pleasant to be, for once, distinctly the giver and not the recipient. Thus everything promises to end well, and much depends on this evening.

I must travel to Stockholm on Saturday, because a man I must see is taking off early Monday. St. flies to Berlin on Sunday and is taking this letter with him. He has to go to Headquarters first, but intends to arrive in Stockholm Wednesday evening. By then I must already have fought the main battle. It is a little unfortunate but perhaps has the advantage of bringing a new impetus on Thursday.

Here, with the [general] staff, everything is very nice for me. Again I eat with the C.-in-C.,[1] am treated well, and hear everything I want to know and in exchange only have to listen to the general's stories, which are sometimes quite nice. In any case it is a very small price to pay. People, however, have not become better; on the contrary. Only Steltzer's staff are still unchanged and sound. . . .

[*continued*] *19 March 1943*

This is the last part of my letter, for tomorrow morning I depart and at midday St. is travelling to Berlin with the letter. Tomorrow night I'll be in Stockholm, where I'll be staying at the Strand Hotel again.

Yesterday evening, or, rather, last night, went on till 3.30. Fortunately I was very much better and so I had no trouble sticking it out. It was very satisfactory again and we have made a good deal of progress. It is so pleasant that all the joint planning[2] goes so easily and I only wish it were as easy nearer home. But it isn't.

Today the weather is glorious and the whole splendour of the harbour in Oslo Fjord is spread before me. On such days I always think: How long until I can come here with you and show you all my friends, and how will the world look then?

This morning I concluded one part of my official business successfully, this afternoon there will be a postlude with various high gentlemen, the chief, the Generaloberst, and so on. It will swallow up the whole after-

1. Falkenhorst.
2. For European cooperation and federation after the war.

noon. In the evening we eat at 7.30 and at 8.15 I'm going with St. and some of his people to a gathering with some artists from Soest. I don't expect much from it, but it has been arranged by Steltzer's staff and I don't want to exclude myself. But on the ground that I have to travel the next day and haven't slept much at night, I'll go to bed early.

Farewell, my love, in 10 days I'll be back in Berlin and perhaps I can manage to get hold of the subsequent week-end. Keep well. . . .

The following letter was written by Moltke in English. Although not addressed to Freya, it is included here because of its enormous historical importance. His spelling and phraseology have been retained without editorial alteration.

Stockholm, March 25th, 1943.

Lionel Curtis, Esqu.,
Hales Croft,   or   All Souls' College,
Kidlington,   Oxford.
Oxon

Dear Mr. Curtis,

This letter has a chance of getting into your hands without passing any censor. And I want to take this singular opportunity of giving you an analysis of conditions in my country, and to make some proposals as to how matters could be speeded up.

1.

I have to write a preface to what I have to say. From my experience I distrust judgment and discretion in matters of internal political developments of everybody connected with missions abroad. For one thing we get highly confidential stuff from practically every British and much worse still every American legation or embassy. Probably your people repay us the compliment in tapping the stuff inside our legations; but in the first case such information has killed more than one man whom we can ill spare. I have the impression that diplomats are so used to live in their very limited circles prying on each other and lauding each other that they are naïve as soon as it comes to the facts of life. Indeed one sometimes has the feeling that diplomats lead such a secluded life, that they simply cannot imagine what life really is like on our continent. There are grand words to describe the conditions of life on the Continent; but for lack of imagination what that looks like in reality these words do not really convey anything to the person using them much less to the one hearing them.

There is further caution in the same line, that is the prevalence of the secret service view as opposed to the political point of view. From the point of view of the secret service everything I do and with me many men and women is simply destructive of the third realm, thereby destructive of the chief enemy and therefore laudable. But from the point of view of politics the same rule applies in dictatorships or tyrannies as in democracies: you can only get rid of one government if you can offer another government, and that means, that the mere process of destroying the third realm can only get under way if you at least are able to propound an alternative. This view is not in sight of the man with the secret service point of view, and this lack can have very grave consequences not only for the postwar period but also for the chances of destroying the third realm with assistance from inside.

By the way, this argument has been propounded to me by more than one man from the underground organisations in the various occupied countries.

2.

People outside Germany do not realise the following handicaps under which we labour and which distinguish the position in Germany from that of any other of the occupied countries: lack of unity, lack of men, lack of communications.

Lack of unity: in all countries under Hitler but Germany and France the people are practically united. If it be in Norway or Poland, in Greece, Jugoslavia or Holland the vast majority of the people are one in mind. In Germany, and to a lesser extent in France this is different. There are a great many people who have profited from the third realm and who know that their time will be up with the third realm's end. This category does not only comprise some few hundred people, no it runs into hundreds of thousands and in order to swell their number and to create new posts of profit everything is corrupted.—Further there are those who supported the Nazis as a counterbalance against foreign pressure and who cannot now easily find their way out of the tangle; even where they believe the Nazis to be in the wrong they say that this wrong is counterbalanced by a wrong done to us before.—Thirdly there are those who—supported by Göbbels' propaganda and by British propaganda—say: if we lose this war we will be eaten up alive by our enemies and therefore we have to stand this through with Hitler and have to put him right, i.e., get rid of him thereafter: it is impossible to change horses in mid-stream.—You may disagree with those reasons just as strongly as I do, but you must take them into account as politically effective in making for disunity. Therefore while, practically speaking, you can trust every Dutchman, Norwegian, etc., as to his intentions, you have to probe deep into every German before you find out whether or not you can make use of him; the fact that he is an anti-nazi is not enough.

Lack of men: In our country we have, practically speaking, no young men left, men of the age groups which make revolutions, or are at least its spearhead. You have got young or at least fairly young workers in your home factories, you have your young men training in your own country. All this is different with us; all our young men, even those in training, are far beyond our frontiers. Instead we have got more than 8 million foreign and potentially hostile workers in the country, and their numbers are going to be swelled to 10 millions and not a man younger than the age group of 1899 in the country. The exceptions to this rule are, but for the secret police and the SS, negligeable. And those who still are there and are active are terribly overworked and have no strength to spare. The women, if they are not engaged in war work of one kind or another, are fully occupied— physically but especially mentally—in keeping their houses in order. The worse the economic strain gets the less likely a revolution be-comes, because people are so occupied in simply living. Food distri-bution is fairly all right, though it also takes a lot of time; but if you endeavour to buy anything else you will have an exhausting experi-ence. If you need an envelope, want your shoes repaired, your dress mended, your coat cleaned, if you are so audacious as to ask for nails or a toothbrush, for glue or a cooking-pot, a piece of pottery or glass, if you try to park your child anywhere or need a doctor you will find the fulfilling of any one of these desiderata a full-time job. You have to wait and to run, to stand and to bid, to press and to plead, and in the end you will probably only get what you want if you have some-thing to offer in return, be it services or goods. And all this additional work falls on the women. While the men forget in their job of sol-diering completely what work is like, the women are thoroughly overworked. And that means not only that they are occupied physi-cally with these jobs, they are of course, but the worst is that their head is full of thoughts about stratagems to get what you need, be it a toothbrush or a doctor. When a woman goes to sleep her last thought probably is: "I must not forget that they said they might get some envelopes at three, and the doctor's office said he might be back by 6.30; but what do I do with my child while waiting for the doctor; it may be 9 before I come back." There is no time even to think of the war.

Lack of communication: That is the worst. Can you imagine what it is like if you

a. cannot use the telephone,

b. cannot use the post,

c. cannot send a messenger, because you probably have no one to send, and if you have you cannot give him a written message as the police sometimes searches people in trains, trams, etc., for documents;

d. cannot even speak with those with whom you are completely *d'accord,* because the secret police have methods of questioning where they first break the will but leave the intelligence awake, thereby inducing the victim to speak out all he knows; therefore you must limit information to those who absolutely need it;

e. cannot even rely on rumour or a whispering-campaign to spread information as there is so effective a ban on communications of all kind that a whispering campaign started in Munich may never reach Augsburg.

There is only one reliable way of communicating news, and that is the London wireless, as that is listened in to by many people who belong to the opposition proper and by many disaffected party members.

3.

Some of this devilish machinery has been invented by the Nazis, but some of it has been produced by war itself. But this machinery is used to great effect by the ruling class. Their first aim is to keep the army out of touch with the political trends in the country. They succeed in this to a great extent. None but men on leave and those manning anti-aircraft guns are in the country. When on leave they do not want to be bothered and their relatives do not want to bother them. When out of the country, the information they get by post is very scanty as their womenfolk dare not write to them for fear of repressive measures which are and have been taken. Besides, the soldiers lead a fairly secluded life. Where they are they usually appear in great strength and have only the enemy to cope with. Most officers especially lead a life far above their status in civilian life. The normal soldier does not know more about conditions in Germany than you, probably a great deal less. And besides the soldiers are continuously led into positions where there is no choice but to fight. Their mind is occupied with the enemy as fully as the housewife's is occupied with her requirements. "The German general and soldier must never feel secure, otherwise he wants to rest; he must always know that there are enemies in front and at his back, and that there is only one thing to be done and that is to fight." This remark Hitler addressed to field marshall Manstein, who proposed to fortify some line way behind the frontline.

But even in Germany people do not know what is happening. I believe that at least 9tenths of the population do not know that we have killed hundreds of thousands of jews. They go on believing that they just have been segregated and lead an existence pretty much like the one they led, only farther to the east, where they came from. Perhaps with a little more squalor but without air raids. If you told these people what has really happened they would answer: you are just a victim of British propaganda; remember what ridiculous things they said about our behaviour in Belgium in 1914/18.

Another fact: German people are very anxious about their men or boys who have been reported missing in Russia. The Russians have allowed our men to write home, which was a very wise thing for the Russians to do. Well, these letters are, on their arrival in Germany, locked up or destroyed but not allowed to reach the relatives. About 1000 of these cards had passed the censor through some technical error. The recipients who then tried to answer in the normal way through the ordinary channels were thereupon arrested, questioned, and kept in confinement until they had realized what it would mean to them if they ever talked about the fact that they had received news from their men. Things like that go on in Germany for months and perhaps years and this is a bit of information for which Germans are eagerly waiting; you cannot explain it away, as you could with the example given about the jews, with the argument that the Germans are impolitic and do not want to hear, that they have put jews to death. No, even these facts about the communications from Germans in Russia are neither known nor, where you tell them, believed. And where the facts become known, as with officials dealing with the cards or their relatives, there is a widespread belief, that the cards are faked and that the Führer in his magnanimity does want to prevent the raising of hopes by the beastly Russians which are unfounded and must give way to still deeper despair once the facts become known.

A third fact: We have now 19 guillotines working at considerable speed without most people even knowing this fact, and practically nobody knows how many are beheaded per day. In my estimation there are about 50 daily, not counting those who die in concentration camps.—Nobody knows the exact number of concentration camps or of their inhabitants. We have got a concentration camp only a few miles from our farm, and my district-commissioner told me that he only learnt of the fact that there was a concentration camp in his district when he was asked for orders to stop an epidemic of typhoid from spreading to a neighbouring village; by that time the camp had existed for months. Calculations on the number of KZ-inhabitants vary between 150.000 and 350.000. Nobody knows how many die per day. By chance I have ascertained that in one single month 160 persons died in the concentration camp of Dachau. We further know fairly reliably that there are 16 concentration camps with their own cremation apparatus. We have been informed that in Upper Silesia a big KZ is being built which is expected to be able to accommodate 40 to 50.000 men, of whom 3 to 4000 are to be killed per month. But all this information comes to me, even to me, who is looking out for facts of this nature, in a rather vague and indistinct and inexact form. We only know for certain, that scores, probably many hundreds of Germans are killed daily by the various methods, and that these people die not a glorious death, as those in the occupied countries do, knowing that their people consider them heroes, but an ignominious death knowing that they are classed among robbers and murderers.

4.

What is happening to the opposition, the men "of whom one hears so much and notices so little" as a headline in a paper lately said.

Well, first of all, it loses men, at a considerable rate. The quick-working guillotines can devour a considerable number of men. This is a serious matter, not alone because of the loss of life; that has to be faced, as we will not be able to get out of the quandary into which we have been led without considerable sacrifices in men. The worst is that this death is ignominious. Nobody really takes much notice of the fact, the relatives hush it up, not because there is anything to hide, but because they would suffer the same fate at the hands of the Gestapo if they dared telling people what has happened. In the other countries suppressed by Hitler's tyranny even the ordinary criminal has a chance of being classified as a martyr. With us it is different: even the martyr is certain to be classed as an ordinary criminal. That makes death useless and therefore is a very effective deterrent. Secondly the opposition has thrown sand into the machine. It will probably never be known to what extent this has helped your people. But the extent to which that has been done is very considerable, especially in the higher bureaucracy. There is seldom a week when I do not notice something that must have been done in order to prevent a command from being executed or at least from becoming fully effective.

Thirdly the opposition is saving individual lives. We cannot prevent the ferocious orders from being given, but we can save individuals. And this is done in all walks of life. People who have been officially executed still live, others have been given sufficient warning to escape in time. This is especially so in occupied countries: there is no denying the mass-murders, but once the balance is drawn, people will perhaps realize that many thousands of lives have been saved by the intervention of some German, sometimes a private and sometimes a general, sometimes a workman and sometimes a high-ranking official.

Fourthly the opposition has made many mistakes. The main error of judgement has been the reliance placed on an act by the generals. This hope was forlorn from the outset, but most people could never be brought to realize this fact in time. The same reasons which made it impossible for the french generals to get rid of Napoleon prevent this happening in Germany. To expound the reasons would be too long a process. The main sociological reason is that we need a revolution, not a coup d'état, and no revolution of the kind we need will give generals the same scope and position as the Nazis have given them, and give them today.

Fifthly the opposition has done two things which, I believe, will count in the long run: the mobilisation of the churches and the clearing of the road to a completely decentralised Germany. The churches have done great work these times. Some of the sermons of the more prominent Bishops, Catholic as well as Protestant, have become known abroad, especially two sermons of the Bishop of Berlin, Count Preysing, of May 16th (?) 1942 and December 20th, 1942. But the most important part of the churches' work has been the continuous process by which the whole clergy, practically without exception, have upheld the great principles in spite of all the intense propaganda and the pressure exerted against them. I do not know of a single parson who in a church demolished by British bombs held a sermon with an antibritish strain. And the churches are full Sunday after Sunday. The state dare not touch the churches at present, and in order to get over this difficulty the churches have been re-quisitioned in many places for storing furniture saved from bombed houses; thereby the state hopes to make church-work slowly impossible.

The breaking down of the idea of a highly centralised German state has made considerable progress. While two years ago the idea of a completely decentralised Germany was considered a utopia it is today nearly a commonplace. This will ease the transitory period between war and peace, and may, perhaps, make a meeting of the minds possible.

5.

Two general observations can be added: one on war criminals and one on the threat of communism. The punishment of political crim-inals once the third realm has come to an end will this time be very popular with the German people. You must realize that we have a concentration-camp-population of some 250000, certainly once again that number of men have lost their lives through the nazis' hands, and probably another 250000 have once been in a camp but have been released and fight or work somewhere. These 750000 men and/or their relatives have only one big desire: to kill the person whom they consider responsible for their special case. And this by the quickest procedure possible, if attainable with their own hands. And those who are killing people in occupied countries are to a great extent the same people who have killed or imprisoned Germans, un-less they are drawn from other countries, especially from Latvia.— By the way, most of the most brutal SD-men, murderers, etc., have been drawn either from Austria or from the Sudetenland, the minor-ity are toughs from the smaller Germany, and probably a quite min-ute minority only from Prussia.—Therefore it is a need of the internal German politics to bring these men to justice, perhaps even to death without justice, and the only way in which this could be prevented would be by making these toughs national heroes suffer-ing for Germany instead of being punished by Germans.

The "danger of communism" is in our position very real. But as things are this danger arises mainly in the group of intellectuals and not among the workmen. The reason is that those workers who would go communist are already nazis. And those who are nazi are ready to go communist any day. If one does not take care, one will find all those brutal SA and SS men posing as persecuted commu-nists, who now have to avenge themselves on their opponents. But

those workers who are not nazi now, and that is the majority of the
older and highly skilled workers, are completely fed up with all kinds
of totalitarianism. These are the workers on whom we must build,
not on those who can escape with a simple change of colour without
change of heart. You see, the fight against nazism is not confined to
one class or another: it goes on inside the classes and there are ad-
herents to each creed at all levels of the society, at the top as well as
at the bottom. If there is anything you can say about classes it is this:
broadly speaking, the middle classes are nazi or at least most highly
afflicted by one form of totalitarianism or another, and the lower
ranks of the Prussian nobility as far as it still possesses land is least
afflicted, is in fact practically immune from any kind of totalitarianism. The nobility of the higher ranks from dukes upwards and the
nobility of the South and West of Germany is much more afflicted
by this disease and the urbanized nobility is really part of the middle-
classes. These middle-classes tend, where they are anti-nazi, to be
philo-bolshevist, philo-Russian, etc. They feel uncertain of themselves and hope for the great new strength that shall come from the
East.

6.

Now my plea in these circumstances is for a stable connection between the German opposition and Great Britain and a connection
not based on secret service relations, not used mainly to extract information but a political connection. I do not want this in order to
discuss possible peace terms, possibilities of a post-war world. I want
this connection in order to assist our war against Hitler, our internal
war. I enclose a note I made about a certain event which has occupied
us lately. If we had had a stable connection with Great Britain we
could have discussed common strategy in exploiting these facts. As
we have not got this connection we have to grope about in the dark,
hoping that the information which comes to your people will not be
used in such a way as to discredit and perhaps endanger us.—Occasions like this will recur, and other occasions will make contact
useful. But I hope that this one example will show you what I mean
without further details or examples.

7.

Now, how can this be done technically? We would have to have a
man in Stockholm who knows Central Europe and who, working

under the general guidance of the ambassador, would have special functions to keep in touch with the various underground movements in Europe, especially in Germany, and would have to deal with them on a basis of political discussion and cooperation. We would supply him with addresses here which would contact him with the oppositions in various countries under Hitler. Preferably it should be a man whom I know or about whom I know something, because time is precious and with a stranger it will take some time to get intimate and real personal contact is required.

But there are two main points, one about his position and one about his powers. Although subject to the general guidance of the ambassador, he should be free from all entanglements of secret service work. As far as I can make out, the channels of all secret services of the various nations are the same, and most agents will work for at least two parties. Therefore whatever you put into the secret service of one country will in due course be known to the secret services of all other countries. As a result the secret services of all countries are secret to everybody but its opponent. There may be an all-important time-lag before one bit of information available to one secret service percolates to the other, but in the end it will get there, and there is not much to be thankful for if the guillotine is simply postponed for 3 months.

As to the powers, I have to offer the following remark: the man must be able in certain circumstances to provide one of us with everything necessary to get to Britain and back in a short time, so that if necessary common plans can be discussed *viva voce.*

Well these are the proposals and I hope you will be kind enough to give them a thought. Perhaps they will be brought to you by one of our Swedish friends; if not, they will contain the address of one of our friends, with whom you could put a man you sent here in contact. You will realise that you must please not mention my name in this connection unless it is to a man placed so highly as to be able to decide himself without handing the information with the name on to some superior. The name must most certainly never appear in writing anywhere.

As far as I am concerned I would, of course, prefer to have Michael here in Stockholm, be it as principal or as an adviser to the principal.

I do not feel able to add personal notes to this letter. I have written separate letters to Michael and Julian and have given them all the news. They know that they shall show their letters to you, and perhaps you will be good enough to show them from this letter what you think worth while showing.

I send my love to you both, Yours ever

Last night, when I considered the day already finished, the Baroness[1] demanded to see me. She came and reported: Bergen[2] is being pensioned off, Weizsäcker becomes Ambassador at the Vatican, Steengracht becomes Staatssekretär [Under-Secretary of State]. And a few other changes. You can imagine her state: utter despair and fury. I first assured her that this must be a gigantic April Fool's joke by her Adolf. But she persisted and told me, when I checked back today, that he had confirmed it to her again. The whole thing is really a catastrophe and will look very odd to the outside world too, because even the friendliest assessment of the dear Baron cannot consider him equal to the routine for such a post. . . .

Lukaschek came for lunch. The meal was excellent: soup with a little meat and lots of potato, horse-radish sauce, and afterwards a kind of white sauce dessert, with your juice. L. had had some unpleasant experiences; it's a good thing I saw him again, especially as it emerged that he totally rejects the good Burgomaster,[3] who always claims him for himself.—In the afternoon I was with Conrad,[4] who is well. I did have quite a lot to tell him and he showed himself very well informed on the latest developments in the Jewish question. It looks as if, after all, mixed marriages are to be broken up.[5] I hope he will hear more soon. . . . [6]

. . . Borsig came to lunch. He had little to report, less than I would have liked.[7] . . .

---

1. Ilse-Marie von Steengracht.
2. Carl Ludwig Diego von Bergen, German Ambassador at the Holy See.
3. Goerdeler.
4. Preysing.
5. Cf. n. 1 (p. 262) to letter of 12 November 1942. For the status of mixed marriages and their forcible dissolution at that time, see the sources given in the German edition, pp. 464ff.
6. The handwriting is not decipherable with any certainty in this sentence, and the translation is something of a guess.
7. Borsig had gone to Munich, where he still knew professors from his student days. He wanted to find out whether the activities of the White Rose were continued after the first executions (cf. n. 1 [p. 279] to letter of 18 March) and what the echo was. The answer was disappointing. Sympathizers were now doubly endangered and isolated. Alexander Schmorell, Willi Graf, and Professor Kurt Huber were sentenced to death on 19 April; Huber's execution was postponed until the summer at the instance of his publisher, Graf was kept alive for further interrogations until October. From Cologne Günter Schmölders was not able to report the formation of any oppositional student groups either.

Berlin, 5 April 1943

... This is a warm spring day. In the morning it was still overcast but from 11 o'clock on there was a warm sun. Unfortunately the day was badly rushed. For Husen came at 10, at 11 the man who was to have had lunch with me, who had meanwhile received orders to fly back at once; Diwald,[1] the new man, who studied with Verdross,[2] came at 12; at 12.30 I was with Dohnanyi;[3] Gablentz had lunch with me at 1.15; at 3 & 5 I had meetings; and now it is 5 to 7, and I am sitting at home and waiting for König, who must come any moment. So the day was chopped into little pieces and accordingly produced nothing.

Therefore there is nothing to report. Dieckhoff[4] becomes Ambassador in Madrid,[5] Woermann goes to Nanking—if he gets there. The situation in Tunis is worsening slowly, the others proceed very systematically. Nothing new in the East or from the occupied territories. In short, everything is in suspense: *patiencia victrix.*

Berlin, 7 April 1943

This has been a day full of most unpleasant sensations.[6] Also much current work. I really am up to my neck. And these are all matters in which one would need time and peace to think about what to do and how to do it. What's more, it burdens the conscience, is of paramount importance, and very dangerous. It was a lucky coincidence that Peter came here this morning for 24 hours and I was therefore able to talk about this

1. Lieutenant Otto Diwald had joined the International Law Group on 1 April.
2. Alfred Verdross (1890–1980), Austrian professor of international law and philosophy of law, with whom M. had studied in Vienna.
3. Hans von Dohnanyi was arrested on 5 April, as was his wife, who later reported that M. had warned her husband of his imminent arrest. Her brother, Dietrich Bonhoeffer, was arrested at the same time, as were Josef Müller and his wife. Oster was suspended from office and banished from Abwehr headquarters. The rival counter-espionage office of the SD was now in the ascendant. (See Eberhard Bethge, *Dietrich Bonhoeffer: Man of Vision, Man of Courage*, trans. Eric Mosbacher et al., ed. Edwin Robertson [New York and Evanston, 1970], pp. 685–92.)
4. Dr. Hans Heinrich Dieckhoff, until then Ministerialdirektor in the AA.
5. Hans Adolf von Moltke had died in March.
6. Apart from the arrest of Dohnanyi, it may have been the discovery of the bodies of thousands of shot Poles, mostly officers, in mass graves in the wood at Katyn. The German publicity campaign about it started on 14 April. The Soviet Union blamed the Germans for the shootings (cf. n. 3 to letter of 14 April). In the occupied territories the massive recruitment of forced labour led to increased resistance, which in turn led to German reprisals, hostage takings, executions, and deportations, which included prominent politicians and military men.

matter. I had lunch with them at their house. There was a circus of people all day long.—It is 9.30 in the evening.—It is 11.30. I must stop. Another meagre letter and tomorrow will be bad too: a meeting at 10, one at 12, Adam at 1, a discussion at 3 and one at 5.30, and Eugen at 7.30. In between the matter which has occupied me today like a sauce over it all. . . .

Berlin, 9 April 1943

After two quite meagre letters on the 6th and 7th I didn't write to you at all yesterday. But the day began at 6 and ended at 12, and so it was simply impossible.—As you know, the 6th & 7th were already rather stormy. Towards evening on the 7th other rather disagreeable things happened and when I was about to leave to attend to those, a quite impossible order arrived from Keitel concerning occupied territories. I was consulted too late, was to give an opinion the same evening, refused, and demanded an extension until noon on the 8th. Then I pursued the other troubles, had a detailed discussion with Peter and König, and by 9 p.m. I'd got to the point of attending to that matter.

Meanwhile I had summoned Wengler to the Office, and a secretary, and we brooded there until midnight. In addition I had to telephone all military commanders in the Western Territories. At least the night produced enough progress for me to dictate an opinion by 9, having arrived at the Office again at 8 a.m. on the 8th; at a quarter to 10 I had Bürkner's signature, and then it went out over the teleprinter. Whether it will still do any good I don't know, but firstly I satisfied my conscience and secondly it may after all act as a brake.[1] In any case it worked like a bombshell at FHQ,[2] for they have already applied to me several times for elucidations of our teleprinter message.—So the night was well spent in any case, only unfortunately you got short-changed.

For then all other matters moved on. At 10.45 I had a meeting, which lasted till 12.30, at the office of the Minister of Finance, at 12.45 I went

1. Former Dutch prisoners of war who had been released were to be sent to Germany as civilian workers, thus losing the protection of the Wehrmacht. M. tried to keep the prisoner-of-war status for them and for Dutch soldiers already in police prisons. A compromise was reached. On 29 April General Christiansen, C.-in-C. Netherlands, ordered all former Dutch prisoners of war—the officers had already been reinterned a year before—to report for reinternment in German prisoner-of-war camps. There was considerable unrest, and on the 30th a state of siege was proclaimed. On 6 May the Reich Commissar in the Netherlands, who was not under Wehrmacht jurisdiction, decreed that all men between the ages of eighteen and thirty-five had to report for forced labour.
2. Führer Headquarters.

with Goerschen to see Adam, at 3.30 I turned up at the Office to devote myself to current tasks, but found a message that Bürkner wanted to talk to me, and then I discussed an amazing row between Ribbi[1] and Keitel with him and drafted a letter on it. Then it was 5.15. At 5.30 I had people at my office who occupied me until 7.15 and afterwards I was at Eugen's, where I should have been at 7.30. There I stayed until 11.45.

At Eugen's it was very nice. We both had much to report. He chiefly from Rome. Many details, nothing earth-shaking. A quite negative attitude in the Vatican towards Russia. That was of great interest to me, especially since I'd expected the opposite. Besides, a great hymn in praise of Rösch: he was Catholicism's strongest man in Germany. That pleased me, of course. Otherwise he was well. He and his patron[2] are probably suffering somewhat from their reactionary backers. . . .

I had lunch with Herr Deichmann. We had to discuss all sorts of household matters. Mutz[3] is letting us have a room for Frau Pick. Moreover, the Cohns are threatened with [deportation].[4] That, too, occupied us greatly. C. is travelling to M.D.'s[5] today.

As for matters of general interest, Tunis is now approaching the end, and Italy, contrary to my expectations, seems to be drawing conclusions from this after all. In any case Mussolini is said to have come to Salzburg[6] at his own initiative. I wonder if that will turn out to be the case. It looks at the moment as if Italy and Roumania want to make a separate peace.[7] In any case the political situation looks more critical once more. If I (a) hadn't experienced so many crises and (b) were not so tired, I might get excited about all this. . . .

Berlin, 12 April 1943

Don't you really have too much to do? You sounded a bit like it on the phone. Spare yourself, my love. The time for limitless exertion has not yet come and you must be prepared for it. You above all, for you must always reckon with the possibility that I shall no longer be there, be it physically or merely geographically. Please don't forget that.

1. Ribbentrop.
2. Wurm.
3. Maria Schanda, actress, friend from the Schwarzwald circle.
4. The German word M. uses is *Absendung*, "despatch." Cf. n. 1 (p. 262) to letter of 12 November 1942, and n. 5 to letter of 2 April 1943.
5. Carl Deichmann was going to visit his mother in the Rhineland.
6. He was at Schloss Klessheim 7–10 April.
7. Mussolini's proposal to Hitler was of a separate peace with Russia, to give relief to the Western Front. Hitler would not consider it.

My week-end trip to Hanover was completely meaningless. It was nice but frightfully strenuous and boring, really provincial. Well, why shouldn't something go wrong once in a while. I only regret the time and also it made me tired; and I do find boredom much more of a strain than working.

On the return journey I travelled with a couple named Tetter [?] and 2 boys aged 3 and 2. Nice, harmless business people from Krefeld, the children nice and moderately well brought up. As soon as the woman spoke I knew that she was English, for she made the same mistakes as Mami. Their house and business had gone up in flames and they were on their way to an uncle in Silesia to get some sleep. The children didn't look much affected by it, the mother very exhausted. But when it got dark the older one became very restive and kept saying "Tommy coming soon" and couldn't be persuaded to go to sleep. Then he told me about the burning of his house: "Uncle Jim come and make all flat." She said that despite all the losses there wasn't a shadow of hatred of England: just compare that with '14/'18.

A new week begins today. After I've dealt with all the small rubbish the big jobs follow this week: 2 big court cases, one in Sweden, one in Turkey, the hostage affair.[1] Once all that is in train, I can go on leave with peace of mind, and so I'm hoping to have got that far by Maundy Thursday. . . .

Berlin, 13 April 1943

A heavenly spring day seems to be breaking. There is still a light haze over the land, but one already sees the sun behind it, which will surely be fully visible by 9 or 10. There is still no wind. Everything is growing and the air feels lighter. Perhaps it only feels light to me because at the moment I'm especially pleased by a few things I did 3 or 4 weeks ago. For there is no other reason I can see. In any case, the day is starting as if one could achieve something in it. It is also promising to be stormy enough. . . .

At lunchtime yesterday Peters paid me a long visit at the Office. He gave quite an interesting account of British offensive tactics and had quite a lot else to say too. He really is a nice man. His wife had a relapse after the shock of the air raid of 1 March and is no longer with the Sisters with whom she was staying. That is a heavy burden for him, because he must now look for another place for her to stay.—Reichwein and Friedrich came in the evening. They were in good form and full of pep. But unfortunately Maass has had quite a severe relapse since he is no longer under

1. Cf. letter of 5 June.

constant surveillance. F. got quite furious about him and R. gave a marvellous description of the conversation between F. & M. F. constantly sat
with his back to M. on the pretext of warming his feet at the electric fire.
It must have been beautiful. Nonetheless the hitch is very awkward and
Uncle[1] and his crowd will have to make efforts to make up for it. . . .

Berlin, 14 April 1943

. . . With Adam and Eugen I had a detailed discussion on questions of
foreign policy and to my great joy our differences in the last discussion
had been completely overcome. This was partly because we took a different point of departure, but partly because the military situation had become clearer to them both,[2] and because of the discussion in England
and the conflict between Russia and Poland.[3] Thus, to my surprise, a
synoptic view resulted. In particular they had largely accepted my thesis
on the island.[4] So we moved a big step forward, and now Whitsun[5] looks
quite probable to me.

Berlin, 15 April 1943

An enormously strenuous day is about to end, but I have made real
progress with my programme. In fact I am a bit further along than I expected and, except for one matter, I also got all the signatures I needed.
Unfortunately this one matter has to be signed by Keitel himself and is
on the way to him. I hope it goes well. I have not attended to any current
business for days now, and it looks like it all around me. But I'll dispose
of it easily tomorrow in the course of the day. Unfortunately I have to look
after a lot of small technical detail in the big jobs: duplication and printing of the opinions, proper despatching, etc. I hope it will all be over by
Saturday noon. . . .

I am so full of the work of these two days that I can really think of
nothing else. I have to watch so many people who work for me, and that

1. Leuschner.
2. The surrender at Stalingrad and the imminent German-Italian surrender in North Africa.
3. It was known that the Soviet Union was not prepared to give up the parts of Poland
acquired by the pact with Germany in 1939. On 1 March 1943 the "Union of Polish Patriots"
had been founded in Moscow. The reaction of the "London" Poles to the mass graves at
Katyn led to the rupture of diplomatic relations between the Polish government in exile and
the U.S.S.R. on 25 April. Cf. n. 6 to letter of 7 April.
4. The special position of Great Britain inside and outside the planned European federation.
5. The third and last meeting at Kreisau, devoted to questions of foreign policy and European and international economic policy, and also to the punishment of Nazi criminals.

is very troublesome. And nothing much has happened. Only my plans have become uncertain, because I can't do what I wanted to do in the Government [General].[1] I'm still wondering whether I should go now at all or give it up.—In Tunis the end is approaching. It may drag on for weeks, like Stalingrad, but it is practically all over: no more supplies by sea or air, no rest from enemy planes by day or night, no more planes of our own, no space for operations.[2]

My love, the telephone has just rung again and I must go to the AA in connection with one of my favourite operations, the one for which I did a night shift a little while ago.

Berlin, 16 April 1943

Slowly I'm beginning to see that I'm eating my way through the mess, and in the distance Easter is beckoning like the land of milk and honey. I hope it all works out. It actually looks likely now.

Last night when I suddenly had to stop my letter to you, I was called to the AA in a matter which I'd held up by a night shift at the beginning of the week—or was it at the end of last week. The AA was about to cave in, and I came at just the right moment. So I fortified them with an injection and played the matter into Schlitter's hands and thus hope to have saved it again. And whatever happens, I have saved 10 days of their lives for many hundreds of thousands of people, that is, days of their normal lives.[3] That sort of thing still cheers one up. By 9 I was home, wrung out like a washcloth, and sank into bed.

Today started early. Schlitter came at 10 and we had to work together till 11. Oxé, who has returned from an official trip, took up 1 hour, Diwald, the new man, wanted something, Dr. Bloch's[4] opinion had to be

---

1. On his trip to the Government General, i.e., occupied Poland, M. wanted to see not only Christiansen-Weniger at Pulawy but also Archbishop Sapieha in Cracow—which seems to have proved impossible, at least for the time being (cf. letter of 11 January). The omission of any mention of Cracow in the travel plans discussed in the letter of 18 April could be due to discretion; but the letter of 4 May shows that there was obviously no stop at Cracow on the way to Pulawy. F.M. cannot recall any oral report on a visit to Sapieha, which she would hardly have forgotten. The account in van Roon, *Resistance to Hitler*, p. 213, and in Balfour and Frisby, *Moltke*, p. 258, describes the visit as being concerned with cooperation with the Polish resistance and protection against SS reprisals; both rely on information given by Christiansen-Weniger, who had established the connection but could not be present himself, because he was already suspect as a friend of the Poles, and was indeed arrested later.
2. The capitulation came on 13 May.
3. A delay in their dispatch to Germany. One of the arguments he used was the persuasively "expedient" one that Germany would profit more from their work in their own country.
4. Dr. Joachim-Dieter Bloch of the Kaiser Wilhelm Institute.

looked through and expedited. Wengler also wanted this and that. Suddenly it was 1.30. Schlitter came to lunch, then I had to go to the main building in most unpleasant matters, at 4 Frl. Breslauer came for dictation and has just now left the room at 5.30. Now I'll stay here, at the Office, to finish a matter which I have to dictate tomorrow, at 7 Einsiedel comes for the evening. There you have the day. . . .

Berlin, 17 April 1943

After much hesitation I have decided after all to visit Christiansen[1] after Easter. It is a big sacrifice for me. But he's in such an isolated post that one has to do something for him. I'll discuss the schedule with you tomorrow. I further plan to return to Berlin on 4 May and want to ask if you couldn't come with me. At the end of the week I'd then like to visit relatives in Bavaria with you.[2] What do you say to this project? We'll talk about it on the phone tomorrow.

It is 12 o'clock on Saturday and my desk is completely empty. Not a single paper left here. I am really tremendously relieved. But it was a great effort, I can't deny it. Tomorrow I have another nasty job, which will cost me the whole day; it is to go through certain files and take out certain papers that belong in our files. It is a great nuisance. The 4 days of the new week I hope to spend only on the expediting of my writings.

Last night Einsiedel came, nice and harmless and not extravagant. He had a good day. Trott came with alarming news that can't be correct. It was 11.30 when I got to bed and slept splendidly. This morning Delbrück came, and later Poelchau for quite a while. He has a dreadful lot to do, really a bit too much, and too great a psychological burden. Waetjen is coming to lunch today. . . .

Berlin, 18 April 1943

. . . My travel plans are as follows: In the evening of the 29th get into sleeping car for Vienna at Liegnitz. Depart from Vienna evening of the 30th, arrive Pulawy evening of 1 May, depart Pulawy evening of 3rd May, arrive Berlin 4 May, leave Berlin 7 May midday, arrive Munich in the evening, leave Munich evening 9 May. I've booked a room for us. Can you write a letter for Aunt Katze[3] and ask if we can visit her sometime? . . .

---

1. Cf. n. 1 to letter of 15 April, and letter and n. 2 (p. 272) of 11 January.
2. Those visits were to camouflage political visits.
3. Great-Aunt, Baroness Leonardi, née Countess Bethusy-Huc.

Berlin, 20 April 1943

Today I've had a little more sleep though still not enough. Yesterday was strenuous but went very well, with a lot of coffee and tea at Behrenstrasse.[1] Adam, Eugen, Peter, and Marion stayed till 11.30 and we cleared another bit of the way through the jungle. I am very relieved that we are beginning to make progress again. I wonder if there will then be another sudden push forward. The path, or, rather, the stretch we marked out yesterday, is not yet quite clean. We didn't quite finish, because it was more than we could manage.

It was nice yesterday with Conrad. Both of us had much to report, and however much a good deal of it oppresses the heart, the feeling that everything is moving is a relief. He complained that he no longer had a pulpit[2] and had to accept hospitality. I thereupon agreed with Eugen that we'll try to get him one side of the cathedral.[3] It would really be grand if we succeeded.

The Cohns have to move after Easter but will stay in the vicinity.[4] They were to have moved out yesterday. But it was possible to get a postponement. Unfortunately I contributed nothing to this. But I am glad that it worked out. . . .

On the way to Warsaw, 1 May 1943

Yesterday in Vienna I wanted to write to you, but every minute was occupied, and I had trouble even getting the train to Warsaw. When I got to the station the train was so full that the platform was barred and I, because I had a berth reserved, had to be convoyed through the locked-out crowd by the stationmaster. It was a good thing I had the berth, for otherwise I would have been stuck in Vienna. . . .

Berlin, 4 May 1943

After I posted my last letter to you, we entered the G.G.[5] The train was rather empty and remained so as far as Warsaw. It was reserved for Germans. It seems that Poles are not allowed on express trains. The journey to Warsaw was interesting in that one still saw single cows along the line,

1. The seat of the Bishop of Berlin.
2. The St. Hedwig Cathedral had been destroyed in the night raid of 1–2 March.
3. The Protestant *Dom.*
4. Probable meaning: no deportation, just eviction.
5. Government General.

being tended. I thought that we had already disposed more thoroughly of the Polish stock of cattle.

At 2 I was in Warsaw, having had a fairly decent lunch in the restaurant car. Since I had until 6 before continuing my journey, I wandered through the streets of Warsaw. Actually I was surprised to see how much was still standing. It doesn't look much worse than Cologne or Mainz. The streets are packed. The large number of men of the best age is a surprising sight to us. Occasionally one sees wretched figures, not only beggars, as in the past, but also destitute children, emaciated and sickly people. There were queues in front of pharmacies, likewise in front of an outpatient clinic. But the bulk of the population doesn't look worse fed than ours. And their clothing is still surprisingly good. The shoes are probably the worst. The trams are full to overflowing, the slow passenger trains too. People hang in clusters outside, sit on the roofs, on brakeman's cabins, buffers, etc.

A big cloud of smoke stood above the city and could still be seen a good half hour after my departure by the express train, that means about 30 km. It was caused by a fight which had been raging for some days in the ghetto. The remaining Jews—30,000—reinforced by airborne Russians, German deserters, and Polish communists, had turned part of it into an underground fortress. It is said that they have made passages between the cellars of houses while the Germans were patrolling the streets, and reinforced the ceilings of the cellars, exits are said to lead by underground passages from the ghetto to other houses. I was told that cows and pigs had been kept in those catacombs and large food depots and wells had been installed. In any case it was said that something like partisan fighting in the town had been directed from these headquarters, so that it was decided to clear out the ghetto: but the resistance was so strong that a real assault with guns and flamethrowers was needed. And that is why the ghetto is still burning. It had already been going on for several days when I got there and was still burning on my return journey yesterday.[1]

There were 2 other men in my compartment on the train to Pulawy, who soon started talking and gave a graphic description of the danger of night-time travel by train. They vied with each other in their atrocity tales, and they compared the dangers of different sections of the route. They left me at Deblin after declaring that they were lucky to get off before the most dangerous part. So I travelled on *"well primed"*[2] for an

---

1. Armed resistance in the Warsaw ghetto lasted from 19 April to 16 May. For the official German report see *The Stroop Report: The Jewish Quarter of Warsaw Is No More!*, trans. and annotated by Sibyl Milton, intro. Andrzej Wirth (London, 1980). M.'s mention of reinforcements and livestock seems to be based on rumours.
2. English in the original.

adventure. Once we stopped at a signal on the track in the middle of a wood, and I thought things would start now, but after 10 minutes the train moved on. At Pulawy another man got off with me, Prof. Ries, who belongs to the Institute. As there wasn't a car, I was much relieved to find a travelling companion in him, for it was pitch dark. He got a car by telephone and we drove briefly to Christiansen's, had a schnapps, and then I went to my hotel. Next morning—Sunday—Chr. fetched me at 7.

We had breakfast together. His wife is small and sturdy with sparkling eyes. The house is nicely built, has 2 storeys, Prof. Horn lives upstairs without wife. The house stands, with 2 others, halfway between the station and the town of Pulawy. The landscaping is quite new because everything had frozen. The rooms are furnished with insipid official furniture and therefore lack a personal note, but they are bright and clean. The maid is a nice Polish wench, the coachman and driver, Adamczyk, is a philosopher who drove Russian professors till 1914, then German, then Polish, now German professors again, and who awaits the next generation with composure. The worst thing in the house is the arms. In the evening there is a machine gun in position upstairs, Christiansen has a machine pistol beside him and never leaves the house without a revolver. The partisans are very strong and growing constantly. At the edge of the wood they have put a notice: Off Limits to Germans.

Chr. and his people are very nice with the Poles and relations are obviously good. They give one of Christiansen's people a guard of 5 men for his wife, so that nothing should happen to her when he is away. They live alone on a farm.—The Institute is enormous. The main building is a beautiful castle which once belonged to Prince Czartoryski[1] and, standing on high ground, commands an extensive view over the Vistula. The farming operation has 5,000 hectares, most of it experimental fields. 240 Polish scientists are employed there—I have a pamphlet I'll give you to read. The spirit of this enterprise is excellent and there is no doubt that under Chr. first-rate work has been done for Polish agriculture, because he has succeeded in getting good but disharmonious Polish scientists to work together on immediate practical tasks.

I can't give you a report on the breeding results in detail. The most impressive were a species of poppy with 40% oil and a rape which flowers simultaneously and evenly from top to bottom. In the livestock department a small peasant horse, "Kulik," is noteworthy and above all the Pulawy pig. But all the Polish livestock makes a healthy and sturdy, undemanding impression and with proper feeding a lot can be done there.

1. Adam Kasimir Czartoryski (1734–1823) served Austria after the first partition of Poland and tried to restore Polish independence; his son Constantine (1773–1860) took part in Napoleon's Russian campaign in 1812.

The soil varies, from sand and alluvial land to massive layers of loess. Actually mostly very good, warm humus soil without stones. I was particularly interested in the department of agricultural meteorology, which was said to be occupied also with micro-weather questions, and the fruit-growing department, which is doing large-scale basic experimental research in resistance to frost.

Berlin, 5 May 1943

. . . Last night I visited Eugen with Peter. We talked about the progress they have made in respect of Whitsun.[1] It is satisfactory on the whole. Everything seems to have gone according to schedule.—Eugen's chief[2] is in Berlin today and tomorrow to sign a very good letter.[3] I may see him tomorrow.

I had a talk with Bürkner this morning about the little sailor's[4] fits of weakness and told him this couldn't go on. I'd have to be sure of my backing, otherwise I couldn't do anything useful. B. was reasonable and has given me permission to talk about it with the little sailor alone. That is to happen early next week. I wonder how it will end.

Peter came at lunchtime. We had to discuss our plan of action for the time until Whitsun. In addition we discussed the Kleinöls matter and Wernersdorf-Bresa. Altogether it took 3 hours, so that not much is left of the afternoon, for at 5 I have an appointment at my office, at 6 another. Delbrück is coming in the evening and in between I must go to see Haubach. But I've brought my bike.

6 May 1943

. . . In the evening I wanted to talk to Delbrück. But when I got home I found a message to come to Eugen as soon as possible; he had his chief with him. So I had supper with Delbrück and put him out at 9.

The evening at Eugen's was very long; I left only at 12. There were just the three of us, plus Pressel[5] from time to time. W. again made a very good, wise impression. Yet it is hard to shake off the feeling that his assistants aren't good enough and that therefore the work isn't done care-

1. Cf. n. 5 to letter of 14 April.
2. Bishop Wurm.
3. This does not seem to have happened—cf. letter of 6 May. For Wurm's letter to Hitler of 16 July 1943 see letter and n. 1 (p. 321) of 18 July.
4. Canaris, whose own position was endangered after the removal of Oster and Dohnanyi—cf. n. 3 to letter of 5 April.
5. Cf. letter and n. 1 of 19 June 1942.

fully enough. It is a great pity. We talked about his and our latest plans, and our results were probably satisfactory.

Today, in a few minutes, I'm going to see Conrad, with whom W. has an appointment this afternoon. In the morning Peter, Einsiedel, and Haeften came. Now it is 11.—So it is flying weather, as you might say. Peter and Adam will have lunch with me tomorrow. . . .

Berlin, 17 May 1943

It is 4.30, and I hope that you have meanwhile had a good trip and landed safely at home. It was a great relief to me to know that you had a sleeper and were, I hope, comfortable at least as far as Dresden.—Your husband travelled well and without air-raid warnings; he didn't sleep too well, but is unable to give reasons for this.

Here they'd had 2 air-raid warnings, but without much shooting. Last night, to make up for it, the wicked little angels[1] thought of a new piece of malice: they drop torpedoes in reservoirs and cause dams to collapse. They succeeded with two dams last night, and it causes devastation and reduces electrical capacity. I wonder if they have more of that kind of thing up their sleeves.

Here it was cool, too, when I got out. But it got a little warmer during the day. But it isn't as decidedly warm as last week.—Eddy and Peter were here at lunchtime. It went quite well. But it looks as if we won't need E. because Abs seems to be coming. He intends to be back on 8 June.

My love, what a lovely week I had with you. I express my thanks for the kindly care given me by my spouse. Now she should take real care of herself, herself and her children. The year will become strenuous enough and, moreover, the preparation for Whitsun is a strain too.

Berlin, 18 May 1943

When I woke up this morning, it was icy cold. Only 7°. What can one say to that? It is simply scandalous. What will it do to the bees? I can't imagine that they like it.—The departure of the ARP[2] cars woke me up at 12.45, but they returned after about 45 minutes. I have decided to prepare myself well every evening now, and I don't mean only my soul.

1. Probably an allusion to the story about Pope Gregory I, who, on seeing three flaxen-haired English boys in the Roman slave market and being told they were Angles, said they looked to him not like Angles but like angels. He then took in hand the evangelization of Britain.
2. The cars of the air-raid protection organization used the garage beneath the Derfflinger-strasse apartment.

I now always pack my despatch case full of important things, reading matter, and food. If I do go into the cellar, I want to do it sensibly.

Last night I was alone with Peter and had mainly to report on the week-end.[1] We talked about the various necessary preparatory steps. I went home at 10. The moon shone brightly and the Tirpitzufer looked magical in this lunar radiance. . . .

Berlin, 24 May 1943

What a lovely Saturday/Sunday that was! My heart, how I love to be with you, how truly home it is, and how good that despite the catastrophes everything is bearable for you, because at least you have peace in the house.

Your husband had a good journey. The train was quite empty at Lieg-nitz and really full only from Guben, but even then only so full that all seats were taken. The journey was quite unsensational, I read my *Parlia-mentary Reports* and have finished them except for 3. But it is a lot of work. Also I have read the Keynes Plan and the White Plan.[2]

But my thoughts were always wandering back to you and to the many tasks before you. I thought, in particular, of the bees, the new frames, the new swarms, and the work we did yesterday. I wonder if we did it right, and if both queens stayed on the right side. It is all very exciting. . . .

The farm, too, occupies me enormously: the sheep and cows, the feed and the new planting plans, the building, the well at Wierischau, the new machines, and so on. There is such an awful lot to do, to consider, to plan, that I regret every day I can't be at home. I wonder how it will go.

Waetjen was here for lunch today; I'd given him work to do over the week-end and he'd done a good job. Now, in 5 minutes, I'll go to Peter's with Poelchau; Goerschen is coming to lunch tomorrow. You see there isn't a dull moment.

Berlin, 25 May 1943

. . . Last night with Poelchau was very nice. He, P., is terribly busy with his support operations and asks again for help for his charges.[3] I told him we would certainly send him a sizable quantity of peas. Will you, please,

1. They had spent it in Munich, Stuttgart, and Heidelberg, and there had been a meeting with Bishop Wurm.
2. The British plan for an international monetary and clearing union prepared under the direction of Lord (John Maynard) Keynes and published on 7 April, and the simultaneous plan for world stabilization prepared by Harry Dexter White of the U.S. Treasury.
3. The people he looked after were, apart from prisoners, persons living illegally, like Jews, who had insufficient rations or none.

find out and, if it is possible, send him a hundredweight? His address is: Pastor Poelchau, Berlin N. 65, Afrikanischestrasse 140 B. He knows that he must return the sack at once. Furthermore, I have invited him and his wife to Kreisau for a stay in the summer, as we agreed. He is unlikely to come for any length of time, perhaps only for an extended week-end. . . .

For news there are only thickening rumours about the defection of Italy. Whether they are true nobody here knows; but it is certain that they are negotiating wildly with Italy.

Goerschen came to lunch today. We ate the two pigeons I had brought with me and with them divine mashed potatoes. Carlchen is arriving here on the 3rd and will go on to Holland immediately. G. said that in Switzerland the whole enterprise has already been completely written off.

Brussels, 5 June 1943

I'm writing because I think that in the haste and work of Whitsun there won't be time for a leisurely account.

Monday morning I was at Hilversum, where I was put up at a princely hotel. The headquarters was about 20 minutes away, on the outskirts of the town, and I was immediately equipped with a good Dutch army bicycle to make me mobile. Monday morning I had my first talk with Capt. Janssen, a dyed-in-the-wool Catholic from Aachen, whom I liked very much. He is no heavyweight, and that is a disadvantage, but he is full of good will, which, after all, is the main thing. At lunch I met the most important people immediately, especially the chief of staff, General von Wühlisch,[1] and the very nice older Ia,[2] Col. von Müller. The staff as a whole makes a good impression; it isn't very big, but right-minded people predominate.

In the afternoon I read the relevant files of the Ic[3] and then talked with Wühlisch. He is a recent arrival, but undoubtedly he has the right attitude and tries to prevent shootings as far as he can. I therefore felt I could count on Hilversum to cover my rear, and with that I went to the SD at The Hague. That was the great surprise. First, I was most warmly received, and people gave me a lot of time. The SD General Harster[4] talked

1. Heinz von Wühlisch, chief of staff in the Netherlands since April; committed suicide in internment after the war.
2. First (operational) Staff Officer.
3. Intelligence Officer.
4. Dr. Wilhelm Harster (born 1904), Free Corps fighter, Party member since 1933, SS Gruppenführer and lieutenant general of police, July 1940–August 1943 commander of the Security Police and SD (BdS) in the Netherlands, then in Italy until 1945. 1947 sentenced to twelve years' imprisonment in Holland, released 1953; 1956–63 civil servant in Bavaria; 1967 indicted for murdering Jews and sentenced to fifteen years' imprisonment in 1968; released before his sentence was fully served.

with me for hours during those two days; on the second day he was ill, and I sat at his bedside. He therefore had a chance to dodge the issue but didn't at all and was on the contrary obviously very interested. The same goes for his staff. Despite the alien foundations, the basic attitude, there is therefore in the superstructure an identity of conception and interests which was very encouraging. I'll quote Harster: "Against the guilty I am really harsh, even rigorous, but to shoot innocent people is simply idiotic." "Every execution of hostages is an admission of police bankruptcy; it simply means we haven't caught the culprit, or haven't caught him quickly enough." "I can't expect the population to keep quiet and not help bandits if I start to seize innocent people." "If you want the taking and shooting of hostages totally and categorically prohibited, you can be certain of my support."

Thus this conversation with the SD was a complete success, and I hope to have helped somewhat thereby. Harster, at least, promised me that he'll gradually and very secretly release the hostages still in custody. Nor will the whole thing be a flash in the pan, for after Whitsun I'll put Lt. Diwald on his back; he is to put his complete files at Diwald's disposal, and the way he does this will show whether or not one can count on him. In any case, our parting was most cordial, and he asked me to come back for a closing discussion. All this took 2 days, Tuesday and Wednesday.

At 6 on Tuesday I saw Goerschen at the bank and later we drove to Wassenaar for supper at his house. Our conversation was satisfactory and we arranged a meeting *à trois* the next afternoon with his chief Dutchman.[1] The supper was uninteresting. The Goerschens were nice enough to ask me to stay overnight, sparing me the return trip to Hilversum, with which I'd reckoned. The house is sumptuously furnished but not ostentatious, and therefore nice as a whole. The son, Peter, is meanwhile 15, very tall, and an ardent admirer of Adolf Hitler, with only one wish: to become a soldier as soon as possible. Despite his Dutch citizenship he is ostracized and maltreated at school as a German. Hence the reaction.— The Goerschens get all their supplies from the black market and think they can rely on this because, firstly, everybody lives mainly on black-market food and, secondly, they frequent only black-market dealers who also supply Rauter[2] and Seyss-Inquart.[3]

Wednesday morning I was back with my SD, also Wednesday evening

1. J. H. van Roijen, high civil servant in the Dutch Ministry of Foreign Affairs until the German invasion, then one of the leading figures in the Dutch resistance; after the war Foreign Minister, then Ambassador in London.
2. Hans Rauter, HSSPF (Higher SS and Police Chief) in the Netherlands.
3. Artur Seyss-Inquart (1892–1946), Reich Commissar in the Netherlands 1940–45; sentenced to death at Nuremberg.

at Herr Harster's sickbed. Wednesday lunch I had with Igl and Wicka[1] in a good restaurant to which Igl invited me, where we ate entirely without food coupons: lobster, soup, filet of steak, dessert, coffee. Both were well. Wicka looked well and they obviously had enough money and not too many cares. She talked about life in Holland, which after all is still much easier than in Germany. For there is still enough manpower and the only shortage is of supplies in some places. But they said that food had become much worse in the last 6 months, fabulously expensive, and black-market goods very expensive, too. 30 guilders for one kilo of butter. But if one is prepared to pay one can still get everything.

The meeting at Goerschen's was at 4. The Dutchman is a good man and clearly understands our problems, hates the Germans but is intelligent enough to see that they are not all the same, and that they, too, must be given a chance to live. Besides, it is not we who are the chief target of hatred, but Mussert.[2] We talked for an hour and a half, and I'd guess that we can establish a relationship of trust with this man. For, thanks to my good relations with the SD, I shall in fact be able to give him and his friends real help, if they refrain from active sabotage. In any case, Goerschen has done good preparatory work and it should be possible to form quite a close relation. So I was satisfied with this part of my stay, too, and when I come in July, I should be able to get down to brass tacks.

I got back to Hilversum dead tired Wednesday night, and the whole of Thursday was taken up by reports on my talks with the SD and plans for the use of the results achieved. In the evening I ate with Christiansen.[3] He is an affable merchant-marine captain. Just the type we kept meeting on our trips on English and German ships, perhaps above average intelligence. He therefore hasn't a clue to the higher questions of politics and strategy, because he doesn't know how to pose the questions. He is quite untouched by them. I simply don't understand how such a man can be appointed Wehrmacht C.-in-C. He told me the story of his appointment and of his first week in Holland and didn't at all realize that he was giving a complete explanation why things were bound to miscarry in Holland. They couldn't possibly go well. He described, for instance, his first conversation with General Winkelman, the C.-in-C. of the Dutch armed forces. "W. said, 'I take it for granted, General, that you will keep within the framework of international law and the Hague Convention.' Do you

1. Wicka Breitbarth, née vom Rath, a cousin of F.M.'s, and her husband. They had left Germany and settled in Holland before the war.

2. See n. 2 to letter of 30 November 1940.

3. General Friedrich Christiansen, Wehrmacht commander in the Netherlands. After the war sentenced to twelve years' imprisonment by a Dutch court.

know what I answered? 'General, did you ever at school hear of international law? I didn't. International law is a thing that exists only in newspapers.' " At that the whole group burst into loud laughter. Wühlisch, who
probably saw that I listened intently and critically, said, when we'd settled
in the car for our return trip, "You'll understand how difficult it is to make
political or military headway with such a C.-in-C." Yet Christiansen is a
nice man. He simply lacks certain organs. At the end, by the way, there
was something of a hitch. As he said goodbye he pressed into my hand a
parcel, which I'll bring with me. It was terribly embarrassing, but to refuse it would have been impossible, so here it stands, still wrapped, beside
my suitcase. What do these people think? It's the Göring touch, which
one keeps coming across there.

Paris, 7 June 1943

A little continuation. Thursday morning passed with further talks and
I took my leave before lunch because I wanted to reach a train at 1.25
and hadn't packed yet. So I ate at the hotel. There was tomato soup –.60
guilder, salad 1.– guilder, salmon whose price was not stated, and pud-
ding 1.50 guilder. I had some mineral water with it. And the bill? 40.65
guilders = RM 55.– That was an impressive moment and very enlight-
ening as to conditions in Holland.—At 1.25 I took the train back to The
Hague, had to settle a small item of official business there, and at 3.40
went with Igl to Wassenaar, where I forgot to deliver your letter. But the
house is charming, small, with many rooms: a large living room and small
dining room downstairs; a big bedroom for the parents, a medium-sized
one for the "Donna," and two tiny ones for the little boys on the next
floor; and 3 diminutive rooms under the roof. All very practical and well
appointed. The two sons very nice, Hans speaking German passably,
Thomas badly; good children. Igl happy and as good as free from homesickness. Wicka very well and completely free from homesickness. They
will, I'm afraid, never come back.—They live really well on the black
market, where an egg costs 1.30 guilder, I think, butter 30.– guilders a
kilo. Cheese, sugar, coal, etc., are all available on the black market.—
The neighbourhood is full of "villas" and would be nothing for us, but I
think they like it.

My train to Brussels left at 6, and at 11 I was in bed at the Hotel Plaza,
tired but quite satisfied with the first part of my trip. Next morning—
Friday—I went to see Falkenhausen from 8 to 11 and he discussed the
world situation with me in full confidence. I led him to the questions that
concern us at the moment and found a gratifying amount of agreement,

actually more than I had expected. At 11 it was Craushaar's[1] turn. He was obviously pleased and surprised at the success of my trip to Holland. I very much hope that it will provide real relief for the people in Brussels. To my great joy, the result of my last visit[2] is that since then there have been no more punitive deportations of Belgians. This time I made an extra sally in a particular direction, and Falkenhausen has promised to act in accordance with it. Moreover, I had arranged with Craushaar that he will release the 300 hostages he still has in custody. At any rate, in these days I have secured the liberty of more than 1,000 people, if all promises are kept. I had lunch and coffee with the men of interest to me in departments of the Military Administration. There was a break at 4, and I used it to begin this letter. At 5 a man from the Administration came to have more coffee with me, at 6 I drove to Seneffe with Herr von Becker.[3] He wishes to be remembered—but he really is a very hollow egg. Everything was nice at Seneffe but nothing special happened. After dinner there were card games until 12.30, as usual, and I won 25 francs. Princess Ruspoli[4] was there, a Princess Drago with her husband, who is the new Italian Minister in Brussels, Planck,[5] and some other officers. The food was simple but very good.

[continued] Paris, 8 June 1943

At 1.30 I returned from Seneffe to the Plaza, at 6 had to get up because my train to Lille went at 7.30. Downstairs at 6.45 I met Goerschen, who had come from Paris overnight and wanted to continue his journey to Holland at 7.40. We quickly discussed the results of my last talk with Harster and agreed what he should tell our friends. Then I started for Lille, cold and tired, in rainy weather. The train goes through an incredibly fertile countryside with well-tended fields and gardens and especially well-tended trees and hedges. It is always exciting to see something like that again, for in comparison our best efforts are bungling. Yet I didn't enjoy the trip, because the weather was too beastly and cold. Besides I travelled with nothing but Germans, who were without exception awful.

1. Dr. Harry Craushaar, Falkenhausen's chief of staff and deputy chief of the military administration.
2. In February; but there are no letters extant between 1 February and 4 March.
3. Banker who worked, as did Carl Deichmann, in the trade firm Wodan.
4. Elisabeth Ruspoli, née von der Assche, a Belgian; later imprisoned at Ravensbrück for helping her countrymen.
5. Erwin Planck (1893–1945), son of the physicist Max Planck; former Staatssekretär, private secretary to Brüning and other chancellors of the Weimar Republic. After 1933 worked in industry. Associated with the Goerdeler group. Executed 23 January 1945.

4 signals girls discussed the question whether the Bosporus was in Norway. That's what I call getting one's money's worth. Schmid[1] met me at the station in Lille and gave me breakfast with hot coffee, 2 eggs, and bread, butter, and jelly, things brought to him by local people. For 2 hours I had to brief Schmid and agree on the line to be pursued, but I got the impression from his account that his preparations are good and his results quite nice. Then I discussed the matter of hostages with him too. At 1.30 an actress came to fetch us for lunch and we had an outstanding meal at the "Deutsches Haus." Everything was to be had there. But the clientele was the most amazing part: profiteers, profiteers, and more profiteers. Some in civilian clothes, but some paymasters, lance corporals, NCO's who eat there with an assortment of girls for RM 20.– a head. All obviously people who live by the motto: Enjoy the war, the peace will be terrible!—After lunch we were joined by Hans Heini,[2] who came from Bethune and was nice and clearly happy. He said in his district they were expecting an average wheat harvest of 20 ctr. per acre. At 4.40 I started back to Brussels.

Immediately after my arrival in the evening I had a final talk with Craushaar, and Wend[3] turned up at 9. He looked well and reasonably happy, greatly enjoyed a bottle of red wine the officers' mess had let me have, and talked about his life, which seems to have become more bearable in some respects, though he may, regrettably, be transferred to an active unit from his training school. That, of course, isn't so good. We went to the station together at 10.30. He went to Antwerp, and I sank exhausted into my berth, where I fell asleep at once and didn't wake up until the conductor knocked at 5.30 in the morning. This short but sound sleep was very valuable because there was a rather strenuous day ahead of me.

One arrives in Paris at 6.30, which isn't very thrilling. I went straight to the Ritz with a porter, had breakfast and a luxurious bath, and at 9 went to see Lt. Col. Hartog, the man who looked after me at the C.-in-C.'s. There were all kinds of preliminaries to be gone through there, and by the time I had done it all and had talked to everybody it was 12 and I had to go to see Stülpnagel.[4] I liked St. very much. Not the level of Falken-

---

1. Carlo Schmid—cf. letter and n. 1 of 10 October 1941, and letter of 11 October 1941.
2. Hans Heinrich von Portatius, neighbour at Kreisau.
3. Wend Wendland, M.'s brother-in-law.
4. Karl-Heinrich von Stülpnagel (see n. 3 to letter of 21 October 1941), commander-in-chief in France since February 1942; determined opponent of the regime, old friend of Ludwig Beck, successfully led the plot of 20 July 1944 in Paris (cf. n. 2 to letter of 4 November 1942), tried by People's Court, executed 30 August 1944.

hausen but all the same a good man. I spent all of 1½ hours with him and shall go back again tonight. He certainly has quite the right attitude in the question that interests me, and I'll get good support from him. The mere fact that he trusted me with his most secret report on the subject, which he didn't even give to Falkenhausen, is agreeable proof of his confidence in me. In any case, he assured me that he would not have more hostages shot, whatever his orders.

From Stülpnagel's I could only hurry to the station, quickly eat a bad lunch, and then had to go to St. Germain and the office of the C.-in-C. West,[1] where I had an afternoon appointment with the Ic.[2] He lives in a charming, beautifully furnished house with a wide view across the valley to the wooded hills beyond it. I quite liked the man himself. But he is probably rather a lightweight and will hardly pursue his insights with the tenacity required. But at least he too has the right attitude and will be more of an asset than a liability. I drove back to Paris with him. The route from St. Germain into the city is very beautiful because one drives for miles along an avenue lined with plane trees and first catches sight of the Arc de Triomphe at eye level across a small valley, then climbs up it from below for the second half of the drive. It was a beautiful, warm, sunny day. At 6.30 I was back at the hotel and at 7.30 at Werner's.[3] We ate alone. Both very nice. Nora had done the cooking herself, and well. After the meal the Paris Falkenhausen,[4] a nephew of the general, came and we talked till 11 about our situation, the chances of the church, the significance of the Munich student affair,[5] etc. I talked more than is my wont and said rather a lot. But F. has quite a nice position here among the non-NS Germans, and so I thought that it was quite good to make it clear to them that everybody can and must make a contribution. Otherwise the people here keep waiting for the generals, although they should know better. The last métro goes at 11.15 and so I was in bed at 12.

This morning at 9 it began again. First to the C.-in-C. in Stülpnagel's car, which he'd been kind enough to put at my disposal, to discuss a few things with some men in the department. I felt terribly ostentatious driving past all the saluting sentries, who normally don't let officers' cars through, and then pulling up in front of the Hotel Majestic. When I got out with my umbrella—it was pouring today and that's why I had it with

1. Field Marshal Gerd von Rundstedt (1875–1953).
2. Intelligence Officer.
3. F.M.'s uncle Werner von Schnitzler and his wife.
4. Rittmeister (Reserve Captain) Dr. Gotthard Freiherr von Falkenhausen, bank expert at the German Embassy in Paris.
5. Cf. n. 1 (p. 279) to letter of 18 March.

me—the guards saluted and caused me the embarrassment of having to greet them with raised hand. At 10.30 I was back again at St. Germain, with Rundstedt's chief of staff, General Blumentritt.[1] I quite liked him even if he doesn't reach up to Stülpnagel, let alone Falkenhausen. At least he was ready to enter into my suggestions for circumventing Führer Orders, and that was what mattered most to me for a start. There, too, I was embarrassed by the guards' salute. I dislike the very sound of it. I spent a little over an hour with Blumentritt; then I had to go and see Meier Deterding and was back at home at 12.30, where I wrote the first part of this letter, i.e., as far as the smear. I had lunch with Hartog here at the Ritz. I had invited him because he'd looked after me in such a friendly way and arranged everything for me. Then a general whose name I've forgotten and the young Falkenhausen joined us for coffee, and we sat until 4. At 4 Falkenhausen turned up with his entourage, changed quickly, and we talked about the results of my talks in Paris, since he was going to see Stülpnagel at 5 and I wanted the two of them to do something jointly.

Nora, Carl vom Rath,[2] and his wife, Monica, came for tea at 5, and we had it in a separate salon. Jella,[3] whom I'd wanted to join us, wasn't in Paris. The Little Uncle,[4] who'd intended to come, was detained. I liked Carl though he has a curiously coarse face. His wife seems to be nice, Nora was in great form with a very exciting, enormous hat. I wanted to see Carl because I'd just seen Wicka. . . .

At 6.30 I was back with Stülpnagel, at 7.45 back at the hotel, ate, and now it is 9.15. A cycle-taxi is coming at 9.30 to take me to the station. I'll be terribly embarrassed to let myself be pedalled through Paris by such a slave, but if I don't take it I'll get to the train quite wet from the rain. There are masses of cycle-taxis here, some propelled by one man, some by two.

In the dining hall the Maître, an old man with white hair, mentioned Hans Adolf, whom he'd known as a guest of the Ritz since 1913. He spoke very nicely about him and had particular praise for his fine taste. He also knew Uncle Max[5] and Jella and gave them good marks.

So, my love, now I'm up to date with my report. At midday tomorrow I'll be with Mütterchen in Godesberg for lunch, and the morning after I'll be back in Berlin. In the evening I hope to be with you.

1. General Günther Blumentritt, Chief of Staff to C.-in-C. West.
2. Karl vom Rath (1915–86), cousin of F.M., brother of Wicka Breitbarth; art historian.
3. Gabriele Mirbach, daughter of Uncle Max.
4. Werner von Schnitzler.
5. Magnus Freiherr von Mirbach, with whose family M. stayed during his last year and a half at school.

Berlin, 15 June 1943

How lovely it was with you, my love, and even if we were hardly alone for a minute during the 4 days,[1] you were always there and so it was pleasant all the time. And how well you arranged everything and how beautifully everything went, smoothly, and, so it seemed to me, without intolerable strain for you or your household. Everyone was happy and in good spirits, and that is very important.

We had a very good trip. At Liegnitz we parted with Husen, who saw us leave with a whole compartment to ourselves. I hope he had a comfortable journey, too. On the way we talked some more about what was on our minds and I saw that both of them were obviously satisfied. But mostly we read.—The train was full only between Guben and Frankfurt. . . .

Berlin, 17 June 1943

. . . Yesterday began with your nice telephone call. Then I went straight to a meeting, which lasted till 11 and gave me much pleasure. For I was in the murderers' pit of loyal vassals of the Führer, generals and officers of the OKW, whom I routed in furious attacks. They pointed out to me that what I wanted was incompatible with a Führer Order, whereupon I replied: "But, gentlemen, you can't hide behind a Führer Order. We would grossly violate our duty to the Führer if, sitting quietly at our desks, we lacked the courage to tell the Führer that he was badly advised when he issued that order, and if this cowardice of ours caused the death of our men at the front!"[2] That was roughly the tone and pitch of my harangue to these disgusting toadies, and though they went red in the face one by one, they all turned tail in the end.

Then I paid Husen a brief visit, then had a meeting with Diwald and Wengler until 1, and at 1.30 I was home, where Eugen was already await-

1. The third and last meeting at Kreisau took place during the long Whit week-end of 12–14 June. Those present were, apart from the hosts, Peter, Marion, and Irene von Yorck, Trott, Delp, Gerstenmaier, Reichwein, Husen, Einsiedel. Trott introduced the discussion on foreign policy and economic relations after the war; Husen had written the documents on the punishment of Nazi criminals (*Rechtsschänder*). See n. 1 to letter of 19 June, and van Roon, *Resistance to Hitler*, pp. 338–43.
2. Probably the matter under discussion was the partisan warfare in the South-East, with its massive German reprisals; or it may have concerned the forced recruitment of former prisoners of war (cf. n. 1 [p. 293] to letter of 9 April) or the question of the status as combatants of soldiers of defeated and occupied countries who fought on under British aegis and who, M. argued, had to be recognized, and were protected, as prisoners of war.

ing me, and Adam and Haeften joined us, too late. I had already seen with Husen that the 4 days had an aura of blissful transfiguration; it was the same with Adam and Eugen. Naturally I was very happy about this, for in some respects this transfiguration is more important than the concrete result. But in that respect, too, there was general satisfaction, especially with Haeften, who was much impressed. We discussed the further programme for this summer until about 1st October and then it was 4 o'clock and we had to return to work. Then I had the afternoon, which was painful, because I really had no strength left, and the short evening described above.

Peter is coming to lunch today, in the evening I'll go to Babelsberg, tomorrow I have lunch with a man from the Office, and in the afternoon I want to visit Conrad. Steltzer, with whom I telephoned yesterday, has been out of the army hospital for 2 days but can't travel yet for another 3 weeks.

Berlin, 18 June 1943

. . . Yesterday was a much more colourful day than I'd expected. Early in the morning there came an Alexander Uexküll, husband of the Countess Uexküll I advise in Sweden, with nice stories from the Government [General].[1] Peter came to lunch and we talked about the further programme. It is very full because we want to take a step forward in everything before I go to Istanbul.[2]—Before lunch I visited Einsiedel, who was obviously still very impressed too. But he and C.D. can't resume until the 28th. After lunch we went to Husen's to invite him for tonight and there met Gerstenmaier, who'd been trying in vain to wake him up. Since he hadn't barricaded himself sufficiently, we succeeded in our joint efforts to shake him out of bed.

I didn't get much chance to work in the afternoon, for first came a man to enlighten me on the case against Dohnanyi, and then Schlange. D.'s case looks much better than 3 weeks ago. Canaris was interrogated the day before yesterday and Oster yesterday, and the two interrogations give one the impression that the whole thing will end without substantial sequel.[3] Awful how such a thing, with all its psychological strain, can drag on, indefinitely. . . .

1. Occupied Poland.
2. See letters of 6 and 7 July.
3. It was a false hope. Canaris himself and the Abwehr were now endangered—see Bethge, *Bonhoeffer*, p. 709.

Berlin, 19 June 1943

. . . Last night was very nice with Peter and Husen, and we now have an agreeable sense of fellowship and friendship with him. Therefore what we had to discuss[1]—which was by no means all pleasant—was transacted so smoothly and without friction that we might as well have discussed it at my office. I am very glad of that. . . .

Berlin, 20 June 1943

. . . I hope you can manage to come. It would be particularly nice while Hans is still here. It would be a Deichmann Family Reunion, so to speak. This morning I had your letter from Königszelt. So that wasn't any faster than a letter from Kreisau.

Yesterday's lunch with Goerschen & Carl was very nice. G. is very enthusiastic and does his stuff well. I wonder how it will develop. G. stayed till 4. Then I went to see Guttenberg, who had Delbrück with him, to discuss the DoX[2] case. I'm afraid it doesn't look as good as I thought, everything is still in suspense and there has, rather, been a turn for the worse. And all because the matter was handled very foolishly. It would be easy to handle it well and conclude the case successfully but it seems to me that they'll get it so entangled that everything will go wrong in the end.—At 7.30 I took Guttenberg to his train. . . .

Berlin, 26 June 1943

. . . Krüger was very nice last night and very ready to do something. It is a real joy to be with him.—Conrad was much impressed by our labours and full of praise. He was also satisfied with the result of his trip to Bonn. That is to be the basis for the plenary session[3] in August. What he told

1. Husen's first draft on the punishment of Nazi criminals had been discussed at Kreisau (cf. n. 1 to letter of 15 June); the second one, of 23 July 1943, was now being worked on (see texts in van Roon, *Resistance to Hitler*, pp. 340–47). The moot question was the retroactivity of penal provisions for crimes for which there was no precedent. The principle *nulla poena sine lege* forbade punishment for outrages (*Untaten*) or violations of natural law (*Rechtsschändungen*) that had not been formulated in positive law.
2. The abbreviations of Dohnanyi's name and the cross-out "X" show increasing caution; but M. probably underestimated the danger Canaris and the entire Abwehr were in. Dr. Karl Sack, the Army Judge Advocate, saw Dohnanyi's arrest as the first victory of the SS in its war against the Abwehr. He tried to prevent a trial, but was in the end himself killed, with Canaris, Oster, and Bonhoeffer, in Flossenbürg—and probably on the same day as Dohnanyi in Sachsenhausen.
3. The Bishop of Berlin and the West German bishops were preparing for the annual bishops' conference at Fulda.

me about it sounds very good and I hope it is borne out. Eugen has come back from the South and is also satisfied with the outcome. . . .

Berlin, 27 June 1943

The day is already approaching its end. I haven't written yet. It is a fine, sunny day, and on such days it is especially painful for me not to be at home. I then realize that the day is passing irrevocably.

I got up late because we had a preliminary air-raid warning and I was unable to go back to sleep till 4 o'clock. So I read and thought about Kreisau and all the many things that still have to be done there. The day passed with cooking, eating, *The Times*, some books, and Patience. It wasn't peaceful, because I had no inner peace. Once more I had the feeling that I have only very little time left, and that I must leave such an awful lot undone behind me. These are days when I find it really difficult to maintain my peace.

Now I'm going to visit Husen, with whom I want to discuss the result of my conversation with Conrad. On the way I want to try to find Friedrich. I'll be back for supper and then hope for a quiet evening.

REICHSKRIEGSMINISTERIUM[1]

Berlin W 35, Tirpitzufer 72–76   *28 June 1943*

This is the last letter before my departure. Imagine, there was still none from you this morning. I do hope to find one at lunchtime, when I come home to eat with Guttenberg. He is bound to be late, and so I'll have time to read it.

Last night I went to see Husen and had some splendid tea and cake. Again it was very nice with him. He is a charming man, and the whole house is very characteristic of him and deeply Catholic. They'd celebrated Corpus Christi, and the flowers on the table had adorned the altar in church in the morning. As to work, Husen was also good and promised to take Conrad's points into consideration in the new version.[2] . . .

1. Stationery of the defunct War Ministry.
2. Either of the document on the punishment of Nazi criminals (cf. n. 1 to letter of 19 June) or of the Basic Principles for Reform (see van Roon, *Resistance to Hitler,* pp. 347–54), especially the section on church, cultural life, and education. Preysing had studied law. Both subjects were discussed with him.

Istanbul, 6 July 1943[1]

It is quite early in the morning, 5.15 for you, 6.15 here. Your husband is sitting on a balcony open to the east with a view over the Bosporus and across to Scutari. The sun has just risen and is veiled by curtains. Cool, fresh air is rising from the water. The morning could not have been more beautiful.

But first I want to report how I got here. The plane left Vienna an hour late because the transmission wasn't clear. I had meanwhile introduced myself to Eugen's friend Sister Margarete, and among the passengers there was a man called Zapp, who is married to a friend of Asta's, and so, with Wengler, there were four of us standing about. Sister Margarete had been in Düsseldorf during the big air raids and gave really incredible descriptions. She had evacuated her relatives from there to Holstein. She has been in Istanbul for 11 years and of course knew Christiansen[2] and the Wilbrandts.

Eventually we departed. After an hour's flight we stopped at Budapest for 15 minutes. The lunch looked quite decent, but we couldn't partake of it because we had no pengö, and they weren't taking any other money. Then came the first long lap, 3 hours to Sofia. The flight over the Balkan mountains wasn't really interesting, apart from the beautiful cloud formations we flew through. On the south side of the mountains we came into clear weather. I already had more than enough before we got to Sofia. My head was buzzing from the noise, and total stupefaction had already set in. One gets into a state very appropriate to a hunk of meat. Stop in Sofia also only 15 minutes. We managed to change some German

1. The official reason for this trip to Turkey, from 5 to 10 July, and the second one, in December, was a fleet of Danube ships Turkey had interned in the Sea of Marmara. It belonged to a French company, one of whose directors had fled to England in 1940 and ordered the fleet to steam through the Bosporus when Germany attacked Yugoslavia and Greece in 1941. Under German influence a Frenchman in Paris started a suit against neutral Turkey for release of the ships. Wengler accompanied M. and attended to the negotiations. M. concentrated on the establishment of connections with the Allies, especially with Alexander Kirk, who was now stationed in Cairo. It did not work. There were contacts with the American Office of Strategic Services (OSS), despite M.'s mistrust of secret services. Alexander Rüstow, a German sociologist who had emigrated to Turkey in 1934, was one of the intermediaries. M. also saw old acquaintances there: Hans Wilbrandt, formerly financial consultant for Kreisau and economic adviser of a Frankfurt bank, who had also lived in Turkey since 1934, and Paul Leverkühn, who now worked for the Abwehr. A meeting with Franz von Papen, former Reich Chancellor and now German Ambassador in Turkey, was unproductive. Rüstow's advice was not to attempt to shake the Allied formula of unconditional surrender, but to offer German cooperation in a rapid occupation of Germany by the Western powers (see Balfour and Frisby, *Moltke*, pp. 270–73).
2. Christiansen-Weniger had lived in Turkey for some time before the war.

money to buy some eggs and bacon. There were mountains of eggs lying about. Big pieces of bacon hung in the restaurant, and bottles of egg cognac stood round the walls. The surprising thing about the flight over Bulgaria was that all the fields were still green, while in Hungary they already looked very ripe. The corn, too, in Bulgaria was still quite small. Then came the third lap. 3½ hours to Istanbul. First I read my Bädecker, then I dozed off, and when I woke up the Black Sea was below us. As any sea does: it moved me and gave me a wonderful feeling of freedom. I simply can't see the water without instantly realizing that this same water laps Table Mountain, Sydney, and Shanghai. We flew over the water for so long that I was about to doze off again, when we saw land to the right, which was the coast of Thrace. Soon after we sighted the Black Sea estuary of the Bosporus, flew a few kilometres into Asiatic Turkey, crossed the isthmus, flew over the Sea of Marmara and the Princes' Islands, and landed at an airport about 20 km from Istanbul. The approach, in a sun already giving a reddish glow, was magically beautiful: beneath us lay the Sea of Marmara, the Bosporus, the Golden Horn, and stretched along it the city, with its strange and fascinating silhouette.

Before beginning an account of my harmless adventures I must tell you something about the situation of the city—which admittedly you can also read in Bädecker, but probably won't. . . .[1]

[continued] 7 July 1943

Meanwhile I have seen Hagia Sophia, where the interior disappointed me. It is no longer used for services and is completely bare. Thus one gets no real impression of the space, which now lacks all subdivision. One does not sense its famous proportions and doesn't even feel small, diminutive, as in St. Peter's. In brief, one misses the pull to the supernatural; it is profane, perhaps it has become profane. Besides there is bright light, which is quite disturbing and a profanation to our eyes. There is no mystery in the edifice. I was sorry about this disappointment, for after all the descriptions I had expected a lot. To make up for it there are really wonderful and imposing mosaics in the mosque. The figures in the mosaics are not good but the ornaments are very beautiful. I never learnt anything about ornamentation, and here I see that it is really essential. It seems to me that school drawing classes should include real drill in ornamentation, for it is a thing one can learn. That the people here know something

1. There followed a very long and detailed description, which continued on 7 July. Undoubtedly the letters his famous forebear had written while seconded to Turkey as a young officer were present at the back of M.'s mind.

about it you can see in every shop, at every stall, especially the fruit stalls. Cherries, yellow plums, peaches, apricots are all spread in ornamental patterns, and where this is impossible, as with raspberries, mulberries, currants, single flowers are used for ornament. The mosques altogether are a disappointment for me. They are somehow not sublimated enough for our way of thinking, are very squat, at most have a façade but no beauty of proportion, and often impossible additions have been made outside. The interior even of the mosques that are in use is bare and cold because of the bright light. Nonetheless they are beautiful, but only at a great distance. So to my feeling the panorama of Istanbul is most beautiful when seen from the water, either coming from the Bosporus and entering the Golden Horn, or from the Sea of Marmara, where the Ahmed Mosque with its great width and its 6 minarets makes a specially strong impression.

I like the Turks, much better than, for instance, the Italians—with whom they can hardly be compared. Above all they are proud and not pushing. This makes walking the streets very pleasant despite the crowds. There is no begging, no shoving, no tripping over other people. There is a pronounced consciousness of race. Zita, Leverkühn's employee, is Greek. She does not speak to Turks. The Jews are complete outcasts here; they are addressed with the familiar Thou and no-one shakes hands with them or offers them a chair, even when they are bristling with money and Europeanized. Levantines are children of mixed marriages with Italians or Greeks. Also, the child of a German and a Greek mother is Levantine, too, and socially inferior to Turks. It is all very strange.

Life here is very expensive. A Turkish pound is worth RM 2.– but in reality ½ peace-time mark at most. Only food is reasonable on the whole. There is everything. It's the mountains of really first-class fruit that are most beautiful. Curiously enough, everything seems to ripen here at the same time. Thus there are heavenly cherries, but also melons and peaches. The raspberries are exemplary. One buys them in narrow, high baskets, and the berries are big and dry. All the fruit comes from producers nearby, and a great deal is sold from horseback. Unfortunately one has to be very careful eating fruit, because typhoid, typhus, and paratyphoid are endemic, and therefore one can eat only washed fruit. In the shops one sees textiles of moderate quality, good, very expensive shoes, chocolate and sweets of all kinds in quantity. But I won't bring back much, because baggage is limited to 15 kilos.[1]

---

1. The letter breaks off here. But M. used the opportunity of his stay in neutral Turkey to write to friends abroad, including one in South Africa, Dr. Petronella van Heerden—in English—expressing sadness at his grandmother's death—now the death of both grand-

Berlin, 15 July 1943

... At the Office I found one matter completely bungled and a lot of other work. There is some news again. The offensive in the East seems to have miscarried completely, with very heavy losses.[1] The Italians intend to evacuate Sicily, essentially without a fight and contrary to agreement. The Anglo-Saxons already have 100,000 men on the island, mainly 8th Army men.[2]

Peter was here at lunchtime. Everything seems to have progressed according to plan. Tomorrow I shall have lunch with Willem Bekker, tomorrow night I'll first visit Ulla, then go to see Husen. Karl-Ludwig[3] and Delbrück are coming Saturday afternoon, Friedrich & Peter in the evening. So you see the programme is lively. Einsiedel, C.D., Reichwein, Trott, Haeften, Eugen all are in store for next week. ...

My love, I am full of agreeable thoughts about Kreisau and sorry that you aren't there. I don't like that at all. I feel so much more secure when I know you are sitting at home.[4] ...

Berlin, 17 July 1943

... My head is full of Kreisau. I'd like very much to stay at home entirely for a few years. Perhaps it will happen. Husen, whom I saw yesterday, is going on leave in Tyrol today and will not return until the 8th of August.—

My love, there is nothing new to report from here. The hourglass is slowly running out, and people who haven't looked at it in years are rather frightened now to see how little sand is left in it. I always find it hard to understand how people could have illusions about that.

Berlin, 18 July 1943

The Sunday is as good as over and unfortunately was not at all peaceful but very lively. Things started last night when Adam, Eugen, Peter &

---

parents—and his continuing attachment to South Africa; he hoped to see his friends there soon; but in case he should not be alive when such a voyage was possible again, he had a wish: "See to it that my boys get out. Our South African heritage is [by] far our best and I hope that they will realise the importance of their grandmother and her country to us."

1. A German offensive—Operation Citadel—against the Russian Front at Kursk had begun on 5 July, a Soviet counter-offensive on 12 July; on 13 July Hitler ordered the cessation of Operation Citadel.

2. Allied landings on Sicily had begun on 10 July.

3. Guttenberg.

4. F.M. was visiting her sister-in-law, Dickie Deichmann, who was expecting a child.

Marion, Friedrich, & Haubach were with me—and Reichwein too—and stayed till 1 o'clock. It was a rather productive evening which, however, demanded a continuation. And so things continued at Peter's at 1.30, without Reichwein, and went on until 7 o'clock, then Adam, Peter & Marion, and I went to the Haeftens', and I've just got home at 9.30. There were all kinds of significant differences and it was encouraging to see how strong our common ground was, which makes such differences bearable. . . .

My Sundays are allocated as follows: 1 August Munich, 8 August Friedrich with me, 15 August major battle days in Berlin, 22 August Vienna. Or I may go to Holland again after the 15th and postpone Vienna to the 29th.

Eugen's chief has at last issued his masterpiece.[1] It is a real masterpiece, something quite important, and I am very glad of Eugen's success.—We'll still have a lot of work in connection with it. . . .

Berlin, 19 July 1943

. . . Wengler came from Istanbul today. He had greetings from all concerned and has learnt some quite useful things. In any case my one week was altogether worth while from the official point of view, too.—Today Stauffenberg[2] came to lunch to discuss questions concerning the Institute. It really went quite well, and together we worked out a plan of campaign to reactivate the Institute. It will mean a nice row with Bruns.—His brother[3] who was wounded so badly is already on convalescent leave and has made something of a recovery amazingly quickly. . . .

Berlin, 20 July 1943

. . . Peter is coming tonight. I have to do some work with him alone, and so we reserved an evening for ourselves. I think he has never been here alone for an evening.—I talked to Frau Pick about her departure in case of bombs. She was obviously pleased. . . .

---

1. Wurm's appeal to Hitler and the Reich government of 16 July 1943 condemned the policies—executed and planned—against the "non-Aryans" as conflicting with God's commandments and the foundations of Western thought and life, and it entered a special plea against extending those measures to the so-called "privileged non-Aryans" in mixed marriages. He deplored measures of the regime in occupied countries and at home and described these and the general disintegration of the rule of law as a heavy burden on the people, heavier than the sacrifices demanded by the war.
2. Berthold Stauffenberg.
3. Claus Stauffenberg had lost an eye, his right hand, and two fingers of the left in an air attack in North Africa on 7 April.

Berlin, 21 July 1943

It is still early and today I want, at last, to write to you early, not always when I'm worn out. Peter came last night, and we'd just finished supper when König appeared, bringing some splendid stories from the South. We had to put him out for half an hour because we had a big programme of our own to get through.—The evening was enormously fruitful, and what with dictating, writing, and talking, we had quite a respectable piece of work done by 11.30. We were both well satisfied: I wonder whether this satisfaction will stand the test of daylight. In any case the afternoon was very productive.

At the Office too I can now see the bottom. This morning there are only three more fat jobs, and they are likely to disappear today and tomorrow. Then everything will be up to date again. Reichwein is coming to lunch today and König in the afternoon, and he'll depart for home at 8. The evening I want to devote to diminishing the pile of *Times*es.

Peter told me that the trains to Silesia are incredibly crowded. Probably with people fleeing from bombs. Marion didn't get on the first early train she wanted to take yesterday, Tuesday, and she only managed to get on the second by using her suitcases as steps and climbing through the window. For the afternoon trains there is now a special additional ticket of admission. In view of these conditions I hope that you are not coming via Berlin but going direct. . . .

Berlin, 26 July 1943

. . . My love, saying goodbye today was a bit sad. But I can't stand it when I see that you overdo it. Whether you have chickens and ducks, geese and turkeys, is a matter of indifference compared with the question whether you are well rested and in possession of a well-oiled soul. I like ducks and chickens etc. too, but I absolutely don't want you to worry about defeats on that sector.—But, my love, it was lovely with you as always and you know that it is only with you I am at home and at peace. If only at last I could work in peace at home for once. Not only would it be pleasant, it really is bitterly necessary. . . .

Berlin, when we arrived, was very hot and close and "in danger of an air raid." I still know nothing about Mussolini[1] but want to make enquiries towards evening. In any case two of our men who wanted to go to Rome for negotiations were ordered back at the Brenner.

1. The Fascist Grand Council had deposed Mussolini on 25 July and the King had had him arrested. The new government of Marshal Badoglio instantly entered into negotiations with the Allies.

Here there is, as usual, a lot of work. Wengler has turned up again. . . .

Farewell, my love, I must go to the main building. Keep well, take care of yourself, take care of yourself, never forget that your entire family lives on your good spirits and your patience.

Berlin, 28 July 1943

Please make 3 copies yourself of the main Kreisau texts:[1] C[hurch] & St[ate] & E[ducation], Whitsun '42, Political and Economic Constitution Oct. '42, and Principles of Foreign Policy Whitsun '43. Of course only the agreed main texts and not preliminary papers, like Trott's product. Also I'd like you to ring Marion and ask her to bring these 3 sets of copies to Berlin so that they are here Friday lunchtime. I assume that she's coming here for the week-end because she intended to meet Peter in East Prussia. If she isn't coming, you must send Frl. Breslauer back. Otherwise, Frl. Breslauer can stay over the week-end and work on the books. She should not return before Tuesday morning at the earliest, so that Monday evening we can discuss whether she should come or not.

The situation here has been changed fundamentally by Stalin's declaration,[2] and the longer it takes Italy to reach a separate peace or separate armistice, the more events in Italy will further the ripening process. There is no obvious reason why it should be quick now.

It seems that it was we who achieved Mussolini's abdication, that we wanted Scorza[3] in his place for an unlimited terror regime. The King spoiled that by accepting Mussolini's abdication and then appointing a different successor. Scorza, Musso, and the Party chiefs are in military custody, the Party has been practically liquidated, the Party flag suppressed, the Fasci painted over, the militia ("former fascist militia") subordinated to the armed forces and replaced at all frontiers by carabinieri.

1. See van Roon, *Resistance to Hitler*, pp. 329–39.
2. The latest indication of Soviet policy was the founding on 12–13 July at Krasnogorsk, near Moscow, of a National Committee "Free Germany," whose publications bore the imperial and nationalist colours black-white-red. A "League of German Officers" followed on 11–12 September, which pointed again to Stalin's declaration of 6 November 1942 on the equal rights of nations, the inviolability of their territories, and the guarantee of democratic freedoms. Stalin himself barely changed his ambiguous differentiation of 23 February 1942: "Hitlers come and Hitlers go, but the German people, the German state remains"—even though his Order of the Day on 1 May 1943 stated that it was obvious that only the complete expulsion of the Hitler armies and the unconditional surrender of Hitler's Germany could bring peace to Europe. The dissolution of the Comintern at the end of May 1943 was intended to show that fears of Russian interference in other countries or of their Bolshevization were groundless.
3. Carlo Scorza, Secretary General of the Fascist Party.

Meanwhile Reichwein has been here, with whom I talked for an hour, Eugen & Adam are returning this afternoon, Haubach & Reichwein in the evening. Steltzer is coming next Wednesday. We certainly have 2 stormy weeks ahead of us. . . .

Berlin, 29 July 1943

Just a quick word. I have just come from a meeting at the AA and must in 15 minutes go home, where Leverkühn is having lunch with me. But the afternoon is sure to be stormy again and so I'd rather write now.— It is another hot, close day with overcast or, rather, veiled sky. Berlin is quaking with fear of the expected air raids,[1] against which one feels unprotected and defenceless. Strange how quickly morale disappears.

Yesterday afternoon Adam, Eugen, & Haeften were with me. After 2 hours there was a little pause for supper, and then Reichwein and Haubach came at 8 and we went on with them until 11.30, then a little sleep, at 1 preliminary warning, at 2 the returning vehicles. Today I had Eddy & Einsiedel early, then the meeting at the AA, now Leverkühn, Adam comes at 3, then Einsiedel again. These are curious days, for in some respects I do little or nothing, but then I need an awful lot of time to listen and to see to it that things go on. . . .

Frl. Breslauer should help you put away the things in the boxes and the things she has brought with her, because she knows which of them I have to get at again and which can be stored away. She should also make a list of the files and mark the boxes so that they can be found when needed.[2]—Please return the suitcase with Frl. Breslauer. You could put a few potatoes and some carrots in it. But what I like best at the moment is milk, which unfortunately is going to be finished tomorrow.

Reichwein says he doesn't know where to put his family.[3] I told him that it was uncomfortable with us but that if he wanted to send his family as NSV-evacuees[4] it would be a pleasure for us, and you would certainly try to make all the inconvenience as bearable as possible for his wife. He'll write to you himself.

1. The big raids on Hamburg, which began on 24 July, were not yet over.
2. Frl. Breslauer had copied files for the future. The copies are lost, as are the records of the Abwehr. Cf. letter of 3 August.
3. Rosemarie (Romei) Reichwein went to Kreisau with her four children and stayed there till after the war.
4. Refugees from the air raids whose accommodation was supervised by the National Socialist Welfare Organization (Nationalsozialistische Volkswohlfahrt).

Berlin, 30 July 1943

... I am writing early because there is an enormous programme ahead of me today: lunch with Peter, Haeften, and a man from Stockholm, after lunch joined by Adam and Eugen. For tea: Eddy, Peter, Adam. At 7 Reichwein and Peter, and at 10 I depart. Yesterday Leverkühn came to lunch, then Adam, then Einsiedel, between them Illemie,[1] and at 10 Peter rang up to say he was here, whereupon I went there on my bike and got back at 12.45, just before the air-raid warning. I wonder whether we'll make progress. That will be largely decided over the week-end.

Please don't ring up Monday evening but Tuesday morning. Monday evening I'll be visiting Steengracht to discuss, in general, how idiotic outrages can still be prevented at this late stage. The initiative for this discussion came from him, and I very much wonder how it will go. So I have, as you see, three well-filled days ahead of me. If the week-ends here and in Munich are successful, the time afterwards will be even more crowded.—

Illemie was at Hohenlychen with Adrian, and fortunately his spine is so much better that he doesn't have to go back there. In view of the possibility of air raids starting soon, Illemie wants to send him to Kreisau as soon as possible. With the situation we'll have in 3 or 4 weeks in the air, Silesia will probably be the only more or less safe area apart from the Warthegau.[2]

Your husband is a bit tired today from the disturbed night. But he drinks tea and coffee all day and will have no trouble going on. Otherwise he is very well indeed. And you, my love? Don't let the drought depress you. That kind of thing will happen. Only see to it that the watering is not neglected. I would also water the flower garden properly, for having green and flowers around is good for the soul. The theory that only the vegetable garden counts is wrong. If you help to water the vegetable garden, the Stäsches can help in the flower garden, and in addition I would let one of the girls help with the watering. I really think vegetables and flowers equally important. . . .

Munich, 1 August 1943

My visit to Munich is over. It is 10 p.m., my train goes at 12, but I hope to be in my berth not later than 11. I want quickly to use the remaining time to write to you.—Friday lunch and the afternoon until the train departure at 10 was filled with talks without a pause. It was like a market,

1. Ilse-Marie von Steengracht with her little son, Adrian.
2. Part of Poland annexed to Germany.

and amid all this coming and going the proposal slowly emerged which is to be discussed with Uncle in Berlin over the week-end and which I was to put through in Munich. So I left quite satisfied. But the journey was not very pleasant, because I woke up several times. The man above me was obviously very excited about a girl in another carriage, whom he seemed to have abducted. He was about 48, she 22. It was very funny.

In Munich talks started immediately after my arrival, at about 10, and they really didn't stop except for the intervals for eating. I also took part in the Mass on Sunday, that is, today. Otherwise I really worked without pause. Saturday from 10 to 1 Rösch alone, 1–4.30 König alone, 4.30–9 p.m. Rösch & König. Today 7.30–8.30 Rösch alone, then Mass 8.30–10.30, 10.30–22.00 Rösch, König, and after 18 hrs. Delp. A heavier schedule than usual, as you see. That was necessary in the first place because of the whole programme. Then C.B.'s friend[1] and her colleague from Salzburg were not there, so that I was able to devote myself to our friends without distraction. The result was rather satisfactory, and I have the impression that we can count on them fully. So we have achieved everything here, I believe, that was needed. Moreover they have provided a constant messenger to Berlin for us for the next two weeks. . . .

People are greatly concerned that air raids on Munich from the south may be in the offing. Since Munich is now, in addition, an important traffic junction for supplies to the south, there is concern that it will be attacked from the north, too. At any rate there was an air-raid warning Saturday about lunchtime, and it is said to have caused a great deal of uneasiness.

The Mass at St. Michael's was the first Mass of a newly ordained priest. The Mass, by Haydn, was very beautiful, even if it lacked the richness of other great Catholic Masses. The church was very crowded and the entire Mass took all of 2 hours, with a fairly good though not quite first-rate sermon on the part to be played by the priesthood—to proclaim the truth and to dispense the means of grace. I sat, again, high above the altar in the box, so that I had the whole scene before me. It was rather interesting for me to experience the Sunday activities behind the pulpit. The Fathers all had to hear confession from 6 a.m. onward. They just finished this before the main Mass of the day, and those of them who had no part in the main Mass then got their breakfast. Then last preparations were made: nuns and acolytes and priests hurried about as I climbed up the spiral stairs, and scarcely had I sat down when the whole whirl entered as a well-ordered procession. From then on everything unrolled smoothly, if somewhat stiffly and slowly.

1. Irene Faulhaber.

It is awfully hot here, and between the houses there is a kind of shimmering heat. But in the rooms you know[1] it was cool. We didn't go out to
Delp's.[2] We ate, as always, like princes, and I am now on my way back,
supplied with a box of cigars and sandwiches. The 2 days were strenuous
but satisfying.—Now I wonder whether the others in Berlin have made
progress; I shall hear tomorrow. . . .

Berlin, 2 August 1943

I have come back to a madhouse. The difference in atmosphere between last Friday and today is very funny. Everything is in process of total
dissolution, and in another 2 weeks we'll no longer have any machinery
of government. Yesterday morning Dr. Goebbels favoured his subjects
with the enclosed leaflet,[3] which expresses sheer panic. Not a word of
confidence, of comfort, no call for calm and composure, no hint as to why
these sacrifices are necessary, no intimation that the authorities have
made arrangements to protect the population and to provide for those
who have suffered. Nothing but fear and panic. But the leaflet is nothing
compared with the state of affairs in the ministries. All work is at a standstill. Everyone is packing. Our girls are being sent home today to pack
their things. I had great trouble arranging a postponement of two weeks
for us. Everything is to be done at once, and everything is to be got out
of the way at once.

The consequences are clear. I tried to make an urgent telephone call to
you but had to cancel it when it hadn't come after 1½ hours. 45 minutes
ago I started again and the booking has another 45 minutes to run. The
trains will be overcrowded, luggage is piling up everywhere, and in 2, 3
months' time all regular transport will be a thing of the past. Please don't
come to Berlin. As things are now, you could be very much in the way
here, especially since I may be carted off any day now.

The practical thing to do is this: please send me a sack of potatoes and
whatever vegetables you may have that will keep for some time. Perhaps
some dried beans. I'll send you Frau Pick after the first air raid.—I'm
sending you another suitcase with things in it.—Whether I'll be able to
come home once more in the near future seems to me more than doubtful. It is more likely it won't work. . . .

The week-end here was less successful than mine. But sufficiently successful that work can continue. We'll have to wait and see what comes
of it.

1. Next door to the Church of St. Michael, connected with the Jesuits.
2. Delp's rectory in Bogenhausen, which had served as a meeting place before.
3. None of the enclosures are preserved.

My love, chaos is coming now and our watchword must be: *patiencia victrix*. You'll have to see how you can manage everything and you must be prepared for my possibly not showing up for months. I only hope for a peaceful Christmas. . . .

Berlin, 3 August 1943

. . . We are suddenly the centre of interest; everybody is trying to save our files[1] because they are the only means of self-justification. It is hilarious. Everybody belabours me to evacuate my files and myself without delay. I have the greatest difficulty resisting this courtship, and I may well have to move to Zossen[2] before the end of this week. Ghastly! In this connection I have the following requests: (a) can you retrieve the little cooker and let me have it? Then I can at least make some tea for myself. (2) Could you ask Z[eumer] who has unregistered motor bikes stored with us and try to buy them? I'm already buying what I can here, but so far, unfortunately, I have only a defective one and I must remain mobile at all costs. It is clear that we will have to pay much more than the things are worth.

Conditions at the railway stations are said to be crazy. I'm told that the police use rubber truncheons to separate those who must stay behind from those allowed to travel. The panic is simply indescribable, and it is increased by telling people that there will surely be an air raid the next night, to make them move fast. The conversation in the evening with the Herr Staatssekretär[3] was mediocre. Nothing much really came of it. One gets the impression that he is no longer willing to do much, but accepts the inevitable.

Nothing new otherwise.

Berlin, 4 August 1943

I spent the greater part of last night working on our files with a girl, and we now have a system for ordering them. Everything will be ready by the end of the week, the old files will already be waiting in safety for me to look through them, and the current files will have shrunk to a tolerable bulk so that they are easier to handle and move. The whole team is busy sorting and screening the files according to this system, and Oxé is responsible for destroying all the papers that are only ballast now. Your

1. Cf. n. 2 to letter of 29 July.
2. The Abwehr was in process of evacuation to the army headquarters south of Berlin.
3. Steengracht.

husband meanwhile handles the current work and has a good deal else to do as well.

In the field that interests me most there has been a major hitch: Uncle has joined the club of Their Excellencies,[1] under rather unpleasant circumstances, and this has so much encouraged the reactionaries that we'll probably skid into the Kerensky solution.[2] In that case the hope for a sound and organic solution in our lifetime would be buried; and that unfortunately means a lot. But it has not yet happened and perhaps it can still be prevented. Friedrich is coming on Saturday, and then we'll see whether there is still an effective remedy for it. It is, however, a serious symptom of the immaturity of our people and of our situation. It seems that much more must be laid in rubble and ashes until the time is ripe. What a struggle it is to accept that conclusion. . . .

Berlin, 5 August 1943

. . . There is really no news. The Russians report the capture of Orel today. That is bad. The British are making quite nice progress in Sicily, and we have received no news about the meetings of the Cabinet in Rome. I have the impression that Italy is negotiating in earnest now.

Last night Adam, Haeften, Reichwein, and I were at Peter's, today Poelchau is having lunch with me, in the evening we continue at Peter's. I never get to bed before 12 now.

Berlin, 6 August 1943

. . . Last night Adam and I were at Peter's again, to finish some papers. In essentials it got done; I still have to revise a part, but hope to get round to it this morning so that Frl. Breslauer can finish the final texts[3] by tonight.—Steltzer and Husen are coming today, and they and Friedrich will probably take up my week-end. This week-end will essentially decide whether we definitely separate ourselves from Uncle[4] and adopt the substitute[5] who's been found, or proceed in some other way. In the first

1. Leuschner had joined the Goerdeler group.
2. Cf. letter of 9 January.
3. See van Roon, *Resistance to Hitler*, pp. 347–57, and cf. letter of 10 August.
4. Cf. letter of 4 August.
5. Julius Leber (1891–1945), not a trade unionist but a prominent and experienced Social Democrat. Served in the First World War, took a doctorate in politics and economics, then became a journalist and member of the Lübeck City Assembly. In 1924 elected to the Reichstag, served on Budget and Defence committees. After 1933 spent years in concentration camps, then ran a coal business in Berlin, with his friend, Gustav Dahrendorf. He was in touch with the Goerdeler group and actively engaged in preparations for a coup d'état; some of the conspirators envisaged him as future Chancellor. Arrested in early July 1944, sentenced to death in October, and executed 5 January 1945.

case, the coming week will essentially be devoted to working urgently on the new man, who is far superior to Uncle in character and in decisiveness.

Poelchau came yesterday afternoon. Nice as always. His talks about his job the same as always, only considerably increased in quantity. Yesterday it was the turn of 13 women.[1] His reports on North Berlin rather interesting: complete lethargy, people don't even try to save their possessions, let alone send away their wives and children. He thinks it has reached a point where they would hardly fight fires that might start. They think of only one thing: peace and letting go completely. P. thinks they're so used up that there's not enough left even for communism. Poelchau wants to send his wife and child away at the end of August—unless there is an air raid before . . .

Steltzer has just called up. He is completely bombed out in Hamburg and seems to have lost everything. Stauffenberg's secretary, to whom I've just been talking, needed 6 days to get herself and her family out of Hamburg, where she'd been on leave. They finally left Hamburg by horse-cart. . . .

Berlin, 8 August 1943

I didn't write yesterday, as I told you on the phone. The day was too full, and I wasn't alone for a minute. Kiep had lunch here Friday, Steltzer came at 2.30, Peter at 3, Adam & Haeften at 3.30, then I had to go to the Office and to my own office, and at 8 I was back at the Office, where I had an appointment with Frl. Thiel to finish dividing files, for which I simply had no time during the day. It took so long that I wasn't in bed until 2 o'clock, and I had to get up at 6.15 because there were urgent things to be attended to early at the Office again; they kept me busy till 11. Stauffenberg came at 11, Adam came as he left, Hans came when Adam left and stayed till 1 o'clock. Then I left some instructions on urgent matters and at home I found Peter waiting for me; he and Steltzer had lunch with me, Husen joined us at 2.30, and by the time we were through it was 5.10, and I had to hurry on my bike to Conrad, who expected me at 5; when I returned at 7.30 Friedrich was already here; he stayed till 12.

After this final flurry of a very crowded and almost sleepless week I was really exhausted this morning, although I had slept well and deeply for 6 hours. So I decided to spend the morning in bed, made breakfast on the trolley, read a few psalms and proverbs, and, thus uplifted, went back to

1. To be executed.

sleep for a half an hour at 8.30 and dozed till 11, when Mutz suddenly appeared and sat down beside me to unbosom herself. She left at 12.15, I had a bath, dressed, ate, made my bed, and you see what I'm doing now. As soon as this letter is finished, I'll bicycle out to Peter, from him to Adam's, where Steltzer and Husen will join me, back from there to Peter and the beginning of a night-session with Friedrich, Theo, and perhaps our Substitute Uncle.[1] That, then, is the programme to the minute.

Steltzer is very well and completely cured and has brought quite a bit of news, on the whole good; but as a result of his long absence he is a little out of things and therefore has to be properly reinitiated. He's been completely bombed out in Hamburg, but none of his family were there.— Husen is back from Tyrol tanned and crisp and has very nice stories. He's already been initiated in Munich and pulls splendidly as always. It is very nice to see his engagement in the work. Both Husen and Steltzer are flabbergasted at the panic in Berlin; we saw it growing.

Hans[2] looked well and told rather nice stories from Rome which showed, however, that in Rome they have no idea so far of what's in store. He reported that already all railway stations, bridges, power plants, etc., in Northern Italy have German guards. The real surprise was to find how little he knew, while we here feel that Rome is at the centre of events. Hans wants to return to Rome on Wednesday and is thinking of stopping in Merano.

The Institute will probably be evacuated to Ballenstedt in the Harz Mountains; that means we won't have to house their books.—Saturday lunch with Husen, St., & Peter was tremendously concentrated and fruitful. It all went smoothly and quickly but even so it took 3½ hours. Conrad was in good form after his leave, full of stories from Bavaria and Austria and full of concern about the gathering of his colleagues[3] the week after next; he's afraid that they'll start off in the wrong direction. I presented our new wishes, and we'll meet again on the 12th to talk about that. It will be significant to see what the reaction will be.

Just because the subject was so difficult, the evening with Friedrich was satisfying. He and I are always basically of one mind, and that makes everything else fairly easy. I think we have found a means which will, admittedly, not recover what was there before, but enable us to reach a positive solution.—This evening will show whether that is true. . . .

The military situation on the Eastern Front is becoming threatening.

1. Leber.
2. His brother-in-law, Hans Deichmann.
3. The annual meeting of the Catholic bishops in Fulda. It was to be the last Fulda conference of the war.

That's not good at all. For the Russians to achieve a breakthrough every few days even in summer is contrary to all expectations.

Berlin, 10 August 1943

... Sunday at midday I went first to Peter's, to inform him of the satisfactory talk with Friedrich and the resulting conditions. At 4 Peter and I and Steltzer & Husen were at Trott's, had surveyed the entire terrain by 7, and reassembled at 8 at Peter's, where we were joined by Friedrich and Haubach. Friedrich was in excellent form: clear, decisive, shrewd, tactful, witty; and in this night session, lasting till 5 a.m., the hole torn by Uncle[1] was mended. Friedrich has managed to bring Uncle's associates over to us with him, leaving Uncle alone. This is an enormous advance in practice and theory. Peter will take the recorded deposit of this night to Marion on Sunday, and she must see that you get it soon for safekeeping.

We parted at 5.10,[2] and I bicycled to the Zoo to get your parcel, which had come meanwhile. I took it home but didn't unpack it and sank into my bed about 6 and woke up again at 8. The first thing I did was to open the parcel, which was really magnificent. Now I have a mountain of apples. Heavenly beans and onions and flour and groats are now stored away. Thank you, my love, for the thoughtfully composed parcel. I'll cook beans from it for today's lunch for Steltzer and myself, with applesauce to follow. Since I hadn't yet put away the things Illemie brought, there was a lot to do, I'd only just finished tidying up at 10, when I had to go to a meeting with my most intimate enemies.[3] It turned out to be a major engagement, lasting 2 hours, and in essentials I won a clear victory. In consequence I had to go at once to my chief and to a few other offices, and so it was 1.20 before I got home. That was very late, for Hans Carl came to lunch at 1.30; so he had to assist while I cooked. We had your pigeon.

Lukaschek came at 2.30, Husen at 4, Peter at 5, the last of them left me at 7.30; then I had to go back to the Office to transform my victory of the early afternoon into teleprinter messages; but at 8.30 I was home and by 9 I was in bed. That left no room for a letter.

There is a wild panic here about moving. It is ghastly. Nothing gets done, the people one needs aren't there, or aren't interested in real questions to do with work, only with saving themselves. It is disgusting.

Last night it poured, and this morning is rather cool and very windy. It was the same yesterday. I wonder if you've had rain.

1. Leuschner.
2. At 5.10 a.m.
3. Cf. letter of 22 October.

I'm enclosing a new will. I've come to the conclusion that the right thing is for Caspar to get Kreisau and to know it and prepare for it.[1] We can discuss it sometime. . . .

Berlin, 19 August 1943

. . . C.D. & Peter came to tea yesterday. C.D. is nice, with quite a few details about signs of dissolution in his ministry. Otherwise it wasn't very productive. In the evening there was a Count Lehndorff[2] from East Prussia, very intelligent and nice, who reported rather interestingly on mood and morale in East Prussia. People there seem to be very worried about the future. With L., it seems to me, we have taken a big step forward in East Prussia and he'll try to come back with the possible man[3] at the beginning of the week. I wonder whether that will work out. . . .

Berlin, 20 August 1943

. . . Haubach and Peter had lunch here yesterday. H. was in very good form, just as, in the last few weeks, he has generally proved himself and has grown considerably. I like him better and better. Altogether I am pleased that we got through our friends' severe crisis[4] without a single human disappointment. That is worth a lot, and whatever the final result, we'll have improved our position. Yesterday was really the first time we made progress with Haubach alone.—Krüger came to Peter's in the evening. He is a nice and good man but a certain rigidity caused by his age and his training was rather evident last night. . . .

Here, too, it has got hot, really oppressive. I wonder whether the city is being roasted so as to burn better. Disorganization is growing mightily. The department of the Ministry of Finance where I had an appointment today, for which I was prepared to get up specially, withdrew to Sigmaringen the day before yesterday, without any fanfare. This may mean that the matter which has to be discussed simply can't be dealt with until after the war.[5]—The incoming mail is becoming distinctly lighter, a sign that

1. Caspar was 5¾. The provisions for inheritance were complicated by the Reichserbhof-gesetz for entailed estates.
2. Heinrich Graf von Lehndorff-Steinort (1909–44), estate owner and reserve lieutenant—cf. letter of 28 September. Executed 4 September 1944.
3. The man envisaged as regional commissioner for East Prussia was Graf Heinrich von Dohna-Tolksdorf (1882–1944), retired major general, farmer, and member of the East Prussian Brethren's Council of the Confessing Church. Executed 14 September 1944.
4. Of the Social Democrats and trade unionists.
5. He went to Sigmaringen—see letters of 20 and 21 September.

the machine is slowly ceasing to function. The officials are separated from their files, because some of the officials and some of the files are no longer in Berlin. It is like being on a ship that is shutting off its engines after a long voyage and moving to the quay under its own inertia. Perhaps the machine will be revved up hectically towards the end before standing completely still. If we get a really big air raid on Berlin now, everything will be paralyzed until Christmas.

Berlin, 21 August 1943

Your first letter came today, isn't that fantastic? I'm returning two post-cards. Table Mountain[1] moved me, as always. I wonder whether Caspar and Konrad will ever feel as much at home beneath it as I do.

The town is full of rumours of a Cabinet reshuffle in which Göring will be formally dismissed and greater prominence given to Himmler[2] & Goebbels[3] in accordance with their great activity. That would fit the logic of the situation and would be no surprise. The other news of general interest comes in reports from the East, which continue to be unpleasant. . . .

Berlin, 22 August 1943

. . . Last night Husen came after supper. He isn't going to Münster until next week-end; it couldn't be arranged for this one. Otherwise, he seems to have good news about last week's work.[4] But I don't quite trust the evidence of his informant and will know more precise details only when I've been to tea with Conrad[5] on Tuesday. Still, two things have resulted and are to see the light of day in a week's time.[6] . . .

My love, how I'd like to be at home now. It is 4.30, and you're probably having tea. How peaceful that would be. Here there is no real peace any

1. Capetown.
2. He was made Minister of the Interior on 25 August. This strengthened his hold on the civil service and the courts. See also n. 3 to letter of 12 June 1942.
3. His official increase in power came only after 20 July 1944, when he had some part in foiling the plot against Hitler and the regime. On 25 July 1944 he became Reich Pleni-potentiary for Total War.
4. At the Fulda Conference 17–19 August.
5. Preysing.
6. The Pastoral Letter of the German Episcopate of 19 August 1943 was to be read on 29 August 1943, and the Pastoral Letter on the Ten Commandments of 19 August 1943 read on 12 September 1943. Two drafts of memoranda of the German Episcopate of 22–23 August 1943, protests against the dissolution of mixed marriages and the evacuation of "non-Aryans," remained drafts.

more: the feeling of urgency, of improvisation, never leaves one. And nice though it is at Hortensienstrasse, it is never home,[1] and for Peter, too, it is no longer quite home. Besides, the feeling that all this cannot last long now prevents me from settling in properly. And in the near future I'll be travelling a lot, seeing that I still have to go to Paris, Brussels, The Hague, Oslo, and Stockholm and want to get it all behind me before 1 October.

I wonder when we'll return to anything like stable conditions. I detest this living out of a suitcase, though personally I've so far tasted hardly anything of it. But the very idea of it bothers me.—Luckily I know where I am at home, how everything looks there, and who expects me: my love.

Berlin, 25 August 1943

. . . The air raid two nights ago was pretty awful. In the morning there was no light and no gas, nor is there this morning. Then no transport in the city. Steglitz and Schöneberg got the worst of it: not a house left standing there for long distances. In the South, which I had to cross today, there is very heavy industrial damage. The Arado aircraft works have become an open field haunted by monstrous iron shapes. In an area occupied by huts one only sees several hundred iron stoves now, and other industrial areas look much the same. That therefore must have been well-aimed bombing, while in Steglitz and Schöneberg the bounty was scattered lavishly.

The last two days have been crazy. I really wasn't alone for 10 minutes and therefore started work at Peter's at 11 o'clock at night, when Waetjen & Blessing,[2] with whom we'd had quite a good and helpful talk, had left. At 11.30 there was a warning, but I went on working until 12.30 despite it. Only then did things begin to get unpleasant. I was at least able to start the next day with a job ready for dictation. I left Peter at 7.30 and got to the Office about 9.30, and then I had to go to the doctor. My doctor has been bombed out, and this one did everything I wanted him to do. After that I had a terribly strenuous meeting, and it was 12.30 when I finally got to the Office and my dictation. Then I lunched with Carl and Peter; Husen came in between. At 3 I was with Canaris, at 4 with Conrad, at 6.30 with Steengracht, Goerschen came to see me at 7.30 and drove me to Hortensienstrasse at 9; he was going that way because his train left from Potsdam. You can't imagine my fatigue; even at Conrad's I nearly

1. He was living with the Yorcks because Derfflingerstrasse was more exposed in air raids.
2. Karl Blessing (1900–1971), before the war member of the Reichsbank and the Reich Ministry of Economics, then, because he was persona non grata with Hitler, removed; worked at German Unilever. After the war at the Deutsche Bundesbank, its president 1957–70.

fell asleep, for I was simply exhausted. At 11.30 there was an air-raid warning, but at 12.45 I was back in bed. But I still feel the effects of the previous night and must go to bed early today.

Frl. Breslauer was found last night; she is said to be totally exhausted but unharmed. We telephoned this morning; her house collapsed and burnt down; they have lost everything. For hours they dug out their neighbours, who were buried under rubble, and got out 9 out of 13. Now the three of them are staying with friends in Charlottenburg. I'll have a proper talk with her tomorrow.

Conrad had returned from Fulda in good spirits and full of mischief. The worst was prevented, and what we want is to come at the end of September;[1] but according to C. it has been dry-cleaned, the last spots have been removed, and the colour too. Sad, isn't it, but nothing new.[2]

This morning I went to the place where our division has been evacuated, to see Bürkner. It is rather sumptuous and beautiful; but what mattered most to me was that I got what I wanted. This excursion robbed me of my entire morning: an hour to get there, 1 hour there, an hour back. At 12.30 I was back with Steengracht. That didn't produce much, but perhaps I can still get him to do something.

Peter and Adam had lunch with me. Adam has been surprisingly successful in Brussels, I think. In any case far more so than I expected, and that is very gratifying. And he returned in high spirits. Otherwise, too, he was in good form and cheerful. Borsig and Haeften came after lunch, and at 3.30 I had to go to a meeting at the AA, which took till 5.30. It has mainly to do with another trip to Constantinople.[3]

I'll stop now. It is 7 o'clock and I am dreadfully tired. How nice it would be if we could sleep through this night. My love, I'm leaving tomorrow and shall be at Kreisau in the middle of next week.

Munich, 28 August 1943

I didn't write yesterday or the day before, when there was still a lot to finish at the Office. In the morning there was already a nasty hitch in a matter very close to my heart, and to iron it out meant many telephone

1. Cf. n. 6 to letter of 22 August.
2. Cardinal Bertram, who had suggested a pastoral letter on the Decalogue—which he expected to be harmless—found the final product so political that he refused to sign it. The SD found it objectionable too, especially the commentary on the Fifth Commandment, which condemned the killing of incurables, innocent hostages, prisoners, and people of alien race and descent. The SD also criticized the commentary on the Sixth and Ninth Commandments, which dealt with the sanctity of marriage, including mixed marriages.
3. It did not take place till December.

calls. That took a lot of time. In the afternoon there was another fight over my evacuation. Since dear Bürkner is outside the city, it all had to be done by telephone. Then there was a number of current Office jobs, then Husen and Borsig, Eddy, and a few other people came, and Frl. Breslauer, and finally Wengler and Diwald, who are to keep an eye on matters while I'm away. Before I knew it, it was 6 o'clock, the time when Peter and Adam were to come to Derfflingerstrasse for a final review. Indeed they were sitting there when I arrived and went with me to the station. So there wasn't the least bit of time for a letter to you. . . .

Did I tell you that Reichwein's house is said to have been "atomized"? There is said to be nothing left of it.

We got here 2 hours late. König was at the station, and by chance I met Guttenberg, who took me first to the hotel. Then came the lawyer[1] with whom I had to discuss things, and we went out together. I was back at my base at 10.15 and didn't feel up to writing. Things resumed at 8.30 this morning and now, at 2, there is a lunch break. I'm meeting Rösch at 4; this is his name day, together with St. Augustine's. I'm leaving for Graz tomorrow morning, very satisfied, and am then coming home. I hope to arrive on Thursday at the latest.

Unfortunately I'll have to leave again on Saturday, because I want to go to Schlange's Saturday evening and stay there till Sunday noon. I don't like it at all, but there is just no other way. . . .

Graz, 30 August 1943

Yesterday morning I left Munich at 9, had a quarter of an hour in Salzburg between trains, and spent all the rest of the day on the train here. I arrived at 8.30 in the evening. I sat in 3rd class, which was pleasant for the greater part of the journey, only in the middle stretch was it a bit crowded for 2 hours. It was rather moving to pass Steinach-Irdning and to see the train to Aussee[2] standing there. . . .

After arriving in Graz, I called up my friend Captain Taucher,[3] whom I was lucky enough to reach. He suggested that we meet at the Hotel Wiesler. There were certainly no rooms available there, but I'd never find my way out to him and he really couldn't put me up either. So I stumbled into the dark town of Graz. But I found a nice tram conductress who, despite the fact that I was recognizably from the "Old Reich," gave me such good directions that I found my way to the hotel without delay. To

1. Perhaps Franz Reisert—see letter of 20 September.
2. A recollection of Grundlsee, where M. and F.M. had met at the Schwarzwalds' in 1929.
3. Wilhelm Taucher, professor of economics and friend of the Yorcks.

my own surprise and the utter amazement of the good Taucher, I got a decent room immediately. After cleaning up a bit I went with him to supper at his house, where an ancient housekeeper made me an omelette from 4 eggs and gave me excellent smoked bacon with it. Afterwards I ate mountains of greengages and peaches. . . .

The people here belong to the Styrian type: well built, strikingly well equipped for walking, with very strong, broad necks, and heads atop them that are too small. This last defect is very pronounced here, and I'm afraid the small size allows conclusions as to meagre content. As far as I could gather from conversations on the train, the people of the "Old Reich" are the source of all evil and objects of scorn and deception. To have deceived an Old Reicher is a daring deed, and one boasts of it in the train. And that in the "City of the Uprising of the People."[1] The whole compartment, everyone who entered or left between Munich and Graz, saluted with a snappy H.H.[2]

Last night's talk was bad in its diagnostic aspect, but satisfactory in intent. It is to continue this afternoon, and he may turn up any moment. I want to leave at 4.30 for Salzburg, where I'll arrive at 1 a.m., and to-morrow night[3] want to set sail for home. If I can go right through, I'll be home Wednesday night, otherwise Thursday morning.

Berlin, 6 September 1943

. . . Our community has meanwhile grown by the addition of Eugen, who was bombed out. In the evening the full cast met until 2 a.m. There was an enormous programme to be dealt with, above all the report on my trip and my new instructions for Brussels. Friedrich in top form again. Reichwein rather shaken, evidently by the death of his mother as well as the loss of all his possessions. He seems to have practically nothing left.

This morning the three of us set out, and I found an insane amount of work waiting. There had been rather a muddle, and on a few questions

1. The title—"Stadt der Volkserhebung"—given to the most fervently Nazi town in Hitler's homeland.
2. Heil Hitler!
3. He says nothing about the contents of the talk with Taucher or about the day in Salzburg. Both probably served the search for suitable men to work with in Austria. In Salzburg the former, pre-Anschluss, Provincial Governor (Landeshauptmann) Franz Rehrl was being considered as Regional Commissioner (Landesverweser), a fact later mentioned in Gestapo interrogations after 20 July 1944. It was a statement by Rehrl that led the Gestapo to have "a closer look" at M. in August 1944. Rehrl told them that M. was sent to him by the Archbishop of Salzburg with another, unknown, person and discussed the question of change in the regime with him. M. may have seen Archbishop Rohracher (1892–1976, Archbishop 1943–69) too that day.

close to my heart some perfectly idiotic decisions had been made, simply idiotic.—Peter and Marion came to lunch at Derfflingerstrasse with Frau Pick. . . .

The evacuation of the Office is proceeding rapidly. I expect that when I return from Holland I'll practically rule alone here with another officer and Kiep. There's much to be said for that.—The internal disintegration has assumed grotesque forms. Nothing works any more, and everybody follows the motto *"sauve qui peut."* It is a sad spectacle.—The news from the East is very bad. This goes especially for the centre. One gets the distinct impression that the Russians still have great possibilities. But in a few weeks' time mud will set in and with it a halt, which leaves a pause before the winter offensive. But it won't be more than a very few weeks. . . .

Seneffe, 12 September 1943

. . . The journey was uninteresting and comfortable. First I slept quite a lot by my standards. At 11.21 we were at The Hague. Herr Steinke was already waiting at the station and wanted to know a lot of things. But first I went to see G.[1] so as to be able to make a schedule and I asked Diwald to make an appointment for us with the Higher SS and Police Chief at 12 o'clock. I made the appointment with G. for 1.15 and sent a message to Igl that I wanted to see him at 5 and asked Steinke to come at 3.25. So my programme seemed well organized, and I decided to enquire in Hilversum whether I could see the general there the same evening. So the minute-by-minute schedule ticked off correctly, but at 4.30 I heard that (a) Falkenhausen had already expected me Saturday afternoon and that (b) the general in Hilversum could see me only if I took the train at 5.15. That was sad, because it meant that Igl was short-changed; I saw him for only 50 minutes at the station. He got the animal[2] and said, in the main, that they were all well.

The talk with the SD was terribly necessary and finally successful, on the whole. There has been a personnel change there. The very good man[3] with whom I dealt in the early summer was transferred to Italy quite unexpectedly last week. His successor is an insignificant soft man, who, furthermore, comes from the East[4] and will, I'm afraid, give in to any cry

1. Goerschen.
2. Perhaps a toy for the Breitbarth children.
3. Wilhelm Harster—see letter of 5 June.
4. SS Brigadier Dr. Erich Naumann, Harster's successor as chief of Security Police and Security Service (*Sicherheitspolizei und SD*) in Holland, had been head of Einsatzgruppe B until March 1943.

for shootings. I talked to him seriously, and he assured me that he found my arguments convincing and would discuss them with his staff. But unfortunately the man is so soft that he'll collapse if someone else attacks him tomorrow. Yet perhaps my injection helped a bit.—Elsewhere I had some indirect results, and that was very satisfying and useful.

The evening in Hilversum was less than satisfying, because my chief ally there had to be away that evening. But General von Wühlisch[1] got in full force what I had to convey to him. I really got going and gave him hell. I really enjoyed it.—I spent the rest of the evening with a few other gentlemen of the headquarters staff, who are nice. But the entire staff makes a rather leaderless impression.

At 11 I went to bed, at 4.45 I had to get up again, because my train to Brussels left at 6.10. It was rather cold and I froze in the train. To make up for it, it got frightfully close about an hour before Brussels, and in Brussels there was bright sunshine. As I entered the Hotel Plaza, F.[2] was just leaving for Seneffe and took me with him directly; it relieved me of any planning, which would in any case have been very difficult before I knew F.'s plans. We were 5 at lunch and then there was a siesta. I wanted to see F. before supper. As bad luck would have it, Generaloberst Salmuth,[3] who commands an army here, announced himself and stole F., with whom I'd only been able to talk for half an hour. In the evening we had delicious partridges and then played poker until 2; your husband lost 100 francs.

During this trip, repeatedly, when I found myself too tired to read on the train, I felt for the first time that it is high time for me to take some leave; for in these intervals I can't think of anything worth while any more, only of foolish stuff. One need not always think of something worth while, but this fixation on certain subjects is unpleasant. The only alternative, for me, is Kreisau. I can always occupy myself with that. . . .

[continued] *Paris, 15 September 1943*

As you see, I've got quite a bit further before being able to continue writing. This is a rather quiet day, at least so far. My first appointment isn't till 10.30, and I'm sitting in my princely apartment in the George V with a large view of Paris and start by writing.

The 12th, when I wrote to you in the morning, was *crowded*, too. After breakfast we went partridge shooting and I stuck to F. I was very glad of a 3-hour walk. The countryside is beautifully rolling, fruitful, divided

1. See letter of 5 June.
2. Falkenhausen.
3. Colonel General Hans von Salmuth, commander-in-chief of AOK (Army Command) 15.

into small fields of 2 to 3 acres, and enlivened by small bits of wood, windbreaks, and bushes. It really is a lovely landscape.—Despite the Sunday, there was some work in the fields. The livestock we saw was good; but the pasture was lush, too. Towards the end of the hunt, F. and I walked through a field of vetch and a fallow field where a lot of hedge-mustard was blooming and these two fields were buzzing like mad with bees. I thought mournfully of our hungry colonies.

The hunt itself was unsuccessful; only the gamekeeper who accompanied us got 2 grouse, but the others kept missing very distant birds. There were lots of grouse, but they were terribly shy and always rose at very great distances.—It was hot, rather close, and all sweated like mad, especially those in uniform. At any rate I greatly enjoyed the walk. At the end, 5 minutes before the others came, F. addressed me once more on the questions of interest only to me, and we got a little further.

The others slept after lunch while I read, sitting on the balcony and looking over the countryside, which was still quite summery. From time to time I walked in the garden a little. Princess Ruspoli came at 4 and the general went for a walk with her to hear about the Italian colony's confusion over the recent events in Italy.[1] It must, judging from the few hints I gathered, be very funny.—There was tea at 5, and the visitors all left at 6, and Schulenburg and Dumoulin[2] went grouse shooting once more. My optimistic assumption that I'd now have the general to myself proved unjustified; we were three when we walked in the garden with Frl. von Dazur, the mistress of the house. Our conversation was resumed at 20 to 7, and now I lost no time in coming to our petitions. He listened and then talked about military difficulties of all kinds. Guests came for the evening at 7, and F. and I went to change.

There were a lot of people for supper: a Professor Rassow, who is, I

1. On 3 September Badoglio had asked the Allies for an armistice, which was announced five days later. Hitler, in a clear reference to the Casablanca formula, called it an unconditional surrender. On the next day Rome was occupied by the Germans—not to be liberated until months later. In a broadcast speech on 10 September Hitler dwelt on his friendship with Mussolini, "that great and loyal man"—who was liberated by a German airborne unit in a daring coup de main on 12 September and installed as head of a new "National Fascist Government" by the shore of Lake Garda. The German army took over Italy, which, far from being the "soft underbelly" of Europe, as Churchill had said, became a theatre of war until the German capitulation on 29 April 1945. For the Italians the fall of Mussolini brought the heaviest Allied air raids, German occupation, the disarming of the Italian army by the Germans, and the neglect of the Italian resistance by the Allies (see Elisabeth Wiskemann, "The Italian Resistance Movement," in Arnold and Veronica Toynbee, eds., *Hitler's Europe* [London–New York–Toronto, 1954], pp. 330–37; and F. W. Deakin, *The Brutal Friendship: Mussolini, Hitler, and the Fall of Italian Fascism* [New York, 1962]).

2. Lieutenant Colonel Dumoulin of the AA was a kind of court-marshal on Falkenhausen's staff.

believe, at Breslau University and in any case knows Asta; a very nice General Frantzen, airman and formerly navy; a Professor Wachsmut, doctor and lecturer from Munich; Aschmann [?], who lost his three sons. It was a nice gathering round the table, even though Rassow talked an awful lot and kept lecturing, which is unbearable to me after 10 minutes. Not long after supper we returned to a game of poker; your husband lost the obligatory 100 francs.—Bedtime at 2.

I got up early, went for a little walk, and was in the house for breakfast at 8. We left for Brussels at 8.45. I gave no sign that I had by no means finished with F., although I found it quite hard. As we entered Brussels he said to Dumoulin, "Now, Moltke will have lunch and supper with me," and then to me, "We'll meet in the afternoon, I'll tell you the time at lunch." It struck me as a good sign, for at last I'd waited long enough for him to take the initiative. I had outwaited him, so to speak.—I then went to see Craushaar, the second-in-command of the military administration, with whom I had to have a longish talk. Unfortunately he had no time during office hours, because he had a big meeting, and had therefore kept lunch free for me. He arranged it with F., who released me and asked me to come and see him at 5. Meanwhile it was 10.30 and I hurried to P.W.'s.[1]

I was interested in what he had to tell about the situation of the Belgians, who see that they'll either become a battlefield—if the British land there—or will be left to chaos and civil war if the Germans withdraw some day and the British haven't landed. It isn't a comfortable feeling. . . .

At 1.45 I was at Craushaar's apartment for lunch and we had a gratifying and successful conversation, which was resumed at 3, with the specialist in Craushaar's office, and continued till 4.15. Then I went to see the chief of staff, Herr von Harbou, and from him to F. at 5. Within 30 minutes everything had been settled satisfactorily: in any case I had achieved exactly what I wanted. It was a strange conversation; F. did almost all the talking and talked quite freely. It turned out that he had thought over the bits I'd thrown his way in our three brief exchanges in Seneffe and put them together correctly and had now reached a decision.

I can't get rid of the impression that he had deliberately and systematically tested my patience and endurance by sitting next to me for 2 days and yet giving me no real opportunity. When I'd passed this test like a good boy, all was suddenly dandy. A strange man, but with all the makings of a wise old man.—I went to say goodbye to some people, bought a few flowers for Frl. von Dazur, and at 7 was at the hotel, where P.W. came once more to tell me all he'd thought of since the morning. We went to supper at 7.30. Only Aschmann [?], Schulenburg, and Dumoulin were

---

1. P. W. Müller, friend of Ada Deichmann's.

with us; it was a nice supper, followed by a game of Bridge. Our train left at 11, and the leavetaking was very warm. Altogether, this evening went as though F. wanted to let me know that I was now accepted.

The journey to Paris was particularly pleasant because we were 4 hours late, owing to the sabotaging of a locomotive; instead of arriving ill rested at 6.30, we arrived well rested at 10.30.—From the station I went straight to the military commander's office and after a little preliminary talk with the specialists I was with General von Stülpnagel at 12. There was nothing special. At 1.30 I had lunch with Hofacker, who's leaving here, and then I had to attend to my billeting, which was very successful, too, for this small hotel is really very nice. I am on the 8th floor, have a little balcony with flowers, and across the rooftops look down the Champs Elysées and see the whole inner city. It is Rundstedt's headquarters when he's in Paris, and I therefore have excellent telephone connections, get Berlin in 5 minutes, and so on. . . .

Berlin, 18 September 1943

. . . The trip from Paris was chiefly marked by hunger. I'd had a nice but hardly ample lunch at the Ritz. Then I'd gone once more to see the military commander's people and the SD and when I was through at 6.45, I decided to take another little walk, from the Hôtel de Ville via Notre Dame along the Seine to the Ritz, where I wanted to eat at 8. There was an air-raid warning at 7.30. First one saw tiny silver birds in threes, flying very high. Those were fighter planes, rising. Then the Flying Fortresses came in tight formation: they say there were 180. It was a mighty spectacle. The anti-aircraft guns were shooting and 20–25 little clouds had hardly appeared in the sky when a Fortress came down, and, after another 15 specks of cloud, a second one. Then, because all the bounty of anti-aircraft shrapnel was coming down on us, I went into the basement with some hundred Frenchmen, who'd filled the street with excitement and expectation.

This air raid lasted till 8.45. The métro started again at 9.10. I could only race to the hotel to pack, for my train left at 10.30. By luck I got a car and was at the station at 10.20. I tried in vain to get something to eat there. The sleeping-car attendant gave me 2 splendid pears and consoled me by saying that a restaurant car would be joined to the train from Brussels to the frontier. In Brussels we were already 1½ hours late because a rail had been blown up, and when I started to the restaurant car it was just being disconnected because a wheel had been sabotaged, which made us another half hour late. Luckily I got a connection in Cologne at once and so at least got to Mütterchen's at 7.30.

But Cologne looks fantastic. When you take the train to Godesberg round the inner city you see almost the whole of the cathedral, not only the steeples, as before, for between the railroad and the Rhine nothing remains undamaged. It is a picture of desolation.

I missed the sleeper, because it now leaves an hour earlier. But with a bribe of RM 20.–I got a whole compartment to myself in a train which was really better, because it got to Berlin at 7.15, on schedule.

Now I hear Peter coming and we'll have breakfast.

Berlin, 19 September 1943

. . . There is an awful lot of work at the Office because a lot of quite inexplicable problems turned up in the Italian talks,[1] and there's a good deal else going on, too. So I left Hortensienstrasse at 6 today, had breakfast at Derfflingerstrasse, and then went to the Office. I left there at 1.30, not yet finished, unfortunately, ate something quickly, and now—at 2.10—am expecting Christiansen, who should come any moment. When the gathering disperses it will probably be time for my train; and some time in between Frl. Breslauer is also coming and I must pay another visit to the Office.

Christiansen came at 1 p.m. yesterday. We were three for lunch at Hortensienstrasse and were then joined by Einsiedel, Theo,[2] & Eugen. Agriculture is going to have an incredibly hard future, not only economically but also sociologically and politically. They all took off at 10.30, to get home before the air-raid warning; but there wasn't one and we had quite a pleasant night.—Today we'll continue at midday, with Husen's assistance. Chr.'s train leaves at 7 and mine at 10. . . .

Sigmaringen, 20 September 1943

Here I sit in the "Löwe" and have half an hour before we gather for a preliminary talk before wandering over to the ministry[3] at 3.30. We had a comfortable journey. The sleeper was half empty, and Reisert[4] was awaiting me in Augsburg and we had breakfast together. What a nice man he is. You would like him a lot. Our breakfast and the subsequent

1. Cf. n. 1 (p. 341) to letter of 15 September. On 17 September the British Eighth Army coming up from Calabria linked up with the American Fifth Army at the Salerno beachhead. For German measures relating to the Italian military and civilians see *DGFP*, E, VI, nos. 300, 311, 314.
2. Haubach.
3. The Ministry of Finance had been evacuated to Sigmaringen—cf. letter of 20 August.
4. Dr. Franz Reisert (1889–1965), lawyer—cf. letter of 10 January 1945.

conversation were overshadowed by news that another 12 people, 2 of whom he'd defended, would be executed in the afternoon. On to Ulm at 9.24; approaching Augsburg one gets a very beautiful view of the cathedral keeping splendid watch over the green city. From there on to Sigmaringen through lovely, fruitful land with old centres of cultivation. Unfortunately it poured the whole morning, so that one couldn't see much.

Because we hurried to our hotel in the rain, I haven't yet seen anything of Sigmaringen. After eating I telephoned with Wilflingen, one of the Stauffenberg estates. The Little Stauffenberg,[1] the one whom I recommended to the Little Wolff[2] as teacher, had expressly told me to do that. By chance he happened to be on leave[3] and answered the phone himself. Now I want to go there at 6, if I get through, and spend the night there, returning here in the morning. I'm really pleased about it, although it will be somewhat strenuous.

Tomorrow I'll leave here at 13 hours, be in Munich at 6; there all will gather, and I start back at 10.—We made quite nice progress yesterday afternoon, I think, and Christiansen in particular now sees what will be asked of him. He made a very good impression on all, which was a matter of importance to me. So much is involved in this whole question of agricultural policy, and Peter and I are simply disqualified for it, as undoubtedly interested parties. . . .

Sigmaringen, 21 September 1943

I broke off negotiations yesterday at 5.30 and took a real narrow-gauge train to the Stauffenbergs' at 6.03 [Sketch map follows.] Sigmaringen is on the Ulm–Freiburg line and from Sigmaringen there is a provincial train which runs through the whole Hohenzollern province. I took that first, to Hanfestal, where I had to change, and then to Bingen, and went from there on foot 7 km to Wilflingen. My train couldn't get into the station at Hanfestal, because sacks of seed grain weighing two hundredweight each were to be loaded onto the train on which I came, and the stationmaster and the conductor, whose combined age was over 140, weren't able to handle it. So I transferred the sacks, which at that weight was quite a task even for me. The engine driver turned up later. Then this train departed and mine pulled in.

The trip through the Zollern land is really beautiful. Wooded cliffs rise

1. See letter of 7 July 1942.
2. Ibid.
3. He, too, was serving with the Abwehr.

from water meadows in a valley with little, slow, dammed streams. In most places the final drop from woods to meadow is sheer rock, which makes the whole landscape look quite romantic. The land is sparsely settled, but every settlement is surrounded by fruit trees, and all the lanes, too, are lined by apple and pear trees, which bear excellently. They're drowning in apples here.

Stauffenberg met me at Bingen, which I reached at 7. We marched the 7 km at a fast pace. There isn't a house on these 7 km, and we didn't meet a soul. The ground rises considerably over the first 3 km, and where the outlook isn't obstructed one gets a wide view over the "Rauhe Alb," which looks beautiful but inhospitable, a slightly undulating high plateau rising towards the north with very beautiful colour and light. But one mostly walks through the woods, mostly good, some beech, some spruce, both nicely mixed with other trees, like alder, birch, pine. After 5.1 km the woods end, and the path drops to a little dip in which lies Wilflingen. I didn't see much of it, for it was 8 when we got to the house. The village makes a very nice impression with old houses, mostly half timbered with good fruit trellises.

The house at Wilflingen is a big castle, 3 floors and turrets, with foundations that are probably very old; the present shape dates probably from the end of the 18th century; an enormous church with an onion tower directly beside the house rather hems it in. The rooms are beautiful and large, the furniture old in a nice way. But the house was very dark, with only blue light in the corridors, so that I couldn't see much.

Apart from Stauffenberg's wife,[1] there was his widowed sister, who seems to have kept house for their father until now but is just leaving, and an old aunt. Otherwise we were alone. We sat together pleasantly and talked till 10.30. Then I was good and tired and slept deliciously. I had to get up at 5.15, had breakfast with a thermos at 6, and started on my way at 6.20, to catch the train at Bingen at 7.40. That's why I saw nothing of the fields: it was dark when I came and when I left.

Negotiations resumed at 9 and were finished at 11.30. I am fairly pleased with the result; in any case I achieved more than I expected. What I'm doing now you can see. I want to have a quick bite, and my train to Munich goes at 1. I'll spend the evening in Munich and take the train back at 10.

I must write to the little son[2] so I'll stop.

1. She was British and rejoiced in the copies of *The Times* the visitor brought (Camilla von dem Bussche, 21 July 1980).
2. Konrad was going to be two on 23 September.

Berlin, 22 September 1943

Here I am back in a Berlin that's freezing. How will it be when none of us has any window panes and we can get warm only in bed.—The news I found here was also of a kind that makes one shiver, it is quite alarming. Bad news isn't so bad when the crew is up to it and can take it calmly. But unfortunately one feels that isn't the case here.

The return journey was quite comfortable. I had 4 hours in Munich and met the lawyer from Augsburg[1] and Rösch. What nice, good people they are. Their report held no comfort either, but at least one feels perfectly safe with them. König has been completely bombed out.—They gave me supper, as always rather good, and they gave me sandwiches to take which I didn't need and ate only in Berlin.

My plans now are as follows: Sunday evening[2] I travel to Führer Headquarters for a day. On Wednesday morning[3] I go for 10 days to Oslo & Stockholm, and shall be back around the 10th.—So don't bring too many perishable things, because except for Sunday I'll be eating in Berlin only one other day. If there are shirts ready, 3 or 4 of them would be quite useful.

Today, as always now, we had a high time. Haeften came to lunch with Fritzi,[4] who was very depressed. Reichwein came later and seemed quite satisfied with the Kreisau solution. There was also a crazy amount of work at the Office and in my own office.—My love, I must go: Adam & Eugen are waiting.

Berlin, 28 September 1943

So now I'm back and the first day in Berlin is as good as over. A big programme was got through and I face another hectic day. But I've received a bonus in that I'm not flying at 7 a.m. on Thursday, but at 4 p.m. I gain half a working day, and with it a better prospect of finishing.

The trip was strenuous. We arrived[5] at 10, then there was breakfast, and at 10.30 the morning negotiations started. They went on till 12.45 but were successful inasmuch as we'd practically reached agreement by then. We had found a way to maintain the principles your husband defended without consequences that would be impossible in practice. Then

1. Reisert.
2. 26 September.
3. 29 September—but cf. letter of 28 September.
4. Schulenburg.
5. At Führer Headquarters at Rastenburg in East Prussia. The negotiations concerned Abwehr business.

I quickly had a bowl of soup and left at 1 for Steinort[1] and the Lehn-dorffs', where I arrived at 2.

Steinort is on the Mauersee and the enormous property includes 28,000 acres of water which are being fished. On one side of the house is the lake, on the other a park and then a bog in front of the lake which has become heavily silted at this point and forms a kind of virgin forest, a marvellous area for waterfowl of all kinds: herons, ospreys, seagulls. A flight of ducks several hundred strong sat on a free sheet of water about 300 m away.

The house is not beautiful from the outside: a big box, to which many generations have added, with fine old beams, beautiful old furniture, and a curious and enormous piece of hand embroidery from the 17th century. The whole thing gives the impression of having grown organically.—The Foreign Minister of the Reich was in bed, haranguing the world. The house was in disorder, because the water system wasn't working and the Foreign Minister's bath water had to be warmed at all the fire-places of the house.

At 3.30 there was a nice tea, at 4 I drove back, and at 5 negotiations began again, and at 6.45 they came to an end that was satisfactory to me. Then there was a quick snack, our train left at 7.07 and deposited us here safely this morning. . . .

Berlin, 30 September 1943[2]

Here I sit in the Flughafen underground station, which now accom-modates the Lufthansa check-in. Then one is taken to the airport in a rattling bus. It will be a little while, still, and I want to use this little while to write you a quick line, especially since I didn't get pen to paper yester-day. They were 2 hectic days, and what I would have done if I hadn't had this extra half day I don't know.

The matter that took me to FHQ made more work, Wednesday noon a man came from Adam who stayed rather long and was a fiasco. Adam thought I was very unfriendly to him, for which I was very sorry, because he was a good-natured old gentleman, but he had lemonade instead of blood in his veins and no amount of good nature can remedy that.

The afternoon continued turbulent. Oxé, Wengler, Stauffenberg, Eck-hardt,[3] all wanted something from me, and Peter had entreated me to be

---

1. Ribbentrop's East Prussian headquarters was within reach of Hitler's "Wolfsschanze." The visit to the Lehndorffs' was for discussions on the designation and functions of the Landesverweser, the regional commissioners the Kreisauers wanted to install.
2. Erroneously dated 20.8.43.
3. Ministerialrat Curt Eckhardt of the Navy High Command.

back for supper punctually at 7.15 because Blessing was coming. I was punctual, but Peter didn't arrive until 8. We then talked until 11.30 rather successfully, if not yet altogether conclusively. In the morning I got away, as I'd already done yesterday, as early as 7, packed my suitcase, and got to the Office at 7.45. There I dictated until 10, then Bürkner came; at 11 Oxé and I saw Telschow,[1] the director of the Kaiser Wilhelm Gesellschaft, with whom we had to fight quite hard about our say in the new appointment to Bruns's post.

It was 1 when I got back to the Office, and Hammersen was sitting there, a very nice and good man who's on leave from the staff in Norway. He came with me and sat beside me as I packed, and watched Peter and me eat. Then I had to go to the Office once more, and any moment now the bus will leave. . . .

Oslo, 4 October 1943

. . . Yesterday morning I woke at the Swedish frontier, or shortly before, after a middling night in a sleeper, which was disturbed by a clod in the upper berth. It was an enchantingly beautiful day. It was Harvest Thanksgiving, and at 8.30, having my breakfast at the last frontier station, I thought that you would soon be finishing breakfast and going to church. I wonder whether you had as beautiful a day. In any case, I thought, how much I'd rather be going with you than crossing the Norwegian countryside in a train. But it was very beautiful. A clear autumn sky with a few— That's where Steltzer came and now it is after lunch.—

The foliage here still has much stronger colours than ours, the woods are quite mixed, so that green alders stand beside red maples, above them yellow birches, and halfway up barberries, then clearings with carpets of heather, in between cragged cliffs and again and again water: high up, woods surrounding big calm lakes, which look as though no man had ever stepped on their shores or swum through their waters; brooks which fall fairly steeply and babble along, and then the fjords, some cut into steep walls of rock, some with inviting, settled, flat and lovely shores. The whole picture presents incredibly rich colour and boundless grandeur. I wondered if I might someday travel that way with you and your sons in this autumn splendour; whether I'll then recall my many journeys along this route, and with what feelings I'll think back on them.

And with these thoughts we suddenly stopped; I had to get out of my sleeper and into another train, which took me, quickly and comfortably,

1. Telschow, a Nazi, was managing director of the Kaiser Wilhelm Institute and opposed to Berthold Stauffenberg, whom Canaris had proposed as successor to Bruns, who had died.

while I read *Parliamentary Debates*, to Oslo. I saw that we must soon be there, the train was hurrying through cuts in the rocks and past small villas; I thought it might be a good idea to put on my coat and was just stepping to the window on the corridor side when the train turned a bend and opened up the view of the grand Oslo Fjord lying in the noonday sun in all its glory. This sight is always exciting and a little like the first sight of the Lake of Geneva coming from Berne, though it is even grander.

But before I tell you about Oslo I want to report briefly on Copenhagen. I got there shortly before 7 and was met by a captain with a car. He'd got quarters for me and told me that we must make haste, because there would be nothing left to eat after 8; under the state of emergency[1] Danes were forbidden to be in the streets after 9. That was a foretaste. This evening I sat for a while after supper with the man who met me, but I sank into bed shortly after 9, because he was frightfully boring and I was frightfully tired.—Next morning at 9 I had an appointment with the colonel who was in charge of my business; he took a very friendly interest in me, didn't himself know much about the matters that interested me, but passed me straight on to the Ic, a Herr von Heydebreck, the chief of staff, and the C.-in-C., General von Hanneken.[2] I was announced there for the time from 3 p.m. until the evening. So I was free at 10 and went to see Merete.[3]

But her flat was empty. I had forebodings and telephoned Kim's[4] apartment, where his wife gave me a very halting answer that made me fear the worst. At least I got Kim's office number from her, and after another half hour I had Merete. She had indeed been arrested when the state of emergency was declared, on 29 August, but had been released again after 3 days. In any case she no longer lives at home now but sleeps in different places in succession.

[continued] 5 October 1943

A new morning. I got up early and have a little more time before breakfast.—Yes, I finally found Merete and found that she and Kim were suffering from a sense of complete insecurity. When I assured them that one gets used to it, they just couldn't believe it.—But the day was wholly dom-

1. Imposed on 29 August 1943.
2. General Hermann von Hanneken, commander of the German troops in Denmark, from 11 November 1943 with the status of Wehrmacht commander. For M.'s remonstrations with him see Peter Hoffmann, *The History of the German Resistance*, trans. Richard Barry (Cambridge, Mass., 1977), p. 241.
3. Bonnesen.
4. Bonnesen.

inated by the imminent evacuation of the Jews,[1] the whole town was talking about it, and the political consequences are unforeseeable. The
round-up took place the following night, that is 1–2 October. 3 ships had
entered the harbour in the evening and were to leave the next morning
carrying 6000 Jews to Stettin. The whole operation was organized in a
big way. Hanneken had allowed himself to be persuaded to use the Secret
Field Police, too, and to call up Germans living in Denmark for it. Copenhagen's entire telephone network was dead from 9 till 12. Altogether,
they got only 200 instead of 6000, all the others had made off; one ship
left in the morning with these 200. I talked to Best[2] and Hanneken in the
morning of the 2nd, and both realized that they have shouldered a big
political liability with this measure and were waiting for a reaction.
Meanwhile the Swedes have delivered a note of protest in Berlin and
offered asylum to all the Jews who can get there. In Denmark itself nothing has happened so far, and nothing obvious is likely to happen, but the
reaction will show itself in increased passive resistance by the civil service.

During the afternoon of the 1st I spoke to all military men concerned,
from Hanneken to the Ic, and in the morning of the 2nd, with Best and
his people. Best is not a bad man, at any rate he is intelligent. On the staff
of the German general, on the other hand, Oberstkriegsgerichtsrat
Kanter[3] is the only man who knows his categories. Hanneken is a foolish,
loud man, entirely out of place, fit at most for a barrack square. Best is
vastly superior, and this inferiority makes H. rail against Best like mad.
Thus the conflict between H. and B. is the chief feature of the Danish
situation and in my opinion much of what has happened must be understood as a result of that conflict. In addition H. is soft and lets Best push
him into anything he wants and does quite impossible things. Moreover,
matters of fundamental importance are transacted on the telephone, so

---

1. He uses the German—official—term *Evakuierung.* He had sent a warning about the
forthcoming deportation of the Jews to Kim Bonnesen, who passed it on. But the comprehensive rescue operation was mainly due to the earlier warning by Georg Ferdinand Duckwitz, the German shipping attaché in Copenhagen. See Leni Yahil, *The Rescue of Danish
Jewry: Test of a Democracy,* trans. Morris Gradel (Philadelphia, 1969).

2. Dr. Werner Best, Reich Plenipotentiary in Denmark, as member of the Foreign Service.
Born 1903, co-author of the "Boxheim Documents," a plan for a Nazi takeover exposed by
Carlo Mierendorff in 1931. After 1933 Best enjoyed a quick career in the Gestapo, the
Security Police, and the Reich Security Head Office (RSHA, Reichssicherheitshauptamt),
where, however, he came into conflict with Heydrich. 1940–42 SS Brigadier and chief of
the Administrative Division of German Military Government in France. A Danish death
sentence after the war was commuted to a twelve-year prison sentence, followed by his
release in 1951.

3. Judge Advocate Ernst Kanter. He worked closely with Karl Sack, the Army Judge Advocate—cf. n. 2 to letter of 20 June.

that when I asked for an explanation and justification for some truly stag-gering orders by H., there was no documentation and only the laconic statement: The Reich Plenipotentiary wanted it.

5 October 1943 Continuation

Unfortunately the Danes have to bear the results of this ineptitude, and I think we are putting ourselves into a very complicated and difficult po-sition, in which there are bound to be conflicts with the Danish courts and Danish administrative departments. I therefore left rather disquieted, even though I had quite thorough and altogether satisfactory talks about shootings with all the people with whom I discussed the matter. They all assured me that they realized shooting individuals would do no good and would do enormous political harm. I was most reassured by the fact that Best was quite categorical on this point. But I don't know how long he expects to last, for if he doesn't succeed in getting H. removed, it will never work.

I finished my talks at 12 on the 2nd and then once more met Kim and Merete. Kim has a son now and is a very nice family father. I scarcely saw his wife, who had gone for a walk with the child. Merete had heard from Esther,[1] but only a Red Cross letter. At least it showed that she was well.—Kim seems to be well established in his department and is becom-ing a real civil servant. All the same he still has this boyishness, and that is nice.—Merete is not working for *Politiken*[2] at the moment because she is afraid of being arrested in any new operation, and as a result she is not in very good shape. She is really nervous. I advised her strongly to start work again in any case, but didn't have the impression that she'd be able to bring herself to do it.—Scavenius[3] is living in the country as a private individual.

After an enormous meal I went to the airport at 6.10 on the 2nd, hopped to Malmö in 15 minutes, and there got my train to Oslo comfort-ably. I'd certainly have had a very pleasant trip in it, if at some station the Germans coming by ferry from Denmark had not got on. First of all, they were terribly loud and behaved badly, and one clod climbed into the berth above me. The kind of people who travel on this train are unimaginable! I got up very early and sat in the compartment of the sleeping-car attend-ant, who gets off one station before the frontier; that way at least I didn't have to see these people by day.

1. See letter of 17 March.
2. The paper for which she worked.
3. Erik Scavenius, Danish Minister of State and Foreign Minister July 1940, Prime Minister November 1942–29 August 1943. He had been known as pro-German.

I reached Oslo at midday Sunday. Steltzer came immediately after lunch and I had a long talk with him. He then took me up one of the mountains, from which we climbed down on foot in full view of the majestic Oslo Fjord in its autumn glory. Steltzer has done his part really very well, but he, too, is now showing signs of impatience. We then ate alone and at 8.30 went to see our friends,[1] whom I found rather depressed. There, too, this impatience. Time isn't passing fast enough, the disagreeable winter is coming, the painter's[2] wife is very ill, the friend of another has been sentenced to death. So I had to conduct the whole evening, until 12, more or less by myself and was then thoroughly tired. All the same I woke at my usual time, dressed, and started to read. When Steltzer, who was to have breakfast with me between 8 and 8.30, had not yet come at 8.45, I went to his room and found him sleeping sweetly, telling me that it was only 7.45, because it was now winter time. But then he was ready in a quarter of an hour.

My discussions with the military started at 9—on the 4th. The quality of these men is middling, so that talking to them isn't exactly enjoyable. There was only one likable person, a younger man, Herr von Löbbecke, but he is so egocentric, and has so little interest in general questions as such, that he isn't quite my type either. The nicest younger man, Hammersen, is on leave in Berlin just now, and looked me up there. Still, practical questions went smoothly. I then ate with the top gentlemen, though without the Generaloberst, who was away. They know little about the general picture of the war and think about it even less. Goebbels's speech[3] had cheered them up, and they took the biggest transport disaster of our occupation of Norway, the loss of 30,000 tons of shipping in a British morning raid, quite calmly. They're simply land soldiers, and the occupation of the smallest, most insignificant island is of greater interest to them than a major sea and air operation. Funny people! They don't seem to see all the possibilities implicit in the fact that British aircraft, taking off from a carrier 150 km off the Norwegian coast, can clear out a harbour in 20 minutes, losing only 2 aircraft; that under such conditions at sea and in the air land operations will follow as thunder follows lightning, and that their issue cannot be in doubt either.

After lunch we, i.e., Steltzer and I, went to church, where one of Steltzer's colleagues, who is a pastor,[4] conducts a so-called Berneuchen Mass, i.e., a Communion service, for a very small military congregation, every

2 Cf. letter of 17 April 1942.
2. Henrik Sørensen.
3. Goebbels had made a speech on 3 October in the Berlin Sportpalast.
4. Friedrich Schauer.

Monday. There were only 6 members of the congregation, but the atmosphere was very beautiful and uplifting. I was therefore glad to have been there and to hear a Harvest Thanksgiving sermon at least in this way. We were back at 4.30, and at 5 I went to see the chief of the Abwehr branch. In the evening, when St. had an official dinner, I sat with Löbbecke.—So I've caught up with everything. It is past 8, and Steltzer must come any moment to fetch me. . . .

[continued] Oslo, 7 October 1943

There's been a hitch and I'm still here: my Swedish visa didn't come, and so I have to give up hope for a peaceful day in Stockholm. . . .

Yesterday—no, I still have to tell you about the day before yesterday. That morning I visited the various SD chiefs. It was thorough, a bit difficult at times, but on the whole useful. It was particularly useful that they practically told me they were expecting new severities against the Norwegians, less in response to any military or political needs than because they're considered necessary as a general policy. It was obvious that they themselves don't agree with this, because they regard the liability as greater than the gain. Quisling's position has changed completely in the last 6 months: the attempt to employ him as a politician is past. Instead he is now being transformed into the chief of a body of reliable, trained men to be used in the internal fighting in Norway—not after all to put Quisling in the saddle, but solely to promote German intentions.—So all that was very instructive and the result is that the internal situation in Norway, which 6 months ago seemed stable for the resistance movement, is decidedly shaky today, with a potential for a considerable weakening of the Norwegian resistance.

After lunch Steltzer and I went to tea with our friends, and it went on till 6.30. We had a tremendous amount to discuss. They were nice and open-minded and had good ideas. But they are obviously sick and tired of the war and can't wait for it to end. There was a marvellous tea with highly interesting biscuits; rather, the biscuits were uninteresting, but on them there was a very strong-tasting berry-jam, probably wild berries, in flavour somewhere between red currants and cranberries.

In the evening we were invited to the house of the local shipping magnate; but there wasn't anything of special interest. It was only nice to hear a little man speak continually of "my town house," "my country house," "my farm," "my wine cellar." I believe he acquired all this quite legally as a Hamburg shipowner, but it all sounded too nice.

Yesterday morning I talked with the head of the Abwehr office, who impressed me favourably. In any case, he is better than his predecessor.

I finished there about 11 and from 11 to 1 I went to see various officers involved with my work, the chief of staff, and the Generaloberst to say goodbye. I am really agreeably surprised by my talks with these men. I had expected that the things I wanted wouldn't interest them much. But that was far from being the case. They really showed some appreciation of these problems and on the whole took a much better and more correct line than I'd dared to hope. So yesterday would have been very satisfactory if I hadn't heard at lunchtime that the visa hadn't come. The attempt to get it through nevertheless cost me the greater part of the afternoon and still proved fruitless.—Steltzer wasn't there in the evening. I sat with the Generaloberst and the others until 10 and then went to our friends', where Steltzer picked me up at 12.

This is a heavenly autumn day. If I can't travel today, I'll go on an excursion.

[continued] Berlin, 9 October 1943

... So, my visa didn't come. But I decided to travel all the same and shift my free day to Copenhagen, where I wanted to get the latest information since the lifting of the state of emergency; I also wanted to see Merete again, having said something clumsy to her last week in answer to a question she'd put, something she was bound to misunderstand. In the morning St. drove me once again to a beautiful view over the autumnal Oslo Fjord, then there was lunch, and I left directly after, still in brilliant, colourful autumn weather. After 3 hours I changed into a sleeping car, which took me comfortably to Malmö. I arrived there at 6.45, had breakfast, and went to the airport at 7.45. From there I flew to Copenhagen, arrived at 8.30, and met Merete at 10.—The mood of the town has clearly sharpened. In no occupied country have I seen such looks of hatred directed at German uniforms. People are simply beside themselves. The removal of the Jews has made them all feel unsafe now, and their reaction is very sharp. The soldiers I talked to claimed that all was well. Those innocent angels! They don't know anybody and have no antennae. Towards evening I walked around the town for 2 hours. That was enough for me.—But Copenhagen is beautiful, too, especially in its enormous variety of very beautiful towers. ...

Berlin, 10 October 1943

... It was a blessing that I went to the Office today because I found a few cases which were already in a bad way, and which I tried to put right again by telephone and teleprinter.

... It's a very good thing you aren't here, for after the first meeting there was a second one, then there were a number of telephone calls, and I've only just finished dictating a memorandum for my Führer, and it is now 4.30. The car will be here in 10 minutes to drive me out. So there wouldn't have been a single minute's peace; lunch simply had to be dropped. There is no rest at all today. Preposterous things have been happening again. If only all this didn't always cost more human lives and human happiness. . . .

Berlin, 18 October 1943

How beautiful it was with you, my love. Where am I at home if not with you and your sons. Today, my jubilee Pim, it makes 12 years and 38 & 62.[1] Only we are left. . . .

Last night at 7 I was at Peter's with Neumann,[2] Friedrich, Husen, & Eugen, the last unfortunately rather miserable and exhausted. What ails him isn't quite clear. It wasn't a really productive evening. They were already on the wrong track and couldn't get off it. Since there was the interruption of an air-raid warning, with many fighters in the air and some shooting in the distance, it lasted till 11. I was properly tired, although there was no reason for it, since I'd travelled comfortably.

This morning I saw the army doctor and will probably at last be classified as fit for active service. I assume so in any case, because the man was so terribly gruff and unfriendly. What an odious spirit of mistrust and desire to put people down rules there! It's disgusting!—The day since has been very unpleasant, simply because too much work has landed on my desk, and with all possible haste I can't finish things properly.—In addition an ugly denunciation has come in against Wengler,[3] who is still in Istanbul; it is evidently part of the fight for the director's post at the Institute: they shoot at Wengler in order to disqualify me from having a voice in the appointment. There can't be a word of truth in the story. But it comes in all seriousness from the SD and I can't afford to dismiss it. That cost me the first part of the morning, moving my luggage cost the second. It came punctually and is now in place.

Peter came alone to lunch. We talked about the general situation, and I hope it was useful. I think it was. Husen, Eddy, & Stauffenberg[4] and

1. Twelve years since his and Freya's wedding, thirty-eight and sixty-two since those of his parents and grandparents.
2. Leber, who, like Mierendorff ("Friedrich"), was under police surveillance, hence the pseudonym.
3. Cf. letter of 20 October.
4. Berthold Stauffenberg.

Frl. Breslauer came in the afternoon. Now it is 7.30, and I must begin to think of going home, for yesterday the airmen came at 8.30. . . .

Berlin, 19 October 1943

Only a line, which in any case will not go off until tomorrow morning. The day was filled to the brim and included a very awkward matter: a really disgusting denunciation has been lodged against Wengler, who is still in Istanbul, and though it is utterly idiotic it can't be passed over in silence. It threatens my leave, for if Bürkner, because he's scared, should put Wengler on leave until the matter is cleared up, I can't get away. The affair cost me 3 hours today. I am furious with Wengler, who was to have returned on Sunday, for his enemies are blowing up the whole thing in his absence. . . .

Berlin, 20 October 1943

Today will be stormy, and that's why I'd rather write now, in the morning, before it starts.—So yesterday started with the trouble about Wengler's affair. I had to talk to Stauffenberg about it, to people from the Institute, and above all to the chief culprit, who turned the whole thing on. There are masses of work besides; it just keeps flowing in. Heaven only knows why this should suddenly be so. Yesterday Oxé was rung up by the generals in Belgrade and Agram, who asked that I should come there some time. That's just what I needed! There is nothing useful I can do there any more.

Adam came to lunch, and then there was a man from Munich, which seems to look pretty bad. Delp's house has lost its roof, and the church has been damaged too; the other Bogenhausen church was burnt out. The rest of his report was unpleasant on the whole, and some people down there seem to have turned simply childish.

In the afternoon I went to see Conrad and had a strenuous but on the whole fruitful conversation with him, which lasted 2½ hours. He really is an exceptionally wise man with a sharp mind. At any rate, I liked him very much again, even if his scepticism seems somewhat lowering in a prince of the church. However, it was a good afternoon. At 8 I was at Hortensienstrasse again, where I found C.D. & Einsiedel. A number of things had to be discussed. They have developed quite nicely, and so the evening passed quickly and it was 11.30 when they left.

Today I won't spend much time at the Office. In the morning I have a meeting at the Institute, which will take a few hours, and in the afternoon

I'm going to another long meeting at the SD. There is nothing on in the evening, I think. . . .

Berlin, 21 October 1943

Only a short line, for I must go to a meeting at the AA with Adam and his Unterstaatssekretär, Keppler. I shall appear as leader of the military negotiating team: one lieutenant colonel, one major, and one second lieutenant. I wonder if A. and I will keep a straight face. . . .

Berlin, 22 October 1943

. . . Tomorrow morning at 7 I trek out to Zeppelin[1] to have the whole mess signed by Bürkner, and if I get back at lunchtime I can devote myself to my own office with a good conscience; it needs that badly, too. I want to start the week Monday with a clean desk, and, if things go well, I can then leave on Wednesday.

Christiansen came to lunch today. It always strikes me what a nice and first-rate man he is. He had been in Hamburg and on his farm in Schleswig-Holstein for a week. He related rather unpleasant things about both.

Today was somewhat impaired by my having to depart at 12.30 to bury one of my most intimate enemies from the OKW, Geheimrat Wagner,[2] with Oxé. He was over 70 when he died—I can only say 3 years too late. Much could have been prevented if that tough, stubborn old man had not been there. We always called him the poison dwarf. He was an outstanding criminal lawyer and saw everything solely from the point of view of domestic policy. Well, now he is dead, and his successor[3] is a man with whom in any case I can work much more easily.

Reichwein was in very good form last night. He wants to go to Lake Constance on Saturday. He seems better already since his family has found a home.[4] If he gets two weeks' leave now, he'll probably be quite fit again. I was very glad to get his quite fresh impressions of you and of the move. . . .

---

1. "Zeppelin" was the code name of the new headquarters of the Abwehr near Zossen.
2. Dr. Maximilian Wagner of the Legal Division of the Wehrmacht (Wehrmacht-Rechtsabteilung).
3. Alfons Waltzog.
4. His wife and children had moved to Kreisau.

Berlin, 24 October 1943

... Saturday morning Oxé and I went to Zeppelin to see Bürkner. We arrived at 8.30 on a beautiful, warm autumn day and immediately went to see Bürkner, and when we left him 2 hours later we were fully satisfied. Everything went smoothly. We came back at once and went from the station to Ministerialdirektor Sack,[1] the chief of the Army Legal Department, where my Kriegsgerichtsrat Kanter from Copenhagen was waiting for me. With him and Sack we discussed Danish affairs, which are becoming more acute all the time. We even agreed on a programme, which can be developed further. That took until 2 o'clock, and then I met Peter and Christiansen again for lunch. Chr. had had a talk with Neumann and Husen in the afternoon and was rather satisfied with it. Peter and Chr. left at 5.15.

I was so exhausted by the madly demanding week that I decided to retire to bed. ... When I woke up it was 9, and I dressed to go to the office.

After I'd read what was in the in-tray, Oxé came to tell me that contrary to our agreement Saturday morning Bürkner had suspended Wengler from duty. I lost my temper and told Oxé I wouldn't stay unless this order was rescinded, since (a) I couldn't be expected to work when deprived of my assistants at a critical moment and (b), which was much more serious, I wasn't prepared to have my assistants simply discarded like trash the moment a denunciation, however idiotic, was lodged against them. We then discussed the whole matter until 12.30, partly *à deux*, partly with Stauffenberg. Then I had to attend to some things at my office, ate at home, and it is now after 4 and I must hurry to Hortensienstrasse, where Friedrich is expected at 5.

The Wengler thing is a very dirty business. Apart from that, it comes at the most awkward possible moment for me, for I simply can't leave if there is nobody here who knows something about our affairs. I told Oxé I'd travel anyway if he didn't get the Wengler thing straightened out, that was his affair, he and Bürkner could deal with the mess on their own for two weeks. But in fact I can't very well go. Still, I was so angry that Oxé will finally do everything to get things sorted out again.

Berlin, 26 October 1943

Again only a line. Yesterday Friedrich, Husen, and König came for a very fruitful discussion, which took off especially well between Husen

1. See n. 2 to letter of 20 June, and n. 3 (p. 351) to letter of 5 October.

and Friedrich. F. was in great form. It was 2 when I got to bed, and I had to get up punctually at 6, because Wengler was coming to see me at 8. We then worked on his case till 10; it's getting worse and worse. The whole thing is mean.

At 11 I had a meeting on the Kempinski case, which was very disagreeable and lasted till 1.30; then I was at the Office and now, at 4.30, a man from the AA, who deals with Denmark, has just left me; I must hurry to Conrad's, and Adam comes at 7.30.—Prospects for leave very bad. In no case before Thursday. I'm really very cross about it.

Berlin, 27 October 1943

. . . About me there is really nothing to report but work, work, and more work. And each job more full of responsibility and difficulties than the last.—Luckily the Wengler affair is now getting on the right track: he'll report the charge against himself and we'll try to expedite the proceedings. This, I hope, will prove the groundlessness of the denunciation in a few weeks. Quite a passable man has been appointed to replace him[1] in the meantime, and while I'm away Wengler will sit around the Office on the pretext of finishing reports on his trip. It will probably work out somehow.

Yesterday afternoon and evening we discussed a few things at the Institute. I hope to have got at least 2 important matters well enough founded that I can sleep over it. That long session is strenuous for me, because it's my responsibility to see that something useful emerges; after a long day, I have to tackle 4 different problems in theoretical terms, opposite a different man for every problem, who may have devoted whole days to it. It is a little like playing chess with 4 opponents. In any case my production of paper in the last few weeks, since my return from Norway, has been gigantic. I wonder how it will all read in 10 years' time. Will I still like it?

So, now, my love, I return to work, hoping this night will give me as reward my departure tomorrow.

Berlin, 6 November 1943

. . . My love, it was so beautiful with you, as it always is with you. You know where my only home is. How the 7 days shine from the past. Whether they also promise a future we don't know, but we must be grateful for the past. Look after yourself, my love, yourself and your sons.

1. Probably Dr. Friede of the Kaiser Wilhelm Institute.

It is a consolation that my return was absolutely necessary from every point of view. Oxé has messed up something in the Wengler affair, which I'll only just be able to put right again; altogether there's a lot to be straightened out at the Office.—Furthermore Adam has returned with information he wants to discuss with me, and the immense activity of Neumann and associates has got a bit out of touch with us. Friedrich is coming to lunch today. . . .

Berlin, 7 November 1943

. . . Yesterday Friedrich came to lunch. It turned out that my leave was already inopportune, for they'd forged ahead a bit too impetuously and had lost touch somewhat. I must try to bring my contingent into line with them. It will mean considerable pains will have to be taken to overcome the difficulties.—But *au fond* I am glad that there is suddenly so much impetus.—Adam came in the afternoon. He had spent very interesting days in Stockholm and accomplished a few things too. There he met Steltzer, who intends to come here at the end of the month. . . .

There is a great deal of work here, and I'll certainly only nibble at the edge of it this morning, for there's lunch at Peter's at 1, and the fête will continue until about 6. But then I want to return and put in a night shift.—Oxé is away until Thursday, and so I am quite alone. I want to have meetings tomorrow, dictate on Tuesday, and go out to Bürkner on Wednesday.

They want to train me as a soldier now. 8 weeks basic training. As far as I'm concerned, there's absolutely nothing to be said against it, but all my work will meanwhile go to pieces. I must first see what comes of it. It won't happen so quickly anyway.

Berlin, 9 November 1943

I don't know if you can imagine how it feels to have more and more paper pouring in on you by the hour when you can't cope with the stuff. Here I sit at my desk buried in paper; on all the tables, shelves, and other flat surfaces lie files to be dealt with, and because of these paper mountains I use a large part of my time deciding their relative urgency. Meanwhile telephone calls from all the capitals of our occupied territories and from all departments here are incessant. I'll get on top of it eventually, but it's ghastly.

Add to this the fact that my private preoccupations call for much more attention. Haubach came for lunch yesterday and stayed till 3.30, Friedrich came from 6.30 till 9 o'clock, then Peter and Adam. We are passing through a critical phase on fundamentals; some hope to make the boat more seaworthy by throwing principles overboard and forget that makes the boat impossible to steer.—The matter I indicated to you a few days ago has been born; the child will probably reach you with this letter and a request to include it with your other children[1] immediately. Even Uncle was involved in the birth.

After I'd written the last sentence Eddy & Haubach announced themselves for this afternoon; I have a meeting at 4 which will last till 5.30, and I must dictate, and Wend wants to have some time, too. How can one fit the work into 24 hours?

As you see, there is really nothing to report from here but work, every hour and every minute, yet I am actually quite well.—Incidentally, Weichold was here yesterday, with greetings for you, too, from his wife. He'll eat with us on Thursday. He is obviously depressed.—The Wengler affair is giving trouble and is not making progress. . . .

Berlin, 11 November 1943

In the basement of the OKW, I have an unexpected opportunity to write you. I didn't write yesterday because it was simply impossible. I spent the entire morning yesterday clearing up and preparing myself for the presentation at a meeting with Bürkner in the afternoon. A number of different things affecting Norwegian, Danish, Dutch, French, Italian, Balkan, Polish, Russian, Turkish, Swedish, and Spanish questions. As you see, a tour round the whole of Europe. By the time I'd put this variety in the order in which I wanted to present it, it was, with the inevitable interruptions, 12 o'clock, and I had to go to lunch because my bus to Zeppelin left at 1.30.

I then went out and began my presentation to Bürkner at 2.45; after an hour we went to Canaris, returned after another hour, and then I had an hour and a half with Bürkner only. It was incredibly strenuous, but very fruitful, because both Bürkner and Canaris had enough time, and we made real progress. In itself it was a really good work day. It was 8.30 before I got to Peter's. Steltzer, whom we'd expected, hadn't come; it seems his plane didn't get through.

On matters of substance we're threatened by considerable dangers. Friedrich and Neumann are going astray in ways not unlike Uncle's. It will take great efforts to bring them back to the old line. The efforts will be made, but this is another one of those periodic fits. I hope it passes. . . .

1. No such document is to be found among the Kreisau papers, but see "Observations on the peace programme of the American churches" of November 1943 in van Roon, *Resistance to Hitler,* pp. 367–72.

Berlin, 13 November 1943

. . . I think I'll just have finished everything before I go to Kreisau. But I told Bürkner that I couldn't possibly carry the present workload for a longer period, and that above all I want Wengler back. This has led to firm action at last and the local military court has agreed to investigate. I hope there will be progress now.

Yesterday officials from the SD came again to ask me about the international law on certain questions. This new and intimate relationship strikes me as terribly funny, and sometimes it makes me very suspicious. But these people continue to impress me favourably, and the practical results are very satisfactory. Naturally my whole outfit laughs about it, and Canaris beams. I hope it continues. . . .

Berlin, 14 November 1943

. . . Gerstenmaier had lunch with me. We did a kind of general survey, which was by no means enjoyable, but because of the atmosphere of trust, I, at least, recall the 2 hours with very pleasant feelings. Steltzer, too, was back again, and will probably come again towards evening. Husen comes at 5, Friedrich at 6, and that opens the Big Battle.

I'm afraid I won't be able to bring Friedrich back into line. He has committed himself too deeply. I regret it, for his sake and also as a practical matter.[1] That this aberration was possible shows the lack of maturity, and that is sad and full of potential pain and grief. But facts are facts, even when they are disagreeable.

My love, the day started splendidly with your letters, which came together and gave me great pleasure. I took them directly to the Office and devoured them there.—The news there unfortunately matched my expectations. If one thinks of this mountain of suffering one can despair. And will mankind learn anything from it? If not, then woe betide us!

I'm returning Frau Wilbrandt's[2] nice letter to you. Please write to her at once by air mail and tell her something about us. I'll get her address for you if you no longer have the envelope with it. Please give her my best regards and tell her I am hoping to get away from here during the first or second week of December and would probably have to come to Istanbul then. I'd write also that I have been constantly on the move of late. That all this travelling was, of course, strenuous, but I didn't have so much to do then as usual, therefore had peaceful evenings and could even, sometimes, engage in such activities as Bridge, for which I had no opportunity

1. Cf. letter of 11 November.
2. See n. 1 (p. 317) to letter of 6 July.

at home. Say that Kaspar[1] has become a charming child and I'd very
much like to see him.[2] That that was a decided attraction for me.—Books
at the fireside were, unfortunately, not possible at the moment. All this
you can scatter[3] through the letter. . . .

Berlin, 15 November 1943

. . . Friedrich informed me that he intends to enter the married estate
shortly. It is hard to believe. He is obviously fed up with bachelor life.—
Otherwise the evening with him yesterday was very strenuous. We made
progress enough so that in the foreseeable future the little extra excur-
sions will flow again into the general course.[4] But it wasn't easy, nor is it
finished, because F. was in very high gear and rolled along like an express
train.

Eugen came to lunch; ah yes, I told you.—This morning I dictated
some of the report on the cultivation plan and budget. Always in between
telephone calls and discussions and other dictation. It will reflect those
conditions. But Fräulein Breslauer has to write the draft first, then I can
correct it. There were a few other things to dictate too.—Pape and Peter
came for lunch. Pape's father has died. I think he has really nobody else
in his family. I am very sorry for him. His reports resembled everything
else one hears: excellent morale at the front, especially during withdrawals, because they reach the food depots, and therefore there is more to
eat.—Jowo called up again today, but unfortunately I wasn't in the room.
I don't like these calls at all, but I don't think they are due to personal
worry. Busch[5] has become successor to Kluge,[6] who had to go because of
a car accident.

Steltzer came after lunch today. He is always so beautifully strict and
Protestant. I think with him everything was cleared up too. He and Husen
got on very well together. So it was 4.30 before I got to the Office, ruled
a little there, and am now leaving, at 5.15, because two Viennese friends
are coming at 6. That will fill the evening. . . .

1. The "K" is underlined.
2. A word after this, which could mean "often," has been crossed out and made illegible.
3. This letter was clearly intended to be full of well-distributed and encoded messages. The
underlined "K" could stand for "Kirk," and the journeys and games of Bridge could be
allusions to trips and contacts abroad.
4. Cf. letter of 11 November.
5. Field Marshal Ernst Busch was commander-in-chief of Army Group Centre in the East.
6. Field Marshal Günther von Kluge (1882–1944) became C.-in-C. West in July 1944. The
conspirators had worked on him for a long time, but he could never make up his mind to
take part in the conspiracy. Suicide 19 August 1944.

Berlin, 17 November 1943

Too bad, there can be no getting away tomorrow. I can't leave until Friday[1] at the earliest, for Canaris wants a meeting Friday with Steengracht and Papen,[2] which I am to attend. And that was unavoidable, so to speak, because I am probably the only one who knows exactly what's up.[3] The trip to Istanbul has been fixed provisionally for the 2nd of December.

Yesterday's lunch with C.D. & Einsiedel was very nice. They were both in good shape and surprisingly little affected by recent events. Many people are now grey and listless, but these two not at all. And they also had a few things to say on the subject in hand. So it was satisfactory in every respect. Our evening was also very nice. Haubach came by himself and showed his best side. Remarkable how this man has grown of late. I hope it continues. The objective results weren't bad, and he had quite a few ideas.

This morning I went straight to the Institute and we discussed an opinion on Danish affairs for 3 hours. It was nice and interesting. I think it will be good on the whole. Then I was with Steengracht to talk about Turkish matters. That went well, too, and at the end he invited me to a dinner party tonight. I wonder very much what that will be like. Nothing but clods, a whole collection of them. . . .

Berlin, 24 November 1943

Here I sit in the Office bunker.—Since that first sentence several hours have passed now. I have meanwhile visited Hans Carl's house, which is completely destroyed. A plane crashed on the house with a full load of bombs. It is a heap of rubble and furthermore burnt out. That anyone could still be alive beneath it is therefore out of the question. I went into everything in a talk there with Leoni,[4] and she'll tell you about it today. But meanwhile she's been with little Editha,[5] who was certainly not critically injured and probably not even severely.

1. The 19th. There is no letter between those of the 17th and the 24th. Perhaps he managed to go to Kreisau. In any case he was not at Derfflingerstrasse when it burnt down in the big air raids on Berlin—see n. 3 (p. 366) to letter of 24 November. Marion Yorck reports that he had been living at Hortensienstrasse since March 1943. But M. had used the flat at Derfflingerstrasse during the day.
2. Franz von Papen (1879–1969), German Ambassador in Ankara—cf. n. 1 (p. 317) to letter of 6 July. Reich Chancellor 1932; Vice Chancellor 1933–34; Minister, then Ambassador in Vienna 1934–38, in Turkey 1939–44. Acquitted at Nuremberg.
3. It was again the matter of the Danube ships.
4. Sister of Editha von Hülsen, *Diakonisse*—i.e., Protestant nursing sister—who became the guardian of the orphaned Hülsen children.
5. Daughter of Hans Carl and Editha von Hülsen.

The inner city is a rubble field. There is not a single building standing on Tirpitzufer or in Bendlerstrasse. Tiergartenstrasse, too, is entirely gutted. As far as I can see, there are only 2 houses standing in the so-called Tiergarten quarter, the big House of Tourism and my office in Viktoriastrasse. The Hotel Eden, the whole of Tauentzienstrasse, Budapesterstrasse, Kleistsstrasse, but also Behrenstrasse, Friedrichstrasse, Unter den Linden, Pariser Platz, etc., all that is no more, except for single houses. Thus part of the AA survives, where, incidentally, I met Steengracht. Moabit has been hit very badly. I wonder if Edith[1] is still there. Erika[2] is missing; her house completely gutted, but not collapsed, so that she really should have been able to get out. But she hasn't got in touch yet. Aunt Leno's house is roofless. It has only 2 rooms left. Everything else under water. People seem to have made touching efforts to save things; at any rate there is a lot of furniture, waiting for the next air raid.[3]

What the Office will do with us I don't yet know. I'll try to stay here, but we would have to get new telephone lines. We have one room in the House of Tourism. I won't see Oxé until tomorrow morning, out at Zeppelin, where I'll talk to Bürkner and Canaris. I hope it works out that way.

Your husband is well. A few things have been rescued from Derfflingerstrasse: 2 arm chairs, the little chest with the top, my wardrobe, Carl's chest of drawers in the hall, the refrigerator, and a lot of little things. What's to be done with all this stuff now I don't know, for it can't be moved. Tomorrow I must try to get a total damage certificate in order to hunt up a new apartment.[4]

Berlin, 26 November 1943

Unfortunately my Office section is not yet functional again, because our administrative officer, our chief, etc., are all falling down on the job. Instead of coming now to see that we get new office space, new telephones, new typewriters, cupboards, paper, etc., they all stay blissfully away, and, if and when they come into town, it is only to tell us to do what we think right; and that things here are too dreadful and they're leaving town again. There are no cars for our official use, but even I get a car for private purposes. The whole thing is a scandal and simply shows that we[5]

1. Edith Henssel.
2. Erika von Moltke, a more distant relative.
3. The raids of the nights of 22–23 and 23–24 November were two of five air raids on Berlin that came in quick succession.
4. He now lived at the Yorcks' at Hortensienstrasse 50—and when he was arrested less than two months later that was stated to be his address.
5. Some words that followed, starting with "are ripe for," made illegible.

don't deserve any better.—Since yesterday I've taken matters in hand for myself and shall at last have a desk and a telephone of my own again in the foreseeable future.

Yesterday I went out to see Bürkner and Canaris. The trip to Istanbul is to proceed if burnt passports can be replaced in time and the necessary visas are received. Presumably they'll put steam behind it today.—The excursion cost me almost the entire day. We didn't get back to town until after 4, for it is a mad trip with constant changes; between 2 stations the right track is usable, between the next 2 only the left. But it works, and in the end we even reached Potsdamer Platz, whereas yesterday one couldn't come closer than Schöneberg.

In the city there is no water, light, or gas so far; here outside, only gas is lacking. There is no bread in town either and hardly any food at all. Soup-kitchen food is said to be atrocious: cabbage and water without potatoes. I hope that too will improve with the gradual improvement of traffic and transport. Altogether I expect quite passable conditions in the inner city if we have 2 or 3 days' time.

Editha was found yesterday. Hans Carl will probably be recovered today. I'm going there at 10 o'clock, Leoni comes at 10.30, and we shall then decide everything for the funeral.—Meanwhile I have news of C.D., Einsiedel, Reichwein.

Berlin, 27 November 1943

We have just talked on the phone, but I want to write you a quick line too. I went to Hans Carl and Editha's yesterday morning. To look at Editha's body took all my nervous strength. You could probably have stood it much better than I. She had her fur jacket on, and the shape of her head, her hair and teeth were clearly recognizable. The shelter in which she was buried was a gigantic steel bunker that was squashed. And now massive blocks must be blown out before it is possible even to get in. So it may be days before Hans Carl is dug out. What Leoni and I agreed I told you on the phone.

When I got back at lunchtime the admirable Oxé had already got us 2 rooms with telephone in the House of Tourism. Today we still have to look out for the furnishings—i.e., paper, various cabinets, and so on—and from Monday on work will be more or less possible again. We'll then try first to reconstruct our files. Then we'll send one man to Führer Headquarters and one to the AA. In 2 weeks we should have recovered the main contents of our files again.

The highest civil authorities of the Reich will stay in Berlin. Naturally I am glad of that. All military offices are moving out. The total failure of the military, the inability to improvise, the indifference of the chiefs outside the city to the conditions but also the ability to work of their staffs in town is quite incredible and exceeds all expectations: apart from my Oxé there isn't a single regular officer left in Berlin. We are a reserve officers' club: a director of the Deutsche Bank, and director of the Colonia, a pressman, and I, who keep the show going with girls and orderlies. Nobody out there looks in, nobody bothers about us, they only give us errands to do, which we in turn firmly decline. We have now made ourselves independent, procure our own office supplies, have secured petrol, and rule here as though nobody outside existed. All the military offices are alike: they think of making their lives more comfortable, and are indifferent to everything else.—On the other hand, Ribbentrop and Goebbels, for whom I certainly have no love, concern themselves with everything: they visit their wounded and bombed-out, inspect the damaged sections of their offices, see to it that the office functions again, and Ribbi in particular refuses to return to East Prussia and remains firmly in Berlin.

Whether my trip to Istanbul will come off is doubtful, for the embassies have been bombed out and are not yet working again. I therefore don't know whether we'll get the visas.

[P.S.] My love, stay where you are and don't budge, even if you hear nothing from your husband. Every evening, when the air raids start and we have settled into the cellar, I think, full of tenderness, that your sons are now sleeping sweetly and you are probably seated peacefully at your desk. And that is enormously comforting.

Berlin, 28 November 1943

Frau Pick didn't come yesterday. I don't know what that means. Perhaps she was too much frightened by the very heavy air raid the previous night. I have therefore been unable so far to do anything about the things that are salvaged. I must say it's all the same to me. In any case, I can't get excited about the fact that the refrigerator is still lying outside. I must above all keep my outfit at the Office shipshape, or, rather, get it shipshape, and that is now proceeding nicely. We have now secured enough orderlies and petrol, and so we are slowly beginning to work in an orderly fashion. It if weren't for the evacuees and the sniping everything would soon be in good order. The illustrations of this inadequacy of regular officers confronted with an unforeseen situation is frightening. This way of handling things must end in chaos.

Yesterday Carlo[1] and Julius[2] came at lunchtime. C. left before we'd

1. Mierendorff.
2. Leber.

really got going, and the outcome of the ensuing conversation was singularly deplorable. It marks the end of a hope and gives the Derfflinger-strasse fire a symbolic significance for me. Carlo and Theo[1] are coming again today. If only the whole recipe[2] Julius had let himself be committed to were not so completely idiotic, it wouldn't matter. But it is that.

Hans Carl wasn't dug out yesterday either. I must go there again today. What an awful lot of time all these trips take now; today I haven't a car, and on my bike it takes at least 1 hour there and back. One has to avoid craters, push the bike through heaps of rubble that have fallen across the street, and occasionally get off where the splinters are too bad. It all takes time, and the day is so short. When I come in at 8.30 I have to go first to the bunker, because that is where all the files are kept; then I go to the House of Tourism, which isn't heated and where in any case one can only work till about 3 because there is no light. In between I return to the bunker to eat at 12. At 5 I ride home, where we eat at 6 so that the dishes are done by the time the warning comes at 7.30. Here,[3] too, we have still no gas; in town there is no water either and no light; but above all there is nothing to eat in town, neither in restaurants nor in shops.

This is the beginning of a fine early-winter day. I want to start in a minute, first to the bunker, then to church, then to Hans Carl's and to Goerschen, who is coming here for the day; and I'm expected back for lunch at 1.—I am glad to hear the planting has made such progress. . . .

Berlin, 29 November 1943

. . . You ask how one can stand it all. That isn't so hard. To avoid getting callous is much harder. I am always catching myself at it. That was most noticeable when I saw the remains of Editha and Hans Carl. I overcame my emotion and horror, and then it was quite easy. But that is a false reaction. One should overcome this defensive indifference, one should not put on armour, one must bear it. In order to endure death and horror one tends to kill one's own humanity, which is a much greater danger than not being able to bear it.

Yesterday I saw an impressive sight: In one of the rubble heaps I passed there must have been a carnival shop. Children from 4 to 14 had taken possession; they had put on coloured caps, held little flags and lanterns, threw confetti, and pulled long paper streamers behind them, and in this get-up they marched through the ruins. An uncanny sight to see, an apocalyptic sight.—It was also awful to see people at the gym in Derfflinger-

1. Haubach.
2. German *Rezept*; probably cooperation with the Goerdeler group.
3. At Hortensienstrasse.

strasse being forcibly loaded into buses amid protest and screaming, without being allowed to know their destination. What human degradation.

Friedrich, Adam, and Theo came last night and we had a good discussion, which may have straightened out much that had been distorted the day before. It went well and smoothly, and I think on the whole I carried my points. Well, we shall see.—This afternoon I go to Conrad's, and I'm very curious to see how I'll find him.

My trip will probably remain doubtful until the last moment, because only then will we be sure of having visas. But if we don't go, I hope to come home for a day or two, to get some things.

Farewell, my love. How nice that you celebrated a festive Advent. What a Christmas it will be! I wonder if by then we'll know without any doubt that only there can we hope for help and permanence?

Berlin, 30 November 1943

. . . Yesterday I went out[1] to see Conrad. Unfortunately he was rather affected by events and simply tended to write off Berlin. In fact he had already written it off. That disappointed me a little. His flock seem to be somewhat scattered, and he doesn't seem to know just how he can gather them again. He's too far away from the firing line, for it takes an hour to get there by train. So all that isn't very nice. But I think it has largely physical causes, since he does have a heart condition, and that's hardly what's needed now.

Friedrich came in the evening. At last my weeks of attacking his course have borne fruit, and he has grasped the seriousness[2] of the situation. Yesterday he was quite despondent as a result, and I was correspondingly cheered. In any case I have at last the impression that I can again—or still—achieve something, and thus I am once more full of hope in that respect.

So, now I must go once more to Hans Carl's. There, too, new difficulties have arisen. I may be able to get the Charlottenburg Municipal Court to agree to an executorship.

1. After the destruction of Behrenstrasse, Bishop Preysing had moved to the Dominikus Convent in Hermsdorf, near Berlin.
2. Cf. letters of 11 November and 28 November. A few days later Mierendorff died in an air raid on Leipzig.

Berlin, 5 December 1943

. . . Then Peter, Marion, Fritzi, and I went to church and heard a sermon by Lilje.[1] The sermon was very good on the horror of history, and the gravity of history. A great Advent sermon, which dealt with the Lord's coming at the end of history. Although the sermon was intellectually engaging and stimulating, I must say that I get more satisfaction from going to church at Gräditz, where the feeling of community is much warmer. It convinced me again that, however beautiful a sermon may be, it's the congregation's sense of belonging together that's decisive. I miss it in a big-city congregation.

Fritzi came to lunch and we had your chickens, which were delicious. Fritzi was nice and seems to be on his way back to us again. He is still here now, at 7 in the evening, and he and Reichwein, who has joined us, are discussing elementary schools, while I sit at the desk interjecting a remark every now and then. They've just got to Pestalozzi. I wonder how the day will continue and whether we'll tie Fritzi more closely to ourselves again.

2 hours later: Eugen and Brigitte[2] have come back. The evening seems to be developing nicely. Fritzi is quite relaxed and not mistrustful and probably less jealous, too. I hope it lasts a while now.—In a moment we shall put out the light and light the Advent candles.

Berlin, 6 December 1943

What a pity that I'd already left when your telephone call came today. But you heard that I am well, and I imagine that was what mattered most to you. Everything is still in great disorder here; things are in fantastic confusion, and for the time being we're not getting what we need. That is a great pity. If I go to Turkey now, nothing serious will be done before the end of the year. I don't much like that; but my only choice is between accepting that and not going to Istanbul; and since I must go to Istanbul if it is physically possible, I have no real choice.

Oddly enough, I can't believe in this trip. I can't get rid of the feeling that something will still happen to prevent it. And yet I have my passport, the foreign currency is already in the bunker, and a seat on the plane seems to be assured.

1. Hanns Lilje (1899–1977), Secretary of the Lutheran Council, whom M. later met again in jail when both were prisoners; after the war Bishop of Hanover.
2. Having been bombed out, Gerstenmaier now lived with the Yorcks, too.

Vienna, 9 December 1943[1]

. . . To my eyes the city looked so unnaturally intact: no rubble heaps anywhere, no façades crashing. It took that to show me how accustomed I already was to the ruins. It was a grey day, and from the 5th floor of the Imperial the city looked mysteriously beautiful. . . .

Berlin, 29 December 1943

Our new offices are very pleasant, large, warm, and bright. They are classrooms in a modern school,[2] and I occupy a hall probably meant for 30 pupils. That is very agreeable, and if we keep this house we won't be badly off. In addition we have staff telephone equipment and a teleprinter to ourselves and are thus very well equipped with means of communication. . . .

Berlin, 31 December 1943

. . . I finished my Turkish report last night with proposals on how to proceed further. Today I got Bürkner's endorsement, and now the detailed work begins which is needed to make it all real and get it accepted by others.

Last night there was another matter of conscience, and I wasn't able to

1. No letter to Freya is extant from this trip to Turkey. As he had hoped, he was in Kreisau on the Sunday after the trip and spent Christmas there. Regarding the main purpose for the trip, a disappointment awaited him in Turkey. Alexander Kirk was not in Istanbul, nor could M. fly to Cairo. The American Ambassador in Turkey, who did not want to talk to him personally, only arranged a conversation with his military attaché in the office of the OSS. It was characterized by mutual distrust and M.'s refusal to give military information. A letter he wrote to Kirk, explaining the purpose, modalities, and possibilities of a later meeting, did not reach Kirk and would no longer have done any good. The text is nevertheless interesting and is doubtlessly authentic—see Balfour and Frisby, *Moltke*, pp. 271ff. The authorship of another document is more doubtful. It is a long Exposé on the readiness of a powerful German group to prepare and assist Allied military operations against Germany—see van Roon, *Resistance to Hitler*, pp. 372–75. The authors were almost certainly Rüstow and Wilbrandt (cf. n. 1 [p. 317] to letter of 6 July). An introductory note explains that the paper "defines the attitudes and plans of an extremely influential group of the German opposition inside Germany on the subject of hastening the victory of the Allies and the abolition of Nazism. It has been prepared on the basis of frequent and searching conversations and discussions with a leading representative of this group about the future of a free democratic Germany, cleansed radically of Nazism, and about the maximum contribution that can be made immediately by determined German patriots towards making this Germany a secure reality. . . ." It was clearly addressed to the *Western* Allies. See text and comment in Balfour and Frisby, *Moltke*, pp. 273–81. Cf. n. 2 to letter of 7 January 1944.
2. It was the Lausschule, Lausstrasse, Berlin-Dahlem.

work on it properly because it was already to be presented to Keitel today. I don't like that; once more 220 human lives were at stake.

The little Haeften,[1] the one who used to work with me, was completely bombed out in the last air raid: an explosive bomb tore his house to shreds, but nobody was there, and since it didn't burn, there's hope that a lot of stuff can be salvaged from the rubble.

Last night the elder Stauffenberg brother[2] came. A good man, better than my Stauffi,[3] more manly and with more character.—In the morning I left early to go to Zossen. But the trip took 3½ hours, and so I wasted almost the entire morning. We had to wait repeatedly at smashed-up stations. Luckily I had taken something to read, so it wasn't too bad.

. . . Poor Falkenhausen has some serious trouble. Princess Ruspoli has been arrested and his chief of staff, Harbou, has taken his own life. I am terribly sorry. I only hope that F. gets through the crisis, and on the whole it looks like that. But all the same it is a matter that is better not discussed, so that it isn't blown up by the rumour machine.

My love, I live on the days with you. I am, so to speak, well provided for, but hope that I can renew my sustenance sooner than I fear will be possible.

1. Lieutenant Werner von Haeften (1908–44), younger brother of Hans Bernd von Haeften. Jurist, now at his own request adjutant of Claus Stauffenberg, whom on 20 July 1944 he accompanied to Führer Headquarters in East Prussia and back to Berlin, and with whom he was shot the following night in the courtyard of the headquarters of the conspiracy in Bendlerstrasse.
2. Unquestionably Claus Graf Schenk von Stauffenberg (1907–44), the youngest of the three Stauffenberg brothers, who evidently seemed older than Berthold, the eldest. After recovering from his severe wounds (cf. n. 3 to letter of 19 July), Claus Stauffenberg had on 1 October 1943 become chief of staff for General Olbricht, the head of the Allgemeines Heeresamt (AHA), the General Army Office, dealing with personnel, training, and equipment of the army. Olbricht was equally determined on a coup d'état. Stauffenberg now worked on this systematically, not only on the military preparations, but also in political discussions—e.g., with his kinsman Peter Yorck and with the socialist Julius Leber. On 1 July 1944, as colonel in the General Staff, he became chief of staff to Colonel-General Fromm, commander of the Replacement Army. This facilitated his access to Hitler. On 20 July 1944, during a briefing at Führer Headquarters in East Prussia, he set off a bomb, which, though it exploded quite close to Hitler, only wounded but did not kill him. The failure of the coup attempt and the revenge of the regime cost many lives, including M.'s.
3. Berthold Stauffenberg.

1944

. . . What a year lies before us. If we survive it, all other years will pale beside it. We went to church yesterday morning and opened the year with a mighty sermon by Lilje on Joel 2,21. I think it was the best sermon I ever heard; and it was fundamental for the year 1944. My love, we can only hope for strength to show ourselves worthy of the task this year sets us. And how can we, unless in the midst of all the evil we'll experience, all the suffering and pain we'll have to bear, we are conscious of being in God's hand. You must never forget that, my love.

The telephone brought one piece of joyful tidings: Casparchen's return. Good that he's back and that Konrad is well again too. I hope it stays like that, and I hope that you can celebrate a good Christmas with your sons now.—After the service I went to Franke's. . . .

From there I went to share the goose at Herr Haus's.[2] Your goose was delicious and was polished off joyfully by Haus and his wife, Frau Wolff[3] & husband, Frl. Thiel,[4] Frau Tharandt,[5] Colonel Oxé, and myself. That,

1. Erroneously dated 1943.
2. Captain Haus of the Abwehr Office.
3. Obviously someone from the Office.
4. Anna Thiel, his secretary at the Abwehr.
5. From the Office.

in essence, is the club of those left behind. The party struck me as a success. I had to leave at 3.30, because Husen was waiting for me, and from him I went straight to Waetjen's at Babelsberg, where I arrived at 7.30 because faulty lines had cost me 45 minutes. It was as nice as always with Eddy; we understood each other very well, and I think that he has improved enormously in the last year. We sat together until 12, because I was sleeping there.

The British terrorists[1] woke us at 2.30, let loose a rather scattered attack on Nowawes and South Berlin, and placed 3 explosive bombs in a 150 m radius from the Sarres' house. The chief unpleasantness of this was that in the cellar with us were 3 small children and the immobile father Sarre and Fruli. But nothing much happened, except that window panes blew out all over the house. By the time we'd cleared it all up and were in bed it was 5.30, and although I slept until 8.30 I feel I haven't had enough sleep.—Adam was at Peter's at 12, and then came Julius, with whom we talked till now, 6.30. He is a convincingly good man; but now, with Carlo gone,[2] he is rather one-sidedly practical and sets much less store by forces of the spirit than I.

The week now beginning will bring a tremendous amount of work. Mountains of unread paper are piled up around me, and I still don't know quite how to master it. But I always have in the past; it will probably work out again. Oxé is touching, as always.

Now, incidentally, I'm going to Adam's for the evening and shall meet Einsiedel there. I didn't want to burden Peter & Marion with it. So it will probably be a late night.

Berlin, 4 January[3]

. . . So now I have 10 minutes. I wonder very much how long it will be possible to lead the relatively orderly life we're still leading. Hans was quite surprised at all that's still working and said it hasn't been so in Italy for a long time: there are simply no more trains running, and without a car one is immobile there; he also said that comparatively few telephones are still functioning. Milan, he says, is much more damaged than Berlin, for instance; thus, on the whole, disorganization is much greater. Well, it will all come. The certainty of that makes one thankful for what is still here—that I can sit here by myself in a heated room at a clean desk

1. In view of his detachment about the air raids—there is not a single condemnation of them in the letters—the German *Terrorbriten* is obviously an ironic quotation of official or semi-official terminology.

2. Mierendorff had been killed in an air raid on Leipzig on 4 December 1943.

3. Erroneously dated 1943. The letter is written on the back of a sketch map of half of Western Europe and North Africa.

writing to you, that the light comes through the window panes. I enjoyed this undisturbed night to the full. When I woke at 2 and waited for the siren, though I went back to sleep immediately and then woke again at 6, I was so grateful to have had enough sleep again for once. The day seems so much easier when one's had enough sleep.

Yesterday I had lunch with Kiep in his new apartment, not far from my new Office. It was nice and cosy. It is Kiep's 4th flat since the 22nd of November: 3 were destroyed over his head or at least made uninhabitable. That is really very unpleasant. But because his own house didn't burn but was only blown up inside by a high-explosive bomb, he was able to salvage almost everything, and thinks that, if he gets an emergency roof on the house, the greater part of the furniture will be safe too.—In addition he has difficulties at Wedder[stedt?], where his wife and children were evacuated, because the Gauleiter in Anhalt demands that the Harz region should be cleared of "strangers" and reserved for his dear Dessauers and Magdeburgers. Glorious things are still in store. In any case I see all the time that in Silesia we are better off than is usual elsewhere. . . .

Baruth, 6 January 1944

I've been here since yesterday evening and return to town tomorrow morning. By then I hope I'll have our files in order again and know what's here and what's missing. We did, unfortunately, lose invaluable and irreplaceable things in the fire, particularly my letters and memoranda for about a year, perhaps longer. I'm very glad to have duplicates[1] at Kreisau for the first years at least; that makes the gap less than it could have been.

Yesterday at least I finished reading all that's accumulated, and now I know what has to be done. There are essentially 4 big complexes: treatment of the partisans and Free Corps in the Balkans; Danish questions; Italian questions; and the Turkish affairs resulting from my trip to Istanbul. Afterwards there will be some matters involving the law on prisoners of war and internees. In the next two weeks it should be possible to move all these things a good deal further.

Present plans are for me to go to Breslau in the afternoon of the 21st of January, spend the night there, and attend the Court of Arbitration in the morning of the 22nd. Then I'd come home, at 3 if I'm lucky, but perhaps not before the evening. Oxé would then pick me up, and I'd go on to Vienna during the night from Monday to Tuesday, Tuesday to Wednesday Agram, Thursday to Friday Klagenfurt, Friday during the day to Munich, and in the night from Saturday to Sunday from Munich back

1. These duplicates, too, must be regarded as lost.

to Berlin. That would give me 2 or perhaps 2½ days for Kreisau. In February I'm planning a Western tour and in March a trip either to Sweden and Norway or Turkey. With these little diversions I hope to fight my way through the winter. Making such plans naturally feels funny when a few hours later one may not know where one can sleep, supposing one is still alive. . . .

At 5 I had to set off, packed my things at home, ate a little, and departed with Oxé at 5.25. Unfortunately we were delayed dreadfully, and instead of being organized and settled in at 8 or 8.30, it took until 10.30 and I was too tired to write then. This standing in more or less cold trains is ghastly.—I am staying with the postmaster and his wife, an elderly childless couple who are very friendly to me. In any case, I got a very nice breakfast and a good, clean place to sleep. That, after all, is the main thing. These unfortunates have had people billeted on them almost constantly since 4 years before the war. She said to me quite sadly: since they came here they'd never been alone.

The Solms estate[1] overshadows all else. The whole thing makes a terribly feudal impression, and the stories one hears aren't pleasant. But the officers relish them. The administration is in an enormous building which also houses, in various wings, the former pastor, the Prince's architect, and the accountants and other officials of the administration. Oxé is staying with the architect and is treated like a prince: the wife cooks, bakes, and fries for him the whole day.—The officers' mess is in the new castle, a handsome, two-storey building where one division of the Abwehr has its offices. The food is middling.

I saw only a little of the environs when I went for a short walk. . . .

Berlin, 7 January 1944

. . . All the world is buzzing with rumours of the coming invasion. I wonder whether it will really happen now. I still have a feeling that it will be a while yet. It is partly a question of nerves. Such operations make sense only when they are conducted with such overwhelming strength that their outcome is beyond doubt from the start.[2] As long as that isn't the case, they shouldn't be attempted. . . .

1. The property of Prince Friedrich zu Solms-Baruth.
2. Cf. the similar passage in the Exposé of December 1943 (see n. 1 to letter of 9 December 1943). What distinguishes that is that it came as part of an argument for German cooperation if the Western Allies made an all-out military effort "in such a manner as to make prompt and decisive success on a broad front a practical certainty. This victory over Hitler, followed by [Western] Allied occupation of Germany in the shortest possible time, would at one stroke so transform the political situation as to set free the real voice of Germany, which

Berlin, 9 January 1944

Your two letters of the 5th came today, but I didn't read them until 4.30 because I wasn't alone for a moment. Every day I rejoice in the fact that your two little sons are well again and that all three of you are at peace. If only this peace can be preserved . . .

This morning I first worked a little, then had breakfast with Eugen, went to see Julius on my bike at 10, and stayed with him till 1. It was a useful morning and on the whole satisfactory. But I must make fresh efforts to bring this man into line with us. He is much more like a peasant than Carlo and much less congenial to me. There will therefore be no such spontaneous alignment as gave us stability before. But all the same I am hopeful. Peter will just have to do more and must go there every week.

When I got back at 1.30 Theo was already here and the three of us had a peaceful meal together. We spoke much of Carlo's death. Theo had composed a very fine notice, which appeared in the D.A.Z.[1] on 24 December: It has pleased the Lord of life and death to call Dr. C[arlo] M[ierendorff] from this life. He was killed[2] in the air raid on Leipzig during the night of —————— to ——————. For his friends, T[heo] H[aubach].— The announcement had already caused astonishment, and the *Zürcher Zeitung* carried a long obituary.—Theo has recuperated well and is able again to devote himself to the future. My conversation with him and Eugen was productive and helpful; they have just left, and now I am alone at home and have an enormous amount of work in front of me, which I must get through at all costs. . . .

Berlin, 11 January 1944

There was no pause yesterday or today and so I haven't got round to writing until evening, but now I hope to have a quarter of an hour before

---

would acclaim the action of the group as a bold act of true patriotism, comparable to the Tauroggen Convention concluded by the Prussian General Yorck with the Russians in 1812." The Exposé then went on: "Should, however, the invasion of Western Europe be embarked on in the same style as the attack upon the Italian mainland, any assistance by the group would not only fail to settle the issue of the war, but would in addition help to create a new 'stab-in-the-back' legend. . . ." It is a turn of phrase like "the same style as the attack upon the Italian mainland" that points to an authorship other than M.'s. The comparable passage in this letter reads much more like agreement with the British disinclination to invade Western Europe prematurely, coupled, perhaps, with doubts about the attempt at tyrannicide and coup d'état that several of the Kreisau friends favoured. For the text of the Exposé see van Roon, *Resistance to Hitler*, pp. 372–75, especially p. 374.

1. *Deutsche Allgemeine Zeitung*—the least Nazified German newspaper after the suppression of the *Frankfurter Zeitung* in 1943.

2. The German word is *fiel*, literally "killed in action."

Karl-Ludwig[1] comes. The two days were so incessant because I was hardly ever, and never alone, at my desk. Monday morning I started by dictating the work I'd done on Sunday. Then it was 10, and a man came from the Legal Department of the Wehrmacht; I left when he did, met Frau Pick at 12, Hans at 12.30 and had lunch with him and Mangoldt, then went with Mangoldt to Kempinski's and from there to Hortensien-strasse to pack my things quickly and get to Potsdam, where I arrived at 7.30. We sat till 11.30; in the night there was a small air-raid warning, and in the morning I went straight to a meeting at an office evacuated to Potsdam; then, in a daytime warning with distant machine-gun fire and strips of vapour in the sky, by car with Vesper to Admiral Groos, who is stationed near Potsdam. From Groos, with whom I ate, I went to Husen, who is also somewhere out there, and from him was driven directly to a meeting of the AA, from which I've just returned.

Here I found your letters of the 7th and 8th, that's a one-day improve-ment in the time taken.—I must first say something about an earlier let-ter of yours, on the question of form. Form is absolutely essential and not incidental. To think that content alone matters is a German heresy. I don't want to disparage content. But without form, particularly dogma, there is no way of enquiring closely into content; it remains vague mysticism. Besides, form generally is a help in bridging periods empty of content. It cannot replace content, but it prevents an untimely admission of content-lessness.—Don't misunderstand me; I don't want to raise form to the sky, I only want to point out that it is by no means useless or superfluous; there is a serious and unwise lack of modesty in the opinion that one can dispense with generally valid forms and make one's own. . . .

The Mirbachs were actually well. They live as they have always lived, haven't packed anything, and are determined to live with their things as long as possible and to let everything go up in flames if they must. The atmosphere is as I've always known it, warm and cordial and a little mel-ancholy. Dieter[2] grumpy as always. There was a princely meal; they seem to get supplementary supplies from many sides, i.e., Wernersdorf, Bresa, Jella, and a brother of Max's in Holland. Uncle Max is 68 and surpris-ingly spry for that. It is 20 years now since I lived with them.

The meeting in Potsdam was in a Mendelssohn house, now requisi-tioned, in which I danced in days gone by, a fact I mentioned quite shamelessly. Fortunately nothing has happened to the owner;[3] he lives in the coachman's apartment. It is a splendid, low, long house with a view over the lake and a big park, and beautifully furnished. It is still beautiful,

1. Guttenberg.
2. Son of Magnus and Margarete von Mirbach.
3. Otto von Mendelssohn Bartholdy, a banker who had, however, retired quite young.

because it has only been occupied by the soldiers for a few weeks, but they will ruin it soon enough. Still, it is a small staff, and that may help.

Husen is in a splendid barracks; but it is a grim life. Ciano was executed this morning.[1] The [illegible word] are setting up a war-crimes trial against high officers, in order to curry favour with the Anglo-Saxons, it seems. There's a lot going on in Norway again. That is unfortunate and quite unnecessary. The beginning of the Finnish-Russian negotiations seems to have come to nothing.

Now, my love, I hear the doorbell. It will be Karl-Ludwig.

Berlin, 13 January 1944[2]

. . . Yesterday I didn't write either, my love. A man from the SD came at 9 and sat in our office till 12.30; then I was able to dictate only the most urgent things and had to attend a meeting at the AA at 2; from there I went to the botanical gardens[3] to eat a sandwich, then back to the Office; at 6 I went to see Haubach, who is staying with Carlo's Austrian friend,[4] ate with them, and then the three of us went to see Husen, whom we left at 12. Today started with your telephone call, and after dictating a few things I went to a meeting at the Institute at 11.30, from which I emerged at 3.15, to devote myself, since my return to the Office, to a very important memorandum, which I must finish today. Frl. Breslauer comes for this purpose at 6, and at 8 I am supposed to be with Aunt Leno in Potsdam. Now I am interrupting work on the memorandum in order to write to you. . . .

Last night was nice and satisfactory in substance. I hope that the attempt to take up Carlo's inheritance will be successful in this respect. It will, however, take a lot of effort and work. Husen at any rate was satisfied, and Theo and the other man too. He and Husen are to continue Saturday evening.

Marion returned very satisfied. Unfortunately I have seen both only by the minute, because I am really constantly on the move. I can barely manage to let Peter know what is happening; I do it mostly during 10 minutes at breakfast.—Tomorrow I'll go to Zeppelin[5] in the evening and talk to Bü[rkner] at night. He's resigned to that, because on Saturday he wants

1. Mussolini did nothing to save his son-in-law when a tribunal composed of reliable fascists on 10 January sentenced the members of the Grand Council who had voted against Mussolini in July 1943.
2. Erroneously dated 13.11.44.
3. Hortensienstrasse.
4. Probably Heinrich Gleissner—see n. 4 (p. 229) to letter of 30 June 1942.
5. The central Abwehr Office near Zossen.

to leave to see his family. Thus I gain Saturday morning for work at the Office, and I gain Saturday afternoon by seeing Aunt Leno[1] today. I therefore have some hope that I'll get a good deal of work behind me over the week-end and can finish next week.

My love, I must return to work on my memorandum.

Berlin, 14 January 1944

The letter you finished on the 12th arrived today; so we're back to a 2-day period. That isn't bad.—Eugen has just come in to tell me that there's a preliminary warning and that a big air raid on Berlin is expected. So we are back to early raids; it is not yet 7 o'clock. Last night I saw Aunt Leno in Potsdam and stayed with the Mirbachs, i.e., Uncle Max. Julima is in Silesia, and Dieter is on firewatcher duty in Berlin. But I didn't get there until 12 or shortly before, because it had taken that long with Aunt Leno. We went over everything to do with the children. A lot still has to be cleared up, but slowly one does get a clearer picture of the whole situation. I agreed with Aunt Leno that she should come to Kreisau to defend her rights against Pension Annie in person, unless she hears otherwise from us.—Aunt Leno has got older, but on the whole she is quite well, if one considers what a shock[2] she has just had.

This morning I got up early, at 5.30, and was at Hortensienstr. at 7.30. I had breakfast there and then sat at the Office all morning, mainly busy with dictation. There is a great deal, a very great deal, of work. I only hope that I can clear it up by the middle of next week.—We, that is, Oxé and I, were supposed to have gone to Bürkner today, but Bürkner was called to the Little Sailor[3] and switched our appointment to Monday morning in Berlin. Of course that suits me much better than the ghastly night trip. . . .

REICHSWEHRMINISTERIUM[4]

Berlin W 35   *16 January 1944*

. . . Oxé & I were to have gone to Zeppelin Friday evening; instead Bü[rkner] is coming to Berlin tomorrow morning. That made Saturday morning a kind of bonus. That was very welcome, because I had a lot to clear up and to finish. So I did end the week with a cleared-up desk. Frl.

1. Leonore von Hülsen—see n. 2 (p. 30) to letter of 22 August 1939.
2. The sudden loss of her son and daughter-in-law—cf. letter of 24 November 1943.
3. Canaris.
4. Old stationery.

Breslauer came at 12, and I had things to dictate to her until 1.50; Steinke is coming today at 11, and I hope to get far enough with him by lunch-time that the meeting of a larger group set for 12 o'clock Monday can reach a provisional conclusion.[1] If that is really the end of it, I can prepare myself for the Court of Arbitration; if and when I go to Agram, I shall have finished everything that needed doing. Only with my reading I am badly in arrears. But that isn't so terrible. In any case, I am enormously relieved to see these remaining jobs finished now. I'd be very glad if only there were no heavy air raids for a few more nights, because they always cause so much disorder that more unfinished work accumulates.

Adam was here for lunch yesterday. He is not very well and seems to have a little flu and takes it very seriously and sadly. In any case he was extremely grumpy and annoyed at everything, which amused us greatly, and that made him even angrier. Eugen and I left at 4 to visit Popitz,[2] and stayed there till 8. I found it very interesting and entertaining. He is a bright man, a very clever man, and brilliant in debate. I had the impression that on the whole he, too, was satisfied.[3] Whether anything substantial will come of it I don't yet know; perhaps it will.—By the time we'd had supper and done the dishes it was 9.30, as reported above.

So Jowöchen has lost his safe place and we must find a new job for him quickly. That would certainly be possible if it didn't have to be done quickly, but unfortunately I doubt that it can be quick. In any case, I used my telephone connections yesterday with East, North, and West. Perhaps I can find something for him in the South if I go there next week. The whole thing is serious, for if he lands wrong now, it's not to be expected that he'll find the right channel again. At any rate, I'll go on telephoning today. . . .

I am madly looking forward to the week-end. I hope it works out. . . .

Berlin, 16 January 1944

The day is over.[4] That is, I still have to talk to Peter, but essentially the day is over, and I want to use a quiet minute to send you another line. Eugen has gone to Haeften. Peter & Marion have gone for a walk, it is 6.30, and there is certainly another half hour before a possible air-raid warning; most of the day's work is done.

1. It was still legal work on the Kempinski case, on which M. continued to work even after his arrest.
2. Johannes Popitz—see n. 2 (p. 271) to letter of 9 January 1943.
3. A year before it was Popitz who had suggested the meeting between the Kreisauers and the Goerdeler group, to which he belonged.
4. On this last Sunday before his arrest he wrote twice.

I wonder how things look with you. Are your sons going to bed now? Are you reading to them? Are you doing something else? Is Asta better, or are you worried about her? I only hope that you have peace outwardly, but above all inwardly. My love, if we learn the art of maintaining peace within, whatever happens around us, these sad years won't have been wasted for us. But will we learn it? It is so important to me. If I feel you are at peace, I am already half pacified. If I feel that you are restless, I am quite restless. My dear pole of peace! Where else could there be peace for your husband if not with you and your little sons? I wonder about the people who don't have that and no longer have a mother either. Where are their roots?—Tomorrow evening the moon will be in the same position as on the 22nd of November, and that probably means that the big air raids will start again; one remembers again how to prepare oneself for them and how to depart with a peaceful heart if one has to depart.

This morning I was at the Office to discuss the Kempinski case[1] with Herr Steinke. That was fairly successful, and we virtually finished in 3 hours. But it was hard. Still, it is as good as done, and I hope that tomorrow's meeting will merely wind it up.—The Poelchaus came to lunch. Nice as always, he as steady and calm as always, both of them full of nice stories. We didn't arrive at any very important results.—Then Delbrück arrived, who's been thrown out in the meanest way by his chief and pushed off to the front, as corporal. That in itself isn't so bad as the method. But I hope we'll still succeed in doing something for him.

Steltzer telephoned today to tell me that AOK[2] Norway will put in for Jowo. I hope that is so, and that it works. But I won't cancel the other efforts.—Meanwhile we've had supper, done a lot of telephoning, and Reichwein has been here. It is 10 o'clock and I'm going to climb into bed.

Berlin, 18 January 1944

Yesterday again I didn't write. It is becoming a plague. The reason is partly that if I get home in the evening at a human hour, I must first talk to the others, while at Derfflingerstrasse I was free earlier and was alone. The day itself just races past, and the evening is more or less filled too. Then there is the added clearing up and washing up and that takes time, too. So I sometimes just don't get round to the best occupation of my day, the letter to Pim.

Monday started with a bang, an enormous flow of incoming papers; at 12 I was at my own office with Herr Steinke, from there I went to a meet-

1. Cf. first letter of 16 January and letter of 18 January.
2. Army Command.

ing at the AA at 2 o'clock, which lasted till 5.30; then I had to go to the Office once more, went home on my bike, washed, and went to the Adlon, where I had a dinner appointment with Goerschen. I was back by 11 and still saw Haeften, with whom we talked for another half hour. Today I'm in my school all day, catching up with my work. My desk is virtually empty, only a few things await preliminary decisions from Bürkner, who is coming later. I hope that I'll then have nothing more to do in the evening, because I have a lot of reading.

Jowo's affair, as far as I can see, doesn't look too bad. Steltzer has work for him on his staff; D[illegible], the personnel chief of Army Group North, will also take an interest in the matter, and I hope that Busch will also help. So perhaps the whole thing will end well.—Reichwein came briefly, and has now left for Copenhagen. He seemed quite cheerful and said his family was in quite good shape.—König saw Peter yesterday at lunchtime, when I wasn't free. He had nothing new to report but was in quite good spirits.—Another rather mean attack has been landed on Wengler,[1] and we'll have to parry it. This life among thieves and highway robbers is really a joke and not without its charms; but it will be good when there is an end to it.

Frantz's death is really sad for poor Dosy.[2] One can only say: *Tu l'as voulu, Danton.* The lack of consideration of men in this regard is astonishing. One can't do a thing. I'll write to Dosy.—We'll be telephoning tomorrow morning, and I wonder if you have news of the battle with Pension Annie.

Your husband is well. The Kempinski matter is concluded and signed.[3] There is still a lot to be done for Hans Carl and Rottgart. Once all that is signed I can get down to my preparation for the Court of Arbitration, and that would mean that I've got through the work for my own office too, once more, and can leave without having to worry.—I wonder whether a time will ever come when I have reserves of work done and don't always have to try to catch up with the work with my tongue hanging out. I can imagine that to be very agreeable.[4]

Farewell, my love, I hope to see you very soon. Keep well, look after yourself, give my love to your sons, and, please, continue your affection for your husband, Jäm.

1. Wengler had been arrested.
2. In-laws of Carl Viggo von Moltke.
3. Cf. n. 1 (p. 382) to first letter of 16 January.
4. He was arrested the next day and taken to Gestapo headquarters, Prinz-Albrecht-Strasse. He used his "leisure" there to write a lovely, long, autobiographical letter about his childhood and youth to his two boys—see Freya von Moltke, Michael Balfour, and Julian Frisby, *Helmuth von Moltke 1907–1945: Anwalt der Zukunft* (Stuttgart, 1975), pp. 9–28.

About the Year in Prison—January 19, 1944, to January 23, 1945—Freya von Moltke wrote the following account in August 1989:

On 19 January 1944 Helmuth was arrested. He had warned a colleague, Otto Kiep, that he and a group of other persons would soon be imprisoned for having criticized the Nazi regime at a tea party in the presence of an agent provocateur. They were arrested soon afterwards. When the Gestapo learnt of the warning, they also arrested Helmuth, intent on finding out who had in turn warned him. This was established without Helmuth, but they kept him in jail anyway. He was suspect as a person, and his base of work in the Oberkommando der Wehrmacht was also suspect. He was held in what was called "protective custody" in a prison which was part of the concentration camp Ravensbrück near Fürstenberg, about a hundred miles north of Berlin. The prison was built for the inmates of the camp. Since it lay outside the radius of the Allies' bombing of Berlin, it served the SD for political prisoners as well.

"Protective custody" allowed certain privileges. Helmuth wore his own clothes.—He continued to work for his office.—He could write to me twice a week, and he received letters from me. Those letters were censored, of course.—I was allowed to visit him once a month. It took me about a day's travelling via Berlin from Kreisau.—I could bring additional food. Especially tea and coffee, great rarities in Germany at that time, were very helpful to him in many ways. We met about twenty miles away from Ravensbrück at a police training school, in a place called Drögen, where Helmuth was taken from Ravensbrück by car, and where all interrogations of political prisoners also took place.

We met in the office room in a barrack. There was a bench and a table in one of the corners. The guard was sitting at his desk near the window, busy with his work. We could speak to each other quite freely. I brought a big ledger with me from the farm, pretending to talk business with Helmuth, and we did to some extent. But we were also able to fit in unsupervised exchanges. The guards knew me after some time, also through my letters, which they obviously enjoyed reading. One of them once said how sorry he felt that I had had such bad luck with my geese. When I told Helmuth this, laughing and saying that they were really quite nice men, he said dryly, "Except that they pull out fingernails when they interrogate."

Then, on 20 July 1944, Claus von Stauffenberg attempted to kill Hitler. The attempt failed, along with the planned coup d'état. It had, however, exposed many conspirators, and hundreds of arrests followed. Through endless and cruel interrogations of the other prisoners, the SD had established by mid-August that Helmuth had been closely associated with the conspir-

ators for a long time. He lost his privileges and was interrogated as well, but not tortured.

I did not receive letters any more. I had visited Helmuth once more after the attempted coup; the situation was bad; we agreed on a code, and in one of his last letters Helmuth informed me that he was in grave danger. When, on 29 September 1944, I went from Kreisau to the police school, without a visiting permit, to try to obtain news and, maybe, get through to him, I was told that he had been transferred to Berlin the previous day to appear before the ominous judge Freisler and what was called the "People's Court." I found him at Tegel prison.

This was the prison in Berlin where our friend Harald Poelchau happened to be prison chaplain. He belonged to our group, and had taken part in the group's first bigger meeting at Kreisau (Whitsun 1942). Throughout the Nazi years he stood by countless political prisoners in his sober, unemotional, fearless way, yet feeling deeply. He accompanied Germans and prisoners from other nations right to their execution. At that moment there was not even a glimmer of hope. And there came this chance of close and immediate contact. What luck! Of the many Berlin prisons, just that one! Poelchau had immediately turned to assisting his own friends. Prison walls tend to be more transparent than one would expect. They can be pierced at times; we found that out. For just under four months Poelchau carried our letters in and out, almost daily, and became very close to Helmuth. Because of the great number of cases before the People's Court, it took this long before the case of Helmuth and those tried with him came up. From Tegel, uncensored, Helmuth wrote a report for me on his time at Ravensbrück. It follows here:

Tegel, 28 November 1944

My love, I really still owe you a report on the summer and I'll see if I can do it. On 6 February we were taken to Ravensbrück: Kiep, Bernstorff,[1] Scherpenberg,[2] Kuenzer,[3] Etscheit,[4] and another man, in a Black Maria. At the P.A.[5] I had Herr Witt as my personal guard and Kiep had Herr Motekus[?]. Both came along with us. The day before, the women in-

1. Albrecht Graf von Bernstorff (1890–1945) opposed the regime from the outset and resigned from the Foreign Service in 1933; murdered by the SS on 23 April 1945.
2. Hilger van Scherpenberg, Legation Counsellor; he survived.
3. Richard Kuenzer, Legation Counsellor in the AA, long-standing opponent of the regime; murdered by the SS in Berlin during the night of 23/24 April 1945.
4. Alfred Etscheit, Berlin lawyer connected with the Abwehr and opposed to the regime.
5. Prinz-Albrecht-Strasse, the Reichssicherheitshauptampt (RSHA), i.e., the central office of the Security Service and headquarters of the Gestapo, where he had been taken after his arrest on 19 January and kept and interrogated until his transfer to Ravensbrück.

volved in the same affair[1] had arrived, among whom I only knew Hannah Kiep[2] and Frl. Zimmerman.[3] I got my cell, No. 28, and Kiep was in the adjacent one on one side, and on the other side there were two female SS guards on whom I have reported in my diary. When I was allowed out for a walk in the morning of the 7th, Puppi[4] was looking out of her window, and her cell was so close to the exit that we were able to talk a bit.

In the early days I was careful and guarded, firstly because our guards were numerous—two women SS guards, Frl. Meurer[?], whom I later called "August" for our internal use, and another, who both belonged to the camp, and then for us 6 men and 6 women, 3 SS Untersturmführer[5] and 6 policewomen—and secondly because there were also many SS men and SS girls among the prisoners. But every day I exchanged a few words with Puppi through the window, i.e., she from the window and I from the prison yard. We then each walked separately. From the middle of March on we were allowed to walk with other prisoners, such as had nothing to do with us, and I soon arranged it in such a way that I was let out together with a political girl, Gerti, who came from Düsseldorf and had already been in the camp for 2½ years, and who gave me the first lessons on the different inmates. She herself had been a Red Cross nurse and had been jailed for a political joke, had been sent to the sick bay of the camp as part of the nursing staff, and had had an affair with an SS doctor there who had been sentenced to prison for it, while she was sent to the camp prison in solitary confinement and at times horribly mal-treated: 21 days without food in a dark cell and bent over, with her hands and feet shackled together. They wanted her to confess that the doctor had performed an abortion on her.

The cleaners were 3 women Jehovah's Witnesses who had already served 7, 7, and 3 years: a nice, fat East Prussian, a clever Berliner, and a very cunning and intelligent woman from Bohemia. I soon had a tender relationship with them. On 9 April, Easter Sunday, Gerti was sent away, to Auschwitz. At about the same time the women police disappeared and Puppi, who, as punishment for secretly exchanging notes with Lang-behn,[6] had been transferred to the north side, where Kiep had been since March, was put in cell No. 26, beside mine. Moreover, with Gerti's help I had by now oriented myself enough to be quite sure and to know who could and who could not be relied on. Among those who beautified the

1. The tea party with the agent provocateur
2. Wife of Otto Kiep.
3. Not identified.
4. Marie-Louise Sarre.
5. SS equivalent of a second lieutenant.
6. See letter of 21 June 1941.

summer the following should be mentioned in addition: The man in No. 76, called Poseidon because he was in charge of watering the flowers; a prisoner for the duration of the war, but against whom nothing precise could be proved. He inhabited cell No. 76, was nice, and looked like a technician. Carmen, a Swiss journalist, my age, who had worked for the SD but had defected from it after the Anschluss, was in a cell diagonally below mine. On one occasion she got 25 lashes of the *nagaika*.[1] She told splendid stories. In May or June she was sent back to the "free" camp,[2] where she worked in the sick bay. But she mostly, or frequently, came over on some pretext when I took my walk and was a magnificent source of information for me. Her name is Mori and she is the daughter of a Swiss doctor. In 1940 she was sentenced to death as a spy by the French. The cell below mine held "Schorsch," a gardener of Siemens who, as a free man, had brought letters and things from their wives to concentration-camp inmates, had been "sentenced" to 2 years in a concentration camp, and who, in August, when I had already been put in prison uniform, was sent to the "free" camp for men.

With our two guards, Motekus[?] and Witt, and later Weber, and with the two SS girls, Puppi and I were on very friendly terms, whose foundations were strongly reinforced by food supplies. The best of them was "August." August was rough at first and Puppi claimed that she was treacherous, but I had attached myself to her at once and indeed it turned out that *au fond* she was a jewel, though somewhat man-crazy, but that only served to make my business easier. August was the senior woman in the camp, competent and highly regarded by the camp leader; she was always taken along when new women guards were recruited and was head and shoulders above the other girls. Whenever we wanted anything, I asked August, and 24 hours later we had it. On one occasion I had a conversation about the education of children with August—who had two—and it turned out that she shared my opinion that there was no such thing as educating children without Christian religion and that she therefore had her mother living with her, so that the children did not have to go to the SS kindergarten. So August and I had a very tender relationship.

Then there was the "niner," the man in cell No. 9, surely a man from the former Socialist Workers' Youth, who had travelled all over the world as a wireless operator after 1933, returned to Germany via Siberia during the war, landed in a concentration camp after a few weeks, and was now awaiting the end of the war there.

1. A thick, plaited whip, as used by Turks and Cossacks.
2. The concentration camp itself, as distinct from the adjacent prison. Ravensbrück was primarily known as a camp for *women*.

Then there was "Willi," a steelworker from Graz, who during the Spanish Civil War had fought on the communist side in the International Brigade, then had gone to Russia, and had fallen into our hands as a Russian agent on the Eastern Front. They let him live because he had already been expatriated before the war and had therefore not fought in Russia as a German.

Then there were a lot of changing people: Russian women partisans, nursing personnel of the Russian army, Polish women—two very nice girls from Warsaw, a Ukrainian woman with a baby and sister, SS men, women SS guards of all kinds, all of whom I soon knew, or, rather, all of whom knew me, because after Gerti's and Kiep's departure Puppi and I were the seniors of the prison and also had many privileges. From among those in the sick bay in the free camp I knew Pela Potocka,[1] who worked there and whom I discovered through Carmen, and quite a number of Polish women from the kitchen, who talked with me sometimes when they brought the food.

One day, I think it was May or early June, I returned from my walk in the yard and there was Isa Vermehren,[2] who had just arrived and whom I could therefore at least cheer up with a smile. I at once got the Bohemian Jehovah's Witness to find out where she had been put and it turned out that she was in the cell obliquely below mine, thus below Puppi and next to Schorsch. We established contact by knocking and for a start comforted her and made her part of the community with a quarter pound of butter.

Finally, in early July, a girl in a black dress and with platinum-blonde hair and red lipstick was put into one of the good cells, one of the best, No. 36, which Puppi had inhabited before. When I emerged at noon, she gave me a friendly nod, but I could not make out who she was. She then showed me a cigarette box, which I knew, but which at first I didn't know where to fit in. Deep in thought I returned to my cell, because it was of course very important to know who the new girl was. Suddenly it came to me that they were Falkenhausen's cigarettes and that this must be Princess Ruspoli,[3] who, however, had taken such punishment that I could not recognize her. So I rushed to my window and loudly whistled Falkenhausen's favourite song: "Dans un coin de mon pays," and halfway through the first verse she answered with the second half.

So, that was the crew of the summer until July 20th.

We on the south side had all put our windows "in order," i.e., adjusted

<hr />

1. Member of a well-known aristocratic Polish family.
2. See Introduction, p. 21. Her brother Erich, who had worked in Ankara as Abwehr agent, had defected to the British with his wife when ordered to return to Berlin.
3. See n. 4 (p. 309) to letter of 7 June 1943.

them in such a way that they could be taken out so that one was able to lean out and even put one's head through the grille. When we had to communicate something to each other, we whistled, and each of us had an individual tune. Mine was *"Wem Gott will rechte Gunst erweisen,"*[1] Isa's *"Die Gedanken sind frei,"*[2] that of Elisabeth Ruspoli, called Mary, *"Dans un coin,"* and so on. Puppi, called Erna, didn't have one, because I was able to get her by knocking.

Puppi had a terrible crisis in April and we had many sad talks about it. Her father then sent her a Reformed Bible and we discussed Bible texts thoroughly. From June on we also went out for our walks together and talked about everything from the Bible to organizing food supplies for our fellow prisoners and measures to bribe the personnel, and we always acted together in these matters too. The evening conversations, however, were mostly about a psalm or something similar. We fed the three who were in the cells below us—Carmen, Schorsch, and Isa—copiously, because those three got the bad food. About the middle of June, no, in early June, we succeeded in getting Isa moved to cell No. 27, beside Puppi. I had strongly urged Isa to sing, and she started cautiously at first, and soon it was a regular habit that after everything had been closed down, that is, after 10 in the evening, she sang: first Italian folk songs or something cheerful and finally spiritual songs: Protestant hymns, *"Der Mond ist auf- gegangen,"*[3] and Catholic church music such as, above all, the Gregorian *Te Deum.* The first time she sang it, an Austrian SS man in a cell obliquely below hers sighed loudly and said: "I haven't heard that for 10 years."

Finally in July—and that continued until I was interrogated anew on August 14th—we succeeded, Mary, Isa, Puppi, and I, in being allowed outside once more, towards 9 o'clock, for about an hour. Sometimes we walked up and down slowly, talking. Sometimes we sat and conversed with the personnel, sometimes Isa sang something for us. Often we had No. 76, sometimes No. 9 with us, sometimes someone else from among the crew.

Apart from Puppi's and my food supplies our chief trump was our friendship with August. Puppi's and Isa's initial aversion to August had, after my conversation with her about the religious education of children, yielded to a fast friendship, and from early July on, August brought us three two rolls each, heated up in greased paper, every morning, and occasionally she cooked fresh mushrooms or fried potatoes in the eve-

1. "Whom God would show His pleasure / He sends into the wide world."
2. "Thoughts are free . . ."
3. "The moon has risen . . . ," words by Matthias Claudius.

nings. Thus August did a great deal to enable us to live well. She also did other shopping for us in town.

Food played an altogether great role. After I had connected an immersion heater in my cell to make tea, Puppi sent for a hotplate, and whole dishes, e.g., splendid risottos, were cooked on that. But ham and sausage and bacon from me to go with potatoes, all played a role, and on Sundays we supplied the entire Sunday watch with tea or coffee.

In all this existence terrible things would happen again and again: almost every day some woman from the camp would get 25 lashes of the *nagaika*. It was done in our "cell building." My friends in the kitchen always told me about it the day before, because the prisoner whip-wielders always got extra meat. The women were strapped fast, naked, in the presence of the camp leader and doctor and were beaten by two fellow prisoners. On one occasion a woman was in a cell next to the one below mine who had had 75 lashes, in three instalments. Her back was split open all over, but it was astonishing how fast she recovered. Then there were men who were suddenly asked in the morning "to take a walk round the camp," i.e., to be shot. It happened to Emil, a prisoner in my vicinity, who had an affair with one of the women guards and who refused to divulge her name. A fortnight after his death the girl was in cell No. 24, beside mine, an Austrian from the environs of Vienna, Floridsdorf, I think. But really she was sad and stunned for only 7 days and she then struck up a friendship with No. 9.—Then one day 10 prisoners who had been under investigation for the murder of a fellow prisoner were taken away at 5 in the morning. Quite nice men, actually, and we all thought that the chimney of the crematorium outside my window would be smoking like mad. But then after a week we heard that they were all well and in the Oranienburg camp, where they had to work.—Then we had a British parachute agent, who was taken away to be shot one morning.— Finally there was a man put in the cell with Schorsch who had broken out of the "free" camp; he was taken away one morning and then we heard that he had been hanged in the middle of the camp.—Two Russians who were put in Carmen's cell after her departure, especially pretty girls, by the way, of 19 and 20, were told every few days they were now to be shot, because they had committed sabotage at work.—On the north side, where Willi, No. 9, was, and at one time Isa as punishment for exchanging notes with her sister-in-law,[1] there were daily scenes of beatings and punishment by standing: the women had to stand still in all weathers from 5 in the morning until 10 or 11 in the evening.

1. Presumably the sister of Erich Vermehren's wife, the former Countess Elisabeth von Plettenberg.

Isa, who had been put into No. 8, next to No. 9, communicated with him in Morse and, used to our religious conversations on the south side, had straightaway started asking him in Morse: "Do you believe in God?" His prompt answer was: "No." It was terribly funny, for Isa now tried to convert him by way of Morse signals and soon had to give up. Isa was indignant, too, at Puppi, who was a Catholic, for reading the Bible instead of sticking to the Missal and now did her best to tie her down to the Missal: she was horrified at hearing the Bible called "beautiful"; that was already heretical.—I notice that Elisabeth, called Mary, is being short-changed. I cannot at the moment think of a nice story about her. But she was quite the equal of the other two and a great enrichment. In addition she was especially good at gathering information, because she knew how to ask questions skilfully and calmly.

Information was always important for us. Above all it was important always to learn what new arrivals there were, who was put in vacant cells, where informers were put, why people were moved, what questions had been asked at interrogations. This news service proved very valuable after July 20th, for at least I was spared surprises. I heard about Peter's arrival[1] within 20 minutes, also that Kleist[2] and Schwerin[3] had come with him. The arrivals of Schacht, Popitz, Leber, Haubach, Leuschner, Maass, Wirmer,[4] etc., were reported to us within 24 hours, even with their cell numbers, although everything was done to keep it all secret from us. Hassell,[5] who was treated very badly, already got his first risotto after 48 hours, via the Bohemian Jehovah's Witness. Halder[6] was put in Isa's cell, No. 27, next door to Puppi, and was a prisoner who learnt very fast.

During the night of the 14th of August, at 11 p.m., I was taken away to be interrogated and it was clear that they were after my life. But everything remained as before until the 19th, except that I had, under some pretext, been transferred to the north side shortly before. And so I was able to take leave of all wonderfully during the days from the 15th to the 19th. The three girls promised me that they would visit Freya later and tell her what my last months were like. Mary, above all, intended to go straight from Ravensbrück to Kreisau and to get in touch with the Ansem-

---

1. Yorck.

2. Lieutenant Ewald Heinrich von Kleist had once volunteered to assassinate Hitler; arrested at Bendlerstrasse with Yorck.

3. See n. 2 to letter of 19 October 1941.

4. Joseph Wirmer (1901–44), Berlin lawyer, opponent of the regime from its inception, sentenced to death and executed on 8 September 1944 as one of the chief participants in the preparation of the attempted coup of 20 July.

5. See n. 2 (p. 271) to letter of 9 January 1943.

6. See n. 1 (p. 101) to letter of 14 August 1940.

bourgs from there. On the 19th of August I was put in prison uniform and locked up in a dark cell on the north side, without a book, without writing paper, without my own things, except for socks and handkerchiefs, with bad food and no permission for walks for a week. Nevertheless I stayed in news contact with the others. Later, when I went outside again, we saw each other for seconds, because as I stepped outside I whistled one of our tunes and then quickly waved around the corner when the guards, who were at that time very strict, weren't looking. When they were outside and I had made myself heard, Isa, who had been transferred to the south side, whistled my favourite songs, nothing but Mozart melodies. When I finally left, I happened to see Mary and was able to say goodbye to her, and the Jehovah's Witnesses and August followed me with their eyes, looking very sad.

[*continued*] *29 November 1944*

... I have to add a quick supplement to yesterday's letter about Ravensbrück, to say who else passed through and stayed for a longer or shorter period without playing much of a role in my life there. But perhaps the one or the other will cross your path sometime. Planck[1] was in the cell next to mine when I was on the north side, Alvensleben-Neugattersleben[2] was on my other side, Pechel, the editor of the *Neue Rundschau* [sic],[3] Suhrkamp, the present owner of the Bermann-Fischer Verlag, two brothers whose names which I can't recall at the moment start with a W, publishers from Berlin,[4] Frau Solf and her daughter Countess Ballestrem,[5] Halder and his wife, he for a while next to Puppi in cell No. 27 and a very nice successor to Isa, the sister of Isa's sister-in-law, that is, the sister of Vermehren's wife, whose name I didn't know, but her first name is Gisela,[6] Frau Henschel, the wife of the Legation Counsellor in Ankara, at first somewhat stuffy but then nice, Hermes,[1] Gescher[?],[7] and

1. See n. 5 (p. 309) to letter of 8 June 1943.
2. Werner von Alvensleben (1875–1961), professional officer until the First World War, then banker. Sentenced to two years' imprisonment on 1 February 1945.
3. Rudolf Pechel (1882–1961), writer, until its prohibition in 1942 publisher and editor of *Deutsche Rundschau*; acquitted by People's Court 1 February 1945.
4. The publisher Paul Wasmuth and his brother, a writer.
5. Both involved in the tea party with the agent provocateur.
6. Cf. n. 1, p. 391.
7. Andreas Hermes, Reich Minister of Food and Agriculture and Minister of Finance in the early Weimar Republic and envisaged as possible Minister of Food by the plotters; sentenced to death, but survived.
8. Not identified.

Fehr[?],[1] who were put into uniform with me, and Peter together with Schwerin and Kleist; Leuschner and Maass and Leber and Dahrendorf,[2] Nuschke[?], a trade-union secretary, Gross, another trade-union secretary,[3] and Kunkel, a naval chaplain. With the exception of Popitz, Schacht, Halder, and myself all the men were at some time beaten horribly. Bernstorff and Kuenzer had completely swollen faces for a fortnight, and Kuenzer had to stay in bed for several days. Langbehn was treated worst—now, at the end; in the beginning he had been a special case like me and in the P.A. his manservant brought him an opulent breakfast on a tray every morning; now his hands and feet were shackled and he was beaten in his cell and during his interrogation. . . .

Tegel, 28 December 1944

. . . A remarkable year is drawing to a close for me. I spent it predominantly among people who were being prepared for a violent death and many of them have suffered it meanwhile: Kiep, Frl. von Thadden,[4] Langbehn, Hassell, Peter,[5] Schwerin, Schulenburg, Popitz, Maass[5], Leuschner, Wirmer, and certainly 10 or 11 concentration camp prisoners. With all these people I lived in the same house, took part in their fate, listened when they were taken away for interrogations, or when they were removed altogether, talked with almost all of them about their affairs, and saw how they coped with it all. And I think that here, at Tegel, already about 10 of my group have been executed. Thus death has become a companion of the entire year. And if at first I got enormously excited when "Emil" was asked to come for a "walk round the camp," these violent killings simply became such an everyday matter that I accepted the disappearance of individual men sadly but as a natural event. And now, I tell myself, it is my turn. Can I also accept it as a natural event in my own case? That's the frame of mind in which I arrived here; in fact I thought the detour via the People's Court just a nuisance, and if anyone had told me that death sentences could be simply ordered after an application by the accused and carried out at once, I would have applied for it at the end of September. That's how caught up I was in the atmosphere that one

1. Not identified.
2. Gustav Dahrendorf (1901–54), Social Democrat, former member of the Reichstag; coal merchant after 1933.
3. See n. 1 (p. 401) to first letter of 10 January 1945.
4. Elisabeth von Thadden (1890–1944), founder and head of a Protestant boarding school, 1929–41; after her dismissal on political grounds in 1941, active as a nurse, until her arrest as a result of a tea party she gave that was attended by a Gestapo spy.
5. Yorck.

must not make a *fuss*[1] about dying by execution. And where am I now? The landscape is unrecognisable. Now I definitely don't want to die, there's no doubt about that. The constant work on arguments aimed at avoiding it has been a mighty stimulus to my will to get round this thing. When I think of the many steps, none of them earth-shaking, each one of which seen in retrospect only served the clarification of the arguments, I must say that after the event they prove to have a significant connection and have now produced a respectable defence. (I wonder what Hercher[2] will say about the new version.) All that is a miracle, but it doesn't mean that we can draw any conclusion about the future from it; I am far from doing that, apart from a few hours of weakness. But the accused who was psychologically prepared for non-defence and devoid of any exonerating arguments has turned into a man determined to do everything that can serve his defence and who has a defence worth discussing, which in any case has given him enough inner security that he does not hesitate to write quite impudent letters to H.H.[3]

So the year I spent in the immediate and quite familiar proximity of death ends in a will to resist which is much more determined than it was on 19 January or rather on the 24th of January.—And yet I must be gladly ready to die at any moment, I must maintain this feeling of readiness for it and accept it without any resistance against God, if he orders it. After this time of preparation I must not suddenly be surprised by it, even if it should come by a simple brazen bomb. That is why the admonition to "watch and pray" is so necessary, and yet I keep sinking into sleep when I see that there is still a week's or two weeks' time until the trial. It is really impossible, even for someone who spends as much time on it as I do, to feel the immediate presence of death every moment. Flesh and blood rebel against it wildly.

Now I sometimes think—a thing I haven't done for months—how everything would be if I stayed alive, and I wonder if I would forget it all again or if from this time one keeps a real relationship to death and thus to eternity. I come to the conclusion that in that case flesh and blood would stake all on repressing the insight again and that a constant battle would be needed to save the fruits of this time. We just are a miserable race, there's no doubt about it, only mostly we don't know how miserable we are. Now I know why Paul and Isaiah, Jeremiah and David and Solomon, Moses and the evangelists will never be obsolete: they were not so miserable; they had a stature unattainable by us, unattainable even by

1. English in the original.
2. His defence lawyer.
3. Heinrich Himmler.

men like Goethe, even like Luther. What those men experienced and learnt we'll never understand entirely. One only asks oneself whether in those times such men existed in greater numbers. One has to assume that only a fraction of what existed has been handed down. But how was it possible for such men to exist then? They are like a different human species. And why among the Jews? And why today not among the Jews any more either?. . .

Freya von Moltke:

The letters from Tegel still exist, his and mine; and they belong together. At first Helmuth wrote them in handcuffs. They have as much to do with his death as they have with my further life. They fitted me out for it, and our story still continues. The letters are personal, and I wish to keep them personal. At least as long as I live. When we wrote them, we found that we had almost four months in which to take leave of one another, two people, a man and a woman. The summit of our lives—the hardest time of our lives.

After Helmuth's transfer to Berlin, we first expected that we had very few days left. We had no reason to doubt that he would be condemned to death, and at that time death sentences were mostly carried out on the day of the trial. Then we found we had more time. How much? We never knew for sure. Would the case come up in November, before Christmas? Did we have time into the new year?

The days after the transfer from Ravensbrück, Helmuth was ready to die, ready to pay the price. We always knew this might be demanded. He was then completely free and at peace. As the days went by and more details of other cases got known and the world outside changed, we began to hope again. Two of Helmuth's close friends were also in Tegel prison: Father Delp and Eugen Gerstenmaier. There was enough communication among them for Helmuth to know that they both believed they would survive. (Eugen Gerstenmaier did; Father Delp did not.) Was there a chance for a defence after all? How should it be set up? New tensions arose. Hoping again, Helmuth lost that special peace and freedom: from prison he started to work on a possible defence. Countless steps had to be taken outside, which he suggested and which I carried out. Most of the time during those months, I was in Berlin always on the go or writing to Helmuth. I stayed with Helmuth's cousin Carl Dietrich von Trotha or with the Poelchaus. Dorothee, Poelchau's wife, was just as brave as her husband—I was after all a person to be avoided. Other defendants still alive in other prisons, Helmuth's political friends, had to be informed of his line of defence, and theirs had to be inte-

grated with his. None of those political prisoners were allowed lawyers except a very few days before the trial. And they were chosen and assigned from lawyers acceptable to the Nazi court.

Helmuth placed hope in an interview with Himmler's deputy, SS General Heinrich Müller. I went to the headquarters of the Gestapo in the Prinz-Albrecht-Strasse and arranged the interview with Müller. It felt like walking into the lion's mouth. He promised to see Helmuth, but left no doubt in my mind that they were after his life. After the First World War, he said, "their" opponents survived and took over. They would see to it that this would not be possible this time. He was polite to me, even friendly, as if trying to separate me from Helmuth. No way!—I made that clear to him. Helmuth had his interview, but it was to no avail.

Freisler, the judge, also received me. He talked to me about the never-failing justice of the court. I saw members and employees of the court and the prosecution for different reasons, and asked for permission to visit Helmuth in prison. Four times I met him in prison. For some week-ends I went home to Kreisau to fetch food and get news of the children and the farm, where Helmuth's sister, Asta, was holding the fort. All this is discussed and reported in the letters.

But there is more. There is also the struggle of Helmuth, ready to die and yet hoping for life. There is my holding him yet having to let him go. The tension over so many months became at times unbearable, but we were grateful for every day we had. For Helmuth there were days of deep depression, but he overcame them every time. He became stronger, not weaker. We had always realized that it made sense to risk his life against the evil of the Nazis. We now became willing for him to die as well as to live. In all this we were supported by our faith, faith that came and went like the ebb and flow of the tide. What lay ahead of us was being decided neither by us nor by Freisler and his lot alone.

Then came the days of the trial; Helmuth was brought back to Tegel prison afterwards and described the trial in two long letters. He wished their contents to be known. They were printed for the first time in England in 1947. They now follow.

1945

Berlin, 10 January 1945

My love, just think how good it is that I have been brought back here to Tegel once more, and that the dice, though their fall is already determined, are once more balancing on edge, so to speak. So I can still write a report in peace.

To take the end first: At about 3 o'clock Schulze,[1] who did not make a bad impression, read out the sentences proposed by the prosecution: Moltke: death + confiscation of property; Delp: the same; Gerstenmaier: death;[2] Reisert + Sperr:[3] the same; Fugger:[4] 3 years' penal servitude; Steltzer and Haubach to be dealt with separately.[5] Then came counsel for

---

1. The prosecutor.
2. The judge reduced this to seven years' hard labour.
3. Franz Sperr (1878–1945), retired colonel, Bavarian envoy in Berlin 1932–34, then active in opposition to the regime; took part in Kreisau discussions in Munich and met Claus Stauffenberg in the summer of 1944. Sentenced to death.
4. Josef Ernst Fürst Fugger von Glött (born 1895), landowner, had taken part in Kreisau discussions in Munich and had been envisaged as Regional Commissioner. Got away with a three-year prison sentence.
5. Their trial took place on 15 January. They were both sentenced to death. Steltzer escaped execution as a result of the intervention of Scandinavian friends.

the defence, really all quite nice, none of them vicious. Then the final statements of the accused, which your husband was the only one to do without. Eugen was a bit uneasy, as I noticed during his final statement.

Now for the course of the trial. All this information is, of course, forbidden.[1]

It took place in a small hall which was full to bursting. Apparently a former classroom.[2] After a long introduction from Freisler[3] concerning formalities—that the trial was secret, that note-taking was prohibited, etc.—Schulze read the indictment, only the short text, as in the warrant of arrest. Then it was Delp's turn, whose two policemen stepped forward with him. The procedure was as follows: Freisler, whom Hercher[4] had described quite correctly as gifted, something of a genius, and not wise, and all this in the highest degree, outlines one's curriculum vitae, one confirms or supplements it, and then come the facts which interest him. Here he selects things that suit him and omits entire portions. In Delp's case he started with his getting to know Peter and me, what was first discussed in Berlin, and then Kreisau autumn '42. Here, too, this form: Freisler holds forth and one can insert answers, objections, perhaps new facts; but if it looks as if this could disturb the course of his argument, he gets impatient, indicates that he doesn't believe it, or shouts at one. The build-up for Kreisau as follows: at first there were general discussions more on matters of principle, then the practical case of a defeat was discussed, and finally there was the search for regional commissioners. The first phase might still be tolerable, although it was surprising that all these talks took place without a single National Socialist present but, rather, with clergymen and people who later took part in the 20th of July.—The second phase, however, was already the blackest defeatism of the darkest kind. And the third open preparation for high treason.—Then came the discussions in Munich. They turned out much more harmless than in the indictment, but a storm of abuse came down on the Catholic clergy and the Jesuits: assent to tyrannicide—Mariana;[5] illegitimate chil-

1. Trial and judgment were top secret (*geheime Reichssache*). Poelchau conveyed the letter.

2. It was in Bellevuestrasse, near Potsdamer Platz.

3. Roland Freisler (1893–1945), 1914 army ensign, 1915 prisoner of war in Russia, returned a communist. 1924 lawyer in Kassel, 1925 member of NSDAP (Golden Party Badge 1934), 1932 Reichstag deputy, 1933 Under-Secretary of State (Staatssekretär) in the Prussian, 1934 in the Reich Ministry of Justice. Since 20 August 1942 President of the People's Court, the new court instituted in 1934 to try cases of treason. He was killed in his courthouse by an Allied bomb during the trial of Fabian von Schlabrendorff (q.v.) in an air raid on 3 February.

4. His—officially appointed—counsel for defence.

5. Juan de Mariana (1536–1624), Jesuit, historian, and theologian. In his treatise *De rege et regis institutione* (1599) he declared tyrannicide justifiable in certain circumstances.

dren; anti-German attitude, etc., etc. All this with bellowing of middling quality. The fact that Delp absented himself from the talks that took place in his quarters was also held against him as "typically Jesuitical." "By that very absence you show yourself that you knew exactly that high treason was afoot and that you would have liked to keep the tonsured little head, the consecrated holy man, out of it. Meanwhile he may have gone to church to pray that the conspiracy should succeed in a way pleasing to God."—Then came Delp's visit to Stauffenberg.[1] And finally Sperr's statement on July 21st that Stauffenberg had made hints to him about the coup d'état. These last two points were passed off fairly gently. What was remarkable was that throughout the hearing Freisler mentioned me in every other sentence: "the Moltke circle," "Moltke's plans," "also belonged to Moltke," and so forth.

The following legal principles were proclaimed:

"The People's Court takes the view that the mere failure to report defeatist utterances like Moltke's, coming from a man of his reputation and position, already amounts to treason."—"It is already tantamount to treason to discuss highly political questions with people who are in no way competent to deal with them, especially if they do not in any way actively belong to the Party."—"It is already preparation for high treason to arrogate to oneself any judgment in a matter which it is for the Führer to decide."—"Anyone who objects to acts of violence, but prepares for the case that another, that is, the enemy, removes the government by force, thereby engages in preparation of high treason; for then he counts on the force of the enemy." And so it went on and on. This only allows one conclusion: anyone who doesn't suit Herr Freisler commits high treason.

Sperr came next. He more or less extricated himself from the Kreisau affair—and, quite rightly, somewhat at my expense. But he was reproached as follows: "Why didn't you report it? Don't you see how important that would have been? The Moltke circle was to a certain degree the spirit of the 'Counts' circle,' which in turn made the political preparations for the 20th of July; for it wasn't Herr Goerdeler at all who was the motor of the 20th of July, it was these young men who were the real motor." All in all, Sperr was treated kindly.

Now Reisert. He was treated very kindly. He had had three talks with me, and the chief charge against him was that he didn't notice after the very first one that I was a traitor and arch-defeatist, but he had two more talks with me. The chief reproach against him was that he didn't denounce me.

---

1. On 6 June 1944 Delp had called on Stauffenberg with some concerns that had nothing to do with the invasion or with the conspiracy.

Finally Fugger. He made a very good impression. He had been unwell for a long time and had now recovered, was modest, sure, did not incriminate any of us, spoke nice Bavarian, and never pleased me as much as yesterday; entirely without nerves, while here he had always been terribly scared. He admitted at once that it was clear to him after what he heard today he should have made a report, and he was dismissed so mildly that I thought last night that he would be acquitted.

However, in the other examinations, too, the name of Moltke kept being mentioned. It ran through everything like a red thread and under the above-mentioned "legal principles" of the People's Court it was clear that I was to be done away with.

Perhaps I should give you a brief explanation of the sketch:

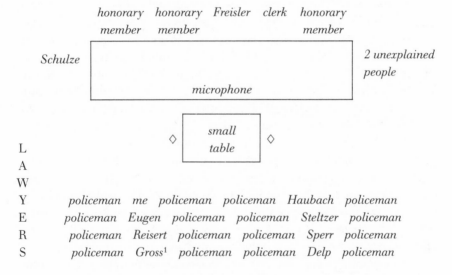

Behind us 5 rows of public

The whole trial was recorded by microphone on steel tapes for the archives. If you felt so inclined, you could, therefore, later on have them played to you. One steps up to the table, one's two policemen too, who sit down on the two chairs to the right and to the left; for Reisert and me, without our having to ask, a chair was provided.[2] Schulze, Freisler, and the clerk in red robes. One incident was typical: for some reason a copy

1. Nikolaus Gross (1898–1945), Catholic trade-union leader and editor. His case was detached with Haubach's and Steltzer's. Trial 15 January, execution 23 January.
2. He had had attacks of sciatica in prison and had difficulty standing; Freisler had conceded the chair.

of the penal code was needed, because Freisler wanted to read something from it; it turned out, however, that there wasn't one to be found.

Now comes the second day. It began with me. It started off in quite a mild tone; very fast, rapid, so to speak. Thank God I am quick and found Freisler's speed child's play; which, incidentally, we both enjoyed. But if he comes on like that with a man who is not particularly quick, he's condemned before he even notices that F. left the personal data behind. Up to and including the discussion with Goerdeler and my position regarding it, everything went quite smoothly and without much ado.

Then came my objection that the police and Abwehr had known about it. Now Freisler had paroxysm No. 1. Everything that Delp had experienced before was a mere trifle in comparison. A hurricane was unleashed: he banged on the table, turned as red as his robe, and roared: "I won't stand for that sort of thing, I won't listen to that kind of thing." And it continued like that all the time. Since I knew anyhow what the result would be, it all left me quite indifferent: I looked him icily in the eye, which he clearly didn't like, and suddenly I couldn't help smiling. This spread to the adjunct judges sitting on Freisler's right, and to Schulze. You should have seen Schulze's look. I think, if a man were to jump from the bridge over the crocodile pond in the zoo, the uproar couldn't be greater. Well, that exhausted the subject.

Now, however, came Kreisau, and there he didn't waste much time on preliminaries, but steered straight for two things: (a) defeatism, (b) the selection of regional commissioners. Both led to paroxysms of the same quality, and when I submitted in defence that it all had its roots in official business, the third paroxysm: "All Adolf Hitler's agencies base their work on the foundation of victory, and that isn't any different at the OKW from elsewhere; I simply won't listen to anything like that, and even if it were not so, every single man has the duty to spread the faith in victory on his own." And so on in long tirades.

But now came the quintessence: "And who was there? A Jesuit Father! Of all people, a Jesuit Father! A Protestant minister, 3 people who were later sentenced to death for taking part in the 20th of July! And not a single National Socialist! Not one! Well, all I can say is: now the fig leaf is off! A Jesuit Father, and with him of all people you discuss questions of civil disobedience! And you know the Jesuit Provincial too! He too was at Kreisau on one occasion! A Jesuit Provincial, one of the highest officials of Germany's most dangerous enemies, he visits Count Moltke in Kreisau! And you're not ashamed of it! No German would touch a Jesuit with a barge-pole! People who are excluded from military service because of their attitude! If I know there is a Jesuit Provincial in a town, it is almost a reason for me not to go to that town!—And the other clergyman, what had he lost there? They should concern themselves with the here-after, and leave us here in peace.—And you visit bishops! What is your business with a bishop, with any bishop? Where do you get your orders from? You get your orders from the Führer and the NSDAP! That goes for you as well as for any other German, and whoever gets his orders, under whatever camouflage, from the guardians of the Beyond gets them from the enemy and will be treated accordingly!"—And so it went on. But now in a key that made the earlier paroxysms appear like the gentle rustling of a breeze.

The result of the examination "against me"—since it would be non-sense to call it "my examination"—: all of Kreisau and all conversations connected with it are preparation for high treason.

Ah yes, I must add: after this climax the end came in 5 minutes: the conversations in Fulda and Munich, all that wasn't taken up any more at all, but F. said, We can skip that, and asked: Have you anything else to say? To which, unfortunately, after a little hesitation, I replied: "No!" And I was through.

Now my summary continues. If the other people whose names were mentioned—not during the trial, by the way, because, once we saw how matters were going, we all took care not to mention any name—have not yet been arrested, it may be because they are regarded as a *quantité né-gligeable.* But if they should be arrested and if they had any knowledge going beyond purely social chat about such questions or were to connect these questions with a possible defeat, then they must reckon with the death penalty. That concerns above all Einsiedel. C.D. & Peters—all the economic part wasn't mentioned and for heaven's sake not a word about it—must remain altogether untouched by the following things: (a) any knowledge about Goerdeler; (b) prepared or systematic discussions; (c) clergymen of any kind; (d) the possibility of an occupation of any part of the Reich, let alone a defeat; (e) discussions of any organizational questions, "regional commissioners," "trade union," "map," and so on.

Einsiedel must say: he was only interested in the problems of a planned economy, which he defended against all kinds of objections, and so he was only there in October '42, and later he only talked with me some-times, purely socially; and he'd been to Kreisau frequently, to recuperate. It would be best if he had a fortnight's holiday there in October '42, and then the others came. It must be considered very carefully, because I'm afraid that Maass was rather explicit. He must simply deny it all. Under the juridical principles applied to us, both of them, C.D. and Einsiedel, will be sentenced to death; for C.D., too, knew and discussed with us considerably more than Reisert. You'd better blot out this paragraph thor-oughly as soon as you've read it, for it would constitute sufficient proof.

In the final resort this concentration on the church aspect corresponds with the inner nature of the case and shows that Freisler is a good political judge after all. It gives us the inestimable advantage of being killed for something which (a) we really have done and which (b) is worth while. But that I should die as a martyr for St. Ignatius of Loyola—and that is what it amounts to in the end, since all the rest was insignificant beside it—is truly a joke, and I already tremble at the thought of Papi's paternal wrath, since he was always so anti-Catholic. The rest he will approve, but that? Even Mami won't agree altogether.

(I've just remembered something else. He asked me: "Do you see that you are guilty?" I said in essence No. Whereupon Freisler: "You see: if you still don't recognize it, if you still need to be instructed on it, it shows that you think differently and have thereby excluded yourself from the fighting community of the people.")

The beauty of the judgment on these lines is the following: It is established that we did not want to use any force; it is established that we did not take a single step towards organization, did not talk to a single man about the question whether he was willing to take over any post; it read differently in the indictment. We merely thought,[1] and really only Delp, Gerstenmaier, & I, the others were regarded as subsidiary figures and Peter & Adam as liaison to Schulenburg etc. And in the face of the thoughts of these three solitary men, the mere thoughts, N[ational] S[ocialism] is so scared that it wants to exterminate everything that is infected by it. If that isn't a compliment. After this trial we are out of the Goerdeler mess, we are free from all practical action, we are to be hanged because we thought together. Freisler is right, a thousand times right; and if we are to die, I am in favour of dying on this issue.

I am of the opinion, and now I come to the practical side, than this affair, properly presented, is even somewhat better than the famous Huber case.[2] For even less happened. There wasn't as much as a leaflet produced. There were only thoughts, without even the intention to use force. The submissions we all made in our defence—police knew, official business, Eugen didn't understand a thing, Delp always happened to be absent—must be struck off, as Freisler quite rightly struck them. And then one thought remains: how can Christianity be a sheet-anchor in the

1. The *raisonnement* of the judgment argued against this: "He did not only think, but gathered a circle in which he discussed and developed plans, and finally he looked round for men for their implementation."

2. The case conducted by Freisler in 1943 against the students of the White Rose group—Hans and Sophie Scholl, Christoph Probst, Alexander Schmorell, and Willi Graf—and their professor Kurt Huber. They were all sentenced to death. (Cf. n. 1 [p. 279] to letter of 18 March 1943, n. 7 to letter of 3 April 1943.)

chaos? This sole thought will probably cost 5 heads tomorrow and later those of Steltzer & Haubach and probably Husen. But because in this trial the trio is called Delp, Eugen, Moltke, and the rest were only regarded as "infected," because it includes nobody who represented anything else, no one who belonged to the workers, no one who looked after any worldly interest, because it was established that I was opposed to large estates and represented no class interests, indeed no interests of my own, not even those of my country,[1] but those of all mankind, Freisler unwittingly rendered us a very great service, if it proves possible to spread this story and to exploit it. And in my view this should be done at home and abroad. For this selection of persons provides documentary proof that it is not plans or preparations but the spirit itself that is to be persecuted. Vivat Freisler!

To make use of this story is not your task. Since we are to die above all for St. Ignatius, his disciples should make it their concern. But you must let them have this story, and it is all the same whom they bring in from among Wurm's people. Pressel would probably be best. I shall discuss it with P.[2] tomorrow. If they find out that you received this letter and passed it on, you too will be killed. Tattenbach[3] must take it upon himself quite unambiguously and, if necessary, he must say that he got it with Delp's last laundry. Don't part with this letter, but only with a copy of it, and that must be instantly translated in a way that it could come from Delp, that is, with him in the first person.

So much for that: the rest will come separately. J.

[P.S.] Obviously Konrad,[4] Dietz,[5] & Faulhaber, and probably Wienken[6] too, must be informed. But leave that to others. Nothing like that is your business. If they are not totally [terrified?] they should be able to make a nice bit of capital out of our death.

1. The German word cannot be deciphered with certainty. It is probably *Landes* (genitive of "country"); but it could be *Ladens* (genitive of "outfit"—i.e., his International Law Group in the Abwehr).
2. Poelchau.
3. Franz Graf von Tattenbach, S.J. (born 1910), who was allowed to visit Delp in prison and was even able to officiate, secretly, at Delp's last vows, despite the pressure the Gestapo had applied to induce Delp to leave the Jesuit order. After the war engaged in charitable and educational work in South America.
4. Preysing.
5. Johannes Baptista Dietz, Bishop of Fulda—see n. 3 to letter of 1 August 1942.
6. Heinrich Wienken (1883–1961), since 1931 Coadjutor-Bishop and Vicar General of Meissen, head of the Commission of the Fulda Bishops' Conference in Berlin—the liaison man to Cardinal Archbishop Bertram in Breslau.

My dear heart, first I must say that quite obviously the last 24 hours of a life are in no way different from any others. I always imagined that one would only feel shock, that one would say to oneself: Now the sun sets for the last time for you, now the clock only goes to 12 twice more, now you go to bed for the last time. None of that is the case. I wonder if I am a bit high, for I can't deny that my mood is positively elated. I only beg the Lord in Heaven that he will keep me in it, for it is surely easier for the flesh to die like that. How merciful the Lord has been to me! Even at the risk of sounding hysterical: I am so full of gratitude that there is hardly room for anything else. He guided me so firmly and clearly these 2 days: the whole room could have roared like Herr Freisler and all the walls could have shaken, it would have made no difference to me; it was truly as it says in Isaiah 43,2: When thou passest through the waters, I will be with thee; and through the rivers, they shall not overflow thee; when thou walkest through the fire, thou shalt not be burned; neither shall the flame kindle upon thee.—That is: your soul. When I was called upon for my final statement I almost felt like saying: There is only one thing I want to mention in my defence: *nehmen sie den Leib, Gut, Ehr, Kind und Weib, lass fahren dahin, sie haben's kein Gewinn, das Reich muss uns doch bleiben.*[1] But that would have harmed the others. So I only said: I don't intend to say anything more, Herr Präsident.

Now there is still a hard bit of road ahead of me, and I can only pray that the Lord will continue as gracious to me as he has been. For this evening Eugen wrote down for us: Matthew 14, 22–33.[2] He meant it differently, but it remains true that this was for me a day of a great draught of fishes and that tonight I am justified in saying: "Lord, depart from me! I am a sinful man." And yesterday, my love, we read this beautiful passage: "But we have this treasure in earthen vessels, that the excellency of power may be of God, and not of us. We are troubled on every side, yet not distressed; we are perplexed, but not in despair; persecuted, but not forsaken; cast down, but not destroyed; always bearing about in the body the dying of the Lord Jesus, that the life also of Jesus might be manifest in our body." Thanks be, my love, above all to the Lord. Thanks also to yourself, my love, for your intercessions, thanks to all the others who prayed for us and for me. Your husband, your weak, cowardly, "complicated," very average husband, was allowed to experience all this. If I

1. Last verse of Luther's hymn *"Ein' feste Burg"* ("A Mighty Fortress"); in the Carlyle translation: "And though they take our life, / Goods, honour, children, wife, / Yet is their profit small, / These things shall vanish all, / The city of God remaineth."
2. Marginal note: "I see that yesterday it was Luke 5,1–11."

were to be reprieved now—which under God is no more likely or unlikely than a week ago—I must say that I should have to find my way all over again, so tremendous was the demonstration of God's presence and omnipotence. He can demonstrate them to us, and quite unmistakably, when he does precisely what doesn't suit us. Anything else is rubbish.

Thus I can only say this, dear heart: may God be as gracious to you as to me, then even a dead husband doesn't matter at all. He can, after all, demonstrate his omnipotence even while you make pancakes for the boys or clean them up, though that is, I hope, a thing of the past. I should probably take leave of you—I cannot do it; I should probably deplore and lament your daily toil—I cannot do it; I should probably think of burdens which now fall on you—I cannot do it. I can only tell you one thing: if you get the feeling of absolute protectedness, if the Lord gives it to you, which you would not have without this time and its conclusion, then I bequeath to you a treasure that cannot be confiscated, and compared with which even my life weighs nothing. These Romans, these miserable creatures of Schulze and Freisler and whatever the whole pack may be called: they couldn't even grasp how little they can take away!

I shall write more tomorrow, but since one never knows what will happen, I wanted to touch on every subject in the letter. Of course I don't know if I'll be executed tomorrow. It may be that I'll be interrogated further, beaten up, or stored away. Please scratch at the doors: perhaps it will keep them from beating me up too badly. Although after today's experience I know that God can also turn this beating to naught, even if there is no whole bone left in my body before I am hanged, although at the moment I have no fear of it, I'd rather avoid it.—So, good night, be of good cheer and undismayed. J.

[P.S.] Hercher, who really is a dear fellow, was a bit shocked at my good spirits; so you see that they were quite irrepressible.

[*continued*] *11 January 1945*

My love, I just feel like chatting with you a little. I have really nothing to say. The material consequences we have discussed in detail. You will get through somehow, and if someone else settles in at Kreisau, you will master that too. Just don't let anything trouble you. It really isn't worth it. I am definitely in favour of making sure that the Russians are informed of my death. That may make it possible for you to stay in Kreisau. Wandering around what remains of Germany is ghastly in any case. Should the Third Reich last, contrary to all expectations, and I can't think so in my boldest imaginings, you must see how you keep the boys from the poison. I should naturally have no objections to your leaving Germany in that case. Do what you think best, and don't consider yourself bound one way or the other by any wish of mine. I have told you again and again that the dead hand cannot govern.—You need to have no monetary worries either, as long as the Deichmann house pays and as long as you keep the Kreisau mortgage—but you must firmly insist that it was acquired with your money, partly with the inheritance from Grandmother Schnitzler, partly with gifts from Aunt Emma[1] (Wodan); then you will always have enough to live on, and even if both should drop out, there will always be enough people to help you.

I think with untroubled joy of you and the boys, of Kreisau and everybody there; the parting doesn't seem at all grievous at the moment. That may still come. But it isn't a burden at the moment. I don't feel like parting at all. How this can be so, I don't know. But there isn't any trace of the feeling that overwhelmed me after your first visit in October, no, it must have been November. Now my inner voice says (a) God can lead me back there today just as well as yesterday, and (b) if he calls me to himself, I'll take it with me. I haven't at all the feeling which sometimes came over me: Oh, I'd like to see it all again just once more. Yet I don't feel at all "other-worldly." You see that I am quite happy chatting with you instead of turning to the good God. There is a hymn—208,4—which says "for he to die is ready who living clings to Thee." That is exactly how I feel. Today, because I live, I must cling to him while living; that is all he wants. Is that pharisaical? I don't know. But I think I know that I only live in his grace and forgiveness and have and can do nothing by myself.

I am chatting, my love, just as things come into my head; therefore here is something quite different. Ultimately what was dramatic about the trial was this: The trial proved all concrete accusations to be untenable, and they were dropped accordingly. Nothing remains of them. But what the Third Reich is so terrified of that it must kill 5, later it will be 7, people, is ultimately the following: a private individual, your husband, of whom it is established that he discussed with 2 clergymen of both denominations, with a Jesuit Provincial, and with a few bishops, *without the intention of doing anything concrete,* and this was established, things "which are the exclusive concern of the Führer." Discussed what: not by any means questions of organization, not the structure of the Reich—all this dropped away in the course of the trial, and Schulze said so explicitly in his speech for the prosecution ("differs completely from all other cases, because there was no mention of any violence or any organization"), but discussions dealt with questions of the practical, ethical demands of Christianity. Nothing else; for that alone we are condemned. In one of

1. Emma Schroeder, née Deichmann, wife of the London banker Bruno Schroeder.

his tirades Freisler said to me: "Only in one respect are we and Christianity alike: we demand the whole man!" I don't know if the others sitting there took it all in, for it was a sort of dialogue—a spiritual one between F. and myself, for I could not utter many words—in which we two got to know each other through and through. Of the whole gang Freisler was the only one who recognized me, and of the whole gang he is the only one who knows why he has to kill me. There was nothing about a "complicated man" or "complicated thoughts" or "ideology," but "the fig leaf is off." But only for Herr Freisler. We talked, as it were, in a vacuum. He made not a single joke at my expense, as he had done with Delp and Eugen. No, this was grim earnest: "From whom do you take your orders? From the Beyond or from Adolf Hitler?" "Who commands your loyalty and your faith?" All rhetorical questions, of course.—Anyhow, Freisler is the first National Socialist who has grasped who I am, and the good Müller[1] is a simpleton in comparison.

My love, your very dear letter has just arrived. The first letter, dear heart, in which you did not grasp my mood and my situation. No, I don't occupy myself with the good God at all or with my death. He has the inexpressible grace to come to me and to occupy himself with me. Is that pride? Perhaps. But he will forgive me so much tonight, that I may finally ask him for forgiveness for this last piece of pride too. But I hope that it is not prideful, because I do not praise the earthen vessel, no, I praise the precious treasure which has used this earthen vessel, this altogether unworthy abode. No, dear heart, I am reading precisely the passages of the Bible I would have read today if there had been no trial, namely: Joshua 19–21, Job 10–12, Ezekiel 34–36, Mark 13–15, and our second Epistle to the Corinthians to the end, also the short passages I wrote down on a slip of paper for you. So far I have only read Joshua and our bit from Corinthians, which ends with the beautiful, familiar sentence, heard so often from childhood up: "The grace of Our Lord Jesus Christ and the love of God and the fellowship of the Holy Spirit be with you all. Amen." I feel, my love, as though I had been authorized to say it to you and the little sons with absolute authority. Am I then not fully entitled to read the 118th Psalm, which was appointed for this morning? Eugen thought of it for a different situation, but it has become much more true than we would ever have thought possible.

Therefore, dear heart, you'll get your letter back despite your request. I carry you across with me and need no sign, no symbol, nothing. It isn't even that I've been promised that I won't lose you; no, it is far more: I know it.

---

1. SS Obergruppenführer (General) Heinrich Müller, Gestapo chief—cf. p. 397.

A long pause during which Buchholz[1] was here and I was shaved; also I had some coffee and ate some cake & rolls. Now I am chatting on. The decisive phrase of the trial was: "Herr Graf, one thing Christianity and we National Socialists have in common, and only one: we demand the whole man." I wonder if he realized what he was saying? Just think how wonderfully God prepared this, his unworthy vessel. At the very moment when there was danger that I might be drawn into active preparations of a putsch—it was in the evening of the 19th that Stauffenberg came to Peter—I was taken away, so that I should be and remain free from all connection with the use of violence.—Then he planted in me my socialist leanings, which freed me, as big landowner, from all suspicion of representing interests.—Then he humbled me as I have never been humbled before, so that I had to lose all pride, so that at last I understand my sinfulness after 38 years, so that I learn to beg for his forgiveness and to trust to his mercy.—Then he lets me come here, so that I can see you standing firm and I can be free of thoughts of you and the little sons, that is, of cares; he gives me time and opportunity to arrange everything that can be arranged, so that all earthly thoughts can fall away.—Then he lets me experience to their utmost depth the pain of parting and the terror of death and the fear of hell, so that all that should be over, too.—Then he endows me with faith, hope, and love, with a wealth of these that is truly overwhelming.—Then he lets me talk with Eugen & Delp and clarify things.—Then he lets Rösch[2] and König[3] escape, so that there aren't enough of them for a Jesuit trial and Delp is added to our case at the last moment.—Then he lets Haubach & Steltzer, whose cases would have introduced foreign matter, be dealt with separately, and finally puts together only Eugen, Delp, & me, for all practical purposes: and then he gives to Eugen and Delp, through the hope, the human hope they have, the weakness which makes their case secondary, and thereby removes the denominational factor; and then your husband is chosen, as a Protestant, to be above all attacked and condemned for his friendship with Catholics, and therefore he stands before Freisler not as a Protestant, not as a big landowner, not as a nobleman, not as a Prussian, not as a German—all that was explicitly excluded in the trial, thus for instance Sperr: "I thought what an astonishing Prussian"—, but as a Christian and nothing else. "The fig leaf is off," says Herr Freisler. Yes, every other category was removed—"a man whom others of his class are naturally bound to reject," says Schulze. For what a mighty task your husband was chosen: all

---

1. Peter Buchholz, the Catholic prison chaplain. He was the last person to see M., who, as Buchholz later reported to F.M., went to his execution "steadfast and calm—even with joy."
2. Rösch was arrested on 23 January, but survived.
3. König went into hiding and was able to evade arrest, but he was very ill and died in 1946.

the trouble the Lord took with him, the infinite detours, the intricate zigzag curves, all suddenly find their explanation in one hour on the 10th of January 1945. Everything acquires its meaning in retrospect, which was hidden. Mami and Papi, the brothers and sister, the little sons, Kreisau and its troubles, the work camps and the refusal to put out flags or to belong to the Party or its organizations, Curtis and the English trips, Adam and Peter and Carlo, it has all at last become comprehensible in a single hour. For this one hour the Lord took all that trouble.

And now, dear heart, I come to you. I have not mentioned you anywhere, because you, my love, occupy a wholly different place from all the others. For you are not a means God employed to make me who I am, rather you are myself. You are my 13th chapter of the First Letter to the Corinthians. Without this chapter no human being is human. Without you I would have accepted love as a gift, as I accepted it from Mami, for instance, thankful, happy, grateful as one is for the sun that warms one. But without you, my love, I would have "had not charity." I don't even say that I love you; that wouldn't be right. Rather, you are the part of me that, alone, I would lack. It is good that I lack it; for if I had it as you have it, this greatest of all gifts, my love, I could not have done a lot of things, I would have found it impossible to maintain consistency in some things, I could not have watched the suffering I had to see, and much else. Only together do we constitute a human being. We are, as I wrote a few days ago, symbolically, created as one. That is true, literally true. Therefore, my love, I am certain that you will not lose me on this earth, not for a moment. And we were allowed finally to symbolize this fact by our shared Holy Communion, which will have been my last.

I just wept a little, not because I was sad or melancholy, not because I want to return, but because I am thankful and moved by this proof of God's presence. It is not given to us to see him face to face, but we must needs be moved intensely when we suddenly see that all our life he has gone before us as a cloud by day and a pillar of fire by night and that he permits us to see it suddenly in a flash. Now nothing more can happen.

Dear heart, this last week, above all yesterday, must have rendered some of my farewell letters out of date. They'll read like cold coffee in comparison. I leave it to you whether you want to send them off nevertheless, or whether you want to add anything by word of mouth or in writing. Obviously I have the hope that the little sons will understand this letter some day, but I know that it is a question of grace, not of any influence from outside.—Obviously you are to give greetings to all, even such people as Oxé and Frl. Thiel and Frau Tharant. If it is an effort to call them up, don't do it; it makes no difference. I only mention them because they are the extreme cases. Since God has the incredible mercy to be in me, I can take with me not only you and the boys, but all those whom I love, and a multitude of others who are much more distant. You can tell them that.

One more thing. This letter in many respects complements the report I wrote yesterday, which is much more sober. Both together must be made into a legend, which, however, must be written as though Delp had told it about me. I must remain the chief character in it, not because I am or want to be, but because otherwise the story lacks its centre. For it is I who was the vessel for which the Lord has taken such infinite trouble.

Dear heart, my life is finished and I can say of myself: He died in the fullness of years and of life's experience. This doesn't alter the fact that I would gladly go on living and that I would gladly accompany you a bit further on this earth. But then I would need a new task from God. The task for which God made me is done. If he has another task for me, we shall hear of it. Therefore by all means continue your efforts to save my life, if I survive this day. Perhaps there is another task.

I'll stop, for there is nothing more to say. I mentioned nobody you should greet or embrace for me; you know yourself who is meant. All the texts we love are in my heart and in your heart. But I end by saying to you by virtue of the treasure that spoke from me and filled this humble earthen vessel:

> *The Grace of our Lord Jesus Christ*
> *and the love of God and the fellowship*
> *of the Holy Spirit be with you all.*
>
> *Amen.*
>
> J.

Glossary

AA Auswärtiges Amt—the German Foreign Office

Abwehr lit. "defence"—the military intelligence service of the German High Command, the full German designation being OKW/Amt Ausland/Abwehr (Ausland = foreign countries)

FHQ Führerhauptquartier—the Führer's headquarters in the field; at various times it had different locations

Gauleiter Nazi Party head of a region

Gestapo Geheime Staatspolizei — secret state police

Kriegsverwaltungsrat official of Military Administration

NSDAP Nationalsozialistische Deutsche Arbeiterpartei—National Socialist German Workers' Party

Obergruppenführer SS lieutenant general

OKH Oberkommando des Heeres — High Command of the Army

OKW Oberkommando der Wehrmacht—High Command of the Armed Forces

SA Sturmabteilung — lit. "assault (or storm) detachment," paramilitary organization of the NSDAP

SD Sicherheitsdienst—Security (or Intelligence) Service of the SS, concerned with both domestic and foreign intelligence; in the latter capacity it rivalled and then eclipsed the Abwehr; domestically it became, together with the Gestapo, an all-pervasive and powerful instrument for information-gathering and terror

SS Schutzstaffel—lit. "protection (or defence, or guard) detachment" of the NSDAP, a paramilitary organization at first regarded as an elite, compared with the SA; after the establishment of the Third Reich, and especially after the purge of June–July 1934, the SS acquired great power and ran the police and the concentration camps. Its military formations, the Waffen-SS, grew to an army of nearly forty divisions during the war

Index

AA (Auswärtiges Amt: Ministry of Foreign Affairs), 31 and *n.*, 32, 34, 41*n.*, 107, 108, 149*n.*, 170*n.*, 210, 221*n.*, 272*n.*, 297, 366; Cultural Division, 221*n.*; German Division (Deutschlandabteilung), 221*n.*; Indian Section, 36*n.*, 149*n.*, 251*n.*; Information Division, 221*n.*

Abetz, Otto, 96 and *n.*, 98

Abs, Josef, 145 and *n.*, 147–8, 150, 165, 167, 189, 191,303

Abwehr (German military intelligence service), 12–15, 21, 42*n.*, 55*n.*, 56*n.*, 173*n.*, 174*n.*, 202*n.*–3*n.*, 205*n.*, 251*n.*, 255*n.*, 258*n.*, 347*n.*, 402; damaged in 1943 raids, 324*n.*, 366–9, 376; endangered after Dohnanyi's arrest, 314*n.*, 315*n.*; International Law Group, 14, 15, 31*n.*, 40*n.*, 46, 141*n.*, 272, 292*n.*; Moltke joins, 12–13; new headquarters in Zossen, 20, 328 and *n.*, 336, 339, 358 and *n.*, 372 and *n.*; and Norway church struggle, 210*n.*–11*n.*; and prisoner exchanges, 267 and *n.*; rivalry with SD, 13, 20, 314*n.*, 315*n.*

Abwehr II, 138*n.*

Abwehr III, 244*n.*

Abyssinia, 137

Academy for German Law, 77, 169, 170

Adam, *see* Trott

Adamczyk, 301

Adenauer, Konrad, first Cabinet of, 145*n.*

Africa, 66*n.*, 118, 133; German-Italian surrender in, 296*n.*; war operations in, 129 and *n.*, 136*n.*, 151, 157, 188, 189, 220, 225*n.*, 227 and *n.*, 261, 262, 265, 267; *see also* German Africa Corps; North Africa; South Africa; West Africa

Agheila, El, 267

Agram, 357

agricultural policy, 172*n.*, 174, 203 and *n.*, 208*n.*, 211, 215, 218*n.*, 344, 345

air warfare, 20, 81 and *n.*, 85, 86 and *n.*, 99, 101, 107 and *n.*, 119, 138, 139, 148, 151, 163, 168, 220, 278, 297, 353; Flying Fortresses, 343; German raids on Britain, 81 and *n.*, 93, 94, 109 and *n.*, 111, 113, 114 and *n.*, 116; raids on Germany, 20, 110–13, 123, 158, 220 and *n.*, 251, 287, 299*n.*, 303 and *n.*, 324 and *n.*, 326, 328, 330, 335 and *n.*, 336, 356, 365–9, 373, 375 and *n.*, 379, 381; raids on Italy, 341*n.*; *see also specific countries*

A NOTE ON THE TYPE

This book was set in a typeface called Walbaum. The original cutting of this face was made by Justus Erich Walbaum (1768–1839) in Weimar in 1810. The type was revived by the Monotype Corporation in 1934. Young Walbaum began his artistic career as an apprentice to a maker of cookie molds. How he managed to leave this field and become a successful punch cutter remains a mystery. Although the type that bears his name may be classified as modern, numerous slight irregularities in its cut give this face its humane manner.

Composed by Graphic Composition, Inc.,
Athens, Georgia

Printed and bound by The Murray Printing Company,
Westford, Massachusetts

Typography and binding design by
Dorothy S. Baker

(continued from front flap)

Almost every day that he was separated from his beloved young wife, Freya, he wrote to her—vivid, detailed, remarkable letters about all he saw, all he knew, all he was doing. Long as they were, they took up little space, because he wrote in a tiny, spidery hand; Freya kept them hidden in her beehives. Betrayed and arrested in 1944, he was imprisoned first at Ravensbrück and then (after the failure of the July 1944 assassination attempt against Hitler worsened the situation of all captured resisters) at Tegel prison in Berlin. Tried for treason, he was condemned to death.

George Kennan has called Moltke "the greatest person, morally, and the largest and most enlightened in his concepts that I met on either side of the battle-lines in the Second World War...The image of this lonely, struggling man, one of the few genuine Protestant-Christian martyrs of our time, ha[s] remained for me over the...years a pillar of moral conscience and an unfailing source of political and intellectual inspiration." On the morning of his death sentence, 11 January 1945, at the age of thirty-seven, he wrote his farewell letter to Freya and his two young sons. Compelling, often heart-wrenchingly moving, and very, very brave, these letters are a major historical document.